Whispers in the Pines

Whispers in the Pines
A NATURALIST IN THE NORTHEAST

Joanna Burger

with Drawings by the Author

 Rivergate Books

An imprint of Rutgers University Press

New Brunswick, New Jersey, and London

Library of Congress Cataloging-in-Publication Data

Burger, Joanna.
    Whispers in the pines : a naturalist in the Northeast / Joanna Burger.
      p. cm.
    Includes bibliographical references and index.
    ISBN-13: 978-0-8135-3877-8 (hardcover : alk. paper)
    ISBN-13: 978-0-8135-3794-8 (pbk. : alk. paper)
  1. Natural history—Northeastern States—Anecdotes. 2. Pines—Ecology—
Northeastern States—Anecdotes. 3. Burger, Joanna. I. Title.
    QH104.5.N58B87 2006
    508.74—dc22

                                              2005019850

A British Cataloging-in-Publication record for this book is available from the
British Library.

Manufactured in the United States of America

For my husband, Michael Gochfeld, who shared many of these adventures with me, and our children, Debbie and David, who grew up during the research and writing of this book.

For my parents, E. Melvin and Janette Male Burger, who showed me plants and animals, regaled me with stories of the Albany Pine Bush, and always encouraged and supported my interests in nature.

For my brothers and sisters, E. Melvin, John A., and Roy W. Burger, Barbara Kamm, and Tina Wiser, who tolerated and sometimes shared my interest in all things wild.

And for my nieces and nephews who helped me see plants and animals through fresh eyes: Kathy Drapeau and Ed Burger; Michael, David, and Daniel Wiser; Jacob and Andy Burger; Ben Kamm; and Erik, Elizabeth, Emily, Allison, and Alexis Burger. And for Greg Drapeau, the fourth generation. May we all appreciate the wonder of a young child watching a Hognose Snake for the first time.

Especially for my Daddy, who passed away during the writing of this book

Contents

Preface

When I was a child, the Albany Pine Bush was a mysterious place to me. My parents told me of the Gypsies who camped there, vagabonds who arrived in the middle of the night and disappeared as quickly, not to return for many months. I imagined them in brightly colored clothes, traveling the countryside by day to sell their wares from the back of pickup trucks, and singing and dancing at night around roaring campfires. It was a wonderful, romantic vision, and I longed to see them for myself. Whenever I was on a sand road amid scrub vegetation, I looked for them and hoped they would be camped around the next bend. While I worried that they would kidnap me if I wandered too far in the pines, I sometimes hoped they would.

The deep Pine Bush was spoken of in hushed tones, for the farmers there could barely eke out a living. The sandy soil was poor, the growing season was slightly shorter than in the Mohawk Valley where I lived. It is colder in the pines than in the lowlands along the Mohawk and Hudson Rivers, and less water was available for irrigation—a must in modern-day agriculture. The farmers in the Pine Bush could grow a few carrots, turnips, and lettuce, but not much else. In contrast, my parents' farm in nearby Niskayuna was fertile and productive, mainly because the Mohawk River flooded every few years, leaving fresh soil and nutrients.

When I was older, I wandered the Albany Pine Bush looking for birds and other animals, secretly hoping to come across my childhood gypsies. The bird diversity was low but density was high, especially in the spring when warblers flitted through the bushes low enough for me to see them clearly. They were easier to identify here than in the tops of the trees in the woods behind our house on my parents' farm. I left the farm and Pine Bush to go to graduate school at the University of Minnesota, and then accepted a faculty position at Rutgers University in New Jersey.

Shortly after coming to Rutgers as a new assistant professor in the Department of Biological Sciences, I headed for the New Jersey Pinelands in the central and southern part of the state. I have spent the last 25 years studying the snakes of the Pine Barrens, particularly the Pine Snake, which in many ways symbolizes the pines. The Pine Snakes of New Jersey are isolated by 600 miles from other Pine Snakes, and so maintain a separate breeding population. They have a rich, striking black and white pattern that makes them avidly sought by snake collectors, and I have lost many of "my" marked snakes to poachers. Over the years, I added Sharp-shinned Hawks, Yellowthroats, and Neotropical migrants to my research interests, often stimulated by the interests of my graduate students.

I will never forget my first impressions of the New Jersey Pine Barrens. I was surprised to find that they were so similar to those in Albany. The image of giant inland seas that left sand dunes and beach sands strewn across the landscape so many thousands of years ago suddenly tied the whole eastern United States together. The feel is the same, the mood the same, and the sense of peace the same. Yet each has its unique characteristics, species, and charm. These are forgotten lands where no one wanted to live or farm for decades.

Many of the pinelands survived early farming development because the soil is poor and water is scarce. While in most of the northeastern United States nearly 90 percent of the forest was cut for farming, the barrens escaped. But the pines have not escaped the more recent housing spurt. Land all along the East Coast became very valuable after mosquito control in the early 1900s made it possible to live and play along the Atlantic Coast. Hordes of people moved to the shore, spilling over into the coastal pinelands. For many people, a pinewoods connotes a plantation of pines planted in neat rows, awaiting a future harvest; the barrens themselves are a very different place.

I am moved to write this book to make the wonder of the pines as real for others as they are for me; to transform the homogeneity that most people see into the subtle heterogeneity that I see. I want to encourage people to travel to pine barrens to share the delicacy of the changing seasons and to see that the subtle colors of the pines are as elegant and moving as the brilliant changes of deciduous forests. The quiet serenity of the Albany Pine Bush is as captivating as the Adirondacks, the endless Jersey shore, the white sand beaches of the Carolinas, or the swaying Sawgrass of the Everglades. Each pinelands is unique because of a slightly different climate, human development patterns, and water and fire regimes. But all share the thread of poorly drained sands, scrub oaks, and scattered pines.

In this book I take you on some of my adventures in the barren pinelands of the Northeast and then wander briefly into those farther south, in the Carolinas and Florida. The barrens are a particular type of pinewoods, where the pines are sparse and sometimes short and interspersed with open patches of sand and low vegetation. The names may differ—the Albany Pine Bush, the Long Island Barrens, the New Jersey Pinelands, but they are related by history, geology, and ecology. For the most part I avoid the large lowland pine forests where the trees are tall and dense, although I mention them occasionally. I have arranged the essays and my field sketches by region, but many of the processes and species are the same.

Acknowledgments

My adventures in the pines have been enriched by many travelers along the way, and I thank them now. In New York, Meg Stewart and Allen Benton introduced me to the ecology of the Pine Bush in courses and field trips while I was an undergraduate at Albany State (whose campus now resides in the Albany Pine Bush). My parents first got me interested in the Albany Pine Bush, my father provided details of how farmers and other people worked the pines, and my nieces and nephews (Andrew and Jacob Burger; Emily, Beth and Erik Burger; Ben Kamm) accompanied me on many a field trip to the Albany Pine Bush Preserve. I enjoyed the company of my husband, Michael Gochfeld, and our son, David Gochfeld, on trips to the Long Island Barrens. Ralph Odell of Natural Resource Protection cheerfully read the manuscript on the Albany Pine Bush and the Long Island Barrens.

In New Jersey, my work with Pine Snakes in the Pine Barrens has been shared with Robert Zappalorti and Mike Gochfeld, and I have appreciated their company and knowledge for many years. Larry Niles, Mandy Dey, Emile DeVito, Eric Stiles, Kathy Clark, Christina Frank, and others shared studies of Neotropical migrants. Henry John-Alder and Linda Seitz discussed their work with Fence Lizards. Several of my technicians helped with literature searches, graphics, chemical analysis, and encouragement, including R. Ramos, C. Dixon, J. Ondrof, M. McMahon, T. Benson, T. Shukla, S. Shukla, and C. Jeitner. Nearly all of my graduate students have worked on Pine Snakes and colonial birds over the years, and I am grateful for their help and insights: Carl Safina, Steven Garber, Susan Elbin, Brian Palestis, Jorge Saliva, and Nellie Tsipoura. Jacques Hill and I worked on Hognose Snakes in the Pine Barrens, as well as snake community structure; and Bill Boarman and I worked on vocalizations of Yellowthroats. Guy Tudor provided information and insights on pine barrens of the northeast. Fred Lesser has been my field companion in most habitats in New Jersey for nearly thirty years, and has influenced my view of nature. Russell Juelg and Carl Anderson provided information on Pine Barrens plants and Pineland regulations. I appreciate the aid of Ricky Lesser and the Ocean Gate-Yacht Basin. David Fairbrothers and Howard Boyd read and provided invaluable comments on this section, and I am grateful. Bert and Patti Murry and Chris and Paula Williams were frequent field companions.

In South Carolina I have wandered the pine hills and Carolina Bays with Whit Gibbons, I. L. Brisbin Jr., Joel Snodgrass, K. Gaines, Cub Stephens, Shane Boring, Chris Lord, M. Kuklinski, and Stephanie Murray. Their insights have been invaluable, and it is always fun to find a Cottonmouth nestled in damp swamps where pines give way to hardwood bottomlands. My sister Tina Wiser and her family provided logistical help in South Carolina and Georgia, and a wonderful home away from home. In Florida my experiences were shared with Mike Gochfeld, Anne Gochfeld, and Alex Gochfeld, and our children, Debbie and David. I especially thank Doria Gordon of the Florida Nature Conservancy for information about invasive, nonindigenous plants, Fred Lohrer for information on Florida pine habitats, and Glen and Jan Woolfenden for showing me the Scrub Jays. In Michigan, I visited the pines with many people, including Mike Gochfeld, Mick Hamas, Harold Mayfield, and others. During the writing of this book, many other people provided information on animals in the pines, including Hank Smith (reptiles), Louis Guillette (alligators), and Barny Dunning (Bachman's Sparrows).

Specific guides, such as J. K. Barnes's *Natural History of the Albany Pine Bush* and D. Forman's *Pine Barrens,* have helped support my own work and observations and should prove useful to the readers of this book. I am thankful to all authors for the work described in the references at the end of the book—may we all continue to study the pine barrens ecosystems and the flora and fauna within.

I thank my editor Audra Wolfe for so many helpful suggestions, and for carefully shepherding this manuscript through Rutgers University Press. I also thank my copyeditor Alice Calaprice for improving the manuscript. It is always a pleasure working with everyone at the Press.

My parrot, Tiko, cheerfully interrupted me when I needed a break, and my chicken, Hester, wandered the backyard, continually reminding me that life goes on.

Finally, I thank my husband, Mike Gochfeld, who has traveled with me throughout the United States and all over the world, providing logistical help, the knowledge of a true naturalist, companionship, and love. He read and commented on several drafts of the manuscript. Our children,

Debbie and David, wandered the barrens with us and helped with many research projects. They grew up as we also matured, and it was always a pleasure to see their wonder and appreciation of the creatures within.

My research over the years has been funded by the National Science Foundation, National Institute of Mental Health, National Institute of Environmental Health Sciences (ESO 5022), U.S. Environmental Protection Agency, U.S. Fish and Wildlife Service, Department of Energy (CRESP, DE-FC01-95EW55084 and DE-FG26-00NT-40938), Penn Foundation, Dodge Foundation, Wildlife Trust, and the Endangered and Nongame Species Program of the New Jersey Department of Environmental Protection. Permits for work with birds, fish, and reptiles have come from the U.S. Bird Banding Laboratory, the U.S. Fish and Wildlife Service, New Jersey Department of Environmental Protection, and New York Department of Environmental Conservation.

INTRODUCTION

1

The Creatures Within

Overhead, a Turkey Vulture sails on rising warm air currents that are calm enough to slow his soaring, yet strong enough to keep him moving without a beat of his black and silver wings. Floating through a pale blue sky, he tilts slightly from side to side, his wings set in a slight upward V. He covers miles each day, searching for a blemish on the land below, scanning for the remains of some unlucky animal, such as a road-killed squirrel or a fallen crow. I follow his flight as he circles overhead and watch him swoop lower to carefully inspect something far below, but then he moves on in a tireless sweep over the pinelands below. The scattered pines frame the dark vulture overhead, and he finally disappears, drifting westward into the deep New Jersey pines, away from the cool ocean breezes.

The soft chipping buzz of a Pine Warbler breaks the silence, as it threads through the scraggly branches of the pines, searching the needles diligently for insects captured by the sticky black pitch. My eyes are drawn downward on the blackened trunk, and I focus on a White-breasted Nuthatch moving methodically downward, inspecting loose bark for hidden insects (fig. 1.1). His movement startles a Fence Lizard, a miniature dinosaur patrolling the trunk for small insects, in a domain now ruled by many larger creatures. In ancient times, giant lizards roamed these lands, fearless rather than fearful. This lizard must be constantly alert to avoid falling prey to a hungry bird or a large snake.

In one long leap the lizard lands head down on a rotting stump, hesitates briefly, and runs underneath, burying deep in the sodden needles and oak leaves caught beneath a fallen log. A black Carpenter Ant creeps over the dead stump, followed by another, and then another, until a small patrol crawls by, and then disappears in the heart of the rotting wood. Above, the needles and oak leaves are still, the lizard hides, the pine boughs no longer sway because the warblers have moved on in their endless search for more insects, the Turkey Vulture is out of view, and the New Jersey pines are still.

1.1. *White-breasted Nuthatch feeding in the pines.*

For nearly an hour no creatures stir, and then a Kestrel darts across the clearing, hovers briefly, and pounces on a grasshopper sitting quietly on a clump of Bluestem Grass. He saw the large grasshopper from a distant perch, while I had not. Surprisingly, grasshoppers make up a significant part of the diet of Kestrels, and unlike other falcons, they kill their prey on the ground rather than in midair. They are a beautiful small falcon that resides in the Pine Barrens year-round, as well as in many other regions throughout North America.

This Kestrel is a male because he has pale blue-gray wings, with a rusty-brown back and tail, and black sideburns on both sides of his buff cheeks (fig. 1.2). Kestrels are actually quite small, not much larger than Robins, which accounts for their habit of eating insects and small mice. They frequently hover on rapidly beating wings, searching for prey, a behavior that inspired Gerard Manley Hopkins's poem "The Windhover."

As with most raptors, the female Kestrel is larger than the male, a fact that has generated much discussion among ornithologists. This difference in size is called sexual dimorphism. In many bird species males are larger than females, but in most hawks, the reverse is true. Some people have proposed that the female has to be larger to protect the young from her mate, a predator who might eat them. When the young are small, the female spends most of her time guarding them while the male is off foraging. He brings prey back to the nest, which she then tears apart to feed them. The problem arises when the male brings food back to the young; the squirming young may elicit the killing instinct of the male, but this is still just a theory.

I am fascinated by the zeal of the Kestrel as he tears apart the grasshopper, limb by limb, eating each in turn. A soft, almost whistle-like cry overhead commands his attention, and dropping his prey, he takes wing, soaring higher and higher. He is joining a female high overhead in an ancient mating dance that takes place entirely in midair. He is far more noisy than she is, crying a loud, insistent "pip pip pip pip pip pip pip," while she simply watches his aerial antics as he displays for her over the pinelands. His cries resound above the pines, and for nearly a half hour he courts her relentlessly. Then the pair sails off into the distance to land out of sight—and I can only imagine what they are up to.

Female Kestrels begin to incubate their clutch with the laying of the first egg, insuring that the young will hatch on successive days. This has the effect of partly controlling the outcome of competition for food among the young— the oldest and largest one always gets the most food. If food is plentiful, all the young survive, but if food is scarce, then only the oldest obtain any, and the younger chicks

1.2. Kestrel in the Albany Pine Bush.

gradually starve. This asynchronous hatching ensures that each year some well-fed young fledge; otherwise, several might fledge, but all would be too undernourished to survive.

The fledging kestrels remain with their parents for several months, learning how to forage by watching them. Though it may not take enormous skills to capture a grasshopper, it is more difficult to learn how to find and capture the small mice they also eat. In late summer, families of Kestrels are common in the pines, and the noisy young often give away their location by moving around rapidly, their exuberant calls and crashing noises making it difficult for the parents to hunt.

I love to watch Kestrels hunting. Their dainty shapes, hovering like tiny helicopters, provide a chance to watch predation, an event usually difficult to witness. Surprisingly, they are very nimble when they move among the tangles of oaks and scrubby pines, but they are equally agile when foraging beside a busy highway. They seem oblivious to the speeding cars and either sit passively on fence posts and nearby trees, or hover for a few minutes over the median vegetation looking for insects or small mice running through trails in the grass.

I wait for another hour, but the Kestrels do not appear again. For a while I watch a pair of grasshoppers mating nearby, contemplating their vulnerability during this time, but they are well hidden deep in the vegetation (fig. 1.3). Rising slowly from my hiding spot among the brushy Scrub Oaks, I make my way through the blueberry tangles, tread softly on the Reindeer Moss, and stop to peer at the smooth sand. Mostly the

1.3. Pair of mating Grasshoppers hidden deep in the vegetation.

sand is stark white, all the organic material long since leached away, swept clean of pine needles and oak leaves by yesterday's winds. The smooth, hard-packed sand has been undisturbed for many years, but once this sandy trail was a busy byway for "pineys" traveling to town for supplies or to sell their meager crops. Centuries before, it was a Lenape Indian trail, leading from inland villages to the estuaries. Indians moved silently through the pines, hunting rabbits, stalking White-tailed Deer, or escaping from their own enemies, be they Cougars or other Indians.

A hundred centuries ago, the land was covered by a giant ice sheet over a mile thick. Its sheer weight forced the land downward, compacting the soils and rock beneath. The hulking ice sheets glided southward, only to retreat once again. Four times over the course of a hundred thousand years the glaciers moved southward, but finally they withdrew northward to the Arctic, maintaining their stronghold for the time being in the far north. If global warming continues, they may disappear, raising sea level to heights that will threaten the pine barrens of Long Island and New

Jersey, both of which are only a few yards above sea level. In their wake, the glaciers left massive mounds of gravel and sand, called moraines, remnants of dunes from ancient seas that survived the scouring of the glaciers. As the ice retreated, arctic plants moved in and colonized the land, creating a cold wet habitat for Mastodons, Woolly Mammoths, and other smaller creatures. People migrated in, following the herds of game. As the climate moderated, the vegetation changed. The spruce muskeg retreated northward, leaving hardwood forests inland, and pines and stunted oaks were left to survive in the harsh coastal conditions.

Farther inland and northward, the pines gave way to tall, majestic trees, as hardwoods claimed the coastal forests, closing out the pines, creating so much shade that the tiny pine seedlings could not flourish. But the sparse pines and stunted oaks remained on the Outer Coast Plains, stretching from Florida to Massachusetts, creating one nearly unbroken pine forest of plants adapted to the sandy, dry, nutrient-poor soils.

The soils are still sandy, still dry, still nutrient poor, and where they remain undisturbed by man and subject to rejuvenating fires, the barrens flourish. Conditions are harsh, in some ways mimicking the arctic environment that left 12,000 years ago with the retreating ice. Only a few species are limited to the pine barrens; many more live only a short distance westward where the deciduous hardwood trees form dense, closed canopies. But the species that live here are well adapted to the barrens habitat. Many are found only in the New Jersey Pine Barrens, eking out a living and coping with the peculiarities of a unique ecosystem.

The lives of many pine barrens creatures are secret, hidden by the darkness of night or the depths of the soil—many by both. They hide in underground dens or burrows by day and prowl the pines by night. Others are up and about during the day, but they are so wary and secretive that they are seldom seen. They can be found only by long hours of careful searching, patient patrolling, and watchful waiting. More often their presence is known by a few scats (droppings), tracks, or other subtle signs lingering in the sands.

Walking slowly, I search for any sign, and finally am rewarded by a faint indentation as if someone had dragged a spoon across the soft sand. I follow the trail for a few feet, and then it disappears because the sand is hard packed, and the weight of the snake that slithered past is not enough to make an indentation. I follow the snake's direction for several yards but am unable to pick up its trail; it must have turned in another direction. Slowly I move in wider and wider circles, searching for some sign of movement or a trail, but there is none.

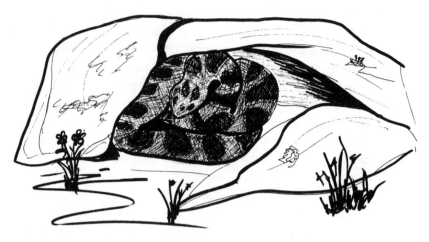

1.4. Rattlesnake hidden in the rocks.

From the size of the impression, I decide the trail must belong to a Pine Snake, the largest snake in the New Jersey Pine Barrens, but it could have been made by a King Snake or even a rattlesnake (fig. 1.4). It is the Pine Snake I search for, that rare denizen of the pines that spends much of its time in underground dens, hidden within rotting logs or concealed under the low branches of pines and oaks, blending in with the needles and leaves. The Pine Snakes in the New Jersey Pine Barrens are a relict population, isolated from other Pine Snakes in the Carolinas and Florida. They no doubt were separated from their southern brethren with the re-treating glaciers, when a small population moved north as far as it could go. For 10,000 years there was no chance for them to breed with Pine Snakes from anywhere else, and they developed unique behavior. The Pine Snakes in the southern United States remained a pale brown and black, while others in Florida grew so dark they are called the Black Pine.

In the New Jersey Pine Barrens, however, the Pine Snake evolved a beautiful black and white pattern that is maintained throughout its life. This striking pattern, along with the snake's relative rarity, makes it highly prized by snake collectors. As the snakes became rarer and rarer, collect-ing pressure has intensified, and they are now on the state's threatened list. Poachers not only look for snakes, but they search the Barrens for signs of snake nests and steal the eggs to hatch them at home. An adult New Jersey Pine Snake is valuable on the black market, especially if she is loaded with eggs.

Poaching is only one problem faced by Pine Snakes; they also contend with habitat loss, habitat fragmentation, and human disturbance. With increasing pressure on Pine Barrens land, largely from developers building malls, golf courses, and retirement communities, unbroken pinelands are decreasing. Although the protection of the Pine Barrens by law has slowed the loss of habitat, it has not stopped it all. Total habitat loss is not the only threat Pine Snakes face, for they must have large unbroken tracts to maintain a viable population. Scattered small patches will not do. One large male may have a home range of several square miles, although females range over a smaller area.

Pine Snakes have another unique requirement: the females need open patches of sand for their nest sites. Pine Snakes lay eggs in underground nests, and their eggs are incubated by the sun-warmed sand. New Jersey Pine Snakes are living at the northern edge of their range, and they need complete sun penetration to the forest floor; otherwise the eggs will not hatch, or the young will be born with deformities or behavioral abnormalities.

It may seem a simple matter to have enough open places for the snakes to nest, but it is not. At one time, these patches were created by fires that roared through the pinelands, opening up the pines to early successional stages. At first, raging fires were lit by lightning, and burned until heavy rains or a river stopped their progress. Later the fires were started by Indians, and a century ago fires were ignited by the sparks from wood-burning train engines.

In the twentieth century, other patches were opened up by "pineys" who cleared small plots to grow crops. The parcels were never large, farming was difficult, and crops did not grow well because the soil was so dry and nutrient poor. Every June, female Pine Snakes came out to dig nests at the edges of the fields, where the sand was not too disturbed and the sunlight was strong. Enlightened pineys always left a border of sand around fields for the snakes to nest in, aware that the snakes ate mice that would otherwise gnaw on the squash or tomatoes.

As more and more people moved into the pines, the effort to control and then suppress fires increased. Large teams of firefighters were at the ready, waiting to pounce on any small fire. Without fire, oaks moved in, the pines grew more dense, and the number of open clearings dwindled. Denied the necessary nesting habitats, Pine Snakes decreased. Few senior citizens or golfers mourned the passing of a few snakes; only the older pineys lamented their absence.

Snakes do not have a large following of people interested in preserving them, not like the hordes of people who work for the preservation of elephants, rhinoceroses, large cats or other furry creatures. Snakes are not as charismatic as the social dolphins and large whales, as spectacular as Peregrine Falcons diving at shorebirds, or as awesome as the predatory sharks that conjure up images of power and ferocity. In fact, for many people, snakes elicit deep fears left over from some previous eon when humans were at the mercy of every large and dangerous animal. Perhaps our fears harken back to biblical accounts of the Garden of Eden, with its seductive serpent representing evil. Snakes invoke all kinds of images; very few people are neutral about snakes—they either love them, or they hate them. Perfectly sane people become unreasonable when confronted by a harmless, foot-long snake basking quietly in the sun. Others find them sensual and exciting, and there is even a popular painting of a naked women clad only in the coils of a large, languid python.

To me, snakes are wonderful wild creatures who slither slowly over the pine needles in search of small rodents or other prey. Their skin is not slimy; it is dry and smooth to the touch. Their muscular bodies undulate with power as they move over and around objects. With a much more acute sense of smell than we possess, they follow the trails of mice or rabbits, or pursue scent trails of other snakes, searching for a mate. They are at the top of the food chain, evolved over the eons as predators able to control the populations of the species they prey upon. In some ecosystems, they are the top predators, like the sharks of the sea, the wolves of the tundra, and the cats of the African plains.

The earliest fossil snakes date from at least the Cretaceous, more than 65 million years ago, but these were advanced forms indicating that snakes had already been around for much longer. It is difficult to find fossils of any sort, much less those of snakes. Too many snakes live in dry habitats—when they die their bones lie atop the soil and are quickly eaten by small mammals in search of calcium in an otherwise nutrient-poor environment.

Judging from either the fossil record or biblical accounts, snakes are ancient, but this fact does not protect them from the onslaughts of the modern world. Sitting in the middle of a deserted clearing in the Pine Barrens far from the sounds of passing cars, it is hard to believe that snakes are threatened, and that some other creatures in this wilderness are in trouble as well, but they are. For me, Pine Snakes typify the New Jersey Pine Barrens, but up and down the East Coast there are many other plants and animals that are characteristic of the pines, some of which are restricted to these habitats. Several vertebrates are specialists in the pines, such as the vibrant, apple-green Pine Barrens Treefrog (New Jersey), the lumbering Gopher Tortoise (Florida pines), the noisy Bachman's Sparrow (South

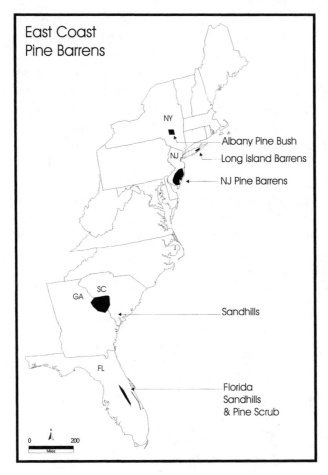

1.5. Map showing the locations of the pine barrens discussed in the book.

Carolina sand hills), the elusive Red-cockaded Woodpecker, and the frenetic Pine Warblers (Albany, Long Island, and New Jersey).

Pine barrens hold their own drama, their own subtle seasonal changes, and have their own unique pulse. To the unpracticed eye the pines are green throughout the year, giving it a sameness. But in the fall the Virginia Creepers turn a vibrant red, the Scrub Oaks turn a rich brown, and migrant birds move through the underbrush in secretive flocks. Raccoons, Red Foxes, and skunks wander the barrens at night, searching for prey. Rare creatures hide their secrets. The Karner Blue caterpillars munch the Wild Lupine in the Albany Pine Bush, Corn Snakes slither under logs in the New Jersey Pine Barrens, while in the pines in Florida, the Florida

Panther makes its last stand. And so I have set out on a journey to under-stand the pine barrens communities that fringe the Atlantic Coast, con-centrating on those of the Northeast, to comprehend the dangers that lie in wait for the animals of the pines and, ultimately, to plead for their sur-vival (fig. 1.5). But I also celebrate the wonderful creatures whose lives are intertwined with one another in a rich tapestry of different colors and pat-terns, who use diverse parts of the pinelands at different times of day or in different seasons, and who have different strategies for survival. For like the Pine Snakes, the pine barrens along the east coast are only just begin-ning to gather protectors, and to give up their secrets to naturalists who once focused only on more charismatic habitats such as tropical rain forests, old growth forests, and, more recently, the seemingly boundless oceans. The pine barrens of the Atlantic Coastal Plain are places well worth visiting, appreciating, and preserving.

2

A Ribbon of Pines

When the first Europeans arrived in North America, they saw vast forests that seemed impenetrable and foreboding, with large predatory animals lurking behind every tree. Cougars, bears, and wolves wandered the deep woods searching for prey, threatening humans and their livestock. Although early written accounts depict the abundance of game, the first colonists did not view the large forest animals as game, although they readily ate them. They did not view the forests as sources of medicines, although they quickly learned from the Indians which herbs to use for common ailments. They felt no reverence, only revulsion and fear for the deep dark forests that stretched unendingly, as far as they could travel. Partly their fear came from the lack of extensive forests in most of Europe. Europeans had no experience with such vast forests, for the trees had been cut down for hundreds of years. The settlers also brought an esthetic vision of neat cottages and endless fields, in which forests had no place. The colonists wanted only to clear and tame the landscape. In the Northeast, the settlers found unbroken deciduous trees, and farther south they found unending pine forests, and they disliked them both.

The colonists set about cutting and burning the forest, peopling the land with "proper Christians," and destroying the dangerous animals. They put bounties on large predators, and within a century eliminated them entirely from the 13 colonies. They wanted to farm and establish villages, and they destroyed the forests in one of the world's greatest blitzes of wastefulness and destruction. In the Northeast, Europeans managed to cut the forests to such an extent that 70 to 80 percent of Massachusetts, Connecticut, and Rhode Island were open lands by the late 1700s—the colonists were very industrious. On Long Island and in New Jersey, the pine barrens were less appealing to the early settlers, the land less fertile, and less land was cleared. The destruction of the southern pine forests took even longer.

The early settlers also found a Longleaf Pine forest that blanketed the Atlantic Coastal Plain from Virginia to Florida. The Longleaf Pines gradually intergraded into a Longleaf Pine–Shortleaf Pine–Loblolly Pine hardwood forests to the west. They wrote of Longleaf Pine forests as vast expanses of open pines with savannahs of grass and other understory vegetation. These forests also fell for timber, pitch and tar, and agriculture.

Pine forests are not unique to the Atlantic Coast. There are many pine forests throughout North America, and indeed throughout the world. Simplistically, pine forests contain pine trees, and pines are the dominant tree. The pine family is the largest and most important coniferous tree group in the world, containing over 200 species. There are about 90 species of *Pinus,* which are widely scattered in the Northern Hemisphere from North America and Europe to Asia, northern Africa, the West Indies, and the Philippines. In the western United States, some species of pines reach gigantic heights, including Ponderosa, Western White Pine, and Sugar Pine, but the pines in the East are much shorter. Many of the pines we see today are in pine plantations, planted for timber or paper pulp.

Pines have been very important for people because most of the trees used in construction since the days of the paleo-Indians have been pines. Pines produce the bulk of pulpwood for paper, as well as derivatives such as rayon, cellophane, turpentine, and plastics (which are now largely synthetic). The tapping of pine sap to produce turpentine or "naval stores" was an early industry in the coastal United States.

The vast majority of pines grow straight and tall and form dense forests with little understory. Light does not penetrate to the ground, and the earth is covered with a deep blanket of reddish brown pine needles. It is these forests that have been extensively cut for lumber and pulp. Pine forests with very old trees are called "old growth," and they have received considerable attention. Old-growth forests, home to the Spotted Owls and other animals that are adapted to them, are charismatic and have a dedicated group of people working for their preservation and conservation.

This book is about a different kind of pine woods—ones we call "pine barrens." They were viewed as barren places where agriculture would not and could not flourish, and where the pines were short and suboptimal for timber. These were places where people could not tame the forests. They had little motivation to clear the land and plant their crops because after a season or two the crops no longer flourished. Instead, people had to learn to harvest the natural products of the barren land, and to make use of the resources hidden within. Small industries developed in some of the pine barrens and scrub pines, but they were limited in scope, although some flourished for over a hundred years.

In this book I describe mainly pine barrens habitats in New York and New Jersey. However, I cannot help wandering to those in South Carolina and Florida because together they give a picture of the variation possible not only in the pines, but in the plants and animals that live there. In each major section I describe the pines in that region, as well as the people and animals in the pines.

There are many pine barrens habitats along the East Coast of North America. The largest ones are the New Jersey Pine Barrens, the Long Island Barrens, and the barrens on Cape Cod in Massachusetts. Many others are isolated in Maine, New Hampshire, Massachusetts, Rhode Island, Connecticut, New York, Pennsylvania, the Carolinas, Georgia, and Florida. Near Albany we have the "Pine Bush," on Long Island the "Barrens," in New Jersey both the "Pine Barrens" and the "Pinelands," in South Carolina and Georgia "Sandhills," and in Florida "Scrub Pine" and "Sandhills." The names may differ, but the structure, environment, and ambiance are similar. Further, there are scattered pine barrens from Ohio to Michigan, and although I will not discuss them here, the habitats are similar and were also created by sands left by massive inland seas.

On the driest, sandiest, most nutrient-poor pine barrens along the Atlantic Coast are the Dwarf Pines, my personal favorites. Only three true Dwarf Pine barrens have trees that are less than 10 feet tall, and these occur in the Long Island Barrens, the New Jersey Pine Barrens, and the Shawangunk Mountains in New York. In these Dwarf Pine Barrens, sometimes called Pine Plains, the Pitch Pine trees are genetically adapted to be short, only about 6 to 8 feet tall and, if transplanted to another habitat, do not grow tall. Centuries of exposure to the truly barren, nutrient-poor, harsh conditions has resulted in a strain of Pitch Pine that is uniquely adapted to these environmental conditions. Other pine barrens farther south have forests where the trees are relatively short, but not this short. The pines in the Scrub Pine habitat of Florida are usually 20 to 30 feet tall.

Most pine barrens in the United States lie on the Atlantic Coastal Plain that stretches from Maine to Florida (fig. 2.1). In its earliest form, the plain was composed of metamorphosed rocks. About 140 million years ago, the old rocks were covered by the oceans. The Coastal Plain was laid down between 135 and 5 million years ago as the sandy sea bottom and dunes of these bygone seas. During this period, the oceans rose and fell several times, and each time more sand and gravel were deposited.

East Coast
Coastal Plain

*2.1. Location of the Atlantic Coastal Plain from
Cape Cod to Florida.*

When the seas were deep over the land, marine animals abounded, and over time, the shells of clams, oysters, and other animals drifted slowly to the sea bottom and were crushed by the sands and ocean above. By about 5 million years ago the seas had retreated for the last time, to near their present levels.

Most of the soils of the Atlantic Coastal Plain are relics left when the last ice sheet retreated some 12,000 years ago. They are sandy, acidic, and porous. The exception is the soil underlying the bogs and swamplands in various pine barrens, which are heavy and poorly drained, perfect conditions for cranberries in the Northeast. When the glaciers receded, pioneer plants and animals that could live on these nutrient-poor soils gradually advanced northward behind the retreating ice. Lichens moved in, softening the soil with their acid secretions, and some mosses colonized. I can imagine the small British Soldier Lichens marching northward, their bright red caps atop silver-gray stalks (fig. 2.2). Typical plants of

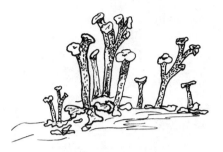

2.2. British Soldier Lichens, one of the first invaders of barrens habitat.

pine barrens include pines, oaks, huckleberries, and cranberries in the North, and pines, palmettos and rosemary in the South. The species are different in each area but the short, scraggly pines and twisted oaks remain.

The open Longleaf Pine forest that stretched over 800 miles from Virginia to Florida is gone, much of it replaced by dense stands of Slash Pine and Loblolly Pine, or by hardwood stands with a few brushy pines. The Longleaf Pine forest once covered over 60 percent of the area—some 78 million acres—but only about 2 percent now remains. Longleaf Pines grew everywhere in their range, regardless of the soil types or climatic conditions. They were far more adaptable and had a wider ecological tolerance than the other trees and shrubs that grew with them.

Much of the pine barrens habitats in the northeast are gone as well. The Albany Pine Bush now comprises only 6,000 acres, down from 25,000 acres a century ago, a loss of over 75 percent. The Long Island Barrens is less than a third of its former size. The New Jersey Pine Barrens fared better, largely because the pines were not suitable for logging, and there was less pressure from urban development, but even so, nearly 50 percent has been lost.

We lost our pinelands for a variety of reasons, not just direct clearing and cutting. Only about 30 percent was directly converted to cropland, pastureland, or developments. The rest disappeared because of the disruption of ecosystem functions; many animals suffered population declines, insects were controlled through pesticides, and birds and other animals that depended on insects declined. Fire was suppressed, and the fire regime was altered. Beavers were once common throughout the pinelands from Maine to Florida, but now they are largely gone, and with them, natural stream damming. In places where they are recovering, they create new wetlands.

In addition to direct habitat loss, three major processes can disrupt the functioning of our remaining pinelands all along the Atlantic Coast: fragmentation, fire suppression, and invasion of nonnative plants.

Fragmentation

Fragmentation and isolation are perhaps the most damaging disruptions because some small areas of pine barrens habitats are already too isolated. As difficult as it is to accept, there is a size limit below which a pine barrens ecosystem simply cannot function, no matter what management regime is imposed. This size threshold is partly related to the requirements of the plants and animals that make up these systems.

Whereas many rare and endangered plants can survive on relatively small patches of habitat, survival is much more difficult for vertebrates, such as some large snakes, birds, and mammals. Many species of medium to large mammals have large home ranges, and there is a minimum population size that is essential for a functioning population. Some species of birds also require large home ranges or territories, including some woodpeckers, owls, and hawks. Some people have argued that 500 animals is an absolute minimum for most species of animals to maintain viable, functioning populations. Whether this is a good or defensible number, we know that a small population of animals can no longer be stable and usually does not contain the genetic variability to maintain itself over time.

The smaller the patch of pine barrens, the greater the amount of edge relative to the center, and this also creates problems for animals and plants that can exist only in pure pine barrens habitats. Edge areas make it easier for a variety of predators and edge animals to move in, competing with and preying on species that have never before existed alongside these edge species.

Fire in the Pines

Before people moved into the pines, lightning started small fires, and when the winds were right and the needles deep and dry, fires spread for many miles. Only when the fire ran into a wide stream or a raging river, or if heavy rains came, did the fire finally die out. Following the last retreat of the glaciers 10,000 to 12,000 years ago, the pine, oak, and heath vegetation moved into the Atlantic Coastal Plain, and fire became a major factor in shaping the ecology of pine barrens habitats, as revealed by studies of pollen in soil cores. The plants of the barrens were adapted to fire, regenerating quickly, while the recurrent fires repeatedly purged the landscape of marauding competitors. In natural succession, oaks invade the pines until fire sweeps through, killing the oaks.

From the Albany Pine Bush to the pines in Florida, Native American Indians living in the barrens and forests burned the pines to open up the habitat for game, to allow better visibility, and to create easier travel. Today, species such as White-tailed Deer, common throughout the Coastal Plain, flourish in pinelands that have some open meadows for grazing. Edge areas between pines and fields are prime places for hunting deer, even today. Later, as the Indians settled down into villages, they burned some pines to clear land for planting crops such as corn, beans, squash, and tobacco. Even when they cut the trees or girdled them, they often burned the brush to clear the ground.

Fires started by Indians burned for many acres since there were limited methods to stop the fires. They often burned pinelands in the fall, when they could drive deer and other game into large V-shaped enclosures for slaughter. Dry summers, particularly in the mid-Atlantic and Northeast, left the ground covered with parched pine needles and oak leaves, which burned easily. The burning of the pines by the Indians is well established not only because of pollen studies, but through the mere existence of the pine forests. Pine barrens vegetation, especially the extremes found in the Dwarf Barrens of New Jersey and the Sandhill Scrub Pines of South Carolina and Florida, can occur only where there is fire at least every 15 years. Otherwise, succession marches on, and the pine forests are replaced by hardwoods.

When European settlers first came to North America, the frequency of fires remained the same. The local Indians continued to burn to clear fields and increase game herds. According to pollen studies, however, the frequency of fire in pinelands increased from the 1700s to the 1900s. This was partly due to railroads because the wood-burning locomotives that traveled through the pines spewed out sparks that ignited the dry tinder.

Since the 1900s considerable effort has been expended to suppress fires in many pine barrens to reduce the loss of life and property. Frankly, I find it incredibly frightening to see a wall of flames rolling toward me, though I'm able to flee in my car. It is therefore understandable that people living in the pines stage small fires before they run wild. Perversely, this suppression has resulted in more serious wildfires. Since there is more time for tinder to accumulate, once a fire has started, it burns hotter, more easily, and more quickly. While in the past, such wildfires burned until they reached a wetlands or heavy rains drowned them out, today many wildfires are stopped by highways, canals, farm fields, or by direct and aggressive firefighting. However, when fires occur with heavy winds, they may jump over roads and continue despite the efforts of firefighters.

All pinelands or pine barrens habitats have a fire regime that maintains the community. The fire regime is a combination of fire size, fire interval, and fire intensity, all of which are affected by soil, hydrology, vegetation fuels, ignition sources, and climate. The fire interval, the time between one fire and the next for a given plot of land, is normally averaged over several centuries.

Fire is critical to maintaining pinelands, particularly the most barren types, because without fire, hardwoods invade. Their seedlings outcompete the pine seedlings, and eventually shade out the pines. The management options, however, may be limited to prescribed or controlled burning, supplemented with control of any wildfires that start. For most pinelands, we no longer have the option of allowing the natural fire regime to run wild. Some exceptions exist where the pinelands extend for many miles, unbroken by human habitation. For example, some of the Dwarf Pine forest in New Jersey persists today as it always has, and some of the larger blocks of pinelands in sparsely populated parts of New Jersey, South Carolina, and Florida have natural fires. But even in these regions, fires and weather conditions are watched very closely to ensure that the fire cannot come too close to human habitation.

Fire interacts with the life cycle of the plants themselves. Fire-tolerant trees, such as most pines, resprout from underground roots or from the trunks themselves if the fire is not too severe. Some also rely on fire to open their cones, sprouting seeds immediately after a fire, and producing cones with seeds within three or four years of sprouting. Less fire tolerant species, such as oaks, Shortleaf Pine, and hickories, can resprout after fires, but they take 20 to 30 years to produce seeds. Thus, if the fire interval is less than 20 years, these trees die out because they do not produce new seeds to sprout and colonize the burned-over area.

Similarly, many understory shrubs and herbs in pinelands do best when frequent fires eliminate competition with fast-growing species that cannot exist with frequent fires. Most fire-adapted shrubs and herbs flourish when there is sun penetration to the forest floor, as there is in the open pine barrens. The seeds of many shrubs will not sprout under a deep layer of needles and leaves that smothers them.

Many plant species in pine barrens habitats are aided by fire because the habitat remains open, with complete light penetration to the ground. Once hardwoods come in, the light levels on the forest floor decline, and the plants are shaded out. In some cases, herbs, grasses, and woody ground-cover plants are threatened or endangered because they are limited to pine barrens communities; in others, the plants that were widespread in open forests are finding their last refuge in pinelands. Some grasses require fire to stimulate flowering and seed production or to kill competing woody plants. The species of herbs, grasses, and woody ground-covers that are adapted to pine barrens habitats vary from New York to Florida, but each habitat is unique. In the New Jersey Pine Barrens, the Broom Crowberry, Pickering's Morning Glory, and Sickle-leaved Golden Aster are all threatened or endangered (fig. 2.3). In Florida's Pine Scrub, several species are endemic and endangered, including Scrub Holly, Silk Bay, Garberia, and Wild Olive.

2.3. Sickle-leaved Golden Aster is a real specialty of the Albany Pine Bush.

Pine barrens plant communities frequently have a diversity of rare moths and butterflies that feed mainly on the ground-cover plants or Scrub Oaks. In the Albany Pine Bush, a delicately patterned butterfly, Edward's Hairstreak, reaches its greatest abundance, and its caterpillars feed only on Scrub Oak. These species will not persist without fire to maintain the community. Similarly, some amphibians and reptiles are limited to pine barrens communities, such as the Pine Barrens Treefrog in New Jersey and other southern pine bogs, and the Florida Scrub Lizard.

Many birds and reptiles are adapted to the open habitats of frequently burned pinelands. Burning improves nesting conditions, provides shelter, and increases food supplies. A fire usually leaves more dead trees for cavity nesters and open sandy places for ground nesters that require them.

There are many types of natural fires: ground fires, crown fires, scorching surface fires, and backfires. As the name implies, ground fires burn along the ground and do not burn the tops of trees, while crown fires burn up into the treetops. Crown fires are higher-intensity fires than ground fires and kill more of the trees. A really hot crown fire in the summer, in a fuel-rich stand, kills trees that are 40 years or older. Less severe crown fires usually allow some mature trees to survive, and even if they burn, they are able to sprout from hidden buds along their trunk. Crown fires kill the shrub understory, but most of these species can sprout from underground roots. Crown fires are most common in habitats dominated by Pitch Pine in the North, by Sand Pines in the South, and by Scrub Oaks throughout the Atlantic Coastal Plain.

Scorching fires kill the leaves and damage the stems because of rising smoke and radiant heat. With more fuel on the ground, a scorching fire kills many trees and most shrubs. Both crown fires and scorching fires kill or damage most trees and shrubs and set back succession by leaving less woody vegetation and more open space. But hot fires also melt the resin that holds serotinous pine cones closed, releasing the seeds.

The least intense fires are called "back fires" and occur when fire moves in the opposite direction from the wind, with the wind holding back the force of the fire. In the summer, back fires can scorch trees and shrubs, causing some damage, but in the cooler months they cause little damage. Because they are less harmful, back fires are sometimes set deliberately in the winter as a controlled burn to eliminate excess fuel. Removal of dead dry leaves, twigs, and other debris reduces the chance of a really hot fire in the future.

For pine barrens habitats, fire is essential. If a natural fire regime cannot be allowed because it may cause loss of life or property, then prescribed burning may be our only option for maintaining the pinelands. Without fire, some pine cones cannot open, preventing the regeneration of pine seedlings and allowing hardwood saplings to move in. Sunlight will no longer drench the forest floor, and eventually the special understory and ground-cover plants of the barrens will die out.

Invasion of Nonnative Plants

Fire has long been recognized as a key element of pine barrens communities, not only in regulating the type and kind of pine community, but in keeping hardwood communities from invading them. The role of invasive or nonnative (exotic) plants, however, has only just begun to be recognized. Even so, generalizations are emerging. Some habitats are more vulnerable to invasive plants than others; disturbed habitats are more easily invaded than undisturbed ones; and dry habitats are generally less easily invaded than wet habitats, which bodes well for the pine barrens.

Although it seems as if dry habitats, such as pine barrens that are on nutrient-poor and dry sands, are less vulnerable to invasive species, it simply may be that fewer nonnative, dry habitat plants (xerophytes) have been imported. People want showy flowers and lush vegetation for their well-watered gardens, and the dry scrub plants that might invade pine barrens habitats are not imported. Gardeners prefer the big, showy, brightly colored blooms of annuals. In the face of burgeoning human populations and water restrictions, some communities are promoting landscaping with plants that need little water. If such dry-habitat plants are ever imported in large numbers, they may well become invasive in their preferred habitats. In Florida, for example, 92 percent of the plants classified as troublesome nonnative invasive plants were intentionally imported and introduced, and 40 percent are still commercially available in nurseries. That means that while some government and private agencies are trying to remove these plants from natural ecosystems at great expense, homeowners are buying them from nurseries to plant around their houses.

Nonnative plants can disrupt delicate pine barrens communities in two ways: by replacing native species, and by disrupting the functioning or fundamental processes of the communities. The replacement of a native plant by a nonnative, or exotic, can be critical, particularly when the native plant is dominant in the pine community. If the replaced species is a pine, a dominant oak, or one of the dominant shrubs, then the habitat can be fundamentally altered and much less appealing to the animal inhabitants.

However, if the nonnative plant also alters the functioning of that system, then the system itself will change. Nonnative plants can disrupt a number of important processes, such as the structure of the soil or vegetation, the cycling of water through the system, the movement of nutrients (such as nitrogen), and the frequency of fire. Invasive and nonnative plants can also change the relationships among predators and competitors.

When some invasive plants move in, they produce more leaves and leaf litter, raising the level of the soil and increasing the depth of groundwater. They may produce large quantities of organic matter, which enters the soil, drastically increasing the organic content and changing the percolation of water through the sand. Some invasive plants handle nutrients differently, making them more or less available to the native vegetation.

Other invasive plants produce toxins that make it impossible for the native species to germinate or grow (called *allelopathy*). Some of these processes also occur with native species in pine barrens habitats, but the species in that community have evolved together and can cope with one another. Many native species, however, have no coping mechanisms for exotic species, and they decrease with the increases in invasive and noxious plants.

One of the most far-reaching effects of invasive plants, however, involves changing the fire regime. Some invasive plants, particularly grasses, produce more vegetation, which creates more fuel. Sometimes, the increased amount of fuel merely results in hotter fires that destroy more vegetation; but in other cases, it decreases the time between fires. Invasive vines can be particularly disruptive because they both produce more vegetation for fuel, and they carry fire higher up the trunks. Fires that would otherwise be ground fires can turn into crown fires, seriously injuring the canopy. When fires do become canopy fires, the fiery vines often break off and soar to nearby trees, igniting them.

Over the last four hundred years we have lost much of our pinelands and pine barrens. Only about 2 percent of the Longleaf Pine forest that once stretched unbroken from Florida to Virginia remains. In the Northeast, we have lost most of the pine barrens habitats, including 75 percent of the Albany Pine Bush, 60 percent of the Long Island Barrens, and 50 percent of the New Jersey Pine Barrens, mostly due to logging and development. Many of the remaining pinelands and barrens are preserved and protected by laws, although these laws are far from perfect. Now the threats are more subtle and will require careful management. Appropriate fire regimes must be reinstituted, and invasive, nonnative plants must be removed or prevented from becoming established. If we are not careful, someday the dwarf pines, sand hills, and scrub pines will be only distant memories. We must be ever vigilant for any changes in the species, in the relative abundance of species, and in the functions of pine barrens to ensure that they remain forever wild for our grandchildren's grandchildren and beyond. We are fortunate, however, in knowing enough about the functioning of these systems to make their preservation and conservation a reality.

THE ALBANY PINE BUSH

The Albany Pine Bush

The Albany Capitol District is a bustling metropolis. It is also the capital of New York State and has a major Hudson River port, 150 miles inland from the Atlantic. But to naturalists and ecologists, Albany conjures up images of the Pine Bush. The Albany Pine Bush is a small and fragmented patch of pine barrens tucked in one of the most heavily populated regions of New York State (fig. 3.1). It is an area of about 40 square miles of sand scrub and bogs covered with Pitch Pine and Scrub Oaks. Superhighways, shopping malls, industries, and housing developments hem in the sands, and any species that strays far away from the isolated patches (called *relics*) seldom survives. Few animals wander in from the edges because the surrounding areas have been covered with concrete and buildings for many years.

The trees in the Pine Bush are short and stunted because the water table is well below the surface, and the sand is quite sterile, with few nutrients. In most parts, the trees are sparse, and the Pine Bush is dominated by shrubs and bushes that are adapted to its relatively arid conditions. The Pine Bush is bisected by trails made by deer and widened by people in search of a few moments of solitude.

This is not the usual place one goes to for wilderness: the wilds of New York's Adirondack Mountains draw much more attention. This habitat, however, is much rarer and far more valuable to the discerning naturalist willing to search for its treasures. Most people once thought of the Pine Bush as wasteland that should be developed so that it becomes "productive," and few people except birdwatchers and botanists ventured there. Now its remnants are preserved, its rare plants and animals saved, its vibrant blue Lupine revered.

I was privileged to grow up only 5 miles from its center, to hear tales of it when I was very young, and to explore its secrets as a teenager. When I was in college at Albany State, my first research project was to compare the foraging behavior of Great Blue Herons in a backwater near

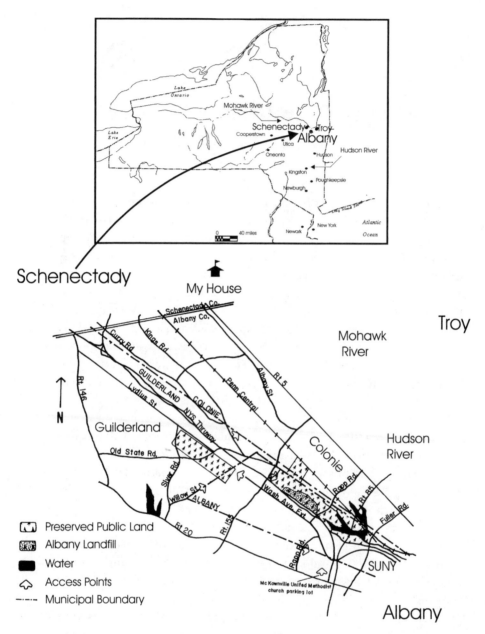

3.1. *Location of the Albany Pine Bush, and of the house where I grew up in Niskayuna, New York.*

my parents' farm with those in a pond in the Pine Bush. Today, you can still see the Pine Bush pond as you drive north on the Northway, just after exiting the New York State Thruway. Back then, only a narrow sugar-sand road passed by the pond, and I was alone as I timed their foraging success using different behaviors. Sometimes the Great Blue Herons stood for an hour without moving, staring at the water, and at other times they walked slowly forward, stirring up fish with their movements.

I often left the Pine Bush swamps and ponds in the evening after the Woodcock called. These birds liked the alder thickets at the edges of the damp and wet swamps. In the late evening or early morning, I would watch a male strut around the ground, erecting its tail, its bill pointed downward, resting on its chest. After giving a raspy "preent, preent, preent, preent," it suddenly flew over 200 feet into the air, spiraling higher and higher. When it was so high I could barely see it in the dim light, it gave a three-syllable note, "chickaree, chickaree, chickaree." Just as suddenly, it plummeted to earth, its wings making a whistling, twittering musical note as it descended to land just where it started. Such a spectacular display must have been impressive to some shy female Woodcock nestled in the grass, or to another male who might have thought about claiming a territory nearby.

I can well imagine this place a few centuries ago, when Mohawk Indians silently slipped through the pines in search of deer and other small game. This was a well-trod region not far from the point where the Mohawk River joins the Hudson, and many different tribes of Indians passed through. They usually camped a distance from the river, where they could be safe from other tribes and not so exposed on the main trail along the rivers. The deer paths through the pines made it easier to trap deer and follow their movements. Arrowheads, broken pieces of flint, and clay beads attest to the vibrant past of the Pine Bush.

The land undulates gently, reminiscent of the dunes along the beaches of the Atlantic. Indeed, the sands below the pines are ancient dunes left behind from huge glacial Lake Albany following the recession of the last ice sheet. Lake Albany, formed where the present-day Hudson and Mohawk Rivers converge, extended as far north as Glens Falls. It existed from 20,000 years to about 10,000 years ago, although its actual lifespan is in dispute. Some archaeologists believe it was around for a much shorter time.

The last glacier began to retreat about 20,000 years ago, but at its peak, 3,000 feet of ice covered Albany. As it retreated, it revealed a landscape with seven layers; the lowest Ordovician bedrock was sandstone and shale that formed below the inland seas some 500 to 400 million years ago

Table 3.1. Geologic Timescale Showing When Major Groups Evolved or Appeared in the Record

Era	Period	Time in Millions of Years Ago (shown is time period started)	Origin of Major Groups
Cenozoic	Quarternary	1.8	
	Tertiary	66	Humans
Mesozoic	Cretaceous	138	
	Jurassic	205	Birds
	Triassic	240	Mammals
Paleozoic	Permian	290	
	Pennsylvanian	330	Reptiles
	Mississippian	360	
	Devonian	410	Amphibians
	Silurian	435	
	Ordovician	500	
	Cambrian	570	Fishes, shelled animals

Note: The Quaternary contains the Holocene (current) and the Pleistocene epochs.

(table 3.1). On top of this was glacial till, well-sorted sand and gravel, roughly sorted sand and gravel, lacustrine sand and clay, lacustrine sand, and the windblown sand and floodplain deposits from glacial Lake Albany. About 12,000 to 13,000 years ago, Lake Albany began to recede and dry up, leaving many smaller lakes. A delta formed where the Mohawk River entered the Hudson River, and the Pine Bush is on this delta. When the glaciers retreated further, the delta was exposed, and huge sand dunes formed with the blowing winds, covering the old Lake Albany bed. Some of the dunes were 70 feet high, although most were only 20 to 30 feet. Some stretched for 1,000 feet before they faded into the landscape. Large blowouts in the sand left depressions, relieving the monotony, and creating swamps, shallow ponds and bogs, only a few of which remain today. Eventually the dunes were covered with arctic mosses, lichens, sedges, willows, and alders. Spruces and firs colonized, further stabilizing the dunes, and finally, White Pine, Pitch Pine, and oaks moved in. These plants provided sustenance for grazing Mammoths, browsing Mastodons, Giant Beavers, and Woodland Caribou, whose remains have been found in this region.

A warmer period about 6,000 years ago allowed Fowler's Toad and the

3.2. *Box Turtles moved into the pines after the glaciers retreated, and are still common today.*

Midland Painted Turtle to move eastward along the Mohawk Valley into the Pine Bush, and the Box Turtle, Spadefoot Toad, Worm Snake, and Hognose Snake moved northward from the Atlantic Coastal Plains of Long Island and New Jersey (fig. 3.2). The species all remained that were typical of the Adirondack Mountains, such as Yellow Birch and Wood Frog.

The Pine Bush escaped the fate of most regions in the Northeast because it was not a particularly good area for farming. In the 1700 and 1800s, when much of the Northeast was cleared for farming, these lands remained wild because the soil was infertile, and there were few streams to serve as a source of water. Furthermore, the sandy soils dry out rapidly after a rain, leaving little water reserves for growing crops. A few attempts at farming were made, but to no avail. The Pine Bush was viewed as wasteland for most of this century, and it is only recently that its value has been recognized. Popular interest in saving the Pine Bush has come nearly too late for many species; the area left to save is small and fragmented. There is little wild land left that can still be bought up and added to the preserve. The Pine Bush is one of New York's most endangered habitats, and only 2,300 acres have been protected in the Albany Pine Bush Preserve, on the edge of New York State's capital city.

The Pine Bush Preserve is surrounded by malls, houses, businesses, and the Albany campus of the State University of New York. It was created by the New York State Legislature in 1988, rather late compared to some of the other protected pine barrens regions. It was already too late to preserve a larger area, and too late to provide any buffers between the city of Albany and the preserve. The preserve suffers from the effects of nearby urbanization, and newcomers often have trouble finding it among the malls and office buildings that surround it. Several trails run through the preserve for hiking, cross-country skiing, and nature study. Although it once spread over an estimated 25,000 acres in east-central New York, today the Pine Bush (both protected and nonprotected) covers only 6,000 acres.

Pitch Pine is the dominant tree in the Albany Pine Bush, along with Scrub Oak. A variety of other trees are present, including Red Oak, Black Oak, White Pine, and Quaking Aspen, although there are few of each, and they are scattered for apart. Some species of plants, such as Yellow Swallowwort are found nowhere else in New York. Wild Lupine with its lovely blue flowers, is a signature plant of the Albany Pine Bush. Its leaves serve as a food source for the caterpillars of the endangered Karner Blue Butterfly.

Animals that are typical of the Albany Pine Bush include Cottontail Rabbit, Opossum, Raccoon, Red and Gray Squirrel, Red and Gray Fox, and White-tailed Deer. Rodents include Meadow Voles, Red-backed Mice, Short-tailed Shrew and Star-nosed Moles. Fowler's Toad, Black Racers, and Hognose snakes are common in the sandy areas. Nesting birds are less abundant than they once were, but include Blue Jay, Cardinal, American Crow, Baltimore Oriole, Brown Thrasher, Catbird, Hairy and Downy Woodpeckers, Mockingbird, Rufous-sided Towhee, and Prairie and Pine Warblers (fig. 3.3). Prairie Warblers are common, returning in late May from their winter stay in the Bahamas and West Indies. The Albany Pine Bush is the northern extent of their range, and they rarely breed elsewhere in New York State. Prairie Warblers nest in June and July, preferring recently burned areas that are typical of the pines.

When pinelands are situated in the middle of commercial and residential areas, it is impossible to allow fire to burn uncontrolled. Historically, however, natural wildfires swept through large expanses of the Pine Bush near Albany, creating conditions that select for the early successional plants typical of pine barrens communities. Without these periodic disturbances, the Pine Bush will disappear and be replaced by the more typical hardwood forests of the Northeast. The Albany Pine Bush Preserve Commission conducts controlled burns to maintain the Pine Bush community, but it is difficult because of the popular belief that fire suppression is important and good. A belief, that for many of us, goes back to our powerful childhood images of Smoky the Bear.

3.3. Pine Warblers are common in the Albany Pine Bush, the Long Island Barrens, and the New Jersey Pine Barrens. Remarkably, they have done quite well and feed on insects nestled in the needles.

Since the 1940s, fire has been actively suppressed in the Pine Bush because of danger to nearby residential and commercial areas. Gradually, the Pitch Pine canopy closed in, the grassy understory was crowded out because of dense oak bushes, and the native herbs disappeared because of low light levels. Wild Lupine, the host plant of the endangered Karner Blue Butterfly, is dying out in many patches. As soon as the New York State legislature created the Albany Pine Bush Commission in 1988, it instituted a policy of controlled burning and asked the Nature Conservancy to oversee the fires. In such an urban area, the danger is not only from fire itself, but from excessive smoke that can be a nuisance to area residents and an immediate danger to drivers on nearby superhighways.

First, the Nature Conservancy conducted small burns of one to three acres to learn how fire moves through the pines, when it is best to burn, and what areas should be burned. Then it moved on to larger fires, aided by special laws to allow burning the woodlands. Over time, local residents and businesses were persuaded that burning is essential to maintain the treasure they harbor in their midst, and public support has mushroomed. Local landowners often participate when they want to burn areas of their adjoining property, creating even more early successional lands. Fire breaks, water, and fire retardants are used to contain the fire, and specially trained firefighters guard the borders.

Because the preserve is so small and is surrounded by residential and business communities, there is a continual onslaught of exotic and invasive plants that move in from roadsides and gardens at the periphery. The commission uses mechanical and chemical removal to stop the spread of such plants. Two trees are invasive in the Albany Pine Bush: Black Locust and Quaking Aspen.

Black Locust is not native to the Pine Bush; it normally occurs in the southern Appalachians and the Ozarks. In the early twentieth century it was widely planted throughout the Northeast because it was fast growing and provided shade. It was introduced to the region for use as posts, railroad ties, and mine props and in shipbuilding. The wood is heavy, hard, and strong. Black Locusts are subject to the attacks of the Locust Leaf Miner and a Locust Borer, which damage and weaken the trunks. The bark is often eaten by Cottontail Rabbits during the winter months, and the seeds are eaten by birds, including Mourning Doves and Quail. Livestock, however, have been fatally poisoned by eating the inner bark. Once it was planted on lawns, it spread along the roads, and then it moved into disturbed areas of the pines. Black Locust successfully invaded the Pine Bush because it has nitrogen-fixing nodules on its roots that allow it to thrive in the nutrient-poor soil. This gives it an edge over other trees, which have to compete for the little nitrogen that is naturally available. Today, Black Locusts have spread over 10 percent of the Albany Pine Bush Preserve, certainly a cause for concern. It is difficult to control Black Locusts because burning or cutting only stimulates the stumps and roots to sprout, causing them to spread even more. Research by the Preserve Commission has shown that the only way to control the locusts is to cut them and apply a herbicide to the cut trunks. Careful application of the herbicide only to the locust stumps avoids damaging nearby native vegetation.

Aspens are another invasive tree, and they are more of a problem because they are native to the pinelands. They are outcompeting other native Pine Bush vegetation because they grow from an extensive underground root system, allowing them to produce many dense trees in one spot; this is called *clonal spread*. Historically, fire controlled the spread of aspens, but with fire suppression, some clumps or clones have spread dramatically by underground roots or suckers. The twigs are browsed by deer and the buds are eaten in winter by grouse. Now the commission is controlling aspens by girdling them. Girdling trees involves peeling off a portion of the bark in a complete circle around the tree, usually in May through July. Trees that are girdled cannot carry as much water or nutrients to growing leaves, and over a two- to three-year period, they gradually die, opening up the canopy so that Blueberry, Wild Lupine, Scrub Oak, and Pitch Pine can move in. Once the aspens are removed, regular burning by the Pine Bush Commission can keep their populations low.

The real advantage of the commission is that it can set policy and rules for the preserve, which otherwise is controlled by six different political entities: the towns of Guilderland and Colonie, the city of Albany, the Nature Conservancy, the New York State Department of Environmental Conservation, and the state Office of Parks, Recreation, and Historic Preservation. Many pine barrens habitats are endangered for this very reason; no one entity has legal authority over all of the habitat, and each entity can develop the land as it sees fit, with no overall master plan. Although the commissioners can set rules and policy for the Albany Pine Bush Preserve, they do not have complete legal control, even of the land within the preserve. In addition, much of the pine barrens land is outside the preserve, and the commission has almost no control over this land. It is striving to increase the area protected by working with landowners, by buying high-quality parcels when they become available, and by managing the preserve so it can function well ecologically. In 2005 a new parcel was added to the preserve, a tribute to the governmental agencies and conservationists working to enlarge the Pine Bush.

The Albany Pine Bush exists because many different legal entities are committed to its preservation, and hundreds of volunteers work tirelessly to keep out invasive plants, help with prescribed burns, and protect the endangered plants and animals within the preserve. They also build fire breaks to prevent fires from spreading into nearby residential areas, collect and distribute native seeds, and pull up invasive herbs before they can become too established.

As I wander the preserve on a sunny but cold winter day, I am impressed by the number of people who enjoy the trails and natural beauty. Some carry binoculars and amble slowly over the trails, searching the trees and

3.4. A male Pheasant runs across the grass after catching sight of people nearby.

shrubs for any unusual movement, pausing to check out the chickadees and kinglets; others walk quickly and hardly notice the wilderness around them. Groups of small children pull sleds and head for the hill where a well-used trail is icy. The trail circles the crest of a large basin, then descends among patches of knee-high oak and withered stems of Bracken Fern. It passes through a dense copse of aspens, their bark peeled off in a circle around the base. Had I not known of the deliberate girdling of the trees to kill them, I might have guessed it was the work of some ravenous animals.

Movement catches my eye, and I pause to watch a Ring-necked Pheasant scratch around in a small patch of grass under the Pitch Pine where the snow has blown away (fig. 3.4). The undulations of the ancient dunes that form the sand here make it easy for the wind to sweep snow from some of the ridges, providing places for birds and small mammals to forage. Pheasants are quite rare now; they are no longer stocked by the state Environmental Conservation Department. They are a bird of more southern climates, and often have trouble during the cold, hard winters.

Only a few yards from the main path, another smaller trail leads off into sleepy barrens where people seldom venture. Black-capped Chickadees flit through the pines, picking the few remaining seeds from the partly opened pine cones still clinging to the trees. A lone Blue Jay calls loudly, warning of a Red-tailed Hawk circling overhead. I can barely hear the nearby traffic, and in the solitude I can almost imagine the Mohawk Indians wandering through the same pines, searching for game to tide them over during the harsh winter.

4

People in the Albany Pine Bush

The Pine Bush was not always as small as it is today. It was once part of a dune field that extended from south of Glens Falls to Delmar, south of Albany, created by an inland lake some 12,000 years ago. Small bands of people we now call paleo-Indians entered the region following the retreat of the glaciers, which left in its wake a changing and variable climate. Where they came from is a matter of much debate—we don't really know. Recently, Dennis Stanford from the Smithsonian Institution and others have suggested that the paleo-Indians who made Clovis point arrow heads came from Europe, and not from across the Siberian land bridge. The Clovis points from eastern North America are remarkably similar in every detail (including their method of construction) to those found in France from the same period. This controversy, however, will likely go on for many years.

The earliest inhabitants were nomadic hunters who lived in a tundra-like habitat at the edges of the glaciers. Initially, the land was covered with lichens, mosses, sedges, grasses, willows, and alders, with clumps of spruces and firs, which provided grazing and browsing opportunities for Mammoths, Mastodons, woodland Caribou, and Elk, whose fossil remains have been discovered in the region.

Evidence indicates that the paleo-Indians hunted caribou in the Pine Bush, and probably hunted other animals as well. A small hunting camp-site in the Pine Bush has yielded scrapers, knives, and a side scraper used for striking fires; the materials were brought up from a quarry in southeastern Pennsylvania, indicating that these nomadic Indians traveled quite a distance. Fluted Clovis points found in the Pine Bush, indicative of early paleo-Indians about 12,000 years ago, are two to five inches long. Nearly 30 percent of Clovis points are found in low swampy ground or along rivers. They were used to kill big game such as Woolly Mammoths, Ground Sloths, Mastodons, caribou, and Giant Beaver that concentrated in these regions. By about 9,000 years ago, the arrowheads were already smaller, indicating a decrease in the size of the game that was hunted.

The flora of the Northeast did not stabilize until about 6,000 years ago, allowing adaptations by the few inhabitants. The Archaic Period, from 5,500 to 3,300 years ago, was a period of hunting, fishing, and gathering. Little archeological material exists from before 3,000 years ago, but there are many finds from more recent periods, which seem to mirror the rapid increase in population of the region. Archeological finds tell us little about the inhabitants' lifestyle, but it is assumed that these Indians were fishermen and big-game hunters. Whereas the paleo-Indians probably traveled in groups of eight to twelve, the Archaic Indians lived in bands of up to a hundred people. They must have fished with nets because many small, pebble sinkers have been located. Very likely they used bone hooks and fishing spears, but the acid soil of the Pine Bush has destroyed all bone artifacts. Whatever animals they could find, they killed with arrowheads one to three inches long attached to spears. Bow and arrows were not known, but they hurled darts with the atatla or throwing stick, weighted with a bannerstone for greater efficiency.

When I was eight I found a perfect black bannerstone on my parents' farm and gave it to my father, Melvin. I refused to let the state archeologist have it, despite his pleadings (fig. 4.1). It was a beautiful, smooth satiny-black tool that I imagined was used for slaying Mastodons and

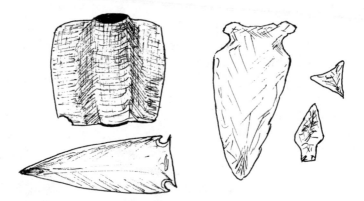

4.1. When I was six I found a perfect black bannerstone (top left) used by the Mohawk Indians to weight throwing sticks, as well as a number of arrowheads that ranged in age from about 9,000 years ago (left bottom, 3.5 inches long), to 4,000 years ago (middle), and to 3,000 years ago (right, 1–1.5 inches long). The smaller ones were used to kill birds.

Mammoths, though it more likely was used to kill deer. It had a small chip at the bottom corner; my father thought the chip might have been necessary to balance it correctly. I discovered it within the long-dead trunk of a very large oak tree along the river, and often wondered how it came to rest there. Had some other little girl used it and hidden it for a later hunt?

About 3,000 years ago, the Indians hunted animals in the pines, including Black Bears, Cottontail Rabbits, Opossums, Woodchucks, Gray Squirrels, Gray Foxes, and White-tailed Deer, as well as a number of birds such as geese, ducks, and Wild Turkeys. By then the Mammoths and Mastodons were gone. From bone remains found in their ancient garbage dumps (called *middens*), deer must have been the primary source of meat. One midden site contained the bones of 1,498 deer, 274 Passenger Pigeons, 87 Gray Squirrels, 73 Wild Turkeys, 67 Box Turtles, 26 Woodchucks, 24 Black Bears, and 21 Bullheads. These animals were killed with flint arrowheads attached to shafts by resin from the pines. This lifestyle sounds exotic and provides wonderful images of hunters slipping silently through the pines. But the middens show that these Archaic people ate mainly acorns, which are highly nutritious when roasted over heated stones to drive off the toxic tannic acid. The women gathered around campfires to grind the acorns into a mush with stone mortars. Acorn meal is 25 percent fat, compared to 1 percent fat in wheat flour and 2 percent fat in cornmeal.

Gradually these bands of Indians in the Albany region began to live in small villages, and agriculture soon followed, with some clearing of the land. This is referred to as the Woodland Period and lasted until the Europeans arrived. Initially the Indians hunted the pinelands as they had found them, but later they burned the pines to keep the habitat open to encourage an increase in the number of deer and other game. These early inhabitants of the pines may well have used the openings as a passageway rather than a place for permanent villages.

Prior to the arrival of people from Europe, the Mohawk Indians of the Iroquois Nation roamed the Pine Bush region of New York State, claiming the right to hunt and fish undisturbed. They fashioned bows and arrows from Red Cedar and strung them with deer sinew. The women made pottery and used Cattails, reeds, and other materials to weave nets to catch fish, although sometimes they speared them. While the men were at war, the women cleared the land with fire, axes, and wooden rakes. They tilled the soil with wooden hoes and spades, or fastened the shoulder blades of deer to wooden handles with resin and deer sinew.

4.2. *Orange Milk-weed is a favorite of butterflies in pine barrens habitats.*

They grew corn, beans, and squash, dried blueberries and sunflower seeds for later use, and collected acorns for mush.

The Mohawk Indian women also gathered medicines from the pines. The pitch of Pitch Pine was applied to boils and burns as a salve, put in cuts to keep them clean, and a teaspoon twice a week prevented constipation. They burned pine needles to get rid of fleas. A White Pine infusion was used to stimulate slow children to walk, encourage fat people to breathe better (and thus lose weight), and discourage colds and coughs. The same infusion served double duty as a powder for chafed babies. The bark of very young White Pines cured cramps and stiffness of the limbs and prevented typhoid. To cure "female troubles" the women boiled the leaves of Scrub Oak into a bitter tea. The Indians had a peculiar use for Orange Milkweed: they smashed the roots, mixed them with warm water, then spread the paste over their legs and feet (or shoes). If you stepped in the tracks of your opponent he would develop cramps and not be able to run after you as quickly (fig. 4.2). While the leaves of Dogbane were woven into nets and ropes, the roots were mixed with boiling water to make a tea that could purify the blood, act as a laxative, and clear up yellow eyes. Cinnamon Fern were used for colds, headaches, malaise, and rheumatism or pain in the joints—one root was boiled with three quarts of water (fig. 4.3). The small tubers on the roots of Cinnamon Fern, called Bog Onion, were also eaten. Bracken Fern was used for prolapsus of the uterus; New Jersey Tea root was made into a tea for suppressed menses, as well as for abortions, colds, and diarrhea; the root bark was ground up to make a powder to put on sores, including venereal sores and those on the roof of the mouth.

From the marshes and swamps the women gathered Spatterdock for swollen abdomens, smallpox, and consumption. Interestingly, Spatterdock roots were mixed with cold water for a few hours, and then this water was sprinkled wherever a recently departed person lived to pacify the ghost; a good-sized piece of root was also hung outside the house to keep the ghost away. Spatterdock root attached to the outside of houses warded off witches as well. From the edge of the marshes the women dug the roots of Marsh Marigold as an emetic against love charms; the roots were steeped in water, and taken early in the day to induce vomiting. High fevers and chills could be cured with a tea made of Pitcher Plant leaves (fig. 4.4). The list of ills cured by plants of the pines is endless, as nearly every plant was used; huckleberry seems to be the exception—only the berries were eaten (although some berries were used for dye).

The Mohawk Indians were the eastern gatekeepers for the Iroquois Confederacy, protecting their tribes against intruding Indians from elsewhere. Their warlike nature led to the general supremacy of the tribe in the region, which persisted at the time the Europeans arrived. A key role

4.3. Cinnamon Fern was used medicinally, and the roots were eaten by the local Indians.

the Pine Bush played for the early Indians of the region was the provision of a crossroads for camping while on long journeys. Small bands of Indians camping among the pines could hunt game there, away from the Hudson or Mohawk Rivers where they might be discovered. Sometimes they camped near the rivers, but never at the confluence where the two met, for that was a dangerous place—too many enemies might lurk nearby. They always went a few miles up or downstream to camp.

I can attest to the importance of the rivers and pines as a crossroads for travel because as a child I spent many a day hunting for arrowheads on my parents' farm beside the Mohawk River, a few miles upstream from the junction of the Mohawk and Hudson Rivers. To keep me interested while I weeded crops or picked vegetables, my father showed me the chipped pieces of flint and arrowheads that were partly buried in the soil. Usually only a tip showed above the dirt, but I developed quite a search image for these treasures, and my arrowhead collection is still one of my most prized possessions. The arrowheads were left by Indians who camped along the river and stopped for a few days to fish or hunt before continuing their journey. My young nieces and nephews have fewer chances of finding arrowheads because the small pieces of black plastic my father and brother Roy use for weed control make it more difficult to distinguish the tip of an arrowhead. Also, the fields have been thoroughly searched by my father, brothers, and sisters and me—Melvin Jr., Tina, and I often competed to see who could find the most perfect arrow-

4.4. Pitcher Plants, which are carnivorous, grow in wet boggy areas amid Sphagnum Moss.

head. Still, my nieces and nephews look for them because floods and plowing can always dislodge some treasure hidden below the surface.

These Indians must have been traders because I found a variety of arrowheads on the farm, less than five miles from the Pine Bush. Some of these are finely carved and exquisite and date from 7,000 to 9,000 years ago. Others that date from 5,000 to 6,000 years ago are smaller, cruder, and less well formed. The more recent ones from 1,000 to 2,000 years ago are again finely crafted and small. I was thrilled as a young teenager to have a "real scientist" from the Albany Museum date my collection, and was amazed to learn that these arrowheads came from Indians who lived or traveled from Pennsylvania and farther southeast. Some of my arrowheads are over two inches long, while others are less than an inch long and were obviously used for smaller game. Large spearheads are three and a half inches long, and I tried to imagine the large animals they hunted with these, particularly since they were the oldest.

As a young teenager I sat on a wooded knoll at the end of our farm, hidden from the fields by a thicket of Black Locusts and oak trees. I imagined a young Mohawk Indian girl sitting on the same spot, wondering where her life would lead her, just as I wondered. I found tiny triangular arrowheads there, as well as small pieces of smoking pipes made of clay, attesting to ancient camping sites. The oak trees were old enough to have provided cover for these small hunting bands, but the faster-growing locusts were relative newcomers. I watched White-tailed Deer through the eyes of that young Indian girl, amazed that the small arrowheads could fell them.

For most of the pre-European-settler days, the pinelands served as a passageway between the Hudson River and the Mohawk River, a short-cut that avoided the confluence. The region of the Mohawk River that flows from present-day Schenectady to Cohoes was full of rapids and was not navigable, and the Indians found it easier to travel overland, carrying their canoes with them. Going directly across the pinelands cut off quite a distance, and once they reached Schenectady, they could go by boat over the Mohawk to Rome and farther west.

Henry Hudson sailed up the Hudson River in 1609, marking the beginning of Dutch occupancy. In the colonial period, the Pine Bush also occupied a strategic trade route. In 1614, the Dutch built Fort Nassau on an island at the mouth of the Norman's Kill, which facilitated trade up the river, across to the Susquehannah Valley. A second fort, Fort Orange, constructed of pine wood in 1624, opened up the region for fur trade with the Indians along the Mohawk River. Fort Orange was the major fur-trading post in North America during the seventeenth and eighteenth centuries. In a good year, 40,000 furs were shipped to the Netherlands. The Indians called this place "Skanehtade," which meant "beyond the Pines." Since the Mohawk Indians controlled both the Pine Bush and the confluence of the Mohawk and Hudson Rivers during presettlement days, they were well placed to continue doing so when the Dutch arrived. They served as the gatekeepers, but now they traded with the Europeans to the east and the Indians to the west. Sometimes fur traders short-circuited the Dutch traders at Skanehtade, and tried to buy furs cheap in the Pine Bush before the Indians reached the fort. Alarmed by this unfair practice, Albany officials passed ordinances forbidding trading outside the city gates. Because the Pine Bush was so important as an early trade route, both the Indians and the early European settlers argued over its ownership.

In 1629 Kilian Van Rensselaer purchased nearly one million acres of land that included Fort Orange, and he became the patron (serf lord) of all who worked these lands. Finally, in 1652, Peter Stuyvesant simply declared Fort Orange and its residents independent, renaming it

Beverwych—"Town of Beavers"—later to be called Albany. In 1661, Schenectady (from Skanehtade) was founded to the west, making an overland pass through the pines even more necessary. The Schenectady stockade was built with Pitch Pines from the Pine Bush, the Indian trails were widened enough for wagons and sleighs, and the trail was called the Albany-Schenectady Road, or the King's Highway. Initially Albany maintained a monopoly on fur trade, forcing the residents of Schenectady to go to the Pine Bush to conduct their illegal trade, gathering at particular sand dunes to do so.

In 1664 New York became an English colony, but this did not change how either the Mohawk Indians or the European settlers used the pines. The English immediately granted charters for towns, including Albany. They also passed an ordinance prohibiting the removal of sand from the Pine Bush along King's Highway because graves were being exposed. In addition to its value as a trade route, the Pine Bush provided firewood for the town of Albany. It was a large burden to gather enough firewood for the militia, so the administrator of Albany levied a tax on all inhabitants. They had to provide three hundred loads of firewood for the blockhouse each year or face fines. The firewood was important for the defense of the whole area, and controversies over who had the rights to the wood in the Pine Bush continued into the middle of the 1700s. The people of Albany were granted the privilege of cutting firewood, and troops stationed nearby also depleted the forest.

Continual fighting took place among the French, Indians, and settlers in the late 1600s and 1700s. In 1690 the French planned to attack Albany, but because of extreme cold, they attacked the unguarded village of Schenectady instead, killing most of the residents. The French continued to burn and kill, frequently attacking Mohawk Indian villages in the Pine Bush between Schenectady and Albany, making travel on the King's Highway impossible without regular patrols.

In the early 1700s, the threat of Indian attack was still very real, and anyone residing outside of the Albany stockade was in danger. A few taverns developed along the King's Highway, providing a safe haven and overnight accommodations for travelers going between Albany and Schenectady. By 1747 the Albany fort was in very bad shape: the wood was rotting and needed replacing. The woodcutters had to go farther and farther afield, however, because the nearby wood in the Pine Bush had been depleted. The French and Indian Wars of the 1740s and 1750s transformed the Pine Bush forests into even more of a barrens because of the ravages of fire and timber cutting.

By the 1770s, travelers noted that the soil was very sandy and produced mainly brush and only a few pine trees. Because there was little
brush, and so few trees, the Dutch and English calvaries used it as a suitable route to traverse without fear of ambush. Almost no one lived there,
and it was visited only by a few woodcutters and berry pickers. By the
1780s the Pine Bush provided an ideal hiding place for spies, Tories, run-
away slaves, and other fugitives because the scrub had again grown tall
and dense. They lived in miserable huts in the woods, eking out a living
trying to farm, make baskets, or begging along the King's Highway. Oddly
enough, they did not resort to highway robbery. The Pine Bush reverted
to being primarily a trade and communications route. The first stagecoach from Albany to Schenectady went through the Pine Bush in 1793
at a cost of three cents a mile. The stagecoach ran once a week, but
two years later it ran daily.

In the early 1800s Pine Bush wood was used to fuel steamships on the
Hudson River. An average steamboat on the Hudson made 72 trips a season, using seven cords of wood per trip. Albany residents were alarmed
by the amount of wood used by the ships, noting that any citizen or
stranger should not be permitted to "cut more wood on the commons"[1]
than is necessary for building or heating their own homes. This is one of
the first mentions of the word "commons" in America, a concept made
famous in the 1970s by Garret Hardin. Mostly, people went to the higher
regions to pick blueberries, including my grandmother, who spoke of going to the Pine Bush as a child to pick them. It was a major trip back then,
requiring a full day in a horse-drawn wagon, and was filled with excitement and anticipation (fig. 4.5).

Sand is a valuable resource for making glass, and in the late 1780s
Leonard de Neufville from Amsterdam, Holland, established a glass factory on a tributary of the Norman's Kill in the Pine Bush. He failed, but another entrepreneur immediately set up a glass shop near Guilderland and
was at first quite successful. A vast area of forest was cut for wood to keep
the furnaces burning, but this factory also failed, and by 1815 the pine
barrens was again abandoned and left to grow back up into pine trees and
oaks. Thereafter, sand from the area was used for fill and as molding sand
until the 1940s when artificial molding sand was developed.

One of the industries that sprang up in the pines and the surrounding
region was the mining of molding sand for operating foundries in nearby

[1] From D. Rittner, "Man's activities in the Pine Bush. Pine Bush: Albany's Last Frontier." Pine Bush Preservation Project, Albany, New York, 1976.

*4.5. It was a long day's journey by horse for my grandmother
to go to the Albany Pine Bush to pick blueberries, but she said,
"Well worth the trip."*

towns. When the massive glacier retreated, it left an 8 to 15 foot layer of
unusual sand called "molding sand," a very fine-textured sand with high
clay content. It also left the usual piles of sand and gravel, and over time
the winds covered the molding sand with soil or dunes. Molding sand was
easy to shape when it was wet, but when it dried it was very hard. It could
be used to construct molds for making cast-iron objects.

Most books on the region list molding sand as a small, fleeting industry
of the pines and environs, but it actually dominated the area for nearly
100 years. The presence of iron in northeastern New York State, the abundance of molding sand in the Pine Bush and surrounding region, and the
availability of limestone for flux established Troy as the major iron and
steel center of the nation by the Civil War. The local foundries even made
the armor plates for the *Monitor,* the famous Civil War fighting ship. The
Monitor traveled to Virginia, where it had the distinction of being involved
in the first battle in the world of ironclad warships in 1862.

The sand molding industry was at its peak from 1860 to about 1910,
when it disappeared because the local molding sand was finally depleted.
During that period, however, the Pine Bush and environs had the best
molding sand in the country. My father told me of the bustling molding
sand industry in the area when his father and grandfather were farming.
Beds of molding sand underlaid many of the local farms, and the upper
soil or sand was stripped away to reach the layer of molding sand. When
they were not farming, the local farmers rented out their teams of horses
for hauling the sand. One of the liveries was located just across the river

from my parents' farm. In those days, the Mohawk River was not a barrier because the channel had not been deepened, and my father recalled walking across the river, hopping from rock to rock.

Both my grandfather and great-grandfather hauled molding sand to the ironworks, and Grandpa Burger even had a small streak of the sand on his farm that was mined. Before it was mined, the Belted Kingfishers used to dig their burrows there because it could be excavated when it was wet, and the burrows then dried, making a nest cavity that would not collapse on their young. The streak of pale yellow to light tan molding sand on Grandpa's farm was about eight feet thick, and when it was completely mined, it left a gaping hole. Now the farm is gone, bulldozed level, and covered with houses and well-manicured lawns.

"On each trip to the ironworks a team of two horses could haul about two cubic yards of sand in a wooden box. The box was constructed with an opening or chute at the bottom so that the team could just unload the sand and return for another load," my father recalled. There were businesses that ran the horses and mules necessary to cart the sand to the Burden Iron Works, but they always rented whatever local horses were available. In the summer the horses were busy on the farms, and in the dead of winter they hauled ice to be shipped farther south. During the rest of the year they hauled molding sand.

Great Uncle John Finley was a pattern maker, critical to the whole process. While I remember him as a very old, slightly stoop-shouldered white-haired man, he made excellent patterns for armor, horseshoes, bells, boilers, pot-bellied stoves, pans, and other objects that were shipped all over the country. His skills were still important long after the Burden Iron Works had closed its doors. He told me about working there many years ago.

"It was hard work," Uncle John said, "but I loved making the patterns for the iron works."

"What was your favorite?" I asked.

"The bells because I loved the sounds." Uncle John was a musician, as were many of my older relatives.

"What about the armor," I wanted to know, thinking of knights and maidens on horseback.

"It wasn't as much fun as the bells, and the pans were a little boring."

"Did you go by horseback?" I inquired, still thinking it was wonderful to ride horses.

"Of course, but it was simply a way to get there—better than walking. Sometimes, we came home very late. There were more woods around then, and we usually stopped to listen for the Great Horned Owls." Maybe the owl he listened to was the great-grandfather of the very same owls I heard on my mother and father's farm in the late winter.

The sand molding business depended upon the cast-iron works— where the iron was poured into the molds to make goods. The iron was mined down in the Catskills from Iron Mountain, on the west side of the Hudson River, and brought by boat to the Burden Iron Works in Troy. The finished products were transported all over the country by rail.

My father remembered the Burden Iron Works, located in Troy on a tributary of the Hudson River. Initially built in 1809, it was named the Troy Iron and Nail Factory in 1913, and in 1922 it was taken over by Henry Burden, who invented several machines to increase the iron output. Pig iron was made in blast furnaces in which iron was melted, heated by burning charcoal, an industry that also abounded in the New Jersey Pine Barrens. Pig iron was repeatedly heated and hammered into wrought iron to make nails, horseshoes, stoves, and armor. Water-driven hammers pounded the pig iron into wrought iron.

The Burden Iron Works built the largest water wheel in the country to mechanically power the presses. My mother, Janette, still has a faded picture saved by her father of the old water wheel, and it is very impressive. Water from a nearby creek was diverted into a large passage through the building to the water wheel. Constructed of wood, it was about eight stories high. The rim of the wheel was about 20 feet wide with a series of 28 slats around the rim of the wheel, each slat with four buckets. When the buckets filled with water, the wheel moved faster and faster. A small staircase led up to the axle for repair, and wooden spokes radiated from the axle. The frame was of wrought iron because cast iron was a little too brittle. Long after it was no longer in operation it was still a local attraction. When the factory had long disappeared, gears were strewn around the grounds and the wheel remained, too massive to be easily torn down.

After the Civil War, the Pine Bush was still thought of as "forlorn, miserable, and an unsatisfactory combination of sands, swamp, and aridity as the Union can produce."[2] However, farming always took place around the edges of the Pine Bush, particularly in the lower places where some humus collected. In the lower spots, the water table is quite close to the surface, and the farmers had a ready supply of water for their crops. They

[2] From D. Rittner, "Pine Bush: Albany's Last Frontier." Pine Bush Preservation Project, Albany, New York, 1976.

grew tomatoes, melons, and corn, and some of these same crops are grown today on the few farms that remain on the edges of the Pine Bush. It is always colder in the Pine Bush, and so the farmers had to worry about frost killing freshly planted seedlings in the spring, and vegetables in the fall. Mostly the farms have been crowded out by residential developments, but a few still survive.

Some Shakers settled on the edge of the Albany Pine Bush in the 1800s, and they immediately set about learning the medicinal benefits of the local plants. In 1831 the first Shaker herb catalog was printed in Albany, listing 120 herbs with medicinal value, and an additional 22 roots, barks, berries, and seeds of potential use. Some of these grew in the Pine Bush, but most grew along the edges in disturbed areas, and many were invasive plants brought over from Europe.

Some of the plants collected in the pinelands included Wintergreen, used to increase the flow of urine, and Butterfly Weed (fig. 4.6) for treating pleurisy, indigestion, and for promoting perspiration. In the wetter places, they collected Skunk Cabbage used for asthma, convulsions during pregnancy, hysteria, and whooping cough, and they picked Indian Hemp for rheumatism, asthma, and syphilis. On the edges of the Pine Bush, they collected Coltsfoot for asthma, coughs, and as a poultice; Goldenrod for stomach sickness and during convalescence from severe diarrhea, for cholera, dropsy, and urinary difficulties; Lobelia as an emetic; Mullen as a sedative; Pearly Everlasting for bowel complaints, coughs,

4.6. The large orange and black Monarchs are always a pleasure to see. They frequent any habitat that has flowers for nectaring and milkweed for the larvae to eat.

colds, and mouth ulcers; White Oak bark for chronic diarrhea, dysentery, and sore throat. The list of remedies for diseases barely recognizable today goes on and on.

Two of the Shakers' five best-sellers, Deadly Nightshade and Dandelion, could be found on the edges of the barrens where the sand was disturbed. Deadly Nightshade, which is extremely poisonous, was given for convulsions, neuralgia, gout, and other painful conditions of the nervous system, while Dandelion was used for constipation, dropsy, and diseases of the skin and liver. Belladonna, another name for Deadly Nightshade, was used by Venetian ladies to dilate their pupils to give them a glamorous, wide-eyed, and innocent look. Today we recognize that this practice must have led to increased rates of cataracts because the pupils were forced open, exposing the eye to increased UV light.

Today, we also use the Pine Bush as a car trade route. After all, the New York State Thruway, Northway, and U.S. 20 go right through the Pine Bush. Indeed, the early European settlers used the same trading routes as the Indians, widening them for travel by horse. They continued to be improved until the twentieth century, when we paved them. Most modern roads in the region follow old Mohawk Indian trails. The State University of New York at Albany has its main campus in what used to be Pine Bush, and I often use their tall buildings as a compass when I lose my way in the pines.

The Albany Pine Bush holds a special appeal for me, because as a small child I dreamed about its wonderful wilderness, imagining that Indians still roamed the pines, furtively tracking the bears I hoped resided there. In fifty years the prevailing view of the land has changed from "a wasteland" to a "treasure" requiring intense protection. Land around Albany is so valuable for development that the remaining Pine Bush is very endangered. There is, however, a dedicated group of people working tirelessly to save the Albany Pine Bush, to maintain its functions, and to allow fire to run through the pines as it did so many centuries ago. The burn will open up the canopy so the oaks, Wild Lupine, and obscure ground-cover plants can flourish, providing habitat for the Karner Blue Butterfly, Edward's Hairstreak, and other sensitive species.

The Butterfly Count and the Karner Blue

A warm breeze ruffles the tops of a few stunted pines, their needles brushing softly together. Billowing white clouds mar the brilliant blue sky. A fairly dense understory of Scrub Oaks gives way to more open sand, where the sunlight plays off the small white flowerheads of New Jersey Tea. Six or eight tea plants form a dense clump, a patch of delicate white in a sea of greens. Dancing from head to head are a number of small gray butterflies, and our attention is riveted on them. As we peer intently, more silent shapes materialize, for they blend in perfectly with their background. Suddenly two of the insects spiral upwards, twisting and turning a dozen feet overhead, then plummeting back into the oaks.

It is early July in the Pine Bush, time for our annual butterfly count. Like birdwatchers, butterfly enthusiasts have started annual butterfly counts to establish the distribution of butterflies in the United States and to document changes in their abundance. Butterfly counts occur around July 4 each year. The Christmas Bird Count is a major activity—a cross between scientific data collection and outdoor recreation. The first bird counts were done in 1900, making them one of the oldest sporting events in the nation. From late December to early January, tens of thousands of birdwatchers go afield for a day to count as many birds as possible within a 7.5 mile radius of a chosen point. More than 1,500 circles are scattered over North America. The "circle," as it is affectionately called, remains the same from year to year, and only birds within the circle can be counted. The number of participants increases each year, and the number of hours people are afield varies with latitude and weather, and, of course, determination and commitment. When it is cold and windy, fewer people come out to brave the elements, but there are always a few hearty souls. While in graduate school I participated in a Christmas Count in northern Minnesota. The temperature did not go above zero all day, the winds blew at a steady 20 miles an hour. Today we dignify our plight with a wind chill of −40 degrees. Eight of us worked all day to count four individuals of as many species. No other Christmas Count can ever be so bleak—but we reveled in our plight.

It is possible to use these data scientifically, however, for every count includes information on the number of participants and the number of hours spent afield, both walking and driving. Christmas bird counts are an important source of information on declines and shifts in bird populations across North America. They, and the breeding bird counts, provided some of the first indications of declines, and without them, it would have been difficult to make the argument of massive declines.

By contrast, butterfly counts are fairly recent, dating back only to 1975. The participants are often birdwatchers who have tired of cold winter counts when few species are about, and who have simply adopted a new set of interesting animals to watch, learn about, and count. Now they can watch birds from dawn to 9 or 10 A.M., and then switch to watching butterflies leisurely in sunny fields amid colorful flowers and swaying grasses. The pace is slower, the walk is shorter, and the butterflies are in grasses and flowers at waist level. The delicate colors of butterflies are lovely, and their behavior is equally interesting. When butterfly activity wanes in late afternoon, attention turns back to birds. One can really punish oneself by continuing after dark to find frogs and owls. Less adventuresome souls can watch butterflies from the comfort of their backyard swings—butterflies can be drawn to even the smallest garden by planting a variety of host plants.

Butterflies are creatures of summer and sunshine. The butterfly counts are generally in late June and early July when the greatest number of species are most likely to be out and flying about. In the Northeast, not all species will be flying in July—a few occur only in early spring, and others occur in late summer, but the greatest diversity is in July. The counts are gaining in popularity as more and more people expand their interests to include butterflies.

Butterfly counts have followed the bird count tradition in that the count area is a circle with a 15-mile diameter, and all butterflies must be counted on one designated day. Most circles have been chosen to include a variety of different habitats to increase the chances of getting a high count of species. Much thought and discussion goes into choosing the circle, for once chosen, its real value is in repeated counts, year after year. Trends can be established only with many years of counts. In 1975, the first count year, there were only 30 butterfly circles and counts, but by 1995 there were 296 involving 2,946 people. By 2003, this group grew to at least 3,963 people in 471 butterfly counts, showing that butterfly counts are clearly on the upswing. In contrast, 1,623 bird counts took place in 1995, with 37,000 observers throughout the United States, and by 2003–4, the numbers had risen to 1,996 counts with 55,431 people.

It is nearly 90 degrees outside and there is little air movement in the pines. The mosquitos and other small biting insects fly about, landing all too often on our arms and legs. Slowly Mike, my sister Barbara, and I, escorted by our young nephews and nieces, make our way over the sandy trails, peering intently at the vegetation. My husband, Mike, is a physician who teaches toxicology and environmental medicine, but his real love is nature, from butterflies and birds to African antelope. His pace is slow and steady as he walks along, but he misses few things, and his keen observations and eclectic interests are a wonderful counterpoint to my natural history interests. Barbara is not impressed by the small, pale butterflies we are counting, but she enjoys the outdoors and shares the children's enthusiasm.

When we walk down a slight hill I watch in amazement as Jacob, Erik, Beth, Ben, Andy, and Emily bend over the low bushes, carefully counting each butterfly. They skip through the Scrub Oaks to scare up the hidden hairstreaks, oblivious of the dense tangles that tug at their legs and pants. At this age, they are very intent and their eyes are incredibly sharp. They are steadfast in their approach and concentrate with a single-mindedness I cannot mimic.

Although some butterflies are flying about, most are resting in the shade, nectaring at New Jersey Tea or searching for places to deposit their eggs. Looking for butterflies requires developing a search image for small triangular shapes among the leaves and branches, or "leaves" that are just not the right color and turn out to be butterflies. We wave a small stick to gently brush the tops of tall shrubs to encourage any butterflies lingering there to take wing.

Our small binoculars can focus as close as four feet, necessary to identify butterflies that are hard to distinguish, just like birds. We have more time to identify the butterflies, however, because they normally remain where they are. When they do fly, we hope they will fly only a short distance before they alight again. Some, of course, dart off into the distance, and a few soar gracefully higher and higher, landing on the very top of a pine tree. Others flutter erratically along, looking like they are about to flop to the ground, but they never do.

Stalking butterflies requires us to move very slowly so we won't scare them. Another cardinal rule is never pass in front of the sun so that a shadow falls on the butterfly—the butterfly will surely fly off in response. Staying away a respectable distance is also important. Butterflies have evolved with the continual pressure of predation from birds, lizards, and other animals, and they respond to rapid movement or a shadow because it might signal an approaching predator.

As the sun rises higher, more and more butterflies take wing, and keeping track is a challenge as they flit by us in all directions. Like the bird counts, we have to make sure that each one is counted only once. The Pine Bush is crisscrossed with trails, and we lose ourselves in the meandering paths. We can allot only four hours to the Pine Bush, for we must visit other, wetter habitats to add species that do not occur here.

We are searching mostly for Edward's Hairstreak, a beautiful little butterfly. The males are either a dark blue above with a narrow black margin on the wings, or they are a vivid silver blue above. The females are usually a gray-brown above, with just a touch of blue, and orange margins at the lower wing. When they sit still on the delicate white flowers, however, only the undersides of their wings are visible. Their undersides are a pale brown with a series of small black dots, the ones on the edges of the wings are tipped with orange. A delicate light blue fringes each wing.

In 1994 our count of over 200 Edward's Hairstreaks was one of the highest counts for the nation, and we found nearly all of them here in the Pine Bush. This is another feature of both bird and butterfly counts— everyone likes to get the high count for a species, even if it is an incredibly common one. Eventually we all know what everyone else saw, because the counts are announced in a magazine published by the North American Butterfly Association, and the high counts for each species are listed in a separate table.

As we walk on, we begin to realize that there are more hairstreaks than last year, and we are excited about the possibility of finding so many. Mike and I both give in to our competitive bent; it is fun and intoxicating to get the highest count, to beat out the competition. We even want to surpass our own record. We become even more diligent, and walk off onto the tiny side trails of open sand, covering the territory well.

"How do you know you aren't counting the same butterflies over and over?" Barbara asks, skeptically.

"Because we walk along each trail only once, to ensure that we do not count the same butterflies more than once," I replied, "When we have to backtrack we don't count."

Our eyes search even the dark corners of the shrubs where it is hard to pick out the shapes of the dancing butterflies. The hairstreaks are especially fond of New Jersey Tea, and every clump has a least one hair-streak, some have six or eight. This small shrub flowers from late May through July in the Pine Bush, although it blooms slightly earlier in the New Jersey Pine Barrens. The flowerheads that are just opening are a delicate pale yellow, but they are soon bleached by the sun to a pale white, which is preferred by the hairstreaks, perhaps because the older flowers produce more nectar. Some large clumps of New Jersey Tea have a dozen or two hairstreaks lurking on the tiny white flowers. Another butterfly that likes New Jersey Tea is the Mottled Duskywing, whose caterpillars eat it exclusively.

We count every species, of course, and are especially keen on finding new ones. The first one of each species is greeted with glee. Long ago a critic of bird counts noted that there are many species for which only one individual is found, as if the counters did not bother to find more once it was "on the list." This may be a fair criticism.

Along a trail that is especially open we find a small clump of Butterfly Weed, with bright orange flowerheads gleaming in the sun. Butterfly Weed, a particularly pretty member of the milkweed family, is very at-tractive to butterflies. A brilliant orange and black Monarch flits about, going from flowerhead to flowerhead (see fig. 4.6). In comparison to the small hairstreaks we have been counting, the Monarch looms very large and is almost gaudy. We stop to admire her beauty, and to watch her extend her long black tongue to sip the nourishing nectar. She must gather enough energy to allow her to lay eggs, and soon flies, testing the milkweed leaves, and right before our eyes she glues a tiny white egg to the bottom of a leaf. Monarch caterpillars feed only on milkweed leaves.

As we round a bend, an unusual patch of color catches Mike's eye. "Come quickly, look what I have!" he says.

Sitting on a log is a Hognose Snake, basking in the warm morning sun. In only a few hours it would have moved out of the sun on its own, searching for a cooler place. Since snakes are cold blooded, they regulate their body temperature behaviorally by moving in and out of the sun, into deeper shade, or even underground to avoid the heat of midday. But for now it is soaking up the warm rays. When sufficiently warmed up, it will slither off in search of a toad, worm, or insect to eat.

We watch in silence, from a distance, afraid to move lest we interrupt his basking. At first our nieces and nephews stand behind us, but within seconds they peer around, and soon are standing in front, bending for-ward to get a closer look. I have found that most children are fascinated by snakes, particularly when they first meet them without their protective and often fearful parents.

The snake's head lays seductively on one of its thick coils, oblivious to our steady stares. Its position is not random. No doubt it has chosen the log because it reflects the warm rays of the sun, and the tangles of New Jersey Tea provide protection from the wind. Hognose Snakes are a relatively short, stocky snake with a wide head and body, but this Hognose is nearly three feet long. This one is a brilliant yellow with a slight tinge of red, with black splotches along its body. Its upturned snout looks vicious, but it is not. This upturned nose helps it burrow through the sand in search of toads, its primary food. The Hognose must have eaten many toads to have grown so large.

Unable to resist taking a photograph, I move a few inches closer, and the Hognose galvanizes into action, sending our nieces and nephews scrambling for the bushes. Quickly it rears up, raising its head four or five inches above the log. It flattens the sides of its head and neck, and looks like a small, fierce cobra, giving rise to its common name of Puff Adder (fig. 5.1). Slowly, it weaves its head from side to side, hissing, taking aim for a strike—or so it implies. It wiggles its tail, making a slight rustling sound like a rattlesnake. The Hognose Snake is a master at deception, and usually its behavior is enough to frighten off humans or other predators.

We are all riveted to the spot, unable to hear anything but the pounding of our hearts. Beth and Erik stand discreetly behind me, but Emily and Ben peer around, keenly interested in snakes and other reptiles. I have to hold Emily back because she wants to pick it up; she is very tactile and can hardly restrain herself. Equally fascinated, Ben wants to

5.1. *Hognose Snakes are also called Puff Adders because they rear up and flatten the skin around the head to appear quite large and ferocious.*

watch without disturbing it. Older and wiser, Jacob stays back, amused by the interest of his younger cousins.

As I move a few inches closer, the Hognose continues flattening its head until it looks like a wedge, and the tail-rattling grows louder. It becomes even more frantic, moving its head back and forth, and up and down. We remain transfixed, but not enough to prevent me from taking a picture or two. Quickly it lowers its head and moves off a few inches, only to raise up and begin the performance again. It never will strike, of course, for this is a distraction display meant to convince an "enemy" that it is fierce and should be avoided. Two dark spots on the back of its head look like giant evil eyes. Finally, it falls to the ground in a fit of writhing, puts out its tongue, flops over on its back, and remains motionless, apparently dead to the world. It doesn't work—we know that it is merely "playing dead." After taking a few more pictures—for this is one of the largest Hognose Snakes I have every seen—we reach out and turn it over so it is right-side up. A dead snake is supposed to be upside down, however, and the Hognose turns itself over on its back once again.

We move on to counting more butterflies. It will not do to tarry and miss getting the highest count of Edward's Hairstreaks for the country— a task that would be impossible without our nieces and nephews. Momentarily, when their attention wavers, I distract them with hunting for the sweet blueberries that grow in the lower, wet spots. The berries are quite small and a deep blue, but they are far sweeter than the large, succulent-appearing, but often mealy berries we now buy in supermarkets. The children are repeating what their great-grandmother did nearly a century ago. For her it was a full-day adventure in a horse-drawn cart, while it took us only 15 minutes to drive here. Andy spots a passing butterfly, and we are off searching again.

We are between Karner Blue broods, and will not see one today. This butterfly was the original impetus for creating the Albany Pine Bush Preserve. The Karner Blue was first described by the novelist Vladimir Nabokov, who characterized the Albany Pine Bush as "a sandy and flowery little paradise" on his last visit.[1] Nabokov often stopped at the Pine Bush on his way from Cornell University, where he taught, to Harvard University, where he studied butterflies in their collections. The Karner Blue that he used to describe the species, known as the type specimen,

---

[1] The Nabokov quote is from D. Nabokov and M. J. Bruccoli, *Vladimir Nabokov, Selected Letters, 1940–1977* (New York: Harcourt Brace Jovanovich, Bruccol Clark Layman, 1989).

came from Karner, an old whistle stop for the New York Central Railroad in the Albany Pine Bush. The Karner Blues are quite small, with a wingspread of only about one inch. The topside of the male is pale silvery blue with a narrow black margin, while the female is grayish brown to slightly bluish. She has irregular bands of orange crescents just inside the very narrow black border of her wings.

Once "millions" of Karner Blue Butterflies swarmed in the Pine Bush near Albany, surrounded by vast tracts of fire-maintained pines on the glacial sands. Early naturalists wrote of catching 30 Karner Blues in one sweep of a butterfly net, impossible today for almost any butterfly. Light-blue clouds of butterflies swarmed in late July, and a 100 at a time drank from tiny mud puddles, a behavior that is called "puddling." Many different species of butterflies gather at pools to drink—usually it is the males that gather. Nowadays it is rare to see such large groups puddling because loss of habitat and pesticides have reduced the numbers of many butterflies. Today, 1,000 Karner Blue Butterflies in any area is considered a good population and represents the minimum number that is sufficient for the population to persist. In the last two decades Karner Blues have declined dramatically throughout their range, and the eastern race was federally listed as endangered in December 1992. The Karner Blue has become the charismatic cry for preservation of fragile barrens environments in several states, including New York. They are a symbol of vanishing landscapes. The same process that produced the unique plant communities in the barrens also produced very specialized insects adapted to these communities alone, and the Karner Blue is one of them (fig. 5.2).

Karner Blue Butterflies are in trouble partly because they have a low dispersal rate, poor colonizing ability, and their caterpillars eat only one plant, the Wild Lupine. Lupine have purplish blue, sweetpealike flowers, and are really quite lovely. Furthermore, unscrupulous people have collected the Lupine to sell. Because their numbers are so low, even the collection of a few Lupines harms the population of butterflies. Collection of both butterflies and Lupine is illegal without a permit from the U.S. Fish and Wildlife Service, but poachers collect them anyway. Merely carrying a net into the Albany Pine Bush Preserve is grounds for arrest.

Habitat loss and fragmentation were the first and foremost causes of the decline of the Karner Blue Butterfly because it occurs only in oak and pine barrens, habitats that are viewed by many as worthless. Karner Blues were always restricted to these habitats, but as the pine-oak barrens shrank, so did the butterfly's range. In the East, they can be found primarily in remnant populations in sand barrens in the Massachusetts

5.2. Adult Karner Blue Butterflies nectar on New Jersey Tea, which is quite common in the Albany Pine Bush.

and Albany Pine Bush, in barrens near Saratoga airport in New York, and in limited areas in New Hampshire. They are also in Minnesota, and in a few scattered areas in Indiana and Wisconsin. A few small populations exist on powerline right-of-ways extending from the Albany Pine Bush north to Glens Falls, in a region known as the Hudson Valley sand belt. Now and then one turns up on isolated patches of Pine Bush soils, such as my brother Johnny's farm in Niskayuna, but this is rare. Karner Blues have disappeared from Ohio, Illinois, and Ontario.

Conservationists believe that tens of thousands of acres are necessary to maintain a number of healthy, intertwining populations of Karner Blue Butterflies—known as a metapopulation. The smaller the area, and the smaller the population of Karner Blue Butterflies, the more likely it is that a wildfire or other catastrophic event will wipe out the whole population. In a very large continuous habitat block, wildfires burn only a small patch, and adults from nearby patches can recolonize the burned-over areas. The populations of Karner Blues normally move around the entire landscape as each area is in the optimal, early successional stage they prefer. The Albany Pine Barrens Preserve is too small to maintain a metapopulation.

Since Karner Blues suffer high mortality in burned-over areas, it is extremely important for adjacent habitat to contain a population of Karner Blues so that adults can immigrate in to lay eggs following a fire. Fire management requires that only small areas be burned at one time, and that population censuses be conducted to ensure that Karner Blue populations are adjacent to the proposed burn site. Otherwise, the Karner Blues may be wiped out in an area. Burning, however, is absolutely essential to maintain the early successional stage where Lupines and other wildflowers will prosper.

The dependence of Karner Blue caterpillars on Wild Lupine, a native, perennial legume that favors alkaline sand, poses another problem. Lupine has become very scarce in the main area of the reserve. Although the early settlers reported that dense stands of Lupine covered many acres, today only a few hundred Lupine remain in the Albany Pine Bush Preserve, providing scarcely enough food for the butterflies. On many a warm June day Mike and I have searched these sandhills for Lupine, only to find very few scattered plants, not the massive clumps preferred by the Karner Blues. Only two or three Karner Blue caterpillars are usually present on these small clumps.

Wild Lupine is particularly vulnerable to fire suppression because it is not very shade tolerant. With increasing shade, Lupines decrease both in density and growth rates. They may persist for a few years in some shade, but they do not do well. Karner Blues appear unable to carry on their normal life history on shaded Lupine. Even though the absolute number of Lupine plants may seem adequate, their widely scattered distribution results in an apparent food shortage. Caterpillars must abandon one depleted Lupine and walk to the next, limiting their ability to disperse. Up to 80 percent mortality of the small caterpillars can occur during dispersal—they can walk only so far. The caterpillars starve and the Karner Blues perish.

Having only a few widely scattered Lupines also disrupts the behavior of the laying females. If they spend too much time searching for Lupine, they may lay fewer eggs, lay their eggs in inferior habitat or on solitary Lupine rather than on a clump, or be exposed to increased predation. The closing of the canopy decreases the number of Lupines and may reduce the number of other flowers, reducing nectar sources for females during the critical egg-laying period.

A variety of other factors can affect the health of the Lupine stands, including off-road vehicles, acid rain, and overbrowsing. Strangely enough, the removal of off-road vehicles from the Albany Pine Bush may have had a negative effect on the presence of Lupine. Lupines do best during early succession in disrupted soils, the condition that exists following a fire. But in the absence of fires, the off-road vehicles were disturbing the soils just enough to keep out exotic or invasive plants. Now, without either fires or off-road vehicles, some stands of Lupine have been replaced by Spotted Knapweed, an exotic from Europe. It is a delicate balance, because too many off-road vehicles, as well as trampling by horses or people, can destroy the Lupine. It is possible that in the past, the use of the Albany Pine Bush as a trade route by a variety of American Indians, and later by the early settlers, aided in keeping the barrens soil sufficiently disrupted to help maintain an early successional stage. No exotic plants from Europe were present before the settlers arrived.

Several other factors influence Wild Lupine populations. Acid rain, for example, may adversely affect Lupines because they prefer alkaline sands. Therefore, if the acidity of the soil changes, Lupine growth is hindered. Overbrowsing by White-tailed Deer, Cottontail Rabbits, and Woodchucks may also impair growth and seed production of Lupine, thereby affecting the Karner Blue Butterflies. The drifting of pesticides from nearby gardens and lawns into Karner Blue habitat can kill vulnerable caterpillars or adults. Finally, Lupine fanciers sometimes remove Lupines from an area without knowing that they are critical for butterflies. Though they may look lovely in backyard gardens, they are absolutely essential for the butterflies, and their removal is illegal. Moreover, the native species is much less showy than the numerous horticultural varieties one can buy.

One other subtle effect may influence the quality of Lupine as food: the physical aspect of the land. In an undisturbed sand barrens, the ground is undulating, with some high dunes intermingled with flat or rolling habitat. The amount of sunlight varies depending on the aspect. Lupine plants growing on very steep, south-facing sand dunes may die earlier because of the hot searing sun and lack of moisture, reducing the availability or quality of the food. In some sand barrens, only steep dunes remain undeveloped or undisturbed.

The absolute dependence of Karner Blues on Lupine has prompted some states to initiate Lupine propagation plans, which require detailed studies on the biology and habitat requirements of Lupine. Propagating

Lupine is not a simple matter since both physical and biological aspects affect success. For example, removing nearby trees should increase Lupine growth by opening the canopy and exposing the plants to more sun. However, in some cases, this just makes the flowers more vulnerable to browsing by deer, and the plants completely disappear. Exclosures, small fenced areas that keep out animals, are being tried in some areas as a method to preserve the few remaining Lupine. Moving plants to preserves may not always be successful because mature, established plants have long roots that cannot be easily dug up without disruption.

Global warming is yet more troubling for the Karner Blue in the long term. The Blues seem to require from 80 to 120 days of continuous snow cover to prevent freezing, desiccation, or premature hatching of their eggs. In historical times, snow normally covered the Albany Pine Bush for at least 80 or 90 days in winter. With global warming, the necessary snow cover may not be present. The eggs of Karner Blues lie on the exposed sand, and without snow cover they might dry out when the winter sun warms up the sand. The eggs are a delicate pale green with frosty white edges, and they cannot be exposed to full sun for long periods.

Some populations that are farther north in Saratoga County, New York, are faring better than those in the Pine Bush Preserve, perhaps due to their prolonged period of snow cover. In the past, slight increases in temperature meant that the Karner Blue overwintered successfully in pine barrens habitats farther north, but many of these no longer exist because of development. When large tracts of pine barrens are available, species like the butterflies can just move north or south as the climate dictates. However, agriculture, suburbanization, and urbanization have eliminated most of the pine barrens, and what's left of the Albany Pine Bush Preserve is not large enough to enable the butterflies to cope with large-scale global warming.

Lupines are not the only species that are important to the Karner Blue. They also depend on ants. One of the most unusual associations among animals occurs between certain butterflies in the Lycaenidae family (Blues and Hairstreaks) and ants. The Karner Blue caterpillars are attended by ants, up to nine different species, and those that do not have attendant ants seem to have higher rates of predation. The caterpillars produce a sugary honeydew secretion that the ants eat, and the ants produce a substance that repels spiders, wasps, and flies, the primary predators of Karner Blue caterpillars. Though Karner Blue caterpillars attended by ants suffer less predation, not all predators are deterred. Such information is critical to any management plan for the Karner Blue because it means that healthy ant populations must be maintained as well. Edward's Hairstreak also requires these ants.

It has been difficult to determine the minimum viable population size of the Karner Blue. It appears that a population of fewer than 1,000 adults in late July may be insufficient to maintain a viable population. Although every state wants to protect and maintain its population, even if it is below that level, Dale Schweitzer, a New Jersey Lepidoptera specialist, and others feel that federal endangered species money should only go to preserving those populations that are above 1,000 because they have the greatest chance of long-term survival. Small, separated populations may be connected, however, providing they are not more than a few hundred feet apart. Populations can be linked by providing them with paths or corridors; the Karner Blues will fly short distances, particularly if there are other wildflowers or even Lupine along the way. Sometimes brush or a few trees can be cut to make the paths more obvious.

We have very little chance of finding an adult Karner Blue today because the adults fly only from late May to early June in the Albany Pine Bush, and again from late July to early August; in early July they are in the caterpillar stage. Butterflies are challenging to study and census because they are not around continuously. They have four life stages: egg, caterpillar (larva), pupa (chrysalis), and adult. Although all butterflies have these same four stages, there is great variety in how long a given species spends in each stage. Even the total length of the cycle varies: some species go from egg to egg in a month, while others take many months or as long as a year. Weather can affect these events as well.

Species of butterflies that have only one brood (one entire cycle) a year are called *univoltine*, while those that have two are called *bivoltine*. Some, like the Pearl Crescent Butterfly, can have three or more broods a year. In some, the broods can overlap, so usually some adults are flying about. Adult Cabbage Butterflies are always flying, from spring to late fall—so many that census takers often disdain counting them. Since the adults of the Karner Blue fly only in early June, with a second brood of adults flying in late July to early August, it is a "bivoltine" butterfly. Unlike the caterpillars, the adults are able to nectar, or feed, on a variety of wildflowers, including Lowbush Blueberry, Wild Plum, Common Milkweed, Butterfly Weed, New Jersey Tea, and Wild Strawberry. Sometimes they even feed on the droppings of mammals.

In early July, only the caterpillar and pupa stage are present, and these are very hard to find. The caterpillars are green with delicate brown hairs, blending in with the Lupine and less visible to predators, making them difficult to pick out. The caterpillars eat all but the upper layer of each leaf, leaving a translucent window, which sometimes gives a clue to their location. We look carefully, nonetheless, at a small stand of Lupines, but I do not expect to be successful. Surprisingly, Emily finds one—she only needed to hear us say that the caterpillars were impossible to find, and she searched relentlessly. The three-quarter-inch caterpillar has a dark green stripe along its back, with paler stripes along the sides. We carefully place it back on its leaf so that it can continue to eat. In a couple of weeks it will spin a silken pad, attach its body, and form a green chrysalis. A week later the developing butterfly will be visible through the pupal shell, and within hours the new Karner Blue Butterfly will emerge.

The adults that fly in late July lay eggs on or near Lupine, but the eggs are very loosely attached. Many fall to the sand during heavy winds and overwinter on the ground. They hatch the following April after the Wild Lupine has sprouted, providing food for the young caterpillar. Overwintering success is low, however. A given female may lay about 80 eggs, but only 4 of every 1,000 eggs yields a butterfly the following June.

Edward's Hairstreaks are much more successful in the Albany Pine Bush than are the Karner Blues, and there are hundreds of them. Our task is to count every one on the path we normally travel. Like all censuses, we are obtaining a relative count that will indicate whether numbers have increased or decreased from previous years.

Ahead, my nieces and nephews are anxiously searching the clumps of white flowers on New Jersey Tea. They can be very competitive, and each one of them wants to find more than the other.

"These two are stuck together," Emily cries. "Are they injured?"

"Wait, Emily, I'll be right there." I hurry to catch up with her to see what she has. She is pointing to two Delaware Skippers, caught in the act (fig. 5.3).

"They're breeding," I say, hoping she catches on.

"But why are they stuck together?" she asks, clearly not understanding.

"The male is giving her sperm, to make babies," I say, hoping her attention will quickly switch to something else.

"Oh, that," she says disgustedly. "I thought they were hurt. It's icky." With that pronouncement, she moves quickly on, looking for more Edward's Hairstreaks.

"How many do we have?" Andy asks.

5.3. *A pair of copulating Delaware Skippers in early July in the pine bush.*

"Nearly 500," Mike replies. And that spurs them on, for they know we are near the end of our trail, and they want to break 500.

"Here's another one," Ben cries, and they each return to the search.

We walk slowly up and down the undulating dunes, lost in a world where the only sounds we hear are the soft calls of Pine and Prairie Warblers, and the occasional raucous call of a passing crow. We pause to treasure the moment when we pass the 500 mark, and to wonder if we would have the high count for the nation (we did). We watch the warblers pick at the cones on the short pines, hidden in the dark shadows. It is hard to believe that this patch of wilderness that dates back to a time when ancient seas covered the area has survived.

Many years later, I watch in amazement as Allison and Alexis, my youngest nieces, toddle after a Monarch butterfly flitting over the flowers in my brother Roy's greenhouses. It is early spring, and not yet time for our annual butterfly count, but I eagerly await their excitement when they move down the sandhills, searching for Edward's Hairstreaks like their older brothers, sisters, and cousins before them—like countless Mohawk Indian children must have done centuries ago. Today the Pine Bush is guarded by houses, shopping malls, a state university, and the New York State Thruway. The pressure from outside is tremendous and increasing, making it all the more important to protect this sparkling jewel for all our children, and their children's children.

THE LONG ISLAND
BARRENS

People of the Long Island Barrens

The "Barrens of Long Island," as they are often called, are similar to other barrens. They are a mosaic of open Pitch Pine forests with an understory of heaths and shrubby oaks in Suffolk County, New York. They also contain a dwarf forest, located near Westhampton. The Long Island Barrens has received far less attention than the Albany Pine Bush, the New Jersey Pine Barrens, or the Pine Scrub of Florida, largely because it has not attracted as many champions who make it their cause. It has no charismatic species like the Karner Blue Butterfly of the Pine Bush, the Pine Snake and the Pine Barrens Treefrog of New Jersey, or the Scrub Jay and Scrub Lizard of the Florida Pine Scrub. However, it was important for Native Americans and the early European settlers, and it remains a significant barrens habitat today (fig. 6.1).

Beneath the sand and gravel of the Barrens is bedrock laid down in the early Paleozoic more than 250 million years ago. Most of the sand was deposited only 60 to 100 million years ago, although some was left by the retreating glaciers. Some 1.8 million years ago, the Pleistocene Era began, and with it, a period of repeated glaciation when mile-thick ice sheets covered the Northeast. During the last glaciation, sea level was 100 feet lower, extending Long Island some 90 miles to the east. When the last glacier retreated, the climate was similar to the present-day Arctic tundra. Cold-adapted plants and animals moved in following the melting ice, and some of these heath plants remain today in the Barrens. Present-day Long Island first formed some 20,000 years ago as an island. As the climate moderated, spruce-fir communities moved in and were eventually replaced by Pitch Pines and oaks about 9,000 to 10,000 years ago, although the pine-oak-heath communities have been present in the Northeast since the early Cretaceous age. A warmer, drier period occurred between 4,000 and 8,000 years ago, and then the climate turned cooler. These changes in climate caused some shifts in the dominant plant communities. The relative dominance of oaks and pines is in dispute: some

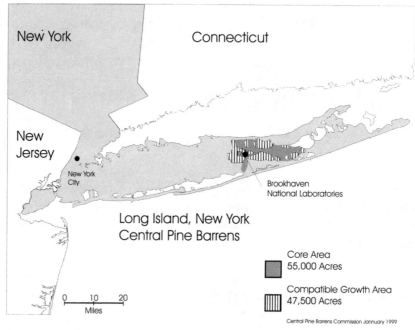

6.1. *Map of Long Island Pine Barrens.*

scientists argue that oaks were dominant, while others argue that pine pollen from cores indicates that pines dominated.

Paleo-Indians moved into the Barrens of Long Island with the retreat of the last glacier about 12,000 years ago. Initially they hunted the large mammals such as Mammoths and Mastodons, but these soon became extinct, no doubt helped by these early hunters. This left them with smaller game such as raccoons, rabbits, and White-tailed Deer. Like paleo-Indians all along the Atlantic Coastal Plain, they used pine logs to make dugout canoes and shelters and collected pine resin to fasten tools together. The earliest Indians lived in small nomadic groups and traveled from the pinelands to the coasts, and then moved inland in search of food. The early paleo-Indian period extended until about 8,000 years ago, when these natives still used fluted projectile points for protection and hunting.

The paleo-Indian period was followed by the Archaic period, when the population increased to the thousands by 3,000 B.C. These Indians developed elaborate burial customs, crafted stone bowls, and made pottery. They began to plant a few crops around their small villages, but even then they moved back to the shelter of the deep pinewoods in the winter. Evidence for some maintenance of garden plots dates to about 3,000 years ago, while true agriculture began there about 1,000 years ago. The fields grew larger, and more and more pinelands were burned or cut to plant crops. Since the sandy soils were so poor, the Indians practiced a slash and burn agriculture. Evidence from charcoal indicates that fires were much more common in areas of the pines inhabited by Indians than in areas without them (fig. 6.2).

Archeologists refer to the period from 700 B.C. to the arrival of Europeans as the Woodland Period, the same as for the Indians living in the Albany Pine Bush. Indians increased their use of pottery and traveled farther afield to gather coastal resources and to hunt. By the time the Europeans arrived, the Indians were burning twice a year, in the spring and fall, and were grow-

6.2. As is characteristic of pine barrens everywhere, the serotinous cones open and germinate only following a hot fire. Then they send up soft green shoots with pine needles.

ing corn, kidney beans, squash, Jerusalem Artichoke, and tobacco, fertilized by whole fish or Horseshoe Crabs they planted with the seeds.

The Indians who lived in the Barrens of Long Island just prior to European contact were related to groups living in Connecticut, Massachusetts, and as far north as the southern tip of Maine. They spoke an Algonquian language, which tied them together culturally. Within this region there was a complex system of trade routes that gave each group the benefit of products from the sea, pinelands, and inland forests. Although each culture had access to many different animals and plants, archeological evidence suggests that they may have obtained up to 90 percent of their meat from White-tailed Deer, a very abundant species in the Barrens of Long Island as well as in more interior forests.

The Indians gathered in large groups to drive deer into V-shaped hedges or walls of brush that were a mile or two long. Sometimes hundreds of men participated in these hunts, and the meat was brought back to the villages to be dried for winter use. In season, waterfowl and geese were shot with bow and arrow, and the pitch from pine trees was used to attach

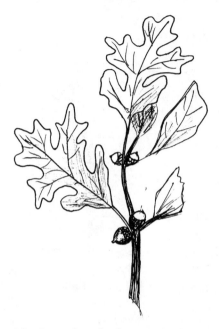

6.3. *A number of oaks grow in the Albany Pine Bush, as well as in the barrens on Long Island and in New Jersey. Acorns were used as a kind of flour by the Iroquois Indians.*

arrowheads to shafts. Wild Turkeys were available during most of the year. As is true of our knowledge of Indians everywhere, much of what we know comes from examinations of the few garbage heaps that remained. Fractured bones, seeds, reed baskets, torn mats, and broken implements found around permanent villages paint a picture of their lifestyle.

Plants from the Barrens were also very important in their daily lives. Dogbane, locally called Indian hemp, grows about four feet tall and has a head of tiny white spherical flowers. The Indians twisted dried Dogbane stems together to make nets and strong rope used for fishing. They also wove these fibers into fine baskets, purses, and large mats for sleeping. Other plants in the pines were gathered for food, including blackberries, grapes, and blueberries, which were particularly abundant in the pines. Acorns were collected and dried for later use in stews or mush, and pine seeds were extracted from cones (fig. 6.3).

Parties of people that lived in the inland pines made seasonal visits to the nearby shore where they harvested fish and shellfish. They dried oysters, clams, and scallops for winter fare and sometimes fashioned shells into spoons. They collected Horseshoe Crab shells for larger scoops and saved the bodies to use as fertilizer for corn seeds they planted in hills. Sometimes they even used the sharp tip of the Horseshoe Crab tail for arrows or spears for fishing. When the mosquitoes and Green-head Flies came out in midsummer, they retreated back into the pines. Visits to the shore also were important for the collection of shells of whelks and Quahog Clams. They cut out white beads from the whelk shells and dark beads from the deep violet of the Quahogs, and then fashioned wampum. Although the use of wampum predates the arrival of the Europeans, the Indians continued to use wampum in trade with fur trappers and early settlers for many years. The regular and seasonal migrations of Indians from the pines to the shore, and farther inland, is a recurrent theme in many pinelands along the Atlantic Coast.

In the early 1500s, Giovannï da Verrazano visited Long Island and reported that open plains extended for up to 100 miles, presumably created partly by the Indians' habit of cutting the trees for firewood and burning other parts of the land. Verrazano's early arrival is memorialized by the bridge named for him that connects Staten Island to Brooklyn. The early European arrivals forced the Indians into smaller and smaller sections of the pines, and in 1666 the Poosepatuk Reservation between Brookhaven and Mastic was set aside for the remaining Indians. It is still recognized today by New York State.

These early European settlers also used the pines, initially for a hunting ground and for lumber, and later for railroad ties and joists for log cabins. The trees of the pines were also cut to make shingles and boat masts. Buckets and boxes, spokes for mill wheels, and coastal pilings were fashioned from Pitch Pine because it resisted decay. Acres of Pitch Pine were burned to make charcoal. A thriving turpentine industry developed in the Barrens, and tar was gathered as wagon-axle grease. To obtain the tar, residents piled stumps, roots, and other waste wood from Pitch Pines into clay-covered earthen mounds. The pile received a slow and controlled burn from the top down, and the tar oozed from the wood into ditches, where it was collected into barrels. Until the 1830s, when coal came into vogue, cordwood was cut as heating fuel in homes; it took an average of 40 cords of wood to heat a home each year. Today, Pitch Pine is still cut to make cargo pallets, but it is too coarse grained and soft for fine woodworking.

Great changes followed the construction of the railroad in 1844, not the least of which was an increase in fires caused by sparks from their wood-burning engines. Other fires were set by arsonists intent on garnering the mandated wages for firefighters set by New York State in the late 1800s. Logging and fires rampant in the 1800s may have contributed to an expansion of pine barrens vegetation.

The twentieth century saw enormous development on Long Island, including extensive roadways that opened up the Barrens to residential development. Roadways have this effect everywhere: first they bring villages and small towns, and then larger population centers spring up along roads. The superhighways opened up the island to hordes of commuters who drive daily to New York City and elsewhere in the metropolitan area. Sleepy shore communities became more accessible, and soon were the "in" place for the rich and famous. Many of these enclaves remain today.

During World War II, Camp Upton was created, which doubled the population of Suffolk County. Today it is called Brookhaven National Laboratory and is run by the Department of Energy. Brookhaven, a monument to our Cold War folly, sits at the edge of the Barrens of Long Island. As with many Department of Energy sites, the public was denied access for nearly 50 years, largely on the basis of national security, thus preserving pine barrens habitat in the middle of one of the most densely populated areas of the world. Though public roads bisect Brookhaven, the vast majority of people speeding by the Barrens seem unaware of its importance. Yet, in surveys I have conducted in the region, maintaining Brookhaven as a preserve or National Environmental Research Park or using parts of it for recreation ranks far higher than converting it to industry or homes. In some sense, people realize its importance, if not its uniqueness. It is a start on ecosystem protection.

Walking through the dwarf pines on Brookhaven last spring, I marveled at the irony of the area. Here was a site built by the Department of Energy to aid in the war effort, dedicated to research on nuclear science, and yet its greatest long-term effect may have been to preserve barrens habitat in the midst of urban sprawl. While the scientists working there may generally be unaware of its ecological importance, the jewel is not lost on the surrounding communities and natural resource trustees hovering nearby. Here the small twisted pines, shorter than I, grow undisturbed by off-road vehicles, hunters, and others who may damage the delicate soil and low shrubs. And here the last remaining Hognose Snakes on Long Island can slither among the lichens and hide in the leaves, waiting for unsuspecting prey.

The population in the central Barrens of Long Island doubled each decade from 1960 to 1990, from 12,500 in 1960 to 57,000 people in 1990, and it continues to grow today. Permanent residences and more transportation routes in the pines created disruptions of many natural communities. Aggressive fire control has also had a negative effect. However, the remaining Long Island Barrens are relatively pristine and a gem onto themselves. Wonderful examples of pine barrens and dwarf forests still exist on an island otherwise crisscrossed with major superhighways and residential communities. The pressures on these Barrens are exceedingly high, but the interest to preserve them has been far less than for either the nearby New Jersey Pine Barrens or the Albany Pine Bush.

When Cranberries Ruled the Long Island Barrens

On a warm sunny day in early June, Mike and I walk the gently undulating sand of the Barrens, listening for the sounds of Tufted Titmice, Robins, and Pine Warblers. The sand slips slightly with each step, revealing a darker unbleached sand beneath the white surface. The soils under our feet are glacial deposits from the last two ice sheets. Immediately after the Wisconsin Glacier began retreating, sea levels were still low, and the outwash plains of Long Island were connected to those in New Jersey and those on Cape Cod. One big sandy plain stretched from Cape Cod to southern New Jersey. As the Wisconsin Glacier retreated even more, sea level rose, and sand bars and barrier beaches formed along the south shore of Long Island and along the Jersey shore.

The retreating Wisconsin Glacier left many species isolated in habitat patches, such as the pine barrens in Cape Cod, Long Island, New Jersey, and Michigan. Prairie Chickens were such a species, and I lament the loss of Prairie Chickens from the Cape Cod barrens (fig. 7.1). Heath Hens, as the eastern subspecies was called, lived in New England and the mid-Atlantic states before the last one perished in the brushlands of Martha's Vineyard in the fall of 1931. Once, a thriving population lived in the coastal plains among Scrub Oak, Sweet Fern, and Alder. When European settlers first arrived, Heath Hens increased in numbers because clearings provided more dancing grounds, where males were able to display to one another. They arrived each day before dawn and danced on small territories not much bigger than themselves. These dancing grounds, called *leks*, were active for most of each morning, then the males dispersed to feed for the day. The dancing increased whenever a female came by. Day after day, the males came to the dancing grounds to wait for the opportunity to mate with a female. Females wandered through, watching each male in turn, judging its quality. When she selected one for a mate, copulation was quick, and she hurried out to the surrounding brushland to lay her eggs and incubate them.

7.1. Prairie Chickens still display on stomping grounds in the Midwest, but the barrens race (Heath Hens) have disappeared from the East.

As the increasing human populations cleared more land, Heath Hens lost the protection of their scrublands among the pine barrens. And they were very edible. Their habit of forming leks during the breeding season and running in large foraging groups at other times of the year made them particularly vulnerable to market hunting—a term reserved for killing birds to sell in the markets of the United States and Europe (either for food or feathers). Heath Hens were hunted to extinction, and the massive efforts of state conservation agencies could not save their dwindling numbers. A small flock of 13 birds on the Vineyard finally perished due to fires, hard winters, and poultry disease. I would have loved to see displaying Heath Hens on my parents' farm in Niskayuna, New York, or in the Albany Pine Bush. In my mind, I can still see the dark silhouettes of Heath Hens dancing in the pine barrens of Cape Cod (fig. 7.2).

Some 400 years ago, the vegetation of Long Island was oak-chestnut forests in the west near present-day New York City, oak-pine forests in the central region, and pine-oak barrens in the east. Originally, there was also a grassy region known as the Hempstead Plains, with only a few, widely scattered Pitch Pines present. This haven for grassland birds, like the Upland Sandpiper, was finally obliterated in the 1960s. To the east was the Barrens, where Low-bush Blueberry, Bearberry, Black Huckleberry,

7.2. Heath Hens as I imagine them in the Cape Cod barrens of long ago.

and Sheep Laurel formed an understory beneath the brushy oaks and scattered pines.

Today, two basic types of pinelands remain in the Long Island Barrens: the Pitch Pine Barrens and the Pine Plains, also known as the Dwarf Plains. As is true of most barrens, these two communities are dominated by very few common species. The tallest trees are Pitch Pines reaching nearly 70 feet, while the shrubs are Scrub Oak, Black Huckleberry, Blueberry, Sheep Laurel, and Bearberry. The sandy soil is covered with Reindeer Lichen, Bearberry, and Beach Heather, arctic plants that invaded just after the ice retreated and still remain. The Reindeer Lichen are only an inch or so high, and their stiff pale green threads crunch beneath one's feet. The lower places contain streams and bogs. On all sides, the barrens grade into oak-dominated forests with very few Pitch Pines.

The vegetation of the Barrens of Long Island is similar to that in New Jersey—not surprisingly, given its history of being connected geologically. But there are some interesting differences: for one, the Blazing Stars are different. New England Blazing Star flourishes in the Long Island Pine Barrens, and its range extends northward (fig. 7.3). In New Jersey we have the Grass-leaved Blazing Star. Pine Snakes are the signature snake of the New Jersey Pinelands, but are absent from Long Island.

7.3. New England Blazing Star, a species that grows in the Long Island Barrens and farther north, but not in the New Jersey Pine Barrens.

As we wander through the Pine Plains, I am taken by the gnarled trunks of the short pines. Some lean to the west, others to the east, as if a whirlwind blew them in different directions. Some trunks are quite straight, while others seem twisted by an angry presence. I am at home among the pines, for there is not a closed canopy above my head, and sunlight bathes the ground. The pines provide some protection from the elements, but it is not clawing and claustrophobic. I can understand why the woodland Indians loved to come here—to feel the warm sun of spring and revel in the openness. There is beauty here for those who look for subtleties; pleasure comes from the absence of people, in the solitude, and in the stillness broken only by a lone Black-capped Chickadee picking silently through the pine needles.

It is challenging to consider the history of the Pine Plains. There is some controversy today about the relative role of humans in maintaining the Long Island Barrens. Most scientists believe that the barrens is a natural ecosystem that was maintained by fire, initially ignited by lightning and later started by Indians. Once Indians began lighting fires, natural fires were less frequent because the necessary fuel was already burned off by the Indians' fires. This key point is often forgotten. Even if most of the fires that ravaged the barrens were started by Indians when the settlers first arrived, it does not mean that fire was not also the primary force before the Indians came.

J. A. Black and J. W. Pavacic have suggested that the Long Island Barrens might be an artifact of human activities.[1] They argue that succession should have resulted in the oaks dominating the pines, eventually shading them out and eliminating them from the forests. The forest should be hardwoods, but Indians—and later European settlers—burned the pines, continually keeping them in an early successional stage. They argue that lightning storms follow heavy rain storms, wet woodlands do not burn easily, and the earliest paleo-Indians did not burn large areas of the pines because their populations were too low. Thus they suggest that early European settlers first encountered a hardwood forest, and that they cut and burned the forests, creating a barrens habitat. This argument is not merely academic: the current management technique to maintain the barrens is prescribed burning.

However, I am not persuaded by the arguments of Black and Pavacic for a number of reasons: very early reports of European settlers describe a plain on Long Island, not a dense hardwood forest. Even Giovanni da Verrazano, the first European to explore Long Island, described expansive pine plains, not a hardwood forest. The presence of a genetic strain of Pitch Pine on the Dwarf Pine Barrens of Long Island and in New Jersey suggests a long evolutionary history of adaptation to environmental conditions. The Dwarf Barrens shown on maps from the early 1800s extended for thousands of acres, and the evolution and spread of a genetic ecotype would have required more than the 200 years since the European settlers had arrived. Pollen from sediments of Deep Pond in the northern

---

[1] From J. A. Black, and J. W. Pavacic, "The Long Island Pine Barrens: An Anthropogenic Artifact or Natural Ecosystem," in *Fire Effects on Rare and Endangered Species and Habitats Conference,* 221–226. Alene, Idaho, 1995.

Long Island Barrens indicates that both pine and oak were dominant for the last 2,000 years, with an increase rather than a decline in Pitch Pine over this period. Although lightning often does accompany heavy rain, as Black and Pavacic suggest, the fact remains that some lightning fires start every year in the vast unbroken tracts of Pine Barrens forests in New Jersey, so why not here on Long Island as well. Also, the presence of so many endemic plants, insects, reptiles, and amphibians argues against a limited 400-year history of Barrens habitat.

Ecosystems are dynamic, the organisms within shift slightly, groups of species live and die, and communities gradually change. These changes in no way diminish the importance of protecting the Long Island Barrens community. Today, the ecosystems that remain in the Barrens are Pitch Pine–Scrub Oak forests, Dwarf Pines, Chestnut Oak forests, swamps, and bogs. These habitats are unique on Long Island and deserve preservation, regardless of their origin. The barrens add to the diversity of habitats on the island, provide optimal conditions for endangered and threatened plants that grow nowhere else in the region, and enhance our appreciation of biodiversity.

Cranberry Bog

While I love walking through the Dwarf Pines, listening for birds and searching for all the variations in the gnarled trunks of the short pines, it is the cranberry bogs I want to see. Wistfully I glance back at the Dwarf Pines, reluctant to leave their solitude. The drive to Riverhead drags me back to civilization as we speed along superhighways, but I am anxious to see the old bogs, mere remnants of their former glory. Bogs form in depressions with little drainage and an accumulation of dead vegetation. The shoreline plants grow out toward the center of the bog, gradually filling in the shallow basin over thousands of years. The floating mass of vegetation shades the water, making it cooler, stopping water flow, and further retarding the decay of vegetation. The partially decomposing vegetation forms peat that releases humic acid, intensifying the acidity of the water. In some of the wetter places a few scattered cranberries grow, nestled in Sphagnum Moss. In others, people have removed the Sphagnum for their gardens as a mulch and soil enhancer. The Indians and early settlers used it as a kind of makeshift tampon and diaper because of its absorbent properties.

Commercial cranberry bogs, such as the Cranberry Bog Preserve in Riverhead, were started in some places. Over the years, other bogs in the Barrens have been destroyed, leaving the remains of Cranberry Bog

Preserve as a rare example of a dwindling habitat. The preserve is part of the drainage system for the Peconic River, and most of its edges are fringed with pine-oak barrens with a White Cedar swamp on the northwest side. A number of rare species of caddisflies, dragonflies, and moths live here, as well as the highly local and abundant Bog Copper butterfly, which is restricted to bogs. Bog Coppers are small butterflies that fly weakly and low over the cranberries and sedges, and as the name implies, they are dark brown with a splash of orange, like the iron of the bogs.

The predominant plant of bogs is Sphagnum Moss, a remnant of a large group that flourished 200 million years ago, as shown by fossil remains. The dense cushions of Sphagnum grow rapidly on top, while the lower portions die and are compressed to the bottom. Because Sphagnum holds great quantities of water, it provides a wonderful place for other plants to grow. Scattered in the Sphagnum are 13 species of orchids, 20 species of ferns, and 59 species of sedges, and it is the only known New York site for Shining Whip Grass.

Pitcher Plant and Round-leaved Sundew are two of the most interesting plants of the bog because they capture and eat insects (fig. 7.4). They developed this curious insectivorous habit to obtain nitrogen, an essential element missing from bog waters. The leaves of the Pitcher Plant look like miniature beer steins, with hollow, stiff leaves that can be three or four inches long. Although the outsides of the leaves are smooth and leatherlike, the insides are covered with reflexed hairs that trap insects. At the bottom of the leaves is a pool of rainwater and sweet nectar that is secreted by the plant to attract insects. Since the hairs curve downward, the insects cannot climb out once they fall in. The reddish yellow Pitcher Plant flowers are an odd, globelike affair, slightly larger than a small plum with small petals, and they are borne well above the leaves on a tall stalk. In the fall their leaves turn a brilliant deep purple, which they maintain throughout the winter.

7.4. Round-leaved Sundew grows in the bogs of both the Long Island Barrens and in the New Jersey Pine Barrens.

Sundews are much smaller than Pitcher Plants and blend in with the Sphagnum.

They catch insects by a method entirely different from that of Pitcher Plants. Leaves radiating from a basal rosette are covered with reddish hairs that exude a sticky substance to catch small insects. Once captured, the hairs slowly bend inward, forcing the insects against the leaf, where digestive juices devour them. Sundews sparkle in the sunlight, the twinkling being due to the sticky drops used to capture unsuspecting insects.

A third group of bog plants, bladderworts, is also carnivorous. These plants grow along the surface of the wet vegetation, and concealed among their small leaves are threadlike segments that contain small sacs with tiny openings to catch minute aquatic animals. The sacs are deflated, but when an animal touches the sac it opens, pulling water and the animal into the bladder. Bladderworts can be quite massive, although they are not obvious because they grow under water. A large plant can nearly fill a pond, containing 150,000 trapped organisms at one time.

The showpiece of the bogs is the native American Cranberry. The leaves remain green throughout the year, and its threadlike vines creep among the other herbs, vines, and even orchids that grow here. The thin woody stems trail along the ground, sending up erect branches covered with small waxy-green elliptical leaves. Tiny little pinkish white flowers look like shooting stars to me, with a yellow pointed cone in the center. Early settlers thought they looked like the bills of cranes and called them "crane berries."

Cranberry cultivation began in New Jersey in the 1840s when "Old Peg-leg" John Webb grew his first crop, selling them at a market in Philadelphia, where he got fifty dollars a barrel. Whalers bought the berries, rich in Vitamin C, to prevent scurvy. The new industry quickly spread to Long Island because of the popularity of the berries for extended ship voyages. To make a natural cranberry bog commercially viable, people crisscrossed the bog with drainage ditches. In the early days, cranberries were grown in relatively dry marshes and picked by women with scoops imported from Cape Cod or New Jersey. In 1885 the Woodhull brothers purchased the bogs near Riverhead and proceeded to flood them. They covered the marsh with a layer of sand, planted the cranberries, and by 1889 they picked their first crop—10 bushels, sold for $1.90 each. By 1892 they were up to 21,600 bushels, which brought $2.00 each.

When the Woodhull brothers finally abandoned commercial cranberry growing, the ditches remained, although the bog was no longer flooded regularly. The ditches drained parts of the bog, allowing upland plants, such as Red Maple, Poison Sumac, and Poison Ivy, to invade. Poison

Sumac is the only sumac that has white rather than red flowers, and it is extremely poisonous to the touch. Unlike Poison Ivy, which is common along roadsides and forest edges, Poison Sumac grows only in bogs and fens. Although some of the edges of the bog still show the signs of commercial ventures, most of the bog has returned to nearly pristine conditions, harboring a wonderful diversity of plants and insects.

Bending over, I gently brush aside the waxy green leaves to reveal the mass of tiny pinkish white cranberry flowers. Since the bog has reverted to its natural diversity, there is no longer a continuous mass of cranberries. The delicate berries are overshadowed by the Pitcher Plants and small sumacs that dot the bog. We have to look carefully to find the cranberries, and we can only imagine what this bog must have looked like when it was covered in a mass of white "crane's bills."

It has been decades since this place was a going concern as a cranberry bog. With time, succession has taken place. Gradually, other bog plants have moved in, and the cranberries are less obvious. Pitcher Plants and Sundews grow in the wetter places: the bog has returned to its former glory.

Ecosystems of the Pines

Leaving the bog, we move on to the upland Barrens, the one most people envision when they think of the Pines. The dominant habitat here is Pitch Pine–oak forest, with Scarlet, Black, White, and Red Oaks intermixed in a mosaic of twisted scraggly trees. The shrub layer contains mostly Scrub Oak, with an almost continuous cover of huckleberry, blueberry, and Bracken Fern. Scattered places contain clumps of Pennsylvania Sedge and Wintergreen. I search the tiny Wintergreen vines for the delicate red berries, but the birds and small mammals must have gotten to them already. The obvious differences in aspect and appearance among different types are mostly a matter of relative abundance of the six dominant plant species.

Although the vertebrate diversity in the Barrens of Long Island is relatively low, as is true of pine barrens in general, some species are common, such as Cottontail Rabbits, Eastern Chipmunks, White-tailed Deer, Raccoon, Red Fox, Masked Shrew, Eastern Mole, and Pine Vole. These species are both abundant and widespread, although shrews are seldom seen unless a cat or wildlife biologist captures one. In some places, Flying Squirrels leap through the trees at night, seen only by those who know exactly where to look. They are protected by their nocturnal behavior.

Oddly, they are moving into areas of suburbia that contain small wood-lots of tall old trees. Once there, they often make a living raiding bird-feeders at night, leading people to wonder what on earth is cleaning out their feeders. The Flying Squirrels cling to the edge of the feeders and fill up before going back to their daytime roosting sites in the hollows of dead trees.

Common birds of the Pitch Pine–oak forest are Mourning Dove, American Crow, Rufous-sided Towhee, Blue Jay, Red-tailed Hawk, and Bobwhite. In areas with taller Pitch Pines, there are breeding Pine Warblers, and on disturbed brush areas, Yellowthroats and Prairie Warblers nest. When oaks dominate the pines, there are Red-eyed Vireos, Scarlet Tanagers, and Baltimore Orioles. In the spring and in the fall, the pinelands host a wide range of migrants, including flycatchers, warblers, thrushes, vireos, and other insectivorous birds. Where the pinelands meet the coast, migrating species funnel through during migration, seeking the safety of the pines to forage before continuing their journey.

Hognose, Black Racer, and Garter Snakes are the common reptiles. Finding these species, however, partly depends upon how well you know where to look, at least for Hognose and Black Racers. In my experience, Hognose Snakes are often far more common than is apparent; they are quite secretive and it is unusual to see them basking in the open. In contrast, Garter Snakes are relatively easy to find, particularly near small streams where they often sit on rocks or logs in the morning sun. In the early spring I have found them peeking out of cracks in rotten logs or from holes at the base of live pines, seeking the warm sun. I was alarmed the first time I saw a writhing ball of nine Garter Snakes, seemingly oblivious to my presence. I watched them for nearly half an hour, until the mass gradually broke up, and I realized I had witnessed a mating dance. Only one male was successfully copulating with the one female in the mass.

Unlike the New Jersey Pine Barrens where many frogs and toads are common, only the Fowler's Toad is abundant in the Long Island Barrens. The toads are relatively hard to find because they often burrow beneath the ground when it is too hot or too cold, seeking shelter from the inclement weather. Only in the spring are they easy to find, when their forlorn trilling is hard to miss.

The transition of Pitch Pine uplands to Dwarf Pine Plains is fairly abrupt, although the two dominant trees are still Pitch Pine and Scrub Oak. On the Dwarf Pine Plains, the Pitch Pines are not more than six feet tall, and some are half that. It is wonderful: even I can look over the top of the pine forest. Within the Dwarf Pine Plain, however, are areas dominated by Black Huckleberry, blueberries, and laurels, known collectively as heaths. These open areas, often devoid of Pitch Pines, may have been created entirely by the activities of the military: these species occur in heavily bulldozed areas. Apparently the underground root systems of the Pitch Pines were destroyed, and invading pines could not compete with the already established heaths.

The Pitch Pines in the dwarf forest are genetically adapted to the soil conditions. They are not short because they are young; some of the three-foot-tall pines in the Dwarf Pine Plains are 30 years old, and 30-year-old Pitch Pines in the upland barrens are much taller. Thus, as with the New Jersey dwarf forest, a genetic strain of Pitch Pines has developed in these regions. The Pitch Pines here are able to produce seeds at a very young age and have a high degree of cone serotony (sealed by pitch, and opening only with fire), making them fire adapted. Their ability to re-sprout from underground roots, trunks, and branches also makes them adapted to a fire regime. It would be interesting to determine if those in the two dwarf forests (New Jersey and Long Island) are part of the same genetic continuum, but this awaits further study.

There are even fewer abundant birds in the Dwarf Pine forests than in the upland pine communities. The common species are Prairie Warblers, Field Sparrows, Brown Thrashers, and Rufous-sided Towhees. Northern Harriers, also called Marsh Hawks, feed in the dwarf pines. This habitat is devoid of any amphibians, and there are few reptiles. There are, however, many species of moths and butterflies, including the rare Buck Moth that thrives in the dense thicket of Scrub Oaks. The moths pupate under the soil, safe from the hot summer sun and autumn fires, and emerge in mid-October as adults. If conditions for emergence are unfavorable, they remain below the soil surface for a year and emerge the following fall. Buck Moth larvae depend on the nutrient-rich, young Scrub Oak sprouts for their food.

Other plant communities thrive in the Long Island Barrens, including Chestnut Oak forests, Pitch Pine–oak heath woodlands, wetlands, shrub swamps, Red Maple–hardwood swamps, and Atlantic White Cedar swamps. Although White Cedar swamps were once extensive on Long Island, only remnants remain because of excessive logging and draining. The largest one is in the cranberry bog discussed above. Here we have the Hessel's Hairstreak, a rare butterfly that is dependent on White Cedar as its host. Preservation of White Cedar swamps is difficult, because we know relatively little about their ecology and maintenance—unlike other communities in the pine barrens—and there are no simple management regimes that will preserve them.

Atlantic White Cedars regenerate only under conditions of full sunlight and moisture, but not flooding. Therefore, regeneration occurs only with the removal of tall, mature trees by logging, fire, high wind, or flooding. Fires and blowdowns were once the most common events in White Cedar swamps, but now they are rare. Fires during low water burns the peat, lowering the forest floor and exposing it to more flooding, which prevents White Cedars from regenerating. It is a delicate balance, allowing the cedar seedlings to generate without burning off too much of the peat, and biologists don't always get it just right.

Most of the plant communities in the Long Island Barrens are fire adapted. Not only are the Pitch Pines adapted to fire, but Scrub Oak is as well, and the oaks recover rapidly from a hot crown fire. Just below the soil surface, the oaks have root collars with dormant buds that resprout quickly after above-ground growth has been killed. Acorn production reaches a maximum when the trees are only five to seven years old, and it slowly declines thereafter. When a fire passes over an area, Scrub Oaks are stimulated to produce four to nine times as much foliage as normal, recovering quickly and outcompeting any other vegetation. There is also an increase in production of protein, phosphorus, potassium, and calcium, providing high-quality food for butterflies and moths that feed on oak leaves. Low shrubs, such as blueberries, huckleberries, and Wintergreen also resprout quickly after a fire.

Hot fires open up the canopy, providing even more sunlight for the species that grow in the understory. Fires sweep through the region every few years, or at the least, every few decades. Without fires, the pine-dominated communities would no longer exist. The Dwarf Pines require more frequent fires to maintain them, on the order of a fire every five to seven years, while the other barrens habitats do well with less frequent fires.

Once, the Long Island Barrens covered approximately 250,000 acres in central Suffolk County, but it has been reduced to some 100,000 acres of relatively undeveloped land, much of it on the federally owned Brookhaven National Laboratory site. The Department of Energy, which owns Brookhaven, in recognition of the unique Pine Barrens habitat on its buffer zone, has declared some 530 acres of land as the Upton Ecological and Research Reserve. The Long Island Barrens is a unique and valuable ecosystem because it contains one of only three true Dwarf Pine forests along the East Coast. Like the pine barrens in Albany and New Jersey, this region is under enormous pressure for development. Over 200 development projects threaten the Barrens from all sides because the land is so very valuable.

7.5. *Tiger Salamanders are quite rare on Long Island today, and occur only in the wet areas of the barrens.*

Even today, with the enormous loss of habitat and with suburbia encroaching from every direction, the Long Island Barrens provides critical habitat. It has over 300 species of vertebrates, 1,000 species of plants, and 10,000 species of insects. Species of concern are the Tiger Salamander, Red-shouldered Hawk, Northern Harrier, and Mud Turtle. Most of the remaining Tiger Salamanders on Long Island are limited to pine barrens, where they prefer vernal ponds that have an open canopy. Jeremy Feinberg has been studying them at Brookhaven for some time and finds that they do best where there is little competition from Marbled Salamanders. Tiger Salamanders try to get their breeding done early, often laying eggs when there is still ice on the pond edges. Feinberg has found clutches even in early January when the temperatures rise. Tiger Salamanders need habitat protection that includes forest as well as vernal ponds, especially since they can travel several thousand yards from their breeding sites (fig. 7.5).

The Barren's unique geological and meteorological history, along with the unusual soil and water levels, make it particularly hospitable to a wide variety of organisms whose survival is threatened by further suburbanization. Any additional loss of Barrens habitat will disrupt migratory routes, destroy food supplies for many animals, and allow more alien plants to invade.

Protection of the Barrens is equally important for the people of Long Island because their drinking water comes from the indispensable Magothy Aquifer that is the sole source of natural drinking water for the over two and a half million people who live on Long Island. Sole-source aquifers are extremely important and need to be protected from contamination. Precipitation infiltrates the land, moving through the subsoil layers, and finally radiates to the north, south, and east, feeding the entire aquifer and diluting any contaminants that have entered the aquifer from other parts of the island. The tremendous advantage of having permeable soil is also a disadvantage, since any pollutants from above can quickly permeate to the lower layers, potentially contaminating the whole water supply. The porous soils do not have the ability to filter out contaminants, and it would take centuries for the system to flush sufficiently.

Unfortunately, although there are several state and county laws that protect the Long Island Barrens, there is no overarching law or master plan that protects it on a landscape scale. This protection exists for the New Jersey Pine Barrens but not for the Long Island Barrens. Each community reviews development plans for its local area, and makes policy accordingly. Most of the relevant state laws pertain to development that affects the purity of the groundwater, prohibits the development of hazardous-waste sites, or protects state-endangered species. Suffolk County has enacted laws encouraging towns and villages to develop "unified policies" with regard to land use, but these have not been adopted.

Even so, a few groups have dedicated themselves to the preservation of the Long Island Barrens, such as the Long Island Greenbelt Trail Conference, and much of the land is already protected by state, federal, or conservation agencies. These groups are developing land use and management plans for the Barrens, and they are well aware of the unique heritage the Barrens represents. Only their watchfulness can preserve the Barrens, protecting this unique assemblage of pine barrens habitats amid a mass of suburbia and development.

THE NEW JERSEY
PINE BARRENS

Truly an Ecological Reserve

I first saw the Albany Pine Bush through the eyes of a young child full of curiosity about the Indians and Gypsies I imagined living there. I first viewed the New Jersey Pinelands 25 years later as a trained ecologist, looking at how ecosystems function. But my heart saw in the Pinelands the same wonderful open pines and low shrubs of the Pine Bush. The lovely and brilliant pale pink of the Mountain Laurel in late May thrills me today as much as it did over 30 years ago when I first saw the dense understory beneath the pines. The excitement of seeing a sleek Black Racer disappearing under the pine boughs, and of a majestic Pine Snake basking in the early spring sun is still as gripping as when I first watched a Hognose Snake playing dead in the Albany Pine Bush.

The New Jersey Pinelands is located in the middle of one of the most densely populated states in the nation and is remarkable for its location, water system, and flora and fauna. Travelers on the Garden State Parkway, which passes along the eastern edge of the Pinelands, often find the region—with its short scraggly pines and a few shrunken oak trees—quite tedious. But the Pinelands is an incredibly diverse and varied ecosystem that has many different habitats, including upland forests, hardwood swamps, cedar bogs, streams, ponds, rivers, salt and freshwater marshes, and bays. To those who take the time, the variations in habitats and communities in the Pine Barrens provide magic and mystery that is as great as in any other ecosystem.

The New Jersey Pinelands comprises about 2,000 to 2,250 square miles of flat, sandy, acidic, sterile soils that constitute much of the Atlantic Coastal Plain in New Jersey. It stretches 80 miles from north to south, and all the way from the tidal marshes along the Atlantic coast west almost to the Delaware River. It encompasses most of the southern half of the state (fig. 8.1). It is the most extensive wilderness tract in the mid-Atlantic states, and much of it has been preserved as the New Jersey Pinelands Preserve.

8.1. Map of the extent of the New Jersey Pine Barrens.

Although the bedrock of the highest regions of New Jersey is more than 570 million years old, most of the rock underlying the Pine Barrens is much younger. Some 225 million years ago, New Jersey, along with the rest of North America, was attached to Africa and Europe in one huge continent called Pangaea. North America drifted away, creating a rift called the Atlantic Ocean. Water covered New Jersey for millions of years. Then North America drifted back into Europe and Africa about 200 million years ago, and the resultant continent was again called Pangaea. During this time the North American continent was subjected to uplifting, called mountain building, with both erosion and deposition. The modern Atlantic Ocean was created about 180 million years ago when North America drifted westward for the final time, carrying New Jersey with it. Large dinosaurs inhabited the swamps and lakes of New Jersey, leaving their footprints in the soft muds. Duck-billed dinosaurs called *Hadrosaurus* roamed the land.

The base rocks of the Pine Barrens were underwater for most of the next few million years, but from 135 to 65 million years ago, sediments that were carried down rivers were deposited on what is now the Inner Coastal Plain. Over eons the seas periodically rose and fell, and each time the seas covered the plains, they laid down sedimentary deposits composed of the bodies of thousands upon thousands of marine organisms and clay, silt, sand, and gravel. Giant sand dunes formed at the edges of inland seas. When the sea withdrew the exposed soils eroded, and most were washed away, only to be rebuilt the next time the seas invaded. These processes continued until about 700,000 years ago, when a global drop in temperature occurred, and the Pleistocene Ice Ages began. More snow fell than melted, and each year it accumulated higher and higher, pressing down and compacting the layers of snow from previous years. Giant ice sheets, enormous fingers of destruction, began moving south. Plants and animals perished in their path or moved farther south.

North America had four ice sheets, called the Nebraskan, Kansan, Illinoian, and Wisconsin. The last ice sheet moved as far south as central New Jersey, pushing debris for miles ahead of the ice. During interglacial periods, the weather warmed, and some of the glaciers melted and re-ceded northward, leaving piles of yellow sand and gravel in their wake. Woolly Mammoths, Mastodons, and Giant Beavers were plentiful, forced southward by the glacial advance. Their remains have been found in New Jersey. When the glaciers were at their peak, sea level was lowest and the tide line of New Jersey was some 100 miles to the east, out in the Atlantic Ocean. Significantly more sandy plains were exposed, and the wide expanse allowed for a great deal of plant migration, partially accounting for the unique flora of the Pine Barrens.

As the glaciers retreated for the last time, sea level rose, leaving a broad expanse of Coastal Plain in New Jersey, part of the Atlantic Coastal Plain that extends northward to Cape Cod and southward to Florida. The similarities among the pine habitats along the Coastal Plain come from these common beginnings. The New Jersey Outer Coastal Plain contains 3,400 square miles, or 45 percent of the land of New Jersey, most of which is

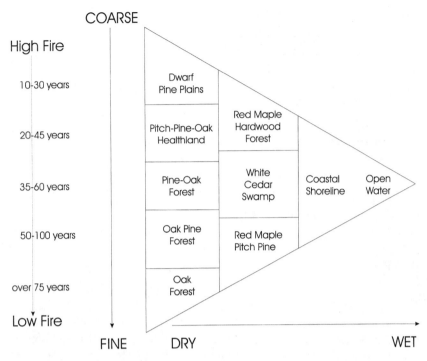

8.2. *Schematic of plant communities in the Long Island Barrens and New Jersey Pine Barrens as a result of moisture, fire interval, and sand type (from Whittaker 1979).*

the Pine Barrens. Elevations in most of the region are less than 100 feet above sea level, and the soils are sandy, poor in nutrients, and dry, a familiar refrain for pine barrens in general.

The soil is made of Cohansey sands, which are loose, coarse, and low in nutrients. The sands are highly acidic, with only a small accumulation of organic material such as rotting leaves and needles, and have highly leached upper layers that are bleached a pure white, overlaying layers of light gray. The sand is 90 percent quartz, along with coarse gravel deposits. There is not enough water for lush vegetation because these soils do not hold the rains. Rain flows easily and rapidly through the loose sands, replenishing the water table and seeping slowly toward the streams and rivers. Eventually the rivers meet the sea, forming gigantic salt marshes and productive estuaries.

Only recently have ecologists begun to realize that the estuaries adjacent to the Pine Barrens are part of the system, for the rains that fall on the pines eventually make their way to the bays, mixing with the salt-water from the ocean to create brackish marshes that are nurseries for

Table 8.1. Type of Forest with the Interval of Fire Required to Maintain That Forest Type in the New Jersey Pinelands

Forest Type	Fire Interval (years)
Oak-hickory at edge of barrens	100–200
Oak-pine forest	60–100
Pine-oak forest	20–60
Pitch Pine–Scrub Oak forest	15–25
Dwarf Pine forest	<20

Note: Dominant tree is listed first.

fish and invertebrates. Many of the fish in the Atlantic depend upon estuaries as nurseries and are vulnerable to changes in terrestrial ecosystems far inland. The slopes in the pines are shallow but high enough for the water to flow to the sea, carrying pollution from the land and severely contaminating coastal waters, impairing fisheries.

The Pine Barrens of both New Jersey and Long Island have been shaped by fire and water (fig. 8.2). Wherever there are frequent fires and very dry conditions, the pines are dwarf; and in wetter areas with less frequent fire, Red Maples move in with the Pitch Pines (table 8.1). The primary pines of the Pine Barrens are Pitch and Short-leaf Pine, and there are a variety of oaks: Scrub, Black, Scarlet, Blackjack, White, Post, and Chestnut. The understory consists of shrubs such as huckleberry. The three main forest types in the Pine Barrens are upland forests, dwarf forests, and lowland forests such as the cedar swamps. These forest types evolved as a result of the water table. Far below the misshapen pines and blueberry bushes lies the Cohansey Aquifer, a giant groundwater system that ties together the uplands and the soggy wetlands of the Pine Barrens. The aquifer has a storage capacity of 17 trillion gallons, and is one of the purest water systems in the world.

Upland Forest

The upland forests occur where the water table is two or more feet below ground level. Pitch Pine is the dominant tree. Also present are some Short-leaf Pines, which can grow as tall as 40 or 50 feet. These are open forests with light penetration to the forest floor; typically Pitch Pine covers at least 30 percent of the ground, and in some places the pines are thick. The upland forests, covering half of the New Jersey Pine Barrens, are unique because they are the most extensive, continuous stand of Pitch Pine in North America. Where the forest has been unduly disturbed, or where fire has been suppressed, the oaks take over and dominate the pines. In abandoned fields, Red Cedars move in, aided by birds who transport their seeds. When birds eat the berries of the cedars, they disperse them in their droppings, and the cedars grow quickly in open areas with abundant sunlight.

The understory of these upland forests is mostly shrubs such as Black Huckleberry, Low-bush Huckleberry, and Mountain Laurel. In the spring, the forests are charming because of the vibrant pink flowerheads of the Sheep Laurel, darker than the common Mountain Laurel that grows in profusion along the Garden State Parkway. In late June and July, the tiny blue huckleberries are a real treat for birds, mammals, and people. Bearberry, Teaberry, and mosses cover the ground in some areas, Pennsylvania Sedge forms patches on the sand between the pine trees, Haircap Moss graces the sand, and tiny lichens cling to the sand in the drier spots. The tiny brilliant red tips of the silvery green lichens richly deserve the name of British Soldier.

Lowland Forest

The lowland forests, occurring where the water table is less than two feet below the ground, can be divided into Pitch Pine lowlands, White Cedar swamps, and hardwood swamps. Wetlands occupy about 30 percent of the Pine Barrens. The Pitch Pine lowlands form along streams or swamps, and as is suggested by their name, Pitch Pine dominates. There are a few oaks, Red Maples, Black Gum, and Sweet Magnolia in the understory, with Sheep Laurel, Black Huckleberry, Sweet Pepperbush, and Dangleberry in the shrub layer. Below the shrubs are Turkeybeard, Bracken Fern, Teaberry, and lots of species of lichens.

Cedar swamps take their name from the Atlantic White Cedar that dominates them. Formerly more widespread, this tall, stately tree was heavily exploited for timber and ship masts in the eighteenth and nineteenth centuries. Many of the bogs in the Pine Barrens were once pure stands of White Cedar, which have largely vanished because of exploitation. There were stands of White Cedar farther north in the Hackensack Meadows, but these have been cut down and completely disappeared. Cranberries are one of the native species in Pine Barrens bogs, and many of the cedar swamps have been cleared for cranberry production on a commercial scale.

Cedars grow in narrow bands along streams, where the water table is very close to the surface. Usually their roots are in water, covered with thick, deep mats of Sphagnum Moss. The slow-moving streams are stained orange from iron ore and White Cedar leaves. Huckleberries, Dangleberry, and Swamp Azalea grow in profusion. Only a few shafts of light penetrate the thick cedar canopy and fall on the Sphagnum, and few seeds germinate. Where the sunlight penetrates the canopy, sundews, Pitcher Plants, a few orchids, and Curly Grass Fern grow in the Sphagnum. Like other elements of the Pine Barrens, White Cedars require fire to maintain them. However, very hot fires result in the replacement of White Cedar by more shade-tolerant trees like Red Maple, Black Gum, and Sweet Bay.

Hardwood swamps occur where cedar swamps have been cut, or where very hot fires have killed the cedars. When the cedars do not regenerate, Red Maple, Black Gum, Sweet Magnolia, and Gray Birch move in, and Swamp Azalea, Sweet Pepperbush, Leatherleaf, and Sheep Laurel abound. Unfortunately, many of the cedar swamps have disappeared from the Pine Barrens and are now hardwood swamps. Cedar was used first by the Lenape Indians for canoes, and later by the early European settlers for shingles. Today the Pine Barrens contain many more hardwood swamps than pure stand cedar swamps.

Dwarf Forest

My favorite habitat in the Pine Barrens is the dwarf forest or "pygmy forest" near the Burlington–Ocean County line, north of Warren Grove. Two such areas are called the West Plains and the East Plains, with a smaller one in between called the Little Plains. These tiny trees grow so close together that they are nearly impenetrable, providing good places for wildlife to hide from people. Here it is possible to stand on the higher ridges and look for miles over the short scraggly pines. Doing so makes me feel positively tall.

The dominant pine of the dwarf forest is the Pitch Pine, and along with Blackjack and Scrub Oaks, it forms a dense forest that is fire dependent. Only the Pitch Pine and the Blackjack Oak, however, can withstand fires at intervals of less than ten years (table 8.1). When the fires have passed and the ground is cool, these species sprout from the root crown just below the soil, and the forest is soon green. Although the trees are only four to twelve feet high, some are very old. The trees here are the same species that occur throughout the Pine Barrens, but the fire-resistant pines have adapted just for these harsh conditions. The frequent fires, along with very old root systems, cause scraggly trees that in some places are only three or four feet high. After fires rip through the dwarf forest, the trees quickly rejuvenate; they grow from underground roots, from root crowns, and from the sides of the blackened trunks. They never regenerate from pine seeds. There are no seedlings following a fire, only green sprouts from the sides of blackened trunks, looking like tufts of angel hair. Although there are some shrubs, such as Black Huckleberry, Lowbush Huckleberry, Broom Crowberry, Bearberry, Teaberry, and *Hudsonia*, these are far less obvious in the dense tangle of the low canopy.

Ecologists love to argue over why the pines are so short and scraggly in the dwarf forest, for the trees are clearly as stunted as trees in the harshest subarctic environments. One explanation seems to be that the short trees are caused by infertile soils, arid conditions, exposure to strong winds, and repeated fires, which occur more often here than in other pine barrens habitats. On average, the dwarf forest burns every 10 to 20 years. This explanation seems very unsatisfactory because some of the pines in Florida burn every year or two, and the trees are tall and straight. The more recent explanation that the trees here are genetically a dwarf form seems more plausible. Even when protected from fire, the dwarf pine race of the Pitch Pine does not grow tall: it simply grows outward and more scraggly.

Fire is the common theme that runs through the ecology of the New Jersey Pine Barrens, as well as barrens everywhere. The vegetation has been shaped by fire. Before humans, lightning strikes caused widespread fires, and then the Indians set the pines afire deliberately. Dry pine needles are highly flammable and burn readily, providing tinder for widely spreading fires. The fires burn off the needles (called *duff*) on the forest floor, and burn up the trees, encouraged by the resins dripping down the trunks. After a fire, the Pinelands look desolate, the Pitch Pine trunks are blackened, and everything looks dead. All the needles, many of the branches, and all the underbrush is gone. On the uplands, fire favors Pitch and Short-leaf Pines. Both have thick bark, and after a fire, they send up new shoots from the base if the top of the tree is killed.

A few months after a fire, small green tufts of needles grow from the base of Pitch Pine branches, and within a couple of years it is difficult to imagine the devastation that the fires had caused. The short scraggly oaks, such as Blackjack, Scrub, and Chestnut Oaks, can also withstand fires. Herbs and shrubs grow from underground stems and manage to survive. When fires occur frequently, there is little chance for a large needle layer to accumulate, and the fires are not overly hot. The underground stems and roots are not damaged by these fires, and plant life can regenerate quickly. Only when fire has been suppressed for many years and a thick layer of dried needles and leaves accumulates will fires become too hot and turn into true wildfires. These can whip through the pines, destroying the trees and root systems, leaving total devastation with little chance of rapid recovery.

Some pines require fires for their seeds to germinate because the cones do not open completely without heat. But more importantly, with a dense layer of needles and oak leaves, the pine seeds do not germinate because they cannot reach down to the moist soil. On the contrary, heavy oak acorns easily penetrate the thick layer of leaves and needles, and they have no trouble germinating and growing under a dense canopy. The amount of leaf and needle litter is very important to the organisms within the soil because it affects soil moisture. For some time, John Dighton and his students have been studying the relationship between the patchiness of leaf litter and the animals living within the soil. They find that larger leaf patches have more oak leaves compared to other leaves or needles, and this influences root growth; diversity in the litter promotes greater root growth.

A number of rare moths and butterflies require pine barrens groundcover plants or oak shrubs, including Dotted Skipper, Pine Barrens Dagger Moth, Pine Barrens Underwing Moth, Pine Barrens Zale Moth, and Variable Heterocampa Moth, and many others. These species decline markedly when fire is suppressed, for they also must have open areas where their food plants can grow. Other species groups, such as snakes, also suffer without some open areas for basking. Pine and Corn Snakes require sunlight that penetrates to the forest floor so they can bask while their eggs are developing in their bodies prior to egg laying.

Without fires, the pinelands would be replaced by hardwoods that can tolerate a closed canopy. An ideal fire interval is 10 to 20 years, and if there are no fires within 40 years, the pines decline. However, with the extensive and recent residential development in the pines, fire suppression becomes necessary. People who move to retirement communities in the Pinelands do not want to look outside their homes and see wildfires ripping through the forests. Loss of property and loss of life must be prevented at all costs. Despite the extensive fire control measures in the pines, there still are thousands of small wildfires each year.

The only solution to the need for fire is to conduct controlled burns, where the area to be burned is carefully selected, the interfire interval is appropriate, and the conditions are optimal to allow for control. This means taking into account the amount of needles and leaves on the ground, how dry they are, the speed and direction of the wind, and the construction of appropriate firebreaks or roads. The system is not perfect, and some wildfires still occur. We cannot control lightning, and once it is started without preparations, fire can run quickly through thousands of acres of pinelands. The suppression of fire had a devastating effect on the New Jersey Pine Barrens, leading to public concern beyond the state.

In the mid-1960s John McPhee wrote a delightful and insightful essay in the *New Yorker* about the New Jersey Pine Barrens, which he later published as a book, *The Pine Barrens*. This fostered interest in the pines across the country, and the flower children of the 1960s eagerly adopted the barrens, wearing "piney power" shirts and hats and lobbying for its preservation. This Barrens had instant appeal because it was an undiscovered jewel that had been sleeping within the middle of the urban sprawl that extends from Boston to Washington. For the first time, New Jersey had something that was a national treasure: a relatively pristine habitat with unique biological diversity.

McPhee's book came at a time when Americans were awakening to the dangers of a technological and chemical society. Rachel Carson had just published *Silent Spring,* and there was a general feeling that we were doing irreparable damage to the environment—an environment all of us live in. Her emphasis was on the direct lethal effect of pesticides on birds, but by 1970, the subtle effects of chemicals on reproduction in birds was also recognized. Entire populations of Bald Eagles, Peregrine Falcons, and Brown Pelicans were eliminated. This led directly to concern for a class of compounds that function as endocrine disruptors, with dire consequences on populations and communities. Although many dismissed Carson's message as hysterical, people gradually began to notice that there were fewer birds, frogs, insects, and butterflies in the environment. Within only a few years, stimulated by a wide coalition of organizations, the country as a whole demanded environmental protection, interpreted very broadly to include protection of human health, nature, and wildlife. Carson's book started the modern environmental movement that resulted in the creation of the Environmental Protection Agency in 1970 by President Richard Nixon, and the need to perform Environmental Impact Assessments before initiating any development. The irony of Nixon being president when many of our major environmental laws and agencies were created is not lost on me.

At least six major conservation advocacies can be easily identified within the United States: (1) species protection (i.e., the protection of migratory birds in the early 1900s); (2) habitat protection; (3) soil conservation in the late 1930s; (4) forest conservation in the 1940s; (5) chemical protection (i.e., regulation and control of pesticides and other chemicals in the late 1960s and early 1970s); and (6) the recent concern that several human activities threaten the health of the environment. This last concern led directly to wide support for the protection and preservation of the pinelands of central Jersey.

In the 1960s and 1970s state and federal agencies began to enact legislation to govern land use and to preserve natural lands generally. In 1978 the federal government designated the Pine Barrens as the country's first National Reserve, representing a national heritage that should be preserved for all people. It was a unique concept, for much of the land remains in private ownership although its use is subject to governmental review. A year later, the New Jersey legislature passed the Pinelands Protection Act that created the Pinelands Commission to oversee and regulate land use within the reserve.

In 1983 the United Nations designated the region an International Biosphere Reserve because of its unique landscape and resources. The National Parks and Recreation Act (1978) included part of Barnegat Bay on the east and Delaware Bay to the south as part of the Pinelands National Reserve. This clearly established that the associated estuarine habitats were truly part of the Pinelands. The U.S. Congress created a Pinelands interpretive and educational program in 1988 in recognition of the importance of the pines. This process continues with the periodic approval of Interpretation Plans to enhance awareness and appreciation of the natural and cultural resources of the region. While the National Park Service leads the effort to develop the interpretive program, many other agencies contribute, including the N.J. Department of Environmental Protection and the Pinelands Commission.

The New Jersey Pine Barrens has a wide range of subtle differences in habitats, from uplands to White Cedar Swamps (fig. 8.3), as well as a large number of rare, threatened, and endangered plants. The list increases

New Jersey Pine Barrens

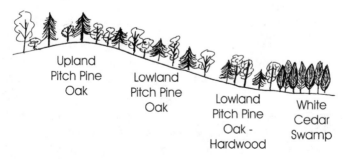

8.3. *Schematic of habitats in New Jersey Pine Barrens.*

8.4. Bog Asphodel is one of the rarest plants of the New Jersey Pine Barrens.

every decade, largely because of human disregard and encroachment. David Fairbrothers of Rutgers University spent much of his life working on these species and has concluded that a 300-year history of bog iron production, glass factories, brick making, and lumbering, not to mention the more recent cranberry farming, has succeeded in disturbing nearly every part of the pines—although fortunately not all at the same time. Few areas have escaped the onslaught. Some activities are worse than others; mining operations usually destroy all ground cover, removing many plants, and consigning others to endangerment.

David, a tall distinguished professor with a full head of snowy white hair, is gentle but dogged in his desire to have a list of endangered state plants and legal authority to protect these species. So far there is no effective statewide protection for plants except in the Pinelands, where 54 species are listed as threatened or endangered. Some plants are protected federally, and the state does have a list of protected, threatened, and endangered plants, but there are virtually no real protections. He knows the locations of the rare plants, where they grow in stable populations that are large enough to survive for years to come, and what measures should be taken to protect them.

"There are nearly a hundred rare and endangered species of flora and fauna in the Barrens," David told me one day. "Even though it is home to over 500,000 people."

"It's hard to believe they still persist," I answered, thinking about all the new retirement communities sprouting up in the pines.

"Bog Asphodel and Knieskern's Beak are known only from the New Jersey Pine Barrens, as are varieties of Grass-leaved Blazing Star, Pickering's Morning Glory and Sand Myrtle (fig. 8.4)," he replied. "The Pickering's Morning Glory is unusual because it creeps along the ground, and the white flowers face upwards forming a dotted carpet (fig. 8.5). Easy to trample without realizing it."

8.5. Pickering's Morning Glory is a state endangered plant that creeps along the ground.

"It's odd," I mused, "for there to be so many endangered plants, when so many other habitats in the state seem more diverse."

"Well, the number of threatened and endangered plant species in the Pine Barrens reflects the colonization history. When sea levels were much lower, there were 100 miles more of the sandy coastal plain, and many species from farther south moved freely into the Jersey pines. Over the centuries, many of these were extirpated from their more southern ranges, either directly by human disturbance, or the loss of habitat."

"I can see that," I said. "People move into habitats they prefer, destroying them first."

"The Pinelands were lucky so few people wanted to live here," he answered. "Unfortunately, that's no longer true."

"But it's not just the endangered species that we should protect, but all the plants that live in this habitat, like the Pine Barrens Gentian (fig. 8.6)," I answered, thinking about the lovely blue flowers.

"We need to protect the entire Pine Barrens communities," David said, "but people much prefer to protect a species they love, like Pine Barrens Treefrogs."

"I can't seem to drum up much interest in protecting Pine Snakes," I responded, "except among the Pineys, and they are disappearing day by day. I don't know what the answer is."

"We just have to keep working with the Pinelands Commission, and with the young kids," he said. "They're the ones who must protect it in the future."

8.6. Pine Barrens Gentian has a deep blue flower.

Fortunately, the Pine Barrens have a chance. The protection of large tracts, and the restriction of development in others, means that we have an opportunity to preserve one of the largest Pine Barrens in the U.S. It is unique in another sense, for the Pine Barrens is the northernmost range for many species, and the southernmost range of others. This means that the species diversity in the New Jersey Pine Barrens is inordinately high for a barrens habitat. Saving this habitat requires the continual cooperation of everyone, including landowners, homeowners, industrialists, developers, and scientists. Scientists are providing the information that can save some of the endangered and threatened species, but it is government agencies, conservation organizations, and the general public that will make it happen. The New Jersey Pine Barrens is a success story, and it will surely exist for our grandchildren's grandchildren.

9

The People of the New Jersey Pine Barrens

A dense stand of Pitch Pine lines the shoreline, and in the small creeks yellow Spatterdock flowers rise above the gray waters, their large oval leaves forming circular patterns on the surface. A few thin cranberry vines dangle into the water, and following them outward, I see a thick mat of vines that goes far across the marsh. The vines are covered with small, pea-sized green berries, for it is still midsummer. In a few months the ripe cranberries will form a vibrant red carpet over the bog.

Except for the absolutely straight edges to the bog, the long narrow ditches, and the nearly level aspect of the bog plants, I might think this area was pristine. Sitting on the edge of a cranberry bog in the New Jersey Pine Barrens, I face the effects of years of farming—a type of farming that takes advantage of the natural ecosystem, but still farming. The earliest paleo-Indians picked cranberries to make dye. I can well imagine them stopping here to search for the berries on their way from the shore to the interior, or from the coast to woodlands farther north. New Jersey has always been a byway because it is so close to so many different habitats.

New Jersey is a state tucked between two metropolitan areas and taken for granted by thousands of travelers who see the blur of towns from a rapid Metroliner, or watch roadsides through the windows of a speeding car. The state was viewed as the road between New York and Philadelphia, a state that somehow failed to develop its own metropolis. We have Benjamin Franklin to thank for this observation that caught the fancy of travelers who seldom stopped in Jersey. Since colonial times, New Jersey has functioned as a corridor, and its economy reflected this role.

By the late 1940s the roads through the state could no longer carry the growing traffic, and plans began for a thoroughfare. The New Jersey Turnpike has shaped the development of the state, often reflecting the worst aspects of urbanization and industrialization. Now, twelve lanes of asphalt roll from New York City in the north, over bridges, past factories, oil refineries, and dense housing, toward New Brunswick, where the tall turnpike offices operate the pike almost in isolation from other state agencies. Gradually the turnpike funnels traffic to six lanes as it passes the turf farms south of New Brunswick and disgorges its dense traffic into Trenton (the state's capital) and Philadelphia. It narrows to four lanes as it passes through the sleepy farms of Burlington County, and finally ends in Salem County, a relatively rural area with a much slower pace.

The turnpike was designed to move masses of travelers from northern New Jersey to states farther south over the shortest and fastest possible route. Industry and commerce clustered near the turnpike, sleepy towns expanded, and land far from the turnpike was left unsettled. This was fortunate for the Pine Barrens of New Jersey, which was nestled between the Atlantic Ocean on the east and the turnpike on the west. The pines were largely ignored by developers and by the shakers and movers who believed that all culture was to be found in Philadelphia or New York City. The people of the pines became more isolated and developed their own modest farms, cottage industries, and customs.

Today, the people of the state, and indeed the nation, revere the Pinelands, which holds the special designation as the first National Reserve. But this respect was not always there. As with pine woods throughout the United States, these lands were largely unappreciated for many decades, relegated to wasteland status because they provided neither fertile farmland nor lush grassland for cattle or horses. Although it does not include the whole Pine Barrens, the Pinelands Reserve covers much of the Outer Coastal Plain, extending from Monmouth County in the north to Cape May County on Delaware Bay. The Pinelands Reserve is 337,000 acres of undisturbed pine woods, bogs, and unpolluted water in the middle of the most densely populated and industrialized state in the nation.

Sitting on the edge of a silent cranberry bog, I can imagine how the people who first arrived viewed the few scattered cranberries nestled in the deep Sphagnum Moss: not much to eat, but the red juice was useful for a dye. The earliest people probably arrived in New Jersey about 10,000 to 12,000 years ago when the last glacier retreated farther north. They met Mastodons and Mammoths that wandered the cooler spruce forests. Gradually these forests disappeared as the glacier retreated, to be replaced by Pitch Pine forests. The first archeological artifacts of Indian occupation date from about 7,000 years ago and were found in the upper Delaware River Valley, and it is assumed that these early people belonged to the Lenape tribe. The Lenape, also known as Delaware

Indians, spoke the Algonquin dialect used by other Native Americans living in Connecticut, southeastern New York, eastern Pennsylvania, and Delaware.

A thousand years ago the Lenape who lived on the fringes of the Pine Barrens treated this land as a hunting preserve. In some places they set fires to keep edge areas open to attract deer, provide winter browse, and allow good hunting. They did not worry about the forest because they knew that the fire did not kill the pines, and they watched tufts of needles sprout the following spring. They used pines and White Cedar to make dugout canoes. They trapped Gray Foxes and captured Black Bears in their dens or dug bear pits for them to fall into. They searched the marshes for Beaver dams, trapping the beaver for food and fur, and they captured birds by luring them in, gobbling to Wild Turkeys, quacking to ducks, and honking to Canada Geese (fig. 9.1). Children contributed by catching fish under stones, and looking for birds' nests and eggs. Garbage dumps, or middens, near old Indian villages show that they ate deer, Porcupine, Gray Squirrel, Muskrat, rabbits, Beaver, hogs, Bobcat, moles, and shrews.

White-tailed Deer were particularly common in the pines, and the Lenape started fires to drive the game toward other hunters hidden in the pines. Some marrow was eaten directly, but most was used as butter. Usually, hunting parties left the villages in the fall and hunted for a month or two in the pines, bringing back what meat they did not eat. Early in the hunt they dried excess meat so it was easier to carry, and they cured the pelts for clothing. They even mixed Black Bear fat with bog iron to make a red dye for their faces.

9.1. *Family of Canada Geese; females nest along the edge of creeks in the Pine Barrens, accompanied by males.*

The Indians used many Pine Barrens plants as well. They ate a subterranean fungus common in the region called Tuckahoe, and I have often wondered if the town by that name in southern New Jersey was named after the fungus. They hiked farther inland to pick persimmons in season, as well as chestnuts, hickory nuts, butternuts, and acorns, and traveled to the shore to gather Beach Plums. To my taste, Beach Plums are a bit tart, but dried they can last even after other fruit has already disappeared. Fruits from the Pine Barrens, such as cranberries, huckleberries, raspberries, and strawberries, were important. Cranberries were eaten, crushed to make dye, and used for medicinal purposes because of their antiseptic powers. The natives ate a number of wild tubers, such as Jack-in-the-Pulpit, Morning Glory, Wild Ginger, Pepper Root, Ginseng, Sweet Flag, and Cattail, grinding them to a mush. I tried mashing up cattail tubers when I read these stories as a child, but my mush tasted bitter. In wet areas, the Indians sowed Wild Rice, which was highly prized. The American Lotus, which today grows in only a few tidal freshwater marshes in southern New Jersey, was a favorite, and the submerged stems and seeds were eaten. Also eaten was Yellow Pond Lily or Spatterdock, for which the Indian had to compete with White-tailed Deer. The Indians also used products of the Pinelands for weaving cloth and making baskets. Cattails were a favorite weaving material because they were strong and could be found in abundance along rivers and streams throughout the pines. The long, thin leaves were tied in bundles and dried in the sun before weaving.

In the springtime, the Lenape moved back and forth within the barrens, fishing for shad in the rivers, and collecting clams and crabs along the bays and estuaries. They built large funnels out of reeds to divert the fish into traps, and they dug for Soft-shelled Clams when the tide was out. In the summer, when the Greenheads and biting mosquitoes came out in droves, they deserted the marshes and estuaries and returned to the pines where they farmed small plots along sandy riversides. In the fall they collected nuts and acorns from the woodlands and hunted deer that came to the clearings to browse on the young trees with tender shoots. The Pinelands served their lifestyle quite well, and they could hunt, fish, trap, and collect wild plants in the traditional manner.

Later the Lenape became agriculturalists who lived in villages, at least during the growing season. Over 1,000 Indian sites have been found by archeologists in and around the Pine Barrens. Although they placed their villages primarily along the rivers, some were deep in the pines. They cleared the pine trees immediately around the villages, and planted crops, primarily corn. They shifted their plots when the fertility of the soil declined, and given the relatively poor soils of the Pinelands, these shifts must have been frequent. Corn was planted in hills of sand, along with one or two bean seeds. They then added Horseshoe Crabs or fish for fertilizer. Some of the corn plants were used like sugar cane—they sucked out the sweet inner core before the plants set corn. Once the corn was ripe, they beat it on rocks and made a mush or porridge. Some corn was dried, placed in baskets woven of rushes, and buried in the soil for winter storage. They had many kinds of corn, including popcorn, sweet corn, multicolored corn, and flint corn, which was hard and lasted longer, and may well be similar to what we call field corn today. In addition, they grew kidney beans, pumpkin, bottle gourd, Jerusalem Artichoke, sunflower, and of course, tobacco. Jerusalem Artichoke produces a lovely sunflower in late summer, and in the fall the Indians dug for the lumpy underground tubers an inch or two across. To my taste they are a little bitter when sliced into salads but are tastier when cooked and mashed with butter. The Lenape farmed a number of potato-like crops, and they baked the tubers in underground ovens.

The first contact between the peaceful Lenape and Europeans came in 1524, when the Verrazano expedition sailed along the Atlantic Coast from North Carolina to Maine. The Lenape were friendly and interested in the boat and its people. This was followed by several Dutch expeditions, and later by the English and Swedes. Although small skirmishes and hostilities broke out from time to time, all sides were drawn together by the desire to trade furs, agricultural products, and beads. Gradually the Dutch infiltrated the Pinelands, considering it theirs.

In the mid-1600s the English wrestled control of southern New Jersey and the pinelands from the Dutch, and some of the hostilities ended. Ultimately, the Lenape were driven out from much of the land and given the Brotherton Reservation in Indian Mills, Burlington County. The reservation was too small to support their hunting, fishing, and farming lifestyle, and gradually they moved into western Pennsylvania.

The Europeans did not find a pristine landscape when they first arrived in New Jersey, although it may have looked like it at the time. The Indian population may have numbered only about 5,000 to 6,000, but it had impacted the landscape markedly. The Indians had regular networks of trails that served as corridors for wildlife, they burned the pine forests to provide open habitat to increase game, and they affected the population sizes of almost all the native wildlife. They also cleared some of the pinelands for farming, and they cut pines for utensils, weapons, canoes, shelters, and fuel.

The early European settlers likewise exploited some traditional foods from the pinelands, foods that were eaten by the Indians, including cranberries, game, and seafood from the nearby shore. Old cookbooks have recipes for wild rabbit pie, fried Snapping Turtle, cranberry pie, hot cranberry tea, and fiddleheads of Cinnamon Fern. As happened in many regions of the United States, the Lenape Indians in the New Jersey pinelands served as teachers because it had been many centuries since the Europeans had to deal with neolithic resources. The relative lack of overt aggression between the Lenape and the Europeans made for the easy transfer of ecological knowledge.

The pinelands was not well suited to the lifestyle of the early Europeans, who generally avoided living there. They wanted to create life as they had known it in Europe. Almost from the beginning, the colonists made a concerted effort to eradicate dangerous animals such as wolves, Black Bears, and Cougars. At the time of the Revolutionary War, the pinelands was classified as "unsettled" and served primarily for hunting, with limited cattle grazing. When the Europeans did venture into the pines, they saw them as a source of raw materials, not as a place to live.

Hunting in the early colonial period was still an important way of obtaining food, but as food became less of an everyday problem for the settlers, the pinelands became a recreational playground. The uppercrust in Philadelphia and New York imitated the English form of fox hunting, including importing the European Red Fox, but the few people who lived in the pines invented their own version. While the uppercrust rode on horseback, the people in the pines walked on foot and used two or three dogs to chase native Gray Foxes. The Pine Barrens version of fox hunting emphasized familiarity with nature since they did not have the advantage of a fast horse, and they had to know both the behavior of the foxes and the behavior of their dogs. This type of fox hunting was also common in the pine woods of Georgia and South Carolina and is still practiced in many of the southern pine forests. Of course, today the prey are Raccoons because they are native and do not have to be imported. Coon hunting is a major sport in the South, and hundreds of hunters gather in coon trials where the object is to have your dog tree a coon. Southerners often shell out thousands of dollars for a good "coon dog," sometimes more than they pay for their cars.

From the early 1700s to the mid-1800s the pinelands were the hub of a number of industries that produced wood, paper, glass, and iron ore.

The name "Barrens" was already well established, for the land was too barren for much agriculture. Lumbering was one of the first industries to get started in the early 1700s because wood was required for building houses and ships, and for fuel. At its peak, there were over 150 sawmills in the pines, mostly in small communities along the rivers, and logging continued into the 1900s. Oaks were cut for shipbuilding, and White Cedars were felled for flooring, beams, sills, and shingles. As early as 1749 Benjamin Franklin worried that overexploitation would leave us with no wood for the future, and warned of the need for conservation. Still, very quickly the largest trees were cut, and the forests were reduced to second growth. Forested areas disappeared even more quickly in other parts of the region, such as the Meadowlands.

Along with lumbering, an industry of turpentine production developed. Slits were made in the Pitch Pine trees to encourage the resin to flow, which was gathered and distilled into turpentine. Roots and trunks were burned to make charcoal, and workers collected the tar that ran out to caulk boats and as an ingredient in shoemaker's wax.

Glassblowing was another of the early industries in South Jersey and the Pine Barrens, one that continues to this day. Sand is basically quartz or silica, which is the main ingredient of glass. Soda and sand from the barrens were mixed together, heated in furnaces, and finally melted down to produce molten glass. The glass from the barrens was green, and the first mason jars used for canning were made from Jersey glass. I remember finding some of these old green jars in my grandmother's basement as a little girl, and I am sorry that I did not rescue them.

In 1739, the first successful glass factory was established at Allowaystown. Thereafter, about 20 glass factories were founded in the late 1700s, and some of these persisted until the 1930s. A very few were transformed into the modern glass industry that still survives around Millville. The early glass industry and iron works in the pinelands were fueled by charcoal, produced by partially burning the pine trees in small pits located throughout the Pine Barrens. If you wander far enough afield, you can still find odd pieces of glass that spilled on the sand. Near the frog pond in my backyard I have a solid piece of clear glass shaped like a bashed-in bowling ball that I collected in the barrens many years ago. Another smaller, jet-black piece the size of a tennis ball sits beside it.

Today some of the sands in the Pine Barrens are still highly prized for glassmaking. The sands are extremely valuable, creating enormous economic pressures to mine them, but the excavation of these sands completely destroys the vegetation, which must be removed before the sands can be mined. Unfortunately, some of the top quality sands are in remote areas where disruption seriously impacts the species living there, such as nesting Bald Eagles.

Clays from the Pine Barrens were used to make bricks and tiles at such places as Mays Landing, Old Half Way, and Union Clay Works. They also made clay pipes, drains, and crude pottery, but these old sites are now in ruins and difficult to find.

Over the years, the production of charcoal was perhaps the largest industry in the pines. Charcoal was made from the common species of pine and the venture was successful because charcoal makers did not require large trees, only lots of them, usually clear-cutting the forest, leaving no pines standing. To make the charcoal, workers dug a shallow pit and placed pieces of sod on the ground and covered it with sand. Next they put the wood to be burned on top, perpendicular to the sand and sod so it formed a tepeelike structure that was 10 to 20 feet tall. More wood was placed on top of this file, leaving a hole or chimney at the top so that more fuel could be inserted. The wood was then covered with turf cut from sandy soil containing Huckleberry and Sheep Laurel, which held the sand together. Finally, this structure was covered with a four- to six-inch-deep layer of sand to form a tight seal. Kindling inserted in the chimney was then set afire. The wood burned slowly, and it took eight to ten days to burn an eight-cord pit. The pits had to be watched continually to make sure the wood did not burn too much.

Initially, the charcoal was necessary to keep the glass and bog iron furnaces burning, but as these industries died out, the charcoal was used for steamboats on the Delaware River and along the bay. Some "pineys" continued to make charcoal the old-fashioned way up into the 1970s, and I once came upon a smoldering pit in one of the back regions of the pines when I was looking for Pine Snakes. The circular mound of smoking sand looked like a miniature volcano ready to blow.

As early as 1675 a bog ironworks was established near Shrewsbury in Monmouth County, although the first truly successful iron furnace was founded in the Pinelands at Batsto in 1766. The Batsto River was dammed to provide a continuous supply of water for the furnaces. The furnace at Batsto produced about 900 tons of iron annually, which required about 12,000 bushels of charcoal to fire its furnaces (this equals about 6,000 cords of wood per year). A well-run bog iron furnace required 20,000 acres of pine forest to keep it running. Workers used a 1,000-acre section each year, allowing only 20 years for the pines to regrow. All they needed to make bog iron was the raw ore found in the streams, abundant water, and plenty of charcoal to fuel the furnaces, and the Pine Barrens provided it all.

There were five furnaces in the Batsto region, along with forges, glassworks, and paper and cotton mills. Since the average pinelands can produce only one-third to half a cord of wood per acre per year, the demand exceeded the growth of the forest. Everything that was one inch or more in diameter was cut for lumber or to make charcoal. Today, we look at the development in the Pinelands with horror, but in the late 1700s and early 1800s much of the pinelands was cut over on a regular basis to fuel the iron furnaces and forges, glassworks, and mills.

Raw bog iron is made naturally by the chemical action of decaying vegetation with iron salts in the stream beds. Pine barrens soils are underlain by a strata of marls that contain a soluble form of iron. The water of the Pine Barrens streams percolates through the marl beds, producing a chemical reaction, and then picks up the iron and carries it to the surface waters. There it oxidizes and is deposited along the bottom or edges of streams as rocky iron ore. Workers dug up the ore and transported it to the furnaces, where it was boiled to remove the water and allow separation of the slag from the iron ore. Gnarled pieces of reddish brown slag can still be discovered around many of the old bog iron plants in the pines. The melted iron was very heavy and was put into "pigs" in sand molds. Later it was called pig iron. This pig iron was made into pots, pans, iron pipe, weights, and cannon balls, the letter being one of the major products.

New Jersey produced thousands of cannon balls and shot that helped win the American Revolution and the War of 1812. Batsto was the hub of iron production, and people who worked there during the American Revolution were exempted from military service. Even today, cannon balls of various sizes lay half buried in the sand around Batsto and in the nearby bogs. Batsto also produced large flat pans for evaporating seawater, leaving salt to supply the Revolutionary Army.

Sawmills provided lumber for the towns that sprang up around the small factories. Sleepy company towns were nestled among the pines where men who worked the forges lived. The women in the households had no option but to shop in the company store, allowing the companies to pay the workers in credit slips, good only at the company store. Since the ironworks required flowing water from the pineland streams, activity ceased when winter came, leaving the people with little to do but hunt, fish, create music, and whittle. This created a culture of poverty similar to that of southern sharecroppers of the twentieth century. Barren land surrounded the towns as the workers cut more and more trees to feed the furnaces.

In the mid-1800s, anthracite coal and iron were discovered in the hills of Pennsylvania, and the ore was easier to extract than bog iron. Coal fueled the furnaces, and the iron industry moved west. Many of the towns that survived continued to produce lumber that was sent to Philadelphia. Once large-scale smelting began in Pennsylvania, the Pine Barrens bog iron industry died out, and by 1848 the furnaces of Batsto were cold. Today Batsto is a ghost town whose only activity is staffing the shops of the historic museum town to preserve a view of old Batsto. The pines gradually reverted to woodlands where few people could eke out a living.

In the 1800s a rather successful industry of making White Cedar shingles for the roofs of houses also existed in the pines. The bark of some scraggly White Cedars had been particularly twisted by the winds, and shingles made from these were highly prized and called "wind shakes." Others, called "dug-ups," were made from logs that were initially buried by nature, but later inventive merchandisers buried cedar logs to create dug-ups. This is akin to modern-day Mexicans burying new ceramics so they will eventually look like pre-Colombian art.

Beginning in the 1870s, Joseph Wharton of Philadelphia, who also founded the Wharton School of Economics at the University of Pennsylvania, began to buy up large tracts of land in the pinelands that became known as the Wharton Estate. His intent was to dam the rivers of the pines to provide drinking water for a burgeoning Philadelphia. The New Jersey legislature got wind of the idea and enacted a law prohibiting the export of water from the state. This made the land economically useless, and it eventually became the Wharton State Forest.

Railroads came to the pinelands in the late 1800s, opening up the land to travelers and developers. But by then most of the industries had moved away, the technologies used in the pinelands were old-fashioned, and it became easier and cheaper to make glass and iron elsewhere. At the beginning of the twentieth century, an awakening interest in natural history brought scores of naturalists to the wilds of New Jersey, many of whom were after plants or rare butterflies for their collections. Train stations served as collecting spots because before the automobile, collectors could get off the train and spend a day on foot, searching the countryside for unusual specimens.

In the late 1800s and early 1900s, the pineys also established a number of other industries: they used salt hay cut from the marshes to make mattresses and mulch. They fished and clammed along the bays, built special duck blinds for "gunning" waterfowl, and made decoys. Some of the decoys made by New Jersey carvers are highly prized today. At a recent auction, a Canada Goose by a Barnegat Bay carver sold for nearly $200,000.

As the metropolitan areas of New York and Philadelphia developed commercially, industrially, financially, and culturally, the Pine Barrens was ignored. The gap widened between the people of the pines and the "sophisticated" people who resided along the turnpike and fled to cities to work. Many people viewed the pineys with distrust, considering them backwoods people who were hillbillies, demented, or worse. They considered the pineys to be hostile, just as likely to shoot you as look at you, and full of mischief. Pineys were considered shiftless because at best they worked the cranberry bogs or made crude glass from the sand, and at worst they lived on deer and raccoons.

When these perceptions became widespread, the pineys withdrew even more, retreating to their woodland homes and gathering in small groups to entertain themselves with their own music. It did not help that the only psychological study in the early 1900s by Elizabeth Kite depicted them as imbeciles with little regard for life. She coined the term "piney," and newspapers often referred to the inhabitants of the pines as "pine rats." The public soon considered the people of the pines as inbred, lawless, criminal, defective, and ignorant, and the rest of the state needed to be protected from them. Some of the Kallikak family lived in the pines, a family long believed to be retarded. I often wonder if this belief wasn't a hoax perpetrated to support the prevailing but erroneous view. People variously believed that the pineys were descended from Tories, "disowned" Quakers, Indians, Hessian soldiers, Revolutionary War bandits, escaped slaves, criminals, and even smugglers and pirates. More likely the pineys were descendants of the workers from the bog iron, glass, and paper industries of South Jersey. The extreme view of pineys as disreputable faded with time, but they were left alone to develop their own folklore and music, free from the rush of suburban life that was becoming the norm in the rest of New Jersey.

The term "piney" was so negative that even the people living there disavowed the name, saying that the "pineys" lived either farther north or farther south of them, depending on where they were from. The folklorist Herbert Halpert, trying to collect songs of the pines in the 1940s, found no one who admitted to being a piney. He believed the negative views reflected a bias of urban people toward rural people—a bias that surfaces every few decades. The local people in the pines made distinctions: "piney" was used for those living in the interior, "clam digger" was reserved for the baymen who lived along the coast, and "rock jumpers" were the farmers of South Jersey. Today, all proudly refer to themselves, as pineys.

Cranberries (in the bogs) and blueberries (in the uplands) are currently the major industries in the pines. Although cranberries grow in the bogs, the early settlers began to grow them in small patches in the wetter places of the pines, often along streams. They created bogs by clearing all the vegetation, leveling it, and digging drainage ditches. Over time, they perfected the ditching system so they could maintain just the right amount of water for optimum cranberry growth, and could also flood bogs for harvesting in October. It takes about five years from the planting of the first cranberry seedlings until there is good production. They also flood the bogs during the winter to keep the delicate roots from freezing. In a natural bog, cranberry roots are normally flooded during the winter, protected by a layer of Sphagnum Moss.

It was not difficult to enlarge these smaller plots to maintain large cranberry farms. With the expansion of cranberry use from a sauce that garnished Thanksgiving and Christmas dinner to a drink that is used year-round, the industry has grown and prospered. Cranberry farming is highly mechanized, and the bogs are flooded in the fall to float the cranberries in a process of harvesting that was invented in New Jersey in the 1960s. The plump berries float to the surface, carrying the vines with them, and a harvester moves over the bed, cutting the berries from the vines. Today, gigantic booms gather the berries and deposit them in trucks, but only a few decades ago men waded in the water, pushing the berries to one end of the bog where they could be scooped up into trucks (fig. 9.2). This is one of the colonial industries that still flourishes, and it is a magnificent and splendid site to see acres of bright red berries festooning the bogs in October. Today the cranberry farmers are organized into cooperatives. Most of the big farmers own their own land but sell and market through the Ocean Spray cooperative, the largest in New Jersey. It is not farmer owned, but has made the farmers successful.

The blueberry industry is more recent, and extensive breeding was required to develop bushes that produced large, lush berries. In the 1910s Elizabeth White traveled the Pine Barrens searching for large-berried bushes she could bring back to Dr. Frederick Coville, who cross-fertilized the plants. Together they produced their first commercial blueberries in 1916. White made the blueberries attractive by covering the small boxes with cellophane, a practice still in vogue today. Whitesbog, a wonderful

9.2. In the mid-1900s men pushed the cranberries to the far end of the bog so that they could be loaded onto trucks. The bogs were flooded so that the berries drifted to the top where they could be cut off.

series of abandoned bogs that are home to a hundred or more Tundra Swans each winter, is named after her father. Blueberry farming has also become mechanized, and today some 8,000 acres of pinelands are devoted to their cultivation.

Although many industries, traditions, and legends of the New Jersey Pine Barrens have slipped away, the Jersey Devil is a delight that remains intact. It is a creation of the people of the pines, and generations of South Jerseyans have searched for the Devil in remote pine woods and swamps. For over 250 years the stories of the Devil have been told from generation to generation, terrorizing young and old alike. As is the way with all legends, the exact origin of the Devil is in dispute, but my favorite is as follows.

In 1735, a Quaker woman known as Mother Leeds learned she was pregnant for the thirteenth time. Cursing her hopelessness, she cried, "I am tired of children, let it be a devil." She lived in an old fishing shack at a site now called Leeds Point on Great Bay. She gave birth to a horribly deformed child, which she confined to the attic (or the cellar) for many years until it made its escape up the chimney (or the outside cellar door). In every version of the story, the child escapes during a raging, violent storm. The actual time of the escape is also in dispute, however. Some pineys believe it was transformed from a normal infant to its horrible devil form during a violent storm, and then fled immediately.

Others hold that the Devil escaped immediately after birth, with a forked, thick tail, huge wings, and a blood-curdling cry. It made directly for the Pine Barrens to hide in the dense, vine-covered, scraggly pine woods, sallying forth to eat young children in the dead of night. By the 1900s many small towns in the pines had their own tales of the frightening works of the Jersey Devil, for by then he had visited most of them. The eerie denizen of the swamps and pinelands started to recede in memory, until 1909.

In the third week of January 1909, the Jersey Devil returned with a vengeance and raided and ransacked some 30 towns in southern New Jersey, or so the residents believed. Several different artists' sketches appeared in the local newspapers. People variously reported a hissing monster, lizard, jabberwock, flying death, flying horse, and flying hoofs that moved through town with great speed. Dogs barked and howled, and grown men hid in fear. His appearance, though itself in dispute, caused schools and factories to close, and people remained at home behind locked doors. Some wondered if the creature was a prehistoric remnant, long hidden in the pines, and some scientists even called it a pterodactyl, a long-extinct flying reptile.

Sightings of the Devil still occur, particularly during storms or when the dense fog from the coast moves into the pines, blanketing everything in ghostly white shapes. It is then that the wailing can be heard by many, and pineys will shudder and lock their doors. A frightening, lonely spirit lurks in the pines, and the Jersey Devil may well embody it. Gnarled and

9.3. Pine Snakes slither through the needles, leaves, and brush, often invisible to the locals walking trails through the barrens.

twisting vines cover the shrubs and wind up to the low pines, and the woods are dark. There are white sand paths that lead through the pines, ancient byways that should have disappeared long ago, except for the silent movement of the Jersey Devil who keeps them open—"the Devil, and the Pine Snakes," the locals say (fig. 9.3). Walking alone in the pines, listening to the wind whistle through the trees, and seeing silvery shadows move in the darkness up ahead, I can well imagine the Devil wandering about.

10

A Spring Chorus

When the first heavy rains of spring sweep across the pines, filling in the low places in the pinewoods far from my home in Somerset, I hear the faraway calls. It is the warmth of the rains, the smell of the fresh earth, and the pull of something remembered from my early childhood. The call of the Spring Peepers is so deafening in my soul that I cannot ignore it. I need to hear their calls, feel the crescendo of the building chorus, and sense the beginning of spring. I can no more deny this calling than I could ignore the banging of an injured traveler at my door. I grab my coat, pick up a flashlight, and Mike and I head for the awakening Barrens.

The drive down Route 18 seems endless. Few cars have ventured out on such a dark, dreary night and we travel quickly. When we reach the sand roads of the pines, we have to slow down, for the drive is more treacherous and no other car lights lead the way. Up ahead I can see the pines thin out and finally disappear in the darkness that is my favorite pond. Even before we shut off the engine I hear the chorus, and I impatiently leap out of the car, flinging on my raincoat and grabbing my flashlight.

Before searching for the frogs, we stop and listen, taking in our first spring chorus. It is every bit as magnificent as my childhood memories, and I marvel that some pleasures never diminish, no matter how many times they're experienced. A thousand calls drown out the patter of the rain, the rushing sound of raindrops hitting the nearby pines, and the torrential rains pelting the pond. Mysteriously, the sounds stop abruptly, and only the rain drones on. Then one Spring Peeper calls, followed by another, and the chorus resumes as loud as ever.

Spring Peepers are tiny treefrogs that live in the tall grasses, low shrubs, and dense trees that line temporary ponds. They have small suction cups on their toes that allow them to cling securely to a small blade of grass or a slippery twig. The suction cups identify them as a treefrog, in the genus *Hyla*. They are pale tan with a dark brown or blackish cross on their backs, which gave them their scientific name of *crucifer*. A few other odd black markings adorn their head and legs, but the cross stands out, making them instantly recognizable among all treefrogs. Spring Peepers are common in the pines where the temporary ponds have not been filled in, and the vegetation still grows in the shallow water and hangs over the banks. Vernal ponds, as they are called, are valuable ecosystems that seldom have legal protection.

It is a warm and balmy night for this time of year, but there could just as easily be ice on the ponds. Spring Peepers begin calling even when ice still lingers on the shaded edges. Although the season is cool and the water is near freezing, warm rains stimulate them to sing.

They have come to the pond for one of the oldest and most primal of rituals. They are here to find a mate, to lay their eggs, to carry on the species, as Spring Peepers have done for eons past. That Spring Peepers call in ponds throughout the Northeast in no way diminishes my delight. It is a pleasing sound enjoyed by many people and ignored by others. Perhaps there are even some who find the din annoying. I still remember a girlfriend years ago who complained that she could not sleep with all that "racket," although she slept soundly with the din of cars near her own house in New York City.

The overhanging vegetation provides excellent perches for calling males, which give a series of high-pitched pipings that continues for several minutes. We creep gingerly along the water's edge, listening intently for a particularly loud shriek nearby. The calls are produced when air is forced from the lungs, passing into the expanded vocal sac at the throat. Each male does not call continuously, but calls in bouts, and we listen for the start of each new bout before creeping closer under the cover of his calls. The vibrations from a careless footfall brings about an abrupt halt in the chorus, and minutes elapse before the frogs start again.

When the male we are searching for stops calling, we stop moving, waiting breathlessly, not wanting to disturb our quarry. We wait in vain, for the male has decided something is not quite right and has hopped silently away. We begin anew, creeping cautiously through the grass, not noticing our sneakers are wet and cold water is trickling down inside our raincoats. The night is warm, and the cool rain soon warms up against our skin. To our left we hear another male, who must be clinging to emergent vegetation, for the call sounds like it is over the water. We edge nearer, moving only when he calls, stopping when he stops. Closer and closer we creep, moving our heads from side to side to get a fix on his exact location. Finally it seems like the call is only inches away. We listen to a full bout, not wanting to interrupt him, hoping he is where we think he is.

He continues calling, and we switch on the small flashlight, pointing it directly to where we hear his call. There he is, less than an inch of pure sound. His throat is ballooned out and nearly the size of the rest of his small body. The balloon expands and shrinks as he calls, and our presence is hardly a distraction. Remarkably, the light does not seem to bother him, and we watch in awe as he continues calling. He is the size of the end of my little finger, and I am amazed at how much sound he produces.

We leave him to his quest and move slowly around the pond. We are now surrounded by displaying Peepers, the calls crescendoing to a full chorus, drowning out all other sounds, all other thoughts. It is early enough in the spring that this is a pure Spring Peeper chorus, with no other interlopers vying for vocal space. Later in the spring, other frogs call, masking the Spring Peeper calls. The spring chorus goes on with hardly an interruption. When the slight drizzle turns to a torrential downpour for a few minutes, the chorus stops, and all is silent. But when the rain relaxes to a slow, soft, steady drip, the chorus begins anew.

Belatedly I realize it is two in the morning, and I have to teach tomorrow. We creep back through the marsh, drinking in the last calls, reluctant to leave this paradise of Spring Peepers. The sand roads are now very slippery, the driving a little more difficult, but slowly we make our way back to Route 18 and the road home. In my heart, however, the chorusing Peepers are as loud as ever, and their calls reverberate for the whole drive home.

The male Spring Peepers come to the ponds first to begin their chorus, and they must wait for the females to be drawn in. It may take a day or two, or it may take a week or two, but eventually females descend from the shrubs and bushes, or from under the leaves and litter, to come to the breeding ponds. Silently they hop from grass blade to grass blade, listening to each male in turn. Although the males sound the same to me, they do not to the female Peepers, who will carefully select a mate.

Once the choice has been made, the pair hop to the water where the female lays tiny eggs. Gently clasping the female around the waist, the male forces the eggs out, fertilizing each one as it floats in the water or attaches to a leaf. This mating posture is called "amplexus." The eggs hatch within a few days, and the tiny tadpoles begin to grow and develop. Mostly the tadpoles hide in the vegetation to avoid becoming food for dragonfly nymphs or other aquatic predators, but they bask in the sun at high noon, soaking up the warm rays that aid in digestion. They have only a few weeks to become frogs, for Spring Peepers usually breed in temporary ponds that dry up with the warmth of summer. This is an adaptation to avoid fish predators. Any ponds in the barrens that are permanent have healthy and voracious fish populations, and tiny tadpoles are quickly eaten.

Spring Peepers are the earliest of several frog species that call from the wetlands of the pines. In only a few days the Chorus Frogs join in. They too are small treefrogs, like the Peepers, but they are not in the midst of the Pine Barrens, occurring in isolated wetlands along the edges. Their choruses are wonderful because they give a rolling "preek" call that crescendos upwards. They make a noise that sounds like running your finger over the teeth of a rusty comb, each frog using a slightly different comb. They are more secretive than the Peepers and are much harder to find because any rustling in the bushes discourages them, and they are silent.

Wood Frogs Join In

In March the Wood Frogs join in—giving a nasal "peent" sound, over and over. To me it sounds more like a crescendoing "zeeeet." One evening during a gentle rain, Paul and Chris Williams and Mike and I creep through a deciduous forest, listening intently to the far-off calls of Spring Peepers. We follow the dirt road, listening to the nasal calls of Wood Frogs coming from small vernal pools. Every small pond has two or three calling males.

"Look, there's an amplexing pair," Mike calls, and we all troop back to watch in awe.

"The female is larger, and a golden brown," Paula notes.

"It must be breeding coloration," I reply, trying to get close enough to photograph the pair. They are oblivious to our quiet movements, and continue long after we leave.

"Here's a Spotted Salamander," Chris says, "just below the surface." We all gather to look at the three-inch-long black salamander with bright yellow dots. Within minutes we find them all over the pond. We have to move carefully, for any rapid movement causes them to dart under the wet leaves.

"Look at the egg mass," I cry. "Here, attached to the sticks. They are salamander eggs." Each black egg is encased in a little pea-sized ball of jelly, and together they form an egg mass that is four inches across.

The Spotted Salamanders live in the upland at the edges of the Pine Barrens, and seldom venture into the barrens. We have come to this particular place because it might have both Pine Barrens and upland species. The usual salamander in the pines is the Tiger Salamander.

10.1. Southern Leopard Frogs breed in the New Jersey Pine Barrens in early to late April.

We walk on, checking each small puddle in the dips of the sand path for salamanders and frogs. This abandoned road creates a series of vernal ponds that, linked together, provide habitat for many breeding frogs and salamanders. The calls from the next pond seem louder, and we are drawn deeper and deeper into the woods, away from the lights of houses and the sounds of highways, drawn to where only the Wood Frogs call, and the few remaining Peepers chorus. It is well into the night when by the light of our small flashlight we pick our way back to the car.

In early April, only straggler Spring Peepers are calling, hoping against hope that some females are still carrying eggs, a condition known as "gravid." In mid-April, when the nights are warmer, Leopard Frogs join the chorus, giving a single, loud, guttural call that they utter at intervals. Leopard Frogs average about three inches in length, are much larger than the treefrogs, and lack pads on their toes (fig. 10.1). Without food pads, they are lousy climbers, so they stay on the ground. In the Barrens, the Leopard Frogs are a bronzy green, with irregular dark olive splotches that have a yellowish border, and their bellies are white. Where I grew up near Albany, the Leopard Frogs are not green at all, but a bronzy brown color. I remember my surprise when I saw my first Pine Barrens Leopard Frog. Bob Zappalorti pointed out that these are a different species—the Southern Leopard Frog, which reaches its northern limit in the New Jersey pines. Leopard Frogs usually sit at the edge of the pond, slightly in the water, and emit their guttural sounds, waiting between each call to see if it attracted a territorial male or an interested female. They too are waiting for a female to select them for mating; then they clasp her around the waist to encourage egg laying, fertilizing the eggs as they are laid. Unlike treefrogs, Leopard Frogs can be seen all year at the edge of ponds or in wet swales.

Green Frogs join the nightly chorus, but they do not stop calling with the dawn, continuing intermittently throughout the day. Green Frog courtship is a laid-back affair, with the males calling every few minutes, first one frog, then several. Then there is a period of rest, as if the croaking and courting were exhausting. In a really good population there may be calls from all over the pond, but usually the calls are sporadic. They sound a bit like the plunking of the A string on my rusty old guitar. It is a wonderful sound, and I never tire of it. They never get bored either, for they go on calling into August. The males engage in frequent wrestling matches that continue for several minutes, and females lay eggs well into late August (fig. 10.2).

Carpenter Frogs and Pine Barrens Treefrogs are perhaps the most interesting denizens of the cranberry bogs and Sphagnum swamps where they breed in the spring. They are not found everywhere in the pines, but are locally common in some ponds and bogs while completely absent elsewhere. They are tied to the Pine Barrens, and unlike the other frogs,

10.2. Green Frogs are one of the few frogs that call both during the night and during the day, seemingly ignoring potential predators. The males sit on leaves in the water and give banjolike calls.

are not found in other marshes and ponds in northern New Jersey. Carpenter Frogs are aptly named, for their chorus sounds like two distant carpenters, banging on nails just a second apart. "Tur-tunk, tur-tunk, tur-tunk." When the chorus is in full swing, it sounds like a convention of carpenters busily trying to build a barn by morning. It is not hard to find a Carpenter Frog when it is calling because they sit in plain sight on floating vegetation, and continue calling despite an approach. If disturbed unduly, it jumps into the water, only to emerge a few feet away, climb on some floating vegetation, and begin calling anew.

The Pine Barrens Treefrog takes the award for being the loveliest little frog in the state and has become the mascot for the preservation of the Pinelands. These tiny amphibians are also found in small disjunct populations in North Carolina, South Carolina, Georgia, and western Florida, making the populations in the New Jersey Pine Barrens quite isolated. They are listed as endangered by the Endangered and Nongame Species Program (ENSP), not because there are so few, but because their breeding localities are limited. Pine Barrens Treefrogs compose a chorus to remember, and near the beginning of May we always make a special foray to Webbs Mills Bog to hear them once again. Although they begin coming to the bogs in early May, the chorus takes a couple of weeks to get into full swing.

The weather is warm and balmy, and Michelle LeMarchant and Guy Tudor have joined us for this pilgrimage. One of the best all-around naturalists in the east, as well as the premier bird artist in America, Guy is a delightful nay-sayer who is sure nature is doomed, along with the rest of civilization. He would have been equally at home in Audubon's or Samuel Johnson's England. With a graying beard, blue eyes, and a wry smile, he spends long hours afield, talking nonstop about wildflowers, birds, butterflies, and the woes of the world. Michelle, in contrast, is quiet and elegant, and moves easily in the New York City art world among Monets and other French impressionist paintings. With long blond hair and a willowy figure, she is equally at home in any environment, be it in gay Paris or on an African plain.

As usual, we search for birds in the early morning and butterflies at midday, and we hope to see snakes at any time. Our high point for butterflies is the over 300 Juvenal's Duskywings we find on the road leading into one of my known sites for nesting Pine Snakes. The Juvenals are sunning in the middle of the sand road, taking in the warmth from the early rays at about 9 A.M. They are quite common in the Pine Barrens from mid-April to early June, when the adults are searching for mates and nectaring on blueberry and Wintercress flowers. They usually disappear toward the end of May, when all have laid their eggs. The larvae feed on oak leaves and overwinter in the leaf litter.

During the rest of the day we search for early spring butterflies: Sleepy Duskywing, Pearl Crescents, Hessel's Hairstreak, Mourning Cloak, Tailed Blue, Brown Elfin, and Pine Elfin. Hessel's Hairstreak is a specialty of the White Cedar swamps, coming down to nectar in the midafternoons on Sand Myrtle and blueberry. We look in vain for snakes, and while disturbing a promising patch of leaf litter, we flush a Jumping Mouse, a species none of us have seen before in New Jersey.

Heading for Webb's Mill Bog

As nightfall approaches, our excitement increases. It does not matter how many times we have found Pine Barrens Treefrogs, we always search for them again. Not all bogs and swamps in the barrens have them, but they are usually quite common in the ponds where they occur. We can always count on Webb's Mill Bog, and we head there.

Webb's Mill Bog is a particularly lovely bog, nestled beside Route 539 in the heart of the Pinelands. Only a short walk through the pines brings us to the edge of the bog, and a wonderful paradise that is seldom visible except by taking long canoe trips down deserted rivers to find the truly wild places. The smell of the cedars, which surround and protect a delightful wetland, permeates the air. The trail leads onto a rough boardwalk that meanders through the bog, passing a dense stand of Atlantic White Cedars with an understory of Sweet Pepperbush, Dangleberry, and Dwarf Huckleberry. The boardwalk was originally constructed so botanists could find rare bog plants without unduly trampling the Pitcher Plants, sundews, and orchids. Many years later the rustic wooden boardwalk was replaced by an awful metal one with high railings. Supposedly someone fell off the wooden one and threatened to sue the state, a sign of the times I find deplorable.

Dwarf Huckleberry, Leatherleaf, Sheep Laurel, and a few stunted cedars grow on hummocks covered with a lush carpet of Sphagnum Moss. Not as lush or deep as it once was, however, for Sphagnum was mined from this bog. Here and there a few bare patches of sand attest to this long-ago stripping. In between the hummocks the ground is wet and the Sphagnum is even denser. Golden Club is a local specialty, and the two inch high plants are in full flower. At the top of tiny stalks are bright yellow flowers on a compact spike, framed by elliptical dark green leaves at the base. Fortunately, these yellow jewels are far enough from the boardwalk to

*10.3. Golden Club forms a vibrant carpet of brilliant yellow
spikes growing in Sphagnum bogs.*

discourage trespassers, and they gleam in the yellow-green glow of late
afternoon (fig. 10.3).

By carefully kneeling on the boardwalk and peering into the moss we
identify three species of sundews: Round-leaved, Thread-leaved, and
Spatulate-leaved. Their small round disks face skyward, waiting to trap
some tiny, unsuspecting insects so they can devour them, obtaining nutrients and nitrogen otherwise absent from the bog. Pitcher Plants, another carnivorous plant, are everywhere, and because they are so much
larger, they are easy to see.

As the last light fades, we head for the car because the mosquitoes have
become unbearable. We must wait for darkness to descend before the
Pine Barrens Treefrogs will call. In the dim light we see a migrant Red Bat
coursing up and down over the road, searching for insects. They are really quite big, larger than a Big Brown Bat. Even the scratching of untold
mosquito bites is not enough to dampen our spirits, and we polish off the
last of the barbecued chicken and gooey brownies while we wait. I always
believe in taking food even though we are never far from civilization in
the Pine Barrens; it is good to be prepared. Guy loves the chicken, and
this has become a staple of our field trips over the years.

Finally we can contain our excitement no longer, and gathering flashlights, cameras, film, and binoculars, we head in. Only a few yards into

the cedars we see a Flying Squirrel soar from one tree to another, a real treat. Although they can be common in some areas of the Pine Barrens, they are nocturnal and are seldom seen. We creep softly along the trail, and out onto the boardwalk. The mosquitoes have died down a bit: either our repellent is working, or we are just too excited to notice. It is a dark night, which will be good for the frogs. Slowly they begin to call, first one, and then another. "Quonk, quonk, quonk, quonk" echoes across the bog. We walk along, trying to find a calling frog that is within reach of the boardwalk, but each time we are frustrated: the "quonks" always come from somewhere else. For over an hour we walk from one end of the boardwalk to the other, our flashlights at the ready, waiting, but none is close by. This is not surprising since they often call while sitting on the pines or cedars at the edge of the bog, far from the boardwalk.

It makes no sense for the male frogs to venture forth, exposing themselves to predators when there are no females about. It is early in the season, and the females may still be quite high in the shrubs or trees. They leave the safety of the vegetation only when they are ready to breed; unlike the males, females don't have to select a territory or display. Time drags on, and finally, reaching the end of the boardwalk, we decide to creep through the bog in the direction of a particularly persistent caller.

We give only a fleeting worry to the bog beneath our feet because of an interesting but curious fact. David Fairbrothers, who has studied Webb's Mill for many years, believes that some trampling of the vegetation is required to keep it in an early successional stage. Too much trampling destroys the delicate plants that grow in the bog, but in untrampled areas Red Maple seedlings and other hardwoods quickly become established. Red Maples shade out the small delicate plants of the bog, and eventually the bog would disappear. Thus the boardwalk is there to keep the vast numbers of ecotourists and plant enthusiasts from trampling the bog, but the few people who venture off the path to find Pine Barrens Treefrogs are probably just enough to keep the bog in an early successional stage. David has watched the demise of other, less-visited bogs, and is anxious that Webb's Mill survives. For forty years he has studied this and many other bogs, providing some of the best long-term data around.

This situation is not unique. In many places managers keep a few cows in marshes to keep down the emergent vegetation that would take over without some grazing. It takes a wise manager to realize the need for such grazing and to maintain the number of cows so that the ecosystem remains in the necessary successional stage for a particular conservation objective. We are slowly losing the bogs of New Jersey that were created by the retreating of the last glacier—gradually they are filling in.

As we creep along, we avoid stepping on the Golden Club and Pitcher Plants. We spread out to triangulate the call, trying to determine just where the tiny frog is. Slowly we move forward toward one another, and the call becomes louder and louder. But it is amazingly difficult to locate, an excellent adaptation to avoid predators. We are more persistent than most predators, however. Sensing our approach, the caller stops for many minutes, trying our patience, but then it continues on.

Finally, as the call seems very near, we gather together, facing in the same direction. We tentatively touch one another, making sure everyone is here. We may have only one opportunity to see the frog before he hops away into dense cover of darkness.

"Is your camera ready?" Mike whispers.

"Let's do it," Guy says. Mike switches on the light and scans a pine sapling in front of us.

There, caught in the beam, sitting on a small pine twig at eye level, is a lovely little Pine Barrens Treefrog (fig. 10.4). A bright Granny Apple green above, with a white belly, he has a vibrant purple stripe extending from his eye to his groin. He is absolutely exquisite, and incredible as it sounds, I forget to take any pictures. Peering at us, he slowly expands his throat pouch and gives one last "quonk," holding his ground. In a few minutes he tires of the intrusion, and slowly begins his series of nasal honks.

We let out a collective breath, for he is not going to flee. Mike nudges my camera, subtly reminding me of my task, and slowly I lift my camera and begin to snap away. Placidly the frog watches, without moving a single muscle. After I take an entire roll of film, we turn off the lights and slosh slowly back toward the boardwalk. Safely on the boardwalk, we wait quietly, and within a few moments "our" male is calling once again. Satisfied that he is safe, we head for the car and home. We sleep well that night, with the wonderful "quonks" of Pine Barrens Treefrogs penetrating our dreams.

The chorus of frogs can seem endless, starting as it does with Spring Peepers in late February and culminating with Green Frogs in June. Green Frogs, however, never quite stop croaking, and their banjolike song can be heard throughout the summer, as if somehow fall will not come if they keep on going. I have found strings of their eggs in Pine Barrens ponds in August, certainly late for a frog. The eggs may make it, however, because the tiny tadpoles only have to survive the winter in

10.4. *The endangered Pine Barrens Tree Frog calls from the cedar bogs, each Frog individually sitting around the ponds.*

the bottom muds, and then they can grow rapidly in the warm waters of the following spring and summer.

The draw of the frog chorus lessens when the weather warms up, and other creatures begin to stir. Snakes bask on warm sunny days in early April, still remaining close enough to their winter dens so they can slither to warmth when the cold returns. I sit quietly on a log, leaning against a pine tree, watching the entrance of a hibernacula. Although I am hoping that a Pine Snake will decide to come up, I am really enjoying spring in the pines. The harsh winter is past, and the pines will soon be home to a variety of vireos and warblers.

Fence Lizards Bask in the Sun

By late April, it is warm enough for the Fence Lizards to make an appearance. They spend a great deal of time flattened against fallen logs, absorbing the warm sun and reflected heat. As the pines begin to warm up, a Fence Lizard crawls out of the safety of rotting vegetation to lie on a sunlit log. It matches the color of the log and its black markings serve to break up its body outline, making it difficult to pick out. Fence Lizards are able to lie absolutely motionless for hours, taking in the sun, heating up their bodies enough to feel energized into searching for prey. They are truly inhabitants of the Pine Barrens, preferring the sandy soil and open places, and they do not occur elsewhere in New Jersey.

Fence Lizards are small, only four to seven inches long, counting the tail. They are a dusky brown, with dark splotches or chevrons of black on their back, and their scales overlap. Tiny ridges on the scales point backwards. The scales on the head seem to have more ridges, and their jet-black eyes and snakelike head look sinister. Only their small size keeps them from being very scary. Imagining them twenty feet long is frightening, and they would be quite impressive predators. As it is, Fence Lizards eat a variety of spiders, termites, grubs, beetles, crickets, and snails. They lie in wait, motionless, until an insect lands nearby, and then they lunge and flip out their tongue so fast the prey doesn't have a chance.

I watch idly as a male basks in the sun. Although it is nearly 65 degrees Fahrenheit, it takes several minutes for him to warm up. He is a particularly fine-looking male with a vibrant deep blue splotch on each side of his throat, and a larger patch of blue on the side of his otherwise white belly. Suddenly he raises his body and begins to do pushups, pumping rapidly up and down, and I turn slowly to see that another male has approached and dared to walk onto his log. They face off, only a few inches apart, each bobbing up and down, and then holding the upward position like athletes awaiting to see how long they can hold a pushup. The intruder finally backs off and dashes into the underbrush, barely touching the leaves and needles in his hasty retreat. It is the beginning of the breeding season, and males may not be quite ready for prolonged territorial clashes.

I am amazed at how fast they can move, and how far they can run in a short time. But they never continue to move; instead, they find a way to avoid the predator by escaping into a hole in the ground or crevice in a log. Endurance is undoubtedly very important to these lizards, especially when they are being pursued by a predator. Fence Lizards have many predators who are only too willing to pursue them to exhaustion. Fortunately, they usually find a convenient crevice first. This need to find a crevice when faced with danger is one of the best explanations for the evolution of territoriality.

Any animal that maintains a territory becomes familiar with the features of that territory, including all the places to hide. When a predator approaches, such as a bird or snake, the Fence Lizard can make an immediate beeline for the closest and safest place. Knowing the safe places to hide saves time when time is critical. Short bursts of running are often required to avoid being someone else's meal. For several years, Henry John-Alder and his students at Rutgers have been examining endurance in Fence Lizards in the New Jersey Pine Barrens. They noticed that running speed and endurance varied among different males. In laboratory experiments they found that endurance was related to social factors such as crowding. Crowding inhibits and isolation accentuates normal male hormone functioning. Endurance also varies by families—some females have offspring that have longer endurance times than those in other families.

Henry comes by his interest in endurance naturally. Small and wiry, with dark salt-and-pepper hair, he is a marathon runner and spends hours testing his own endurance. He regularly runs in 26-mile marathons, and he jogs from one Rutgers campus to another while most of us go by car. Henry and his students have spent a great deal of time watching the territorial behavior of male lizards, their interactions with females, and their ultimate home ranges in the Pinelands. Males that are big have larger territories, and higher levels of testosterone, than smaller males. Having a large territory and higher levels of testosterone does not influence whether a male wins battles against another male, but it does influence his ability to visit females. Visiting females, of course, is directly related to producing offspring and is more important in the evolutionary scheme of things than winning a battle with a male competitor.

The females maintain a rather exclusive territory, while male territories overlap one another as well as the territories of the females. By early May the females are receptive, and the males spend their time trying to visit as many females as possible. The larger male usually wins the female, but if one is not around, she will mate with a smaller male. Males need to know where to find the females within their large home range. The mating period continues until the end of May, when the females lose interest and are no longer so evident. Females lay one clutch of 6 to 13 eggs near the end of May, although a few may lay two clutches. Not surprisingly, the males are much less obvious once the courtship period has passed, disappearing into the rotting oak leaves and decaying logs.

Slowly the Fence Lizard on my log begins to move about, looking for beetles or other insects. The other male has retreated to his own territory, running rapidly over the leaves and leaping onto the trunk of a tree. I can watch both Fence Lizards from my log, and I make a small bet on which one will catch an insect first.

With amazing speed the intruder runs to the opposite side of his log, out of sight, and, fascinated, I watch a large Milk Snake slither slowly toward him. For me, this is a rare experience, actually seeing a hunting snake. One of the lizard's primary predators are snakes, such as Milk, King, and Black Racer. The snake noses around the log, and the snake and lizard dance back and forth. The snake tries to get close enough to make a strike, and the lizard tries to stay on the opposite side. When the snake does not appear over the top of the log, the lizard makes the fatal mistake of peeking over the top to see where the snake is. Too late, the lizard realizes his error, but it is already in the mouth of the snake. It happened so quickly, and so finally, that I am reminded of the constant threats the smallest creatures face.

By June the Fence Lizards are more difficult to see, and usually they are merely a blur moving across the dry mat of dead leaves and needles, or up the trunk of a pine. When they stop moving they disappear before your eyes, melting into the background, blending with all the other browns and blacks on the forest floor. Only an occasional head bob gives their position away.

Most of the frogs have mated for the year, have moved into the vegetation immediately surrounding the ponds, or have returned to the uplands. But not the Green Frogs. They can be counted on to continue their courtship and territorial battles well into the summer. Their clear "A tones" have switched to twangy guitar strings, but they continue nonetheless. Unlike many frogs, they are not shy, but will chorus, court, and mate throughout the day and well into the night, right out in plain sight. On a warm rainy afternoon in late June, the Green Frogs are plunking away on their strings, and the sounds echo across the ponds and bogs of the barrens. Every 10 or 15 feet there is a male nestled in the vegetation, calling every few moments. When one calls, many others answer in turn, and they can work themselves up to quite a frenzy. When they really get going, the males challenge one another by swimming toward an opponent and calling loudly. With their bright yellow throats, the males are quite handsome.

If a male intruder comes too close, he is attacked by the resident, who grabs the intruder around the waist. Frogs do not have much of a waist, but they grab each other around the middle nonetheless. Facing each other, they jump up and down on their hind legs, trying to force the other one over backwards, into the water. These wrestling matches can last for 15 minutes or more, and they end when one of the frogs is forced under the water. Exhausted, the loser releases his grip and swims away.

But within a few minutes he usually returns, and the match resumes. Females seem to pay no heed to these battles, but sit placidly in the water nearby, waiting for an unwary insect to pass by. Sometimes they even leave the battle zone. Females are easy to recognize because they have a snowy white throat, while the male's throat is a bright yellow.

A female must have been paying attention, for by the next morning a great mass of eggs, each encased in a ball of gelatin, has been deposited near the site of the battle. The mass looks like a glop of clear tapioca, and the eggs are small black dots. The calling, courting, and wrestling continues for many more weeks, with females laying three or four clutches during the season. Individual female Green Frogs seem to lay more eggs each year than other frogs, but this may be required by the greater potential for predators. Green Frogs, along with Bullfrogs, are different from most frogs in New Jersey in that their tadpoles need more than a few weeks to metamorphose into adults. Green Frog tadpoles that are hatched in one summer do not normally metamorphose into adult frogs until late in the spring of the following year. Thus, they must breed in permanent ponds, which have many more predators, including fish and dragonflies.

Tadpoles are vulnerable because they have to bask in the sun to warm up and digest their food, yet they must hide from a wide range of predators. Although they can blend in with the muds and mucks at the bottom of ponds, they are visible when they move around in search of algae and other foods. Their behavior is a compromise between trying to remain hidden and immobile to avoid predators, and seeking food and heat from the warm sun.

When the sun sinks lower in the sky in the fall, the tadpoles spend more and more time at the bottom of the pond, where the water is warmer. They bury in the muds, dozens packed together, and wait out the winter. When spring arrives, they again bask in the sun to warm themselves enough to move about and forage. It is a period of rapid growth as there is usually a spring algal bloom, providing abundant food, and the pond waters warm up, making it possible to forage for more of the day. Tadpoles also feed on organic detritus and aquatic vegetation.

Finally, the tadpoles begin to reabsorb their tail and grow legs. In the final days of metamorphosis they spend some of the time in the water and some time sitting on the top of Spatterdock leaves or other floating vegetation. As tadpoles they breathed through gills, but they have now switched to lungs. They bask in the warm sun and survey their new domain above water. But this period is not without peril, for now they face both aquatic and terrestrial predators. Fish, dragonfly larvae, and some turtles search for them from below the surface, while birds and snakes pick them off from above.

We have a nice population of Green Frogs in our pond at home, and in late May or June, when adult male Green Frogs are already in their territories making guitar-string "plonks" to ward off males and attract females, the young nearly-metamorphosed frogs sit about on the vegetation. Sometimes nearly every Spatterdock leaf has one or two. In a good year, there can be over 100 in an area that is 10 yards square. Their diet has switched from algae and vegetation to animal matter, and they are learning to capture small insects.

Slowly a small head appears among the emergent Pickerel Weed, and behind it the water undulates. A Garter Snake slithers across the pond, swimming from one clump of vegetation to another, until it is near a young Green Frog facing the other way. In one quick strike the snake snatches the tiny frog (fig. 10.5). Quickly it manipulates the frog so it can swallow it head first, and then by spreading and elongating its elastic jaws, the snake pulls its prey into its gullet and begins the process of swallowing and digestion. These frogs are so small that they do not even make a lump. The snake moves over the pond, catching one after another, until its meal of six tiny frogs seems enough. It slithers back to the shallows and disappears in the vegetation on shore, perhaps not to eat for another week. Garter Snakes are not particularly common in the Pine Barrens, but where they occur, they can drastically diminish the population of young frogs in a few weeks. Only those froglets that are

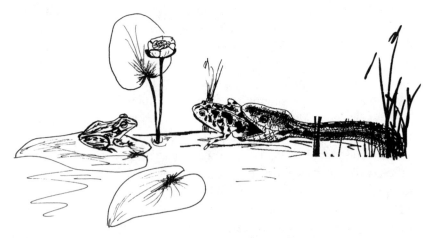

10.5. A Garter Snake preying upon a young Green Frog while a smaller one looks on. The leaves of the spatterdock did not protect the young frog.

wary survive, their perceptions of danger are honed, and they hop away or swim under the water to avoid the snakes. Meanwhile, in the vegetation at the edges of the ponds, there are masses of gelatin holding thousands of tiny black eggs that will be the next generation of Green Frogs. Most will not make it to next summer, but some will, and the cycle will continue.

11

Snake Communities
in the Pines

By late May it is warm in the pines. A pair of Mockingbirds works across a small grassy opening, and a Downy Woodpecker moves slowly over the bark of a Pitch Pine, inspecting crevices for insects. Every once in a while, one of the Mockingbirds spreads its wings rapidly upward, as if it is about to take flight. Instead, it remains on the ground and repeats the wing flashing, searching for insects it has startled, such as grasshoppers, beetles, or crickets. Pitch Pines stand like so many crooked soldiers, each with a wide space around them. The canopy is rather open, as it is in most pine barrens, with sunlight streaming to the forest floor. Clusters of scraggly, misshapen Scrub Oak grow beneath the taller pines. The soil is sandy and well drained and is very dry, not very conducive to promoting a rich understory. Patches of bare sand are bleached white by the sun, interspersed with mounds of pale green lichens forming small prickly cushions.

As we walk through the forest, the Pitch Pines become more sparse, and around my knees is a tangle of Low-bush Blueberry, Huckleberry, Sweet Pepperbush, and Catbrier. We continue downslope into the Pitch Pine lowlands, and it is apparent that we are close to a swamp because the Sweet Pepperbush grows best in low sandy woods near water. The Pepperbush leaves are a rich deep green, but they will not have their white sprays of fragrant flowers until late July. On the ground is a clump of Turkeybeard, with narrow, grasslike, wiry leaves a vibrant green, and a profusion of tiny white flowers on a single 15-inch stalk. Ahead is the silence and darkness of a dense stand of Atlantic White Cedar, with a few Red Maple, Sweet Gum, and Black Gum in the canopy. Skunk Cabbage, cranberries, and various mosses grow in a luxuriant dense ground cover below a few Swamp Azaleas and huckleberries. The pink-tinged white flowers of the Swamp Azalea have not yet opened, but in another week or so the aroma of their delicate fragrance will fill the air.

In the low edges of the swamp we find several Swamp-pinks, their large pink, globular flowerheads standing nearly as tall as I, on stiff, unmoving

stalks (fig. 11.1). They look so odd, as if the pom-
pom flowers were each individually clipped for a
performance. Near the ground a rosette of evergreen leaf swirls form the base of the plant. We are
lucky to find this small colony, for they are a threatened plant species in New Jersey, and it is near the
end of their flowering season.

Jacques Hill, Robert Zappalorti, and I are here to
check our drift fences for snakes, a project we have
been working on since April. Jacques is a tall,
pleasant-looking man with slightly curly blond
hair, Jacques is quiet and gentle, traits I admire in
a man. His sensitive demeanor, however, hides a
fierce and overabiding interest in reptiles, and I
admire his determination and dedication. We are
capturing snakes so that we can examine the differences in their abundance in the dry upland pine
oak forest compared to the moist, lowland pitch
pine lowland forest near cedar swamps. Unlike
many other groups of animals, reptiles and amphibians are somewhat abundant here, and some

11.1. Swamp Pink
flowers are on the top
of a stem that is three
to four feet tall, and
in the deep pines the
vibrant pink stands
out against the
shades of green.

30 of the 35 species that occur in New Jersey are found in the Pine
Barrens.

First, of course, we want to find out which species are present in these
two habitats, and then to determine the relative abundance of each snake
species. Such information is not only of interest to ecologists who examine communities of animals, but also to conservation groups and state
agencies interested in protecting the unique, threatened, and endangered
snakes of the Pine Barrens. Snake community structure is fascinating
because in some habitats, large predatory snakes are the top trophic level
that influence the abundance and distribution of their prey. Changes in
prey abundance secondarily affects the plants or animals they eat, and so
the effects cascade through the pinelands. Where there is more than one
large predatory snake, there may be competition between them, further
changing community structure. Ecologists interested in communities
have devoted most of their attention to top predatory birds because they
are active during the day, are prominent, and are easy to see and identify.
It is more difficult to study most mammals because they are only active at
night. Reptiles have been largely ignored because of their secretive nature. Since many reptiles need to eat only sporadically (once every week

or so), they spend a great deal of time hidden beneath the leaves or debris, within rotting logs, or underground in mammal burrows.

The past bias toward birds sometimes resulted in our managing for the large, charismatic, or endangered species. However, from a management perspective, it is no longer feasible or practical to manage for only one threatened or endangered species. It makes more sense to manage for groups of species that have similar habitat requirements on a landscape scale. This, however, requires a basic understanding of the habitat needs of each species, as well as knowing how different species interact. The first step is to understand how many of each different species are likely to live in the dry upland pine-oak forest compared to the moist, lowland Pitch Pine forest.

In truth, however, I am really interested in finding out how the abundance and distribution of Pine Snakes varies in these two habitats. Pine Snakes are one of the largest snakes in the Pine Barrens (equal in size are the Timber Rattlesnake and Black Rat Snake, their competitors). The beauty of a Pine Snake's black and white color pattern, and their relative rareness, makes them doubly attractive. They are officially listed as a threatened species in New Jersey, due mainly to the loss of habitat through conversion of pinelands to retirement communities, golf courses, shopping malls, and industrial parks. Fortunately, the New Jersey Pinelands Commission now restricts new development in the Pinelands, and only allows and promotes clustered housing construction in noncritical plant and wildlife habitat areas.

Bob Zappalorti, Mike Gochfeld, and I have been studying Pine Snakes for many years in the New Jersey Pine Barrens. I first met Bob at an Endangered and Nongame council meeting in the early 1980s, and we soon discovered a mutual love for turtles and snakes. Tall and muscular with light brown hair now running to gray, Bob is a true gentleman. A self-taught scientist who is deliberate in his actions, Bob takes a long time to decide if someone is honorable enough to take in the field. Once he becomes interested in a particular species, he wants to learn all he can, working tirelessly year after year. We are opposites in many ways, as I always want to plunge full speed ahead into any interesting research question, but we still forged an enduring friendship based on many productive days in the field working on the ecology and behavior of Pine Snakes, Black Racers, and other amphibians and reptiles. Mike joins us when he can, but his medical school duties are more restrictive than are mine at Rutgers. When the warm spring weather finally comes to the pines, I am off to the Pine Barrens to observe snakes again.

Snakes are difficult to study because they are secretive and hard to find just by walking the pines. Old-timers put out boards or sheets of tin to provide hiding places for the snakes. These so-called "sucker boards" often attracted a variety of species, particularly during the hot summer. The trouble with this method of snake collecting is that not all snakes are equally attracted to the boards, and some species are never captured under them. Instead, we have chosen to use drift fences with funnel and pitfall traps for our study.

Last March, Jacques and I walked many areas of the Pine Barrens with Bob, searching for just the right locations to install our drift fence trapping system. Ideally, we wanted to place six fences in dry upland pine-oak forest, and six in moist, lowland Pitch Pine forest that was similar in aspect. This in itself was a difficult task, and we were glad of Bob's advice, for he has spent many years walking the Pine Barrens in search of snakes, turtles, and frogs. Finally, we settled on some sites in Ocean County that contained a mosaic of pine-oak uplands, pine lowlands, and cedar bogs, and set up our drift fence arrays.

Setting up drift fences is time-consuming and hard work. Our overall plan was to place the fences in a Maltese Cross design, the four arms pointing north, south, east, and west, with numerous pitfall and funnel traps placed along the fence. First we had to clear all the vegetation from the places where the fence would be placed, no easy task given all the Low-bush Blueberry, Huckleberry, Catbriers, and other small shrubs, not to mention the trees. The fencing itself is a thick black nylon plastic that is typically used on construction sites to prevent soil erosion. The fencing has to be buried several inches in the ground so the snakes do not dig under it. When completed, our long lines of black fencing looked like a construction site where fencing is used to indicate operations or to keep people out.

We used two types of pitfall traps. First, we buried 50-gallon garbage cans at the end of each fence, with the lip just below ground level so the animals are not stopped by a ridge. We also used 5-gallon plastic buckets buried at 25-foot intervals along the fence, placed on both sides of the arms. When a snake slithers by, it falls in and then cannot climb out the high, slippery sides of the 50-gallon trap. A few leaves placed in the bottom cushion any fall and provide a place for animals to hide. Second, we made funnel traps, which are long and thin and are placed beneath a plywood board to provide shade for the trapped animals. The creature can also hide beneath leaves and other debris placed in the traps. The traps look like an elongated version of the minnow traps that fishermen use along the shore. A snake wandering along the bottom of the drift fence encounters the trap and enters the mouth without realizing that it is a trap. In the end, the funnel traps worked best, and the pitfalls were not as successful because large snakes could climb out. Although we punched holes for drainage, heavy rains raised the water level in the sand and made the pitfalls death traps in which snakes or small mammals could drown. The various traps had to be checked daily so trapped snakes could be returned quickly to their daily activities. We checked the drift fences frequently to release animals, and to make sure that no animal suffered.

Now, weeks later, we are walking along one of the drift fences, searching for snakes. It is exciting because we never know what we will find. Yesterday, Jacques caught a big Pine, two Hognoses, and a few small mammals. Slowly we walk alongside one of our upland sites, peering intently at the base of the fence for any snake that is moving along. We stop to uncover each funnel trap in turn, searching for movement, and then re-cover it so that any unwary snake slithers in easily. Then we move on to the end, where a pitfall trap is still in place, and we find a Box Turtle that wandered by. We pick it up, marveling at the hinged lower shell that allows it to close up completely, hiding its edible legs and head from predators. After a few seconds it slowly sticks its head out, allowing us to see its yellow eyes, which identify it as a female since most males have red eyes. We place it on the ground away from the fence, and within minutes she slowly lumbers off, disappearing among the leaves and needles by a small oak tree. Hognose Snakes have declined in many areas of the Pine Barrens, in lock-step with Fowler's Toads, their primary prey.

We check the rest of the traps of this drift fence, but nothing else is caught, so we move on to the next one, where we find a young Black Racer curled beneath the leaves in one of the funnel traps. In the sun the Racer is a gleaming slate black above and gray below. Its smooth scales give rise to its shiny appearance. This snake was no doubt searching for insects, a small snake, or a Fence Lizard, all of which make up most of its diet (fig. 11.2). We put it in a snake bag to take back to the laboratory where we will measure and weigh it. We will also inject a tiny glass encased micro-chip called a PIT tag under its skin for future identification.

PIT (Passively Induced Transponder) tags are small devices that look like a piece of lead from a pencil, only they are glass. Each tag has a unique number that can be encoded and read with a small radio frequency wand, making positive identification easy and accurate. In the old days we used

11.2. A Fence Lizard basks in the early morning sun, absorbing enough heat to actively search for prey.

to clip scales or brand the scales with an old-fashioned wood-burning tool. PIT tags are easier and much more accurate than counting scales. Although each tag costs over $7.00, it is well worth it. The tags can be painlessly and easily injected under the skin, where they remain for the life of the animal. The basic technology was developed for horses, to prevent unscrupulous owners from switching horses after they were tested for drugs and before they raced. Now winners are tested to make sure they are the horse they are supposed to be. The technology quickly spread to show dogs to prevent loss or theft. Eventually smaller tags were developed for smaller wildlife species, and the technology is now quite widespread.

We move on to the drift fences in the Pitch Pine lowland. It is a little cooler here, and the undergrowth is denser. A burst of feathers and dark color disappears in the brush, and too late we realize we have frightened a covey of Bobwhite. The six or eight quail flew in all directions, an adaptation for confusing predators who cannot settle on which one to pursue. When the predator decides, it is probably too late and the small chicken-like birds have long since disappeared, and all is silent. It is nearly impossible to get a good look at a Bobwhite, although its shrill "bob-whiiite, bob-whiiiite" can be heard in the distance, reverberating through the pine forest. In the 25 years I have worked in the pines, Bobwhite have declined markedly, probably due to increases in predators, including the cats that came with retirement communities. We sneak through the underbrush and eventually see only four of the covey (fig. 11.3).

11.3. Quail skulk along the ground quietly, blending in with the background grasses and leaves.

Anticipation builds as we walk toward the next drift fence. I am really anxious to find a Pine Snake, for I have worked on them for many years, and I never tire of searching for them. Slowly we walk along the fence, checking each funnel and pitfall trap in turn. No one is in the first one, and we move on to the next one. It also is devoid of any snakes, but two Fowler's Toads are hopping around in the bottom of one of the pitfall traps. Both are a greenish gray, with several warts on each of the large black splotches on their moist skin. Since Hognose Snakes specialize on eating Fowler's Toads in the Pine Barrens, the toads are lucky that we came along before a snake did.

Finally we arrive at the last drift fence, and I still am hoping to find a Pine Snake. We search diligently, looking along the bottom of the fence. We find a Hognose Snake here, slowly moving along the fence, searching for an opening that will allow it to continue on its way. Hognoses are rather stocky, dark brown snakes with black blotches. I remember these snakes from my early years in the Albany Pine Bush, and from our trips with my nieces and nephews searching for butterflies. We watch it move up and over one funnel trap. We know that some snakes can avoid our traps, but presumably the proportion that avoid the traps should not vary among the different habitats. Finally, it reaches the large 50-gallon pitfall at the end, and tumbles in, quickly burrowing under the leaves at the bottom. When I pick it up, it writhes and wriggles so much that I accidentally drop it. It immediately gives a few more gasping breaths as if it is dying rapidly, turns over on its back, and ceases to move. It is an old defensive trick, this playing dead, but I enjoy it every time. We also put this snake in a bag for transport back to the laboratory. It is not a bad catch, a Black Racer, a Hognose, two Fowler's Toads, and a Box Turtle, but I am a bit disappointed no Pine Snake was captured. Perhaps on another day. It is quite warm in the pines, and we hurry back to the laboratory to measure and mark the animals; we pride ourselves on their quick release, back where we found them.

Day after day we check the traps, recording the drift fence, funnel trap, and pitfall trap for every creature we capture. One day we are dismayed to find that half of one drift fence has been ripped up, the pitfalls lying upside down on the ground, and the funnel traps gone. We are surprised that vandals came so far back in the pines, away from the road, and we suspect that someone watched us check our traps and later returned to mess up our research. This is one of the hazards of conducting research in the Pinelands. Usually they are deserted, no one is about, and we are safe, but once someone discovers the traps, we are concerned for the safety of the snakes. Although it might just be vandals, it could also be poachers who destroyed our drift fence to hide the fact that they removed the snakes. Sadly, we take down this drift fence and move it to a more secluded site, to prevent further mishap and to protect the snakes from possible poaching.

We are now more careful, and do not stop our car if any other car is on the dirt roads or if we see anyone walking about. Instead, we move on to another site and return later. One day there were several people near the path to our traps, and we quietly left, creeping back through the pines to our car. Jacques is big enough to ward off any unpleasant intruders, but it is best not to tangle with people when we are outnumbered. On another day we had to wait until after dark, and using flashlights once we were far from the road, we checked our traps and removed the snakes. Now, we try to check the traps earlier in the morning, before anyone else is cruising the back roads intent on mischief.

The data mount up, as month after month passes. The autumn is a particularly exciting time because the snakes are on the move, searching for places to spend the winter. Snakes in the New Jersey Pine Barrens normally hibernate from mid-October until mid- to late March, giving us a bit of a break from the sampling. Being cold-blooded, the snakes must seek places below the frost line where their bodies will not freeze once the cold of winter sets in.

October is a fine month in the pines. The daytime temperature is still mild, the oak leaves are just beginning to turn, and the Virginia Creeper is a vibrant red. The mosquitoes are long gone and the weather is delightful. Slowly we move through the pines, checking each drift fence in turn. The lowland sites yield two young Hognose Snakes, a Garter Snake, and two hatchling Black Racers. Not a bad haul, but still no Pine Snake.

As usual, I cannot resist walking beyond our pine lowland sites into the cedar swamp. It is always a world apart, dark, damp, and mysterious. The tall and upright Atlantic White Cedars are so dense that many of the bottom branches have died, leaving only a dense canopy. There is barely enough light to see that the bark is a reddish brown and the leaves are bluish green, small, and compressed against the slender twigs.

I love to stand at the edge and peer in, wondering what lurks beneath the dark waters of the swamp. It is difficult walking beneath the cedars because the roots form hummocks. One minute you walk on the top of moss-covered hummocks, and the next you plummet into a deep pool of cold water, surrounded by a mass of roots and fallen branches. Once I ventured into such a swamp with Bob Zappalorti, and we half-walked and half-crawled slowly through the tangles of High-bush Blueberry, Huckleberry, and Inkberry on tussocks trying to avoid slipping into the deep rusty-brown water. Bob peered under the branches and trunks of each cedar or Black Gum as we passed, and then moved on to the next likely spot. Finally he found what he was looking for: a Timber Rattlesnake coiled and partially hidden in the roots of a cedar. It lolled in a patch of sunlight, with its head resting on its coiled body, just above the water. With their dark brown blotches on a light brown base, these snakes blend in perfectly with the shadows on the fallen leaves of the forest floor. Their shiny black tail and rattle earn them the folklore name of "velvet-tailed rattler." During the cold winter, Timber Rattlesnakes use the moving water, where they hibernate beneath the cedar roots, to prevent freezing. The constantly slow-moving water never freezes, and the rattlesnakes lie partially submerged and immobile, with their heads out of the water to breathe. This is an adaptation used by Timber Rattlesnakes (and Eastern King Snakes) in the Pine Barrens to avoid winter freezing, as the mountain populations of rattlesnakes use rocky fissures or caves for hibernation.

Standing by the edge of the cedar swamp, I can imagine the early European settlers felling the cedars to make ship masts for their vessels and shingles for their houses. I visualize the Lenape Indians a few centuries ago, moving slowly through the cedars searching for just the right log to make a canoe, or gathering sphagnum to use for an antiseptic. Some 12,000 years ago, large Woolly Mammoths moved through, chased by Saber-toothed Cats. We can only speculate what other strange animals lived within the cedar swamps and upland forests back then. I turn around and we move back into the upland to check our other arrays of drift fences. Surely this time I will find a Pine Snake. Pine Snakes are difficult to catch because they are both large enough (often reaching five feet in length) and strong enough to climb out of the pitfall traps, and I have watched a really big Pine Snake slip over a drift fence, taking advantage of a slight crease in the plastic that provided a purchase point.

The leaves of the Blackjack Oak are a reddish brown, contrasting with the rich red of the Virginia Creeper. The needles of the scattered pines are still vibrant green, still able to photosynthesize because the sun is brilliant and the temperatures are well above freezing. A White-breasted Nuthatch flies to the trunk of a tall pine tree and slowly works its way down the trunk, head first. It peers between the cracks of the bark, searching for insects, and finds one every few steps. It spirals slowly downward, and then flies abruptly to the middle of the next tree, to begin searching again. These small black-capped birds live in the pines year-round, and continue to forage even on the coldest days of winter.

Slowly we move along the drift fences, one after the other, searching for snakes. Finally, there is only one funnel trap left. This is my last chance today, and with trepidation, I remove the twigs and brush away the leaves. Curled in the trap is a large Pine Snake with a tiny bulge indicating a recent meal. Maybe it ate before entering the trap, or perhaps it captured a small mouse that fell into the trap. Elated, I reverently remove the reptile and carry it back to the car. It is a lovely, large female with prominent black and white markings. She was no doubt on her way back to a hibernaculum and moved too carelessly through the vegetation and into the trap. Back in the laboratory we measure and weigh her and discover that she is a snake we have previously found several times in the same hibernaculum, close to today's capture site. We release her, hoping to find her next March when we dig up that den as part of a long-term population-monitoring study that Bob and I have been conducting since 1986.

Winter is a time for other pleasures and pastimes; the cold-blooded reptiles are safely underground, most of the birds have migrated south, and the deer have gone deeper into the pines in search of small edible shrubs. I spend my time teaching and writing, and Jack takes the rest of the classes needed for his degree. When the cold winter gives way to the warming days of spring in early March, we embark on another ritual. For years we have been studying Pine Snake hibernacula. It began when Bob built artificial dens as part of a mitigation project to create habitat the snakes lost because of a housing development; the artificial snake dens were built on 100 acres of land donated by the developer as part of a mitigation plan. This March we again find "our" female Pine Snake, buried deep under the ground, more than a yard below the frozen surface with a dozen other Pine Snakes, some Black Racers, and one Corn Snake. She is heavier than when we found her in October, indicating that she must have eaten once or twice before retiring for the winter.

Before the snakes leave their hibernacula in early April, we already have the drift fences in place and are well prepared for another year of sampling. It is essential to collect data for at least two snake activity seasons to allow for any anomalies of a particular year. Finally, however, the second field season ends and we can examine our data. The fieldwork is thrilling and exhilarating because anything can turn up in our traps, but examining the data at the end of a study is also exciting because finally we can answer the question we posed so long ago: What is the diversity and abundance of the reptiles in the two Pinelands habitats?

Over two years, we captured 315 snakes in our drift fences; most were from funnel traps, and only 36 were recaptures (snakes captured more than once). Half of the snakes we caught were Black Racer and Hognose. Although we had expected the Racers to be common, we did not expect to find so many Hognose Snakes. The snakes we found, in order of abundance, were Hognose, Black Racer, Garter, Red-bellied, Pine, and Eastern Worm. Both Red-bellied and Eastern Worm Snakes are secretive and not usually found by merely searching the barrens. We caught more snakes in the lowlands than in the upland pines, but the same species occurred in both habitats. However, some species were more common in the uplands (Corn Snakes, Pine Snakes, Garter Snakes), while others were more common in the lowland pines (Black Racers, Hognose Snakes, Worm Snakes).

Using a formula called the Lincoln-Peterson Index that compares the number of recaptures to the total number of snakes we marked, we estimate that the local population of Hognose Snakes was over 1,000 individuals, the population of Black Racers was over 200, and the population of Pine Snakes was only about 40. We never did catch enough Corn Snakes to estimate their population size. Although all three species are predators, these relationships fit their trophic levels because Hognose Snakes eat mostly frogs and toads, while Pine Snakes—at the top of the food chain—eat Red Squirrels, rabbits, rats, and mice.

Although we were trying to catch snakes, we caught many other animals in our traps, including 11 species of amphibians, 3 of lizards, 2 of turtles, and 15 of mammals. We were pleased with the results because we could also use these data to examine the prey base for our predatory snakes. For the amphibian-eating snakes, we caught over 1,100 Fowler's Toads and 229 Green Frogs. Fowler's Toads were most often caught in

11.4. Fowler's Toads display in the early evening. The males trill together, forming a vibrant chorus.

July and August, during their foraging season when they were away from their breeding ponds. In April and early May, Fowler's Toads gather near any small wet pool or pond, or even a small mud puddle, each male displaying in hopes of attracting a female (fig. 11.4) These data indicate that prey would be readily available for amphibian-eating snakes in most spring and summer months, but more difficult to find in the fall.

For the snakes that eat small mammals, we caught 721 Masked Shrews, 104 Red-backed Voles, and lesser numbers of other shrews and mice. The Masked Shrews seemed particularly uninteresting to look at, but they provide a good meal for small snakes (fig. 11.5). We even caught one Opossum, one Striped Skunk, one Long-tailed Weasel, and two Southern Flying Squirrels. We frequently saw Fence Lizards as we went about our sampling, but we caught only 26, suggesting that they are either good at avoiding being caught or are adept at escaping.

One of the most interesting aspects of our work was the difference in habitat use during the year. In the spring and fall there were more snakes in the uplands, while in the summer more snakes were in the lowland pines. This may reflect their hibernating and thermoregulatory behavior. In the spring they are just moving out of their hibernation sites into the uplands, but during the heat of summer they are mostly foraging and finding places to drink and stay cool in the lowlands. During the fall, snakes again move into the uplands, searching for prey and overwintering sites.

11.5. Masked or Common Shrews were one of the most commonly caught prey items in our drift fences.

We were intrigued that activity patterns varied during the year, as indicated by the number of snakes caught, assuming that we caught more snakes when more were moving about. Black Racers were most active in May and June, Hognose Snakes were most active in July and September, and Garter Snakes were most active in August and September. The activity period of Hognose Snakes in July may reflect their search for Fowler's Toads, their principle prey in the Pine Barrens, as well as gravid females moving away from their nest sites.

Our findings suggest that snakes in the Pine Barrens use a mosaic of available forest habitats that include both upland and lowland pines. Although all species were found in both habitats, some preferred the uplands and others preferred the lowlands. All snake species moved back and forth with the seasons. Of the snakes we caught more than once, a few were captured at least once in the uplands and once in the lowlands. Most surprising was the high population density of Hognose Snakes, and the relatively low number of Pine Snakes and Corn Snakes, indicating why they are listed as threatened and endangered. Low capture rates may also suggest that some species learn to avoid traps, while others used different habitat types away from the drift fences.

We believe that competition between the two most abundant snakes, Black Racers and Hognose Snakes, was reduced by separation in habitat use, months of peak activity, and prey selection. Racers were most active in the late spring and summer in the lowlands, while Hognose Snakes were most active in the late summer and fall in upland habitats. As with most research, our findings left us with more new questions: Why did we catch so few Pine Snakes? Why did we catch more hatchling Black Racers compared to the other species? Is the density of Hognose Snakes consistent year to year, or is it cyclic? These questions can only be answered with more intensive comparative studies—a good project for my future students.

While Bob and I continue our studies of snakes in the Pinelands, Jacques has gone on to study the more diverse communities of snakes in the southwestern United States, but the Hognose and Pine Snakes of the New Jersey Barrens will always hold a special place in his heart. As with all my graduate students, I miss him, but I know he is still searching for other snakes, in other habitats. Now, every time I see a snake slither for cover in the pines, I long to set up longer and taller drift fences with better funnel traps to continue figuring out how the snake communities in the Pine Barrens use their habitat without too much competition. How do large predatory snakes at the top trophic level influence the abundance and distribution of their prey? Do changes in prey abundance affect habitat selection in the large snakes? The Pinelands holds the answers to these questions, and we snake ecologists just have to figure it all out.

12

Where the Barrens
Meet the Sea

Overhead, sunlight is just beginning to tinge the clouds, and a Fish Crow announces dawn with a loud nasal squawk. In the deep shadows from the early morning light, we watch a Green Heron peer into the still waters. He clings precariously to an overhanging oak branch, blending in with the massive tangles of limbs and leaves. He watches a leaf swirl gently in a small eddy and suddenly lunges, spearing a tiny darter. He pulls himself erect and swallows the fish with one gulp. Then he is still again, watching, waiting. The waters are brown and rusty, making it challenging for him to track and capture the tiny fish that make their home near the sandy banks.

In a small pool at the edge of the stream, the water is still and calm. Water Striders, Backswimmers, Water Boatmen, and other beetles move over the water surface. We watch a solitary Whirligig Beetle twirl erratically in circles, creating endless swirls in the stream water. Suddenly he darts forward, skimming across the stream.

As Mike and I drift down a narrow stream on a late spring morning, the pines abruptly give way to a few scattered Atlantic White Cedars, and finally to such a dense stand that the branches overhead have closed above us. The sky has passed from view, the temperature drops 10 degrees, and it is much darker. No clear bank is visible, and not far away, where the water is still, the Sphagnum Moss forms a dense carpet, broken only by low shrubs, Golden Club, Skunk Cabbage, and Pitcher Plants. A few delicate cranberry vines creep over the surface, giving a hint of the vast cranberry bogs created not far away. The shiny green cranberry leaves contrast sharply with the yellow-green carpet of Sphagnum. The gentle flow that carried us this far has ceased, and the canoe stops.

Above our heads, a male Redstart sings softly and then disappears in the cedars. A small flock of insect-eating birds, mostly White-eyed Vireos, Parula and Yellow Warblers, and one Yellowthroat, eyes us, but deciding we are harmless, they continue on. A vireo remains to diligently search a spider web for insects. We are reluctant to move, caught as we are in one of the rare pristine bogs of the barrens. The cedars here are tall and lush, giving no indication of past logging or other human intrusions. The Sphagnum has not been mined, the rare plants are still intact, and the tiny sundews on the bank await unsuspecting insects, as they have for centuries. These insect-eating plants are obtaining necessary nutrients, such as nitrogen, from the insects they capture. We feel closed in, protected, enveloped in a mystical cool world far removed from the bustle of our everyday lives. There is time to reflect and wonder what this bog has seen over the 12,000 years since the ice retreated. What is buried beneath the tea-colored waters? Only the frequent trips of a Parula Warbler gathering nest material is enough to motivate us to put an end to our fleeting presence in their paradise.

We paddle slowly on but soon become "bogged" down amid a tangle of fallen branches, moss, vines, and shallow water. Several hummocks of mud, muck, and cedar stumps impede our progress, and we begin to wonder if we should go back the way we came. We briefly consider trying to stumble through, pulling the canoe behind us, but give up that idea when we see a three-foot Timber Rattlesnake basking on a moss-covered stump. It is incredibly beautiful, and a very rare treat, enough to make us stop and watch him for several minutes. He seems to have caught the only ray of sunlight filtering down through the cedars. He is not the problem, of course, for I know where he is, but I wonder where the other rattlers are?

The bog seems to stretch on forever, or else we are going in circles, paddling by the same hummocks and fallen cedars. We cannot tell in what direction we are going by looking for the sun—it is well hidden behind clouds. We wonder vaguely how wise it was to come here. In my mind, the rattlesnake grows larger and more menacing. Visions of 10-foot-long serpents keep us moving, although we know full well this is impossible for a rattler. We still worry. The damp cool cedars seem to hold their own secrets, and we push on, paddling steadily, not wanting to give in to the fears implied by rapid paddling. The water is absolutely calm, there is no more stream. The cedars now seem to grasp and clutch, rather than to hold and caress. The branches brush the water, the shrubs are more tangled, the hummocks larger and more ominous. The dark crannies are deeper and more foreboding.

Our canoe bumps against a hummock, lodging under some weathered cedar logs above the brown waters. Pushing backwards with a paddle, we bump against cedars. A tinge of fear arises in me as we realize we cannot easily walk out—the waters are too deep, the hummocks make walking nearly impossible, and rattlesnakes lurk among the roots. If we try walking out, our sneakers will surely get stuck, and the going will be rough. Eventually we free the canoe, but there are several paths, and we are not sure where we came from or where we should be going. Breathing deeply, we pause to take in the calmness around us. A Yellowthroat sings a few yards away and flies to a nearby mossy mound to see what we are up to, remaining long enough for us to admire his lovely plumage. He stops to catch an insect, and then is gone.

Watching the Yellowthroat has proved calming and exhilarating, and we can once again see the subtle differences in the network of waterways. The small broken twigs indicate the way we came, canoe marks on the mud banks show us where we hit them, and tiny currents seem to be flowing into another winding pathway. The cedars are still as dense and dark, the mossy hummocks as foreboding, but the path ahead has opened, and we paddle on. Finally, a little light filters through the canopy of cedars, and we see the gnarled trunks of some twisted pines up ahead. There are fewer hummocks, the Sphagnum is sparser, and there are no more Golden Clubs. Suddenly we leave the bog behind, the temperature rises, and the pines open up to reveal a wonderful blue sky with soft billowy clouds. There are shadows, and the mystery of the bog is replaced by the vastness of the Pinelands. The stream widens and deepens, and the waters flow once again. We are able to put down our paddles and drift slowly along, watching the banks and overhanging boughs; we are back in the uplands with scattered pines and oaks. Few creatures are about. We vainly search the underbrush for snakes and lizards, and see a Fence Lizard basking in the sun, but otherwise the barrens are quiet.

Not far away, our stream flows into the Mullica River, one of the few river basins that is entirely within the Pine Barrens. The upper headwaters of the Mullica contain many White Cedar, Sphagnum, and cranberry bogs. As the river runs toward the Atlantic, it is joined by many other streams. These feeder streams have low populations of Sphagnum Sunfish, Banded Sunfish, Chub Sucker, and Northern Yellow Bullhead. The river flows through many old piney towns, with names like Batsto, Pleasant Mills, and Crowleytown. It gathers speed as it goes, widening into small freshwater marshes and finally passing through vast salt marshes on its way to Great Bay and the Atlantic Ocean beyond. In the quiet eddies along the edge, cattails grow, and we listen to the weak dry rattle of the Long-billed Marsh Wren (now called simply the Marsh Wren, fig. 12.1). The Mullica River carries with it the effluent of the pines, tea-colored acid waters, and leaves and twigs.

12.1. Marsh Wrens nest mainly in cattail marshes and in the saltmarshes along the Atlantic Coast.

The New Jersey Pinelands is a product of the oceans, of the vast inland seas that once flooded most of New Jersey, of the retreating glaciers that moved sand dunes and gravel around, and of the forces of coastal storms since that retreat. The Pinelands is also part of the great estuaries that separate it from the seas, being influenced both by storms and tidal waters. In turn, the Pinelands affects the estuaries because streams carry silt, sand, minerals, nutrients, and contaminants.

For most of the time since the European settlement days of the 1600s, rivers were byways for travel, for floating logs, and for carrying agricultural crops to coastal towns. Some, like the Mullica River, separated one kind of agricultural venture from another. North of the river, people grew cranberries and blueberries, and to the south they farmed grapes, strawberries, sweet potatoes and peaches. Now, mostly cranberries and blueberries remain commercially viable.

The paleo-Indians whose identity we do not even know, as well as the more recent Lenape and European settlers, recognized the interplay between the pines and the coast. In the early spring they moved to the estuaries to fish, crab, and clam. When the insects became unbearable, they moved back into the pines, carrying with them fish to dry for later use, at least according to their garbage middens. In the fall they again fished the estuaries before moving inland when the cold winds and snow moved across the bays.

These migrations resulted from the need to obtain food from both the pines and the coasts, and they acknowledged the interconnections between the habitats. It took ecologists longer to study whole watersheds, from the uplands to the coastal bays and estuaries, although even today, many people still study one or the other, without considering them as a whole. On a geological scale, the seas made the Pinelands, shaped them, and provided them with their soils. On the timescale of our lives, it is the Pine Barrens that influences the estuaries by nourishing them with waters from a vast watershed.

We are tracing the path that a Lenape Indian might have taken on his trip to the shore to hunt for ducks or to trap fish. Our canoe is more modern, to be sure, but the images were much the same. Today there are few people who travel the back streams in the Pine Barrens, or wind their way through the narrow channels of the low salt marshes. Luckily, the canoe is light enough for Mike and me to load onto my car for the trip to Great Bay at the mouth of the Mullica. We feel justified in going overland because the paleo-Indians, the Lenape, and the early settlers no doubt did likewise, at least sometimes. We wonder whether the dirt road we drive down to reach the marshes was here centuries ago, or whether it is recent. Most of the early "roads" in colonial times followed the Indian trails.

Reaching the Salt Marshes

Reaching the end of the road, we unload the canoe and shove it into the calm waters. We set off, heading for the barrier island across the bay. We pause to photograph the turtle crossing sign; far too many get hit by thoughtless people driving too fast (fig. 12.2). The salt marsh around us is an endless expanse of swaying grasses, blending into the sea beyond. Light billowy clouds cover the sun, muting the glare. Like a Monet pallette in shades of green, the swirls of color shift with the late morning light. From the narrow salt marsh creek, a steep mud bank leads up to an island covered by Salt Hay that rises well above our heads. At the bend of the creek, three Sanderlings feed on a wider mudflat, lazily pecking at the mud, hunting for tiny crustaceans, avoiding the small snails exposed by the low tide.

Farther along, a Snowy Egret walks daintily through the shallows, searching for fish. Slowly it lifts one yellow foot, stirs the water rapidly, and peers in. It takes three or four steps, jabs, misses, and continues staring into the water. Stirring the water scares fish into moving from the bottom or out of the vegetation, making them more visible. Finally this foot stirring works, and the egret seizes a tiny fish. With one gulp the fish disappears, and the bird slowly begins the process anew. Another egret lands briefly but quickly flies off to try another place.

Snowy Egrets are declining in Barnegat Bay, as are many of the other egrets and herons. Even the number of Cattle Egrets is declining (fig. 12.3). Interlopers that arrived from Africa, Cattle Egrets have increased so much in some southern states that they are considered a nuisance, and people are trying to reduce their numbers. Since Cattle Egrets eat mainly insects, they are

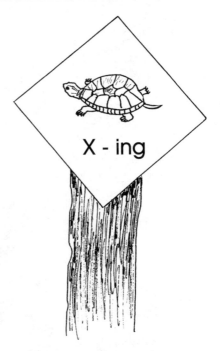

12.2. *Turtle crossing signs prevent some of the slaughter as Diamondback Terrapin cross the roads searching for suitable nest sites.*

not the cause of the decline of the other egrets and herons. Several years of low numbers of small prey fish, coupled with increases of Red Foxes on some of their nesting islands, has resulted in little reproduction. The egrets in the bay nest on low bushes and shrubs that grow on the high parts of salt marsh islands. Normally there are no predators on these islands, but the bay froze during a couple of harsh winters, and foxes wandered over from the mainland. Since Herring Gulls were already on their territory in March, the foxes had plenty of food and remained to dine on egrets and their eggs. Without any tall bushes, all the egrets were nesting at a height accessible to a fox. Eventually the egrets abandoned their colony, but there are few other places in the bay with suitable vegetation for nesting.

Egrets and herons have pollution to cope with, as well as starvation and predators. Mercury levels in the eggs of Snowy Egrets, Forster's Terns, and some other species nesting in Barnegat Bay are well above the levels known to cause reproductive problems for birds. Females can get rid of

12.3. *Cattle Egrets breed in Poison Ivy and other small shrubs on the islands in Barnegat Bay. They are an invasive species that first nested in the United States in the late 1940s.*

some of their mercury burdens by depositing them in the eggs, leaving the developing young with high mercury burdens. Birds can also deposit mercury and other contaminants in their feathers while they are growing, just as we deposit them in our hair. Recently, scientists dug up Emperor Napoleon to determine if he had died from arsenic poisoning. Napoleon was easy to decipher because in those days it was stylish for men to have long hair. The hair closest to his head had the highest levels of arsenic, indicating that someone was feeding him higher and higher amounts of arsenic by the week.

Mercury levels in the feathers of adult Snowy Egrets are also high, indicating that the adults may be suffering subtle behavioral effects. Mercury can cause a lower hatching rate of eggs, embryo malformations, decreased growth of chicks, and lower survival of the chicks. In adults, mercury poisoning can cause reproductive impairment, infertility, and abnormal parental behavior. These effects can be subtle because there are not masses of dead birds lying about, but the subtle effects can lower reproductive success over a number of years, eventually resulting in population declines.

With time, it is becoming clear that mercury may be more of a problem in our aquatic environments than we once thought. Some species of marine fish, particularly top predators like Bluefish, tuna, Swordfish, and sharks, have relatively high levels of mercury. This is because mercury levels accumulate with each step in the food chain, and individuals (and species) that live longer have more time to accumulate mercury. Many states, including New Jersey, have consumption advisories for eating fish from freshwater lakes and rivers, and many of these water bodies are in pine barrens habitats. For example, New Jersey, New York, and South Carolina have advisories for rivers that pass through pinelands, and there are advisories for the Everglades just beyond the pines in Florida.

Many scientists and public health officials have conducted assessments to figure out what the risks are from eating fish, and to whom. There are enormous health benefits from eating fish in terms of reducing cholesterol and associated heart problems. But in some cases, pregnant women and children are advised against eating any of some kinds of the fish because of high levels of contaminants. The mercury problem for humans is primarily for the unborn baby, a time when the nervous system is developing and cognitive functioning can be disrupted. An advisory to reduce fish consumption from rivers and streams is not the end of the world for most people, but it surely is for egrets and herons that eat only fish.

Terrapins: Truly an Estuarine Turtle

Ahead of our canoe, a Diamondback Terrapin lifts his head an inch above the water, looks around for a few seconds, and disappears. Diamondback Terrapin range from Massachusetts to Florida and Texas, and were once so common that they were used extensively for food. Many states passed laws about how many days lobster and Diamondback Terrapin could be fed to slaves. In most places the terrapins declined due to this overexploitation, loss of nesting habitat, and, much later, to increases in boating accidents. Around the turn of the century they were a real delicacy in the fine restaurants of New York, Philadelphia, and Boston, leading to extermination of some populations. To keep the market alive, people tried to farm them without regard to the identity of local subspecies. Terrapins adapted over the eons to live in South Carolina were brought to New York to be farmed, those from the Gulf States were brought to Georgia, and so on. When the market collapsed, the terrapin were released where they were, regardless of their original home. This disregard for natural origins is bothersome to conservation biologists because the gene pools are mixed up, and terrapins are no longer adapted to their specific geographical home. "Will the real New Jersey terrapin please stand up?" How can we protect something that may not be optimally adapted to the Jersey shore?

Diamondback Terrapin are truly an estuarine turtle, always remaining relatively close to land, and never traveling far up into the freshwater creeks or rivers. It is mid-June, just when the females come to the nesting beaches to lay their eggs. Not far away on Little Beach Island, where I studied them for two years, the females are beginning to nest (fig. 12.4). Females swim in with the advancing tides, clamber over the low sandbars, and swim in to shore. They come up to nest during high tide because the tidal waters carry them far up onto the beach, and they have to walk only a short distance to find a suitable nesting site. Also, they can gauge how high to place their nest so their eggs will not be flooded out by succeeding high tides. Most females come up during the very highest tides of the month, insuring that they are well above the highest tides. Females slowly climb out and walk up onto the dunes, searching for just the right nest site. Some females can become 13 or 14 inches long, but most are less than 10 inches, while the males are usually half as large. On the dark upper shell, each scale has a series of concentric rings that gives some indication of age, although it is not perfect. When I studied

12.4. *Diamondback Terrapin digging a hole to lay her 8 to 12 eggs in early July.*

them, I crept over the dunes, searching for females; I stayed well away from them because any vibrations or movement disturbs them, sending them scurrying back to the water.

A nesting female trundles deliberately along the sands, searching for a nest site, testing the consistency with her tongue and then her hind feet. Slowly she scoops out a bit of sand with her front foot, and, deciding conditions are not quite right, she lumbers on. In the next half hour she makes three or four starts, but abandons each one. Finally, she selects a site a yard away from a Seaside Goldenrod, and using her hind feet alternatively, she scoops out a hole that is about eight inches deep. Although she took nearly an hour to dig the nest, she takes only a few minutes to lay the nine eggs and urinate on them to provide moisture. Covering takes even less time. She carefully moves back and forth over the nest, obliterating any signs, making sure it will not be visible to Fish Crows or gulls soaring overhead. I developed quite a search image for the slight signs of a covered nest, and I could find up to 30 in a day.

"There is no way a nest is here," Mike said years ago when I was studying them on Little Beach Island.

"Take my word for it, there is," I said. Slowly I dug down, carefully scooping out the sand with my fingers.

"I can't believe there is a nest there. How on earth do you do it," he asked.

"I've developed a good search image, just like a predator would do. I'm much better at finding them than the local foxes," I replied proudly.

My fingertips brushed against a leathery surface, and I dug more carefully, pulling the sand gently away from the egg mass. Delicately I lifted two eggs for Mike to see. A bit of sand still clung to some, and they were not yet glued together by the liquid the female deposited.

"Why do they cling together?" Mike asked.

"So the eggs don't shift during development. Unlike bird eggs, shifting disrupts delicate development. Then too, the eggs don't shift with the sand."

The eggs hatch in 60 to 70 days, assuming the nest is not dug up by a Raccoon or fox, and the young will dig their way out during the day. The young actually swim toward the surface through the sand, and once they reach the surface, they remain with only the top of their head above the sand, looking to see if the coast is clear. Predators can be a major problem, and when I studied the terrapins years ago on Little Beach, I found that Raccoons and foxes dug up over 60 percent of the nests. Laughing Gulls also harassed the nesting females, hoping to scare them while they laid their eggs. Then the gulls would swoop down and eat the clutch. The gulls also eat any hatchlings they can find, and to avoid being eaten by gulls cruising above the dunes, the young terrapins hide under nearby goldenrod or beachgrass during the daylight and crawl to the bay under cover of darkness. Once in the water, the young terrapins remain close inshore in Eelgrass, Widgeon Grass, and other vegetation of the shallow water for the next few months, eating, and gaining their strength. It is hard to find these baby terrapins; their very life depends on staying hidden to avoid predators.

Having finished covering her nest, the female hurries down the sand dune into the nearest water. Within a few seconds of reaching the water she disappears, not to return for another year. As she is leaving, other females are just arriving. The nesting pattern is repeated over and over, by many different females, and I estimated that nearly 2,000 females nested on the dunes at Little Beach each year.

The head peering at us from this salt marsh creek may well be a female on her way to Little Beach, for it is the most suitable nesting beach in Barnegat Bay and Great Bay. There are very few predators on the island, and no people are allowed. The sand dunes extend well above high tide, and frequent tides keep the vegetation low and sparse, just the right habitat for turtle nesting.

Out of the corner of my eye I catch movement and see the hind end of a Clapper Rail slipping through the Salt Hay. Clapper Rails are another bird species that has decreased in the marshes of the bay, although the causes of the decline are unclear. The habitat is still suitable, the Fiddler Crabs they feed on are still abundant, and they have no new predators. Because their nests are hidden in the grass, they are seldom found by predators. They even build a dome of grasses over the top, further obscuring it from predators flying overhead. Their loud, harsh "kak kak kak kak kak" calls that used to echo mysteriously across the marsh are seldom heard anymore. In the 1970s we could find 40 rails at low tide in the tidal ditches; now few are seen at any tide. I suspect that their decline is partly due to sea level rise—only a very slight change in elevation raises the water level enough to flood our their nests and make many salt marsh islands no longer suitable for nesting.

For most of the early afternoon, we paddle slowly down narrow, winding creeks through marshes without encountering many birds. The marshes adjacent to the mainland are not havens for nesting birds because they are too accessible to ground predators like Raccoons and foxes that can slip into colonies under the cover of darkness. Instead, most nesting birds prefer the solitude and protection of more distant salt marsh islands where water isolates them from mammalian predators, and the mosquitoes, Green-headed Flies, and mud serves to keep most people away. Great Horned Owls nesting on mainland woods, however, will fly several miles to dine on nesting terns and gulls.

Entering Great Bay

Emerging from the mosaic of salt marshes and creeks, we face Great Bay and wonder fleetingly whether it is wise to take the canoe across the open water. This vast open water that protects our beloved colonial-nesting birds from mammalian predators can be dangerous for us if storms come up. The glasslike bay has hardly a ripple, the wind is not even rustling the grass, and the billowy clouds overhead are hardly moving. We should be fine for just an hour or two, and we paddle toward a nearby island where Laughing Gulls nest. We pass a lone man in a small, square-ended boat, slowly pulling in a long rake, scooping up clams in the traditional way. He dumps his haul on the flat bow of the boat and returns to pulling the rake. Barnegat Bay is important to fishermen as well as to birds, fish, and other animals. Fishermen in Barnegat Bay provide New Jersey with 25 percent of its commercial catch of Hard Clams, Blue Crabs, White Perch, and eels, valued at over $3 million annually. It is also important for recreational fishermen and duck hunters, and the sneakbox, a special boat designed for duck hunting, was invented by Barnegat Bay boatmen over a hundred years ago. Keeping the bay healthy is important to all of us, and people with many different perspectives have banded together in "Save Barnegat Bay" associations to preserve the natural and cultural traditions of the bay.

Finally, we face the open water and start out across the bay toward the nesting islands. The water remains calm, and it is easy to paddle. We stop a couple of times just to sit back, rest our arms, and watch the clouds drift overhead. A line of pelicans drifts over the water, and later a small flock of terns hovers overhead, watching the water below for small fish. Still it is hard work, and I feel the strain in my arms. There are no other boats around—it is not a weekend and most people are working. I love the open bay when it is deserted—I like thinking about the vast corridor of humanity that stretches from Boston to Washington, and of this relatively pristine ribbon of coastal marshes and bays along the coast. It is a part of New Jersey that is often devoid of people. I feel that it is somehow mine because I know its secrets, know its fish, turtles, and birds. I know it all, love it all, and know it continues to give up secrets each year. Unlike the weekend warriors that rage over these waters in fast-moving jet skis, I know that each island is slightly different with its own character.

Nesting birds are very selective: not just any salt marsh island will do. Many years ago Fred Lesser and I studied nest site selection in terns, skimmers, gulls, and herons and egrets on these islands. Small changes in elevation result in different habitats, and the birds use these differences to select their nest sites (fig. 12.5). For over 30 years Fred and I have skimmed over Barnegat Bay checking all the salt marsh islands for nesting terns, skimmers, and gulls. Fred loves to band birds—all birds—and

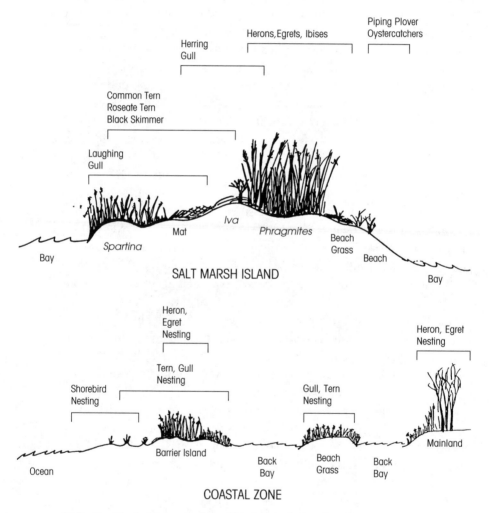

12.5. Nesting habitat selection of birds in salt marshes depends upon only slight differences in elevation.

for him banding is a project in itself. Even now, years later, he still cannot stop searching for chicks hidden in the marsh grass. When I first met Fred he was nimble, quick, and always ready to head out across the bay in a thick fog, as well as in sunny weather. He is absolutely fearless, a wonderful boatman and navigator, and I trust him with my life in the worst storms that can roll across Barnegat Bay. Over the years we have had some really bad northeasters, ones that forced us to land on deserted salt marsh islands or to take refuge in some of the old hunting shacks, long since burned by partying teenagers.

Fred and I discovered that although the islands looked similar to us, they actually differed slightly in aspect, size, elevation, and percentage of the island covered by Salt Hay. We found that most ground-nesting birds choose an island that is just high enough to avoid the spring high tides, but low enough so that predators cannot overwinter comfortably. If an island is high, then rats can live there all year-round, feeding on eggs and birds during the nesting season. Lower islands are free from these mammalian predators because they are overwashed by high tides in the winter. But if the island is too low, it floods during the breeding season, and eggs and chicks wash away. Birds can assess the relative height of an island by the vegetation: islands that are high enough to have cherry trees, Bayberry, or Poison Ivy bushes are usually high enough to avoid the high flood tides of winter. Islands without any vegetation strewn there by the high tides of winter are probably too low for nesting because they will be washed over by summer high tides. It may seem like all the islands are the same to us, but they are not the same for the Common Terns.

The importance of understanding the subtle habitat requirements of birds, and of fish in the bay as well, led the Trust for Public Land and several scientists from Rutgers to examine overall habitat in the bay, trying to figure out which islands are critical for the ecosystem to function well. Ken Able examined the fish populations, while I studied which habitats the birds needed for nesting and foraging. These data were then used by Rick Lathrop to map critical habitats in the bay. Ken heads the Rutgers Marine Laboratory at Tuckerton and has spent many years on the water. Affable, with bright red hair and a ready smile, he is always willing to try something new, be it a new beer or a new way of doing science. Since Rick is often chained to his computer laboratory where he does most of his work, he enjoys getting out and tromping around the marsh with us. He is taller than Ken and I, and so can jump the creeks that we cannot. It is fun to work together, bridging our three very different disciplines, and synthesizing our data to better understand how the bay works.

To most people, all salt marsh islands look the same, but to the birds and fish the habitats on and around the islands are very different, and even slight differences in the size and shape of the islands and the surrounding shallow water make some islands preferred habitat for both fish and birds. Forster's Terns, one of the least common nesting birds on the bay, seem to require undisturbed salt marshes that have not been ditched for mosquito control—making it very important to preserve the remaining pristine marshes. Black Skimmers, on the other hand, can forage in small creeks, but they also prefer creeks that are not disturbed by personal watercraft.

In the last 100 years Barnegat Bay has lost about 32 percent of its salt marshes, due mainly to dredging and filling. Many marshes adjacent to the mainland were filled to provide dry land for houses. People have also created some additional marshes while stabilizing Barnegat Inlet. In the last ten years, however, I have watched many salt marsh islands in Barnegat Bay become less suitable for nesting birds because of increased tidal flow caused by dredging of the channels and very gradual sea level rise. Birds must respond to these changes; as already noted, only slight changes in elevation make islands less suitable for nesting. Many of the islands around Barnegat Inlet that were used for nesting are now deserted because they are washed over by summer high tides, just when eggs are hatching.

The birds not only have to face habitat loss, but the noise and disruption of boats coming too close to their islands. While people seldom walk on the salt marsh islands because they are low, wet, and full of mosquitoes, people operating jet skis (or personal watercraft, to be more specific) often run so close to islands that nesting birds are forced from their nests. Old-fashioned boats cannot come close to salt marsh islands, and the nesting birds have adapted to their presence, but the loud roar of a personal watercraft bearing down on their island is too much for most nesting birds. Only education and laws can ensure that a suitable buffer is maintained around nesting salt marsh islands.

Finally the open water is behind us, and we drift toward a small isolated island. About 20 pairs of Common Terns sit quietly, each incubating a clutch of two or three eggs in nests placed on a long, flattened mat of bleached Eelgrass and Salt Hay on the edge of the island. Most of the nests are near the edge of the mat, close to the upright grasses that provide some protection from the sun and heavy rain. The terns are nestled down in the vegetation, and their silvery backs gleam in the afternoon sunlight; they have a black crown on their head, but otherwise they appear grayish white.

12.6. Laughing Gulls build nests of vegetation so that they do not float away during the high tides, when water surrounds the nest.

Without any resistance the canoe glides quickly along the edge of the island, and suddenly a swirling mass of Laughing Gulls plays over our heads. Their long calls and "gakkering" can be heard across the smooth water. In early June they are mostly incubating, having established their territories a few weeks earlier (fig. 12.6). They sit atop the massive piles of dead Eelgrass and Salt Hay that they call nests. They are magnificent gulls with jet black heads, dark gray backs, and immaculate white bodies. Their dark brown eyes are set off by narrow white patches that ring the eye, and their vibrant red bill is only just beginning to fade. They look quite similar to Franklin's Gulls, the species I studied in the freshwater marshes of Minnesota over 30 years ago. Since then, along with my graduate students, I have studied many aspects of the behavior and ecology of Laughing Gulls.

Each nest is only a yard or two from its neighbor, as if the inhabitants wanted to be close together, while many parts of the island are deserted. The Salt Hay has been trampled down between the nests, indicating past territorial clashes among neighbors. Each nest has a large ramp of dead brown vegetation that serves as a landing platform for a returning mate.

Later in the season this ramp gives the chicks more space to wander about without having to leave the safety of the nest.

The chicks have the best of both worlds. They can sit on the nest in the cool morning taking in the sun, then benefit from the cool breezes, and finally, in the midday heat they can creep down to the edge of the nest and sit in the shade of the grass. The chicks are brownish gray balls of fluff with dark splotches, making them blend with both the nest and the shadows in the grass. Although they can walk around easily within hours of hatching, they are completely dependent on their parents for food and protection for more than a month. While one parent sallies forth to find fish, Horseshoe Crab eggs, and insects to feed the chicks, the other one guards them from aerial predators such as Herring Gulls and hawks. The parents take turns feeding the hungry chicks whose demands for food grow greater every day. In only five weeks the chicks reach adult size, but still they beg for more and more food.

Suddenly the babbling noises of the colony cease, and the whole mass of gulls rises in unison, swooping out over the water in complete silence. While the gulls fly out, a swirling mass of Common Terns rises high in the air, circling around a dark object overhead. As we watch, a Peregrine Falcon makes a dive at a Common Tern that comes too close, flies under the tern, suddenly whips upside down without checking its flight, and grabs it from below. One of the defenses of Common Terns is to dive and attack aerial predators, but there is a cost of coming too close. Most predators are not agile enough to catch a tern in midair, but Peregrines certainly are. The Peregrine keeps going, disappearing across a far marsh, heading toward its nest tower, and the birds soon settle down. No one seems to mourn the passing of the tern, and the long calls and gakkering of gulls resume.

Peregrine Falcons were once extirpated from eastern North America, mostly as a result of pesticides. DDT and other contaminants led to low hatching success, and in some years, almost no young were raised. Eventually the populations crashed, and the birds disappeared entirely as breeders in eastern North America. In the 1960s, Tom Cade and his colleagues at Cornell University started a captive breeding program. They produced a stock of birds for reintroduction and have slowly been building populations back up along the East Coast. Young Peregrines were introduced to the wild in towers where they were fed in such a way that they could not see who fed them. This method is called "hacking," and one important aspect is that the birds spend many weeks looking out over the marsh before they are able to fly, allowing them to imprint on the habitat. Another important aspect is that they never see the people feeding them, and so do not imprint on them.

The first Peregrine young were hacked in New Jersey in salt marshes in Barnegat Bay. Several times a day people crept out to feed them, walking far around the marsh so the young could not see their suppliers. Finally the day came when the young flew away, but they did not go far, and for weeks they remained near the hacking tower, sometimes seeking food, sometimes using it for a night roost. Hacking was a success, and now several pairs breed in coastal New Jersey on towers provided for their use. Although historically they never did nest in salt marshes and were seen there only during migration, they have adapted well, and now it is easy to see a Peregrine stooping majestically after terns or Sanderlings along the shore.

The light breezes of early evening blow across the bay, warning us that it is time to go home, and we slowly paddle across the water. It has been a long day, and I am tired of paddling. The water is still smooth, and we have been lucky with the wind and the weather. There is an urgency now, not just in our realization that we must get to shore before it is too dark, but in the hurried flight of small flocks of terns and gulls heading back to their nesting colonies. Many have mates waiting at the nests, anxious to go off in search of a meal of their own. Incubation shifts often occur in the early evening. The birds hurrying back will no doubt spend the night incubating, to be relieved at dawn. We need to get there before the darkness makes it impossible to identify the creek that will lead us to our car—in the darkness we could make a wrong turn.

We reach the mouth of the creek in time to see a pair of Black Skimmers moving across the water. They are called skimmers because they fly just above the water with their knifelike lower bill slicing the surface, hoping to catch a fish. Skimmers are mostly nocturnal and start to fish in earnest at dusk. Slowly they skim across the water until the creek becomes very narrow, then they turn, and come back, skimming along the opposite bank. They will continue feeding after dark, for their eyes are especially adapted for nighttime vision and their feeding method is tactile. They are one of our favorite birds. Mike and I started to study them together long before we married, and *The Social Behavior of the Black Skimmer* was the first book we wrote together.

New Jersey is remarkable. Not only do we have the most densely populated state with heavy industrialization, but we have some of the most diverse and stable populations of colonially nesting birds along the Atlantic coast. The populations are holding their own, and because there

12.7. Rose Mallow grows along the edges of the small rivers and streams, producing lush pink flower in August. Once in a while one is white, but mainly they are a delicate pink.

are so many protected islands in most of the estuaries, the birds can switch from one nesting site to another when conditions warrant it. The productivity of the estuaries partly reflects the nutrients that wash down from the Pinelands watershed, as well as the purity of the waters.

The last light of evening is fading fast, creating long shadows across the creek and the canoe. The brilliant tips of the Salt Hay look like tiny spears, and hordes of mosquitoes are rising from the grass. Near the dock a small stand of Rose Mallow glistens a lush pink (fig. 12.7). We pause to wonder how many Lenape made this same journey, looking for bird eggs to eat. They traveled in a pine dugout, bailed out their canoes with Horseshoe Crab carapaces, and fished with lines made from deer sinew; but the pleasures of being out on a calm day with the setting sun sending shimmers of light across the water is surely the same.

13

Landscapes for Neotropical Migrants

Sitting quietly in the pines at the edge of a small marsh, I listen to the loud "whitchity, whitchity, whitchity" of a male Common Yellowthroat. In the tangle of shrubs at the edge of the pines, a small dark olive bird with a bright yellow throat and a black face mask pauses briefly to advertise its territory while it moves slowly over the branches, searching for food. He flies to the top of the tangle and calls again, "whitchity, whitchity, whitchity," and is answered from a short distance away. The other bird is not visible in the brush, but his call is still clear. Farther off I can hear three or four other Yellowthroats, but their calls are not quite as pure and seem a bit muffled. Yellowthroats have relatively small territories and defend a space that may be only about 200 feet in diameter. They not only nest within these territories, but they gather all their food there as well. Because the territories are relatively small, they defend them fiercely, usually with songs rather than fights.

Like many passerines, the Common Yellowthroat relies heavily on songs for communication, but remarkably, they have only one major song type. They do not have a large repertoire of songs, nor do they imitate other species. They rarely give a flight song, preferring instead to perch in the tangles and sing loud and clear to defend their space. By not sitting prominently on top of the vegetation or flying in the air to give a song, they run the risk that their song will be modified by the tangles of vegetation.

Since they have only one major song, there are few messages they can transmit with it. They can, however, use the loudness of a song to determine how far away the singer is; a faint song indicates the potential intruder is quite far away. Another method of obtaining information from the song is by listening for any change or degradation of the song that occurs with distance or obstructions. The quality of sound might be greatly reduced if it has traveled through dense vegetation, much like we hear music through a thick wall. Birds can distinguish between the songs of neighbors and those of nonneighbors, and they respond differently. It's not just that the songs of nonneighbors are softer because they come from farther away, but they are somewhat changed by the intervening vegetation. It is impossible to know whether they are responding to the loudness or to the degree of degradation. Some birds, like Western Meadowlarks and Red-winged Blackbirds, respond differently to degraded songs than to normal-sounding songs.

Some years ago, Bill Boarman and I examined the songs of Yellowthroats to determine whether they could distinguish between normal and degraded songs (fig. 13.1). A friendly, affable character, Bill came to graduate school from California, where everything is much more laid back than it is in the East. He wore his sandals nearly all year, stepping gingerly through the wet snow, insisting that he was really quite comfortable. His eyes always twinkled when we discussed research, and I knew then that he would someday find the perfect research animal. He has returned to his beloved southern California, where the food is "sufficiently hot" to impart some flavor, and is busy studying the Western Gopher Tortoise in the desert.

13.1. Male Yellowthroat displaying to a female.

We recorded the songs of Yellowthroats when we were four different distances from them, resulting in different degrees of degradation. We then played back the four different song types at the same distance from the territory of male Yellowthroats. The males responded differently to the four song types, even though they were played from the same place in their territory and were equally loud. They seemed to be detecting differences in the song quality as a function of the song degradation. The birds answered less often to the songs that were the most degraded, which would normally have reflected a bird that was a greater distance away. In other words, even though the song was being played within their own territory, they reacted as if the intruder was quite far away, as it should have been.

The Yellowthroat I watch moves slowly through the tangles, searching for small insects. These birds are "searching" predators that obtain their food by carefully examining the suitable habitat. Most of the time this one is not in view, but I can track its progress by its voice and by the jerking of leaves. Yellowthroats are relatively inflexible in their exploratory patterns; they never sit and wait as some hawks do, but usually move deliberately over the branches. Slowly moving through suitable tangles of tall grass and brambles increases their opportunities to find prey, and switching from tangle to tangle further increases their chances. Since they have relatively small territories and they obtain nearly all of their resources within the territory, they have to choose territories wisely.

I am not here to study Yellowthroat songs or territories today, nor to watch their feeding behavior, but to think about how groups of birds use the barrens. Their song is part of the ambiance of the pines, fitting in with a mosaic of habitats. Unlike many other barrens habitats along the Atlantic Coast, the New Jersey Pine Barrens is extensive, with some large blocks of well-preserved pine forests, such as Wharton and Brendan T. Byrne State Forests. There the dense pines run for many miles, with only a few sand tracks through the forests. Scattered clearings in these forests, remnants of farm plots long abandoned, provide the only openings for animals that prefer edge areas. These dense forests also provide wonderful habitats for "interior-nesting" birds that do not do well except in the center of large tracts of forests, species like Tufted Titmouse and Ovenbird.

Compared to other areas of New Jersey, the Pine Barrens has relatively few birds. Of the over 400 species sighted in New Jersey, only 150 have been seen in the pines, and only about 50 are very common. This is partly due to the low diversity of different trees, partly to the lack of hardwood trees, and partly to the lack of abundant water. With a low diversity of

13.2. Whip-Poor-Wills often sit on the ground, blending in with the sand and old leaves.

trees and shrubs, there are fewer habitat niches, both for foraging and for nesting.

In the Pine Barrens, Yellowthroats often nest at the edge of wet cedar swamps, along with Eastern Wood Pewees, Catbirds, Yellow-throated Vireos, Redstarts, and Song Sparrows. Parula Warblers also nest in the cedar swamps, but they fly long distances in the uplands to find Old-man's Beard, a lichen they use for building their nests. As with other pinelands, most breeding birds are more common in the upland than in the lowland barrens areas, including Rufous-sided Towhee, Pine Warbler, Prairie Warbler, Brown Thrasher, and Whip-Poor-Will (fig. 13.2). Carolina Chickadees are very common, flitting from pine to pine, searching the trunks and branches for insects. These species prefer the open Pitch Pine glades, and their abundance decreases when hardwoods invade. Eastern Bluebirds and Common Nighthawks move into recently burned areas; without fires they decline, and both species have declined drastically in the last 30 years. In early March the first bluebirds return to the pines, and I usually find them in old burn areas or in fields long since abandoned by farmers who eked out a living in the early 1900s.

Wild Turkeys are also native to the pines, along with Ruffed Grouse. When Indians roamed the woods, Wild Turkeys were very common and extensively hunted. The early European settlers quickly grasped the value of the turkey, especially during the fall and winter when other game was less abundant. Although turkeys were exterminated in the pines by overhunting, an aggressive restocking program by the state's Division of Fish and Wildlife has brought these magnificent birds back, but in many parts of the pines they are still having difficulties. In only a few years their populations have increased, and it is not unusual to see two or three courting males with eight or ten hens. In the fall and winter the scattered flocks coalesce, and the flocks fan out through the pines, flying ungracefully up to roost in the tallest trees when the light declines in the late afternoon.

Where the hardwoods have moved in, there are other nesting species, such as Downy Woodpecker, Blue Jay, Carolina Chickadee, Red-eyed Vireo, Screech Owl, Tufted Titmouse, Ovenbird, and Black and White Warbler. With a greater diversity of trees, there are probably more insects, and the number as well as the diversity of birds increases. These habitat preferences are not hard and fast, and like other communities, the birds reflect successional stages.

The rivers and shallow lakes running through the pines attract a few birds that wander in from the nearby coastal marshes. In the summer, Snowy Egrets stand quietly in shallow water, searching for unwary fish, and Green Herons cling to low overhanging branches, peering into the water for small fish and frogs. They remain so still it is hard to believe they are alive, but their aim is deadly once they spot a small unwary fish in the shadows. Now and then a Great Blue Heron fishes along the shallows, but they are rarer, and the fish are usually too small for their tastes.

In the abandoned sand and gravel pits, Belted Kingfishers build nests in the light yellow sand banks and fish in nearby streams and lakes. They sit quietly on overhanging branches above the water, watching and waiting, and finally they sally forth, peer down once more, and dive straight into the water to come up with a small fish. Where branches are not available, they hover rapidly on beating wings, searching the water. They are not above fishing in small goldfish ponds behind people's houses, but they quickly deplete such a pond and have to return to the lakes and rivers.

Where there are cattails and other emergent vegetation, Red-winged Blackbirds nest, feeding on the insects emerging in large black clouds over the marshes. Tree Swallows and Purple Martins swoop gracefully over the water, picking up insects. They usually nest in abandoned woodpecker holes or other depressions in trees, but they also accept birdhouses people build for them. Purple Martins are extolled for their mosquito control prowess by vendors of Martin apartment houses, but this is probably overrated, and most Martin houses are quickly colonized by freeloading House Sparrows. Martins are large, elegant swallows with a dark purple iridescence. Thus utter gurgling call notes, and anyone is fortunate to have a colony nearby.

A few clearings near abandoned farmhouses or around housing developments attract more common suburban birds like robins, Starlings, Chipping Sparrows, and English Sparrows. Some birds, of course, are widespread. Almost always, Turkey Vultures soar on thermals above the pines, looking for carrion. Kestrels perch on pines or old telephone poles, searching the ground for grasshoppers or other large insects. The plaintive "bob-white" of the Bobwhite never ceases to thrill me in the early spring, the songs of the nesting warblers and vireos are music in the early summer, and the calls of migrant flocks in the fall warn of the winter ahead. In the last ten years, some of these species have declined. It is harder to hear the Bobwhite and to see a hovering Kestrel, and I mourn for them.

It is the Prairie Warbler, however, that I think of as a pine barrens–scrubland bird. Whoever named the Prairie Warbler seemingly got his habitats mixed up, for they are not a prairie grassland bird at all but live in old slashings left from logging, abandoned fields, and pastures, and any other habitat that has thickets and tangles. The species was named by Alexander Wilson, a nineteenth-century pioneer in ornithology. He was a contemporary of James J. Audubon and, like Audubon, was an artist. Wilson first found the species in the barrens of southwestern Kentucky, an area known locally as "prairie country." Open pine barrens were often called prairies, particularly when the understory was thick grass. People focused on the extensive grasses, not on the few scraggly or taller pines.

Watching a Prairie Warbler move through the scrubby underbrush in an abandoned farm plot, I marvel that these birds are so pervasive. They occur every place that has scrubby underbrush, especially in pine barrens. The bird bobs its tail slightly as it moves, although not as much as a Palm Warbler. I cannot tell whether this is a male or female, for unlike many birds, they have the same coloration. Both have an olive-green back with dark streaked sides and yellow underparts. Quite a snappy little warbler. The Prairie Warbler sings a series of seven or eight syllables— "zee zee zee zee zee zee zee"—each one slightly higher than the last. Before it is through, I always expect its voice to wear out since the pitch goes up so rapidly. Only when he calls is the male obvious, for then he perches on the top of a shrub, making it easier for other males or his female to see him. Otherwise he stays down in the dense tangles of undergrowth.

Prairie Warblers hide their nests in the dense underbrush in the crotch or fork of shrubs, usually within three feet of the ground. They use grasses, feathers, shreds of bark, plant down, and even small bits of plastic to fashion a neat little nest with a well-formed cup. The female lays three to five eggs and incubates for only 10 to 14 days, one of the shortest incubation periods known. She incubates on her own, but her mate sometimes helps with feeding the young. In New Jersey, Prairie Warblers have only one brood, but farther south they sometimes have two. The nesting pair faces many obstacles, including parasitism by Brown-headed Cowbirds that are always looking for nests in which to deposit their own eggs.

Because they nest so low, they are also plagued by snakes, Raccoons, and other ground predators. They have fared rather well, however, largely because the fields, farms, and old logging plots abandoned by people grow into the scrub pine–oak habitats they prefer. Prairie Warblers are delightful, they are like an old familiar friend that is still interesting and charming, and they are all the more engaging because they occur in many of the pine barrens habitats from Albany to Florida.

The similarities in birds in the New Jersey Pine Barrens, the Long Island Barrens, and the Albany Pine Bush led Paul Kerlinger and Craig Doremus to compare the breeding bird communities in these habitats. They found that five species dominated all three habitats, accounting for over 60 percent of the total birds counted on transects in all three places. Rufous-sided Towhee was the most abundant bird in all three, and Prairie Warbler was the second most abundant in the Long Island and New Jersey Barrens, and I find it pretty common at Albany as well.

In most hardwood forests along the East Coast, there are many more species that make up 60 percent of the birds, and the presence of only five very abundant species indicates a degraded or depaupered forest. When the forest has become fragmented and degraded, a greater variety of common, nonspecialist species can breed. Since pine barrens were historically very harsh environments for birds, the relatively high abundance score for the top five species in the New Jersey Pine Barrens (70 percent) and the Long Island Barrens (77 percent) confirms that they are more pristine than the Albany Pine Bush (60 percent), a conclusion we could have reached simply by noting the fragmentation and urbanization around the latter.

Data from past studies in the 1950s showed that populations of Prairie Warbler, Pine Warbler, Ovenbird, and Brown Thrasher all declined markedly over the last 40 years in the Albany and Long Island Barrens, while the populations remained healthy in the New Jersey Pine Barrens. The habitats in both Long Island and Albany have been drastically reduced, fragmented, and invaded by nonnative plants, allowing species such as Mockingbirds to increase in numbers. Mockingbirds and other species adapted to edge areas increased both along the edges and in the interior. In the mid-twentieth century, Mockingbirds extended their range northward, reaching Long Island around 1960 and Albany about ten years later. In New Jersey, Mockingbirds were already common by the 1940s, but they still are absent from much of the Pine Barrens.

Disturbingly, the Brown-headed Cowbird showed the largest increase of any edge species. They found cowbirds on over twice as many transects at Albany as in the New Jersey Pine Barrens. Cowbirds parasitize the nests of all common pine barrens birds, including Rufous-sided towhees, Pine and Prairie Warblers, Ovenbirds, and Brown Thrashers, and nest parasitism might have contributed to population declines of these species, particularly in the Albany Pine Bush. Some female cowbirds only lay one egg in the nest of their host species, but some return to lay a second egg, and a few females even kick out the eggs of the host. Since the incubation period of cowbirds is less than that of most of their hosts, the cowbird chick hatches first and often ends up throwing out the other eggs. The cowbird chicks are also larger, making it doubly hard for the host's chicks to compete for food from their own parents.

Increases in Brown-headed Cowbirds are a greater concern for Pine and Prairie Warblers than for other birds because they are similar taxonomically and ecologically to the Kirtland's Warbler in Michigan—the species whose drastic decline was largely attributed to cowbird parasitism. Kirtland's Warbler is also a species of pine barrens, and it was unable to cope with cowbird parasitism when cowbirds moved into its habitat. Cowbirds are species that thrive on edge areas and moved into the Michigan pine barrens only when development and farming provided edge corridors through the dense pines. Slowly they moved through the corridor, nesting farther and farther into the dense pines.

In some places more than 90 percent of Kirtland's Warbler nests were parasitized, resulting in no warblers being fledged. Very aggressive management involving the trapping and removal of thousands of cowbirds has succeeded in halting the decline, but few Kirtland's Warblers remain, and the species is on the U.S. Endangered Species List. Management included restoring a fire regime, actively protecting nests, and removal of all cowbirds.

Nearly 35 years ago I wandered the Michigan pine barrens with Harold Mayfield searching for Kirtland's Warblers. An engaging white-haired gentleman of the old school, Harold was delighted to show me "his" special bird. Slowly we strolled through the pines, listening for their calls, talking about the old-time ornithologists he knew many years ago. He gave me a feel for how ornithology has changed over the years, and of the vast natural history information possessed by these early naturalists. Today many professional ornithologists are interested in "questions" and often forget that it is birds we love, birds we want to protect.

The dire plight of the Kirtland's Warblers had just been recognized when I visited, and aggressive management had started. Large tracts of central Michigan pinelands were charred from recent burns, dead barren trees jutted into the blue sky, and the pines were nearly devoid of bird calls. The elimination of all cowbirds was not yet completed, but such removal (trapping followed by killing) was viewed as providing the only chance Kirtland's Warblers had for survival. We stopped to listen at every place where the warblers had territories and walked over many many acres. Finally we found a male perched on a low stunted oak. He stayed for only a fleeting minute, but that was enough to convince me of their rarity, and that their only chance for survival was aggressive management. Even then it was clear that the pine barrens of eastern North America are in a great deal of trouble, and without our vigilance these fragile communities will disappear. Today, the nesting areas of Kirtland's Warblers are carefully guarded, and all nests are monitored. They are censused by counting the number of males that call: a high of 766 calling males was recorded in 1995, with 733 in 1997, and 1,202 in 2003.

The drastic decline of Pine and Prairie Warblers in the Albany Pine Bush is disturbing and warrants great concern. They are integral members of the breeding avifauna of the pine barrens, and the health of their populations is evidence of the overall health of the barrens. They serve as indicators of habitat stability or disruption. Like most warblers, they leave the pinelands in the fall, and head for warmer climes.

The New Jersey Pine Barrens, however, are not as cold in the winter as the northern Highlands of New Jersey, and many species migrate a few miles south to spend the winter in the pines. Carolina Chickadees, Carolina Wrens, and Mockingbirds move through, searching for berries and fruits still clinging to the shrubs and vines. Slate-colored Juncos come from farther north. Mourning Doves, House Sparrows, and Blue Jays can be common in the Pine Barrens in winter. Although some species move into the pines for the season, few use the Pine Barrens as a primary migration route, preferring instead the ridges or the coast. There are, however, impressive numbers of Sharp-shinned Hawks and some warblers, such as Myrtle Warblers, that move through the barrens in April and May, and again during the fall migration.

It is mostly young Sharp-shinned Hawks that migrate through the Pine Barrens in the fall, for the adults stick to what in New Jersey passes for mountain ridges, where they coast southward riding the stiff updrafts that build along the ridges (fig. 13.3). A few immature Sharpies, as they are affectionately called by bird-watchers, manage to migrate south along the inland ridges with adults, but most take the coastal route or cut across the Pine Barrens.

13.3. *Adult Sharp-shinned Hawks mainly migrate down the mountain ridges and through Hawk Mountain, while young hawks come through the Pine Barrens toward Cape May.*

Lookouts, such as Hawk Mountain in Pennsylvania and Raccoon Ridge in New Jersey, are famous for the concentrations of southbound raptors that pass by in the fall. Cape May Point stands out as a hawk concentration point with large numbers of coastal migrating hawks, particularly falcons. On clear fall days when the winds are right, the hawk-watching platform at Cape May holds a capacity crowd, which in no way diminishes the thrill of seeing hundreds of hawks migrating overhead, some barely skimming the trees.

Several years ago Larry Niles and I decided to figure out just what young Sharp-shinned Hawks were doing when they migrated south in the fall. Larry, with dark salt-and-pepper hair, moves carefully and cautiously, but his demeanor hides his fierce determination and foresight.

He is deeply dedicated to understanding how bird populations use different habitats, both temporally and spatially, and now heads the New Jersey Endangered and Nongame Species Program. He wanted to put radio transmitters on Sharpshins and follow them as they moved from the Pine Barrens through the deciduous forests on the Cape May peninsula. He also wanted to find out where they congregated and where they crossed Delaware Bay on their way south. We enlisted Kathy Clark to help, and sailed into the project. Kathy is reserved and careful, picks up each thread of a research project to carry it forward, and the three of us worked well together.

Lots of people have studied migration, but they have concentrated on long-distance patterns. We were interested in how birds make daily decisions about whether to fly on, or stay for a while longer. Would the hawks use time of day, wind speed, wind direction, or visibility, or would they be more influenced by their own body condition? If they decided not to migrate on a certain day, which habitat would they choose to forage in? The more we thought about it, the more questions we posed. How would they decide whether to fly across Delaware Bay from Cape May? The shortest distance across the bay is about 15 miles, from the very tip of the point to Mispillien in Delaware—otherwise it is longer. It was exciting just to ponder the various options, to try and put ourselves in the position of the young Sharpies, to imagine ourselves sailing high above the pine trees, heading for Cape May and the long flight over Delaware Bay.

We decided to use only female Sharpies because they weigh more than males, and the transmitters would be less of a hindrance. We set about trapping two Sharpies each day and fitted them with a small tail-mounted transmitter weighing less than 2 grams. Since the females weigh from 150 to 210 grams, this was not unduly stressful. Birds were immediately released, and tracking began. Flying birds were tracked from a moving vehicle, and the location of each hawk was noted every time it changed location. We stayed with the birds from dawn until dusk or until they stopped to roost for the night. We then used maps and ground surveys to distinguish the different habitats: pine forest, deciduous forest, mixed forest, herbaceous, agricultural, and so on. It involved a tremendous amount of fieldwork, classifying the habitat type of every small block in the whole region. With detailed habitat maps for the area from the Pine Barrens to Cape May, we were able to locate the Sharpies' positions exactly.

With practice, it was possible to determine what the hawks were doing by subtle changes in the radio signal. We could distinguish perching, flying, migrating, roosting, and hunting, and we verified our designations

13.4. Sharp-shinned Hawks spend a good deal of time hunting, but only a short period actually stooping for prey.

by observing the hawks (fig. 13.4). Long-distance flights were called migratory, while shorter stop-and-fly behaviors we designated "flying." We used information on wind, temperature, and visibility from the weather station in Atlantic City.

It was thrilling and exciting to hold a female Sharp-shinned Hawk in our hands, put on the transmitter, and watch her sail up into the sky, look around, and head for the coast. It was even more sensational to track her signal through the vast forests and marshes of southern New Jersey. Of course, we followed the birds until they reached their nighttime roost, so we could usually find them the next morning. Slight changes in signal told us what they were doing, and we were often close enough to watch them hunt or see them pick a roosting site for the night.

Sharpies spent nearly 80 percent of their time hunting or perching, and only 5 percent actually migrating. They usually perched for about 45 minutes and then hunted for half an hour. Then they found a nice tree to rest for a while before setting out to hunt once more, and so the days passed. Time of day mattered, however, and they spent more time hunting in the morning and late afternoon, and more time perching in the early afternoon. They migrated at nearly all times of the day.

As we all expected, the Sharpies migrated when the visibility was good and when the winds were generally from the west. They seemed anxious to reach Cape May Point, however, and birds in the barrens or deciduous woods spent only 37 percent of the time hunting while those already at the Point spent over half of their time hunting for food. Perhaps they were just waiting for the right conditions to begin the long trip across the bay, and so they had time on their hands—or rather, their feet.

The Sharpies spent 98 percent of their time in forests, avoiding the more open habitats. Although they could choose from pure pine forests, pure deciduous forests, and mixed pine-deciduous forests, the Sharpies preferred the mixed forests, but liked the more closed forests with a dense understory rather than the open forests. They also chose to be in Atlantic White Cedar more than expected on the basis of how much cedar habitat was available. This is not astonishing since Sharpies hunt partly by surprising their quarry. It is much more difficult to sneak up on prey in open habitats, such as the heart of the Pine Barrens.

It is spectacular to watch a hunting Sharpie. These birds can sit motionless and then strike by flying into dense vegetation. If they do not connect at first, they can still grab their prey by making short flights that will panic a small bird into the open, making them vulnerable. Their broad wings are short and rounded, allowing excellent maneuverability in dense cover. I have watched a Sharpie at the top of brambles climb down swiftly through the branches to snag a sparrow in the bush. We were amazed at how much time the young spent hunting, often nearly 40 percent of the day. The high rate of hunting may reflect migratory needs, as they have to store fat for the next leg of their journey. Or it may be that they are in a place where immature passerines concentrate, providing an unusual food supply that is too good to pass up. Or they may not have mastered hunting skills yet, and it takes them longer to find enough food.

By examining the conditions under which the Sharpies set out across Delaware Bay on migration and comparing them to the conditions that occurred during the rest of the time, we showed that good migration conditions existed only about 30 percent of the time. It is dangerous for the young hawks to set off across the bay, since the weather could change quickly and it is energetically costly to have to turn back. The hawks are understandably cautious. Once they reach the tip of the peninsula, they have to wait for better conditions before crossing, and they may as well hunt while they wait. Sometimes they got discouraged and moved farther north along Delaware Bay, hoping to cross where the bay was narrower.

Considering our results in terms of the Pine Barrens, it seems the Sharpies prefer to hunt in the cedars and pines where there is a dense understory of oaks, huckleberries, and other shrubs. When they finish hunting, they move to taller, denser pines, looking for a perch with some cover but good visibility of the surrounding forest. They also wanted to find perch sites that provided some protection from both adverse weather and other predators. They use a diversity of habitats, moving freely between them.

The project never really did end, and many years later, Christina Frank, Larry, and I started out to repeat the study. Christina is finishing a Master's degree at Rutgers, one of a stream of wonderful students Larry and I have worked with over the years. In the meantime, even more habitat in South Jersey has been lost, and the hawks have fewer places to roost and forage. The hawks have also declined, and we are anxious to see whether their habitat choices are the same.

Sharp-shinned Hawks and Yellowthroats are not alone in having particular habitat requirements for migrating, nesting, and foraging. Many species of warblers, vireos, and other passerines do as well. Over the past two decades, concern over the well-being of these birds, as well as other small passerines, has come to the fore. Saving "Neotropical migrants" has become the cornerstone of many conservation programs.

For years in the 1970s, bird-watchers were complaining, saying "this wasn't a very good migration year," then "it is not like it used to be, we don't get the big waves anymore." Since few birders keep quantitative records, their perceptions were ignored. Bird banding stations, however, did have such data for some species, and the information began to accumulate. The alarm was sounded when people taking the annual bird censuses began to notice an overall decrease in Neotropical migrants on the breeding grounds, which was echoed when people began to look at migration records from key stopover places. When the reports began to accrue, the global plight of Neotropical migrants became clear. Many species of migrants are facing drastic declines and possible extinction.

Many of the species that nest in the Pine Barrens are Neotropical migrants, including Eastern Wood Pewee, Yellow-throated Vireo, Yellowthroat, Redstart, Prairie Warbler, and Red-eyed Vireo. Like Neotropical migrants everywhere, they have decreased, and their decline may be due to losses of habitat in their nesting range, as well as to the loss of overwintering habitat in the New World tropics, or neotropics.

Although the declines were initially ascribed to problems on the wintering grounds, this is way too simplistic, and some species have declined despite an apparent abundance of habitat on their wintering grounds. The declines came partly after heavy pesticide use in forests resulted in declines in insects, with direct effects on birds. Clearly, the availability of both breeding and migrating habitats must be examined, and for this, New Jersey is critical. To some extent, most of New Jersey is coastal, including the Pine Barrens. Birds migrating in an easterly, a southerly, or southeasterly direction hit the coast of New Jersey and are funneled southward through the Highlands and the Pine Barrens to Cape May. New Jersey hosts the bird traffic out of New England as well as those flying directly south. While the Pine Barrens is not as good a funnel point for birds as Cape May, it does provide migratory habitat for a number of Pinelands birds.

In central and southern New Jersey, 40 percent of the habitat for Neotropical migrants has been lost in the last 30 years, mostly to residential development. This is an alarming rate, and it is made worse by fragmentation of the habitat. A 1,000-acre forest provides much better nesting and migratory habitat for birds than 20 forests of 50 acres each, which in turn are better than 20 forests of one-acre each. Development regulations favor fragmentation, for developers can clear large acres of forest for housing as long as they leave a certain percentage green.

The isolation of forest patches is a major cause for concern for Neotropical migrants and other species that require forests. When the interior of forests are opened to the outside, other trees and weeds move in that are not shade tolerant, disrupting the habitat further. Cowbirds become more abundant, parasitize the nests of vulnerable species, and even dump out the eggs of the nest owners, thus reducing their reproductive success. Interior-nesting bird species have to face changes in the vegetation, increases in competition, and increases in predation by cats, dogs, foxes, Raccoons, and other species that move in.

The New Jersey Endangered and Nongame Species Program has initiated a program to study the effects of habitat fragmentation and human activities on Neotropical migrants. Spearheaded by Larry Niles, the program is leading the nation in understanding how fragmentation affects nesting Neotropical migrants. Larry's mild manner is deceiving, for he is a bulldog within the state's Division of Fish and Wildlife, fighting tirelessly to incorporate good, cutting-edge science into management and regulation. Working with Larry is always a pleasure and the best kind of collaboration between university and government. Recognizing the importance of local support, he started working with local government and community leaders long before it became fashionable. He developed a landscape project that aims to preserve and protect ecosystems on a land-scape scale—ecosystems that are large enough to protect assemblages of birds, reptiles, and amphibians, rather than merely one threatened or en-dangered species. In this regard he is leading the nation. Mandy Dey and Eric Stiles are collecting some of the data to serve as a baseline for the landscape project.

Mandy and Eric were my graduate students at Rutgers. They have con-ducted many transects throughout the southern deciduous woodlands and the Pinelands to census birds, using the data to develop measures of species sensitivity to disturbance, indices that will help design landscape-scale plans so that communities can preserve their Neotropical migrants, and with them other species that require large tracts of unbroken forest.

Tall and lanky, with a ready smile, Eric is intense and persistent. He is interested in the effects of fragmentation on reptile and bird distribution and works for New Jersey Audubon, protecting the state's avian resources and habitats. Mandy is typical of today's young biologists, clinging tena-ciously to our society's ideals of a young, attractive woman seeking to make a difference in the world—and she is making inroads in wildlife management, typically a male-dominated world. Her determination to combine hard field data with satellite imagery and computer models will move us far toward understanding how Neotropical migrants function within a landscape of different habitats, for the pinelands is a mosaic of dissimilar communities.

Remarkably, although the New Jersey Pine Barrens is disturbed by the forces of suburbanization, there is little industrialization and urbaniza-tion, especially when compared to other parts of New Jersey and to the Albany Pine Bush and the Long Island Barrens. Few paved roads bisect the pines: large tracts are completely free from roads and other human activities, and thousands of acres burn every year in both natural and prescribed burns. Prairie Warblers, Rufous-sided Towhees, and Oven-birds are as abundant as always, and the secretive species that nest in the dark White Cedar swamps still creep through the underbrush, searching for insects or calling serenely from the tangles.

14

Strange Things Happen
in the Dead of Night

I have come to the Pines by myself—one of the few times. Usually I have
two or three graduate students with me, or Mike, or Bob Zappalorti. It is
early in the morning at the beginning of September, and all of my students are busy with classes and Mike is teaching. Like most herpetologists,
Bob is not an early riser, and he much prefers the warmth of the day, just
like his beloved snakes and Fence Lizards, or the solitude of night when
the frogs are chorusing. Besides, he has a project elsewhere to finish.

Within minutes I leave behind the paved roads and retirement community, with its one-story houses, each the same size and shape, on the
same size lot. There are only three or four different house designs in many
of these developments that have sprung up in the pines. Each house is
neatly tended, with brilliant red geraniums or white and pink impatiens
near the front walk. The lawns are recently mowed, and not a weed seems
to epist there. I think of these people as interlopers who cleared the pines
for their houses, objecting violently to the thought that snakes might
wander about their yards, especially ones that may be as long as five feet.
Never mind that Pine Snakes are completely harmless, or that they lived
here for thousands of years, or that they feed on unwanted mice.

It is just 7 A.M., and the early morning sun is casting long shadows
from the pines. The forest is sparse, and the ground is dappled with shadows and light. There is no wind, and the branches of the pines are silent.
Against the morning sky, the pines in the barrens look forlorn, as if they
had lost many branches and half of their needles to some catastrophe.
The Low-bush Huckleberries no longer have berries for it is late summer,
and they were eaten by birds long ago, or fell to the ground. There is so
little water and nutrients in these soils that most bushes never reach the
knees, and the berries are usually tiny. Despite their small size, they taste
sweeter than commercial berries.

I wander quietly along, soaking up the silence. There are few birds here,
and in the last throes of the breeding season, they are silent. Most of their

14.1. Female White-tailed Deer feeding ahead of me on the trail.

young have long since fledged, and they are free of all parental duties. They can linger a little longer in the protection of the thick pines, roosting until the warm rays of the sun wake them. The pines close in behind me, and slowly I make my way along the narrow sandy trail used by herds of deer passing silently through the forest. As if on cue, branches up ahead sway slightly, brushed by a small doe. She bends to eat some grass, unaware of my presence (fig. 14.1). I hold my breath, but then she stops to peer at me, and both of us freeze, watching and waiting. I stop breathing, caught in her gaze, not wanting to move a single muscle. She is quite small, typical of Pine Barrens deer. The browse is not very lush in the barrens, food is scarce, and there are no farm fields to plunder as there are in many other parts of New Jersey. Pine Barrens deer usually weigh half as much as those that live in suburban areas of northern New Jersey.

The spell is broken by the scream of a Blue Jay, and the deer turns. Raising her tail in a white flag of retreat, she bounds up the trail, rounds a bend, and is gone. Biologists argue about the meaning of this white flag display, but it is usually given only when a deer has plenty of time for escape. It serves to warn other deer of danger and to inform the predator that it has been discovered. The Blue Jay stops scolding, and the pines are silent again.

I came here by myself to search for emerging Pine Snake hatchlings. I want to sit by a snake nest for hours, waiting and watching for the young snakes. Few other people have the patience to do this. I do not want to be pressured to leave before dusk and so I have left my usual companions at home. Pine Snake eggs take anywhere from two to three months to hatch, depending on whether there is complete sun penetration to the forest floor. The eggs are five to six inches below the ground in a nest, and they depend on the sun warming the sand to incubate them. Eggs that are closer to the surface experience warmer sand and hatch in less time.

A mile or so from the road I come to a clearing left by an old farmhouse, the fields long since abandoned and overgrown. The old piney no doubt had a small vegetable garden, now gone to seed. Nothing remains except the clearing. The house was burned down years ago by kids, and only a forlorn, unpruned lilac attests to the house's location. A few pines are scattered about the clearing, their lower branches brushing the sand, holding the needles in a deep mat. Mostly the sand is covered with sparse lichens and Low Bush Huckleberry.

Patches of bare sand here are hardened by rain and by years of not being disturbed. Few people come here, only an occasional hiker or biker pass through. In some open places the bikers have wheeled around in circles and churned up the sand. It takes only a few turns with a bike or an off-road vehicle to disturb the sand so much that Pine Snakes can no longer dig nests. The bikes loosen the vegetation, and make the sand so soft it is called *sugar sand;* this sand is easy to get stuck in, even with a four-wheel drive vehicle. The soft sand collapses as the female Pine Snakes dig, and they are unable to dig long tunnels that lead to their nests. Even if they could dig a nest, the sand would collapse on the eggs, smothering them without a proper air space above the eggs. There is an old two-tire path through the center of the clearing, once used to reach the homestead. Mostly it is overgrown with short grasses and lichens, but the tire tracks are still visible years later. The pine barrens are quite fragile, and it takes many years for the signs of traffic to disappear.

In early July, Bob and I found several Pine Snake nests here, and we left them to hatch on their own. The nests were easy to find in July because there were fresh dirt piles by each entrance, characteristic of many burrowing mammals. Most people pass these burrows, assuming they belong to a skunk or some other small mammal. We have a search image for Pine Snake nests, however, and can tell the subtle differences. One of the nest openings is in an abandoned tire track, although the nest is off to the side at the end of a four-foot-long tunnel.

Although we dug up the nests to record clutch size, measure the tunnel length, and examine the size and depth of the nest, we recovered the nest carefully. To ensure that there was an air space above the eggs, just as we found them, we put a piece of plexiglass over the nest before we covered it with sand. The airspace heats up during the day, keeping the eggs warm at night. It also provides some room for the hatching young— it takes nearly 24 hours for a snake to hatch once it breaks the surface of the egg. This is not surprising since it takes nearly as long for a bird to break free of its shell once it makes a small hole with the egg tooth on the tip of its bill (a day or two after hatching, this egg tooth falls off). The plexiglass sheet was not much bigger than the nest, allowing space for the young hatchlings to dig their way out along the sides. At first, a few people objected to our procedure, but with time, we showed them that hatching rates were similar or higher than those in undisturbed nests, and the controversy disappeared. Success was often higher because our digging dispersed the top layers of sand with the female's scent, making it more difficult for predators to find the nests.

When I checked yesterday, only one of the five nests here had a small hole at the sand surface. One subtle trail leads from the nest to the underbrush indicating that one hatchling has left on its own; the others should still be within. According to my notes, this nest has nine eggs. I am anxious to see just how the young hatchlings behave when they emerge from a nest. For several years I hatched Pine Snake eggs in the laboratory (fig. 14.2). After we fed the hatchlings in the laboratory, we placed the young back in their original nests in the field and watched them emerge on their own, but I want to see how similar that is to the real thing. I am prepared to sit here in the pines and wait for them to emerge—all day if necessary. I have a sleeping bag in the car, and might just sleep in the pines if it looks promising. I can see three nests from my vantage point, and I have two other nests to check in this clearing.

The sun rises higher and its warmth penetrates the pine boughs above my head. I watch as the rays reach toward the nest, slowly edging closer

14.2. Pine Snakes usually lay a clutch of 8 or 9 eggs that take about 60 days to hatch. Once the young break a hole in the egg, it takes another 24 hours before they emerge.

and closer as the sun rises higher and higher. The sand is getting warmer, I can feel it through my flannel jacket. In the far distance I hear the roar of a motorcycle, but it passes. Then I hear another, and it seems to be coming through the woods. From the sounds of it, there is more than one. Frantically I look around for a good hiding place, but the pines here are quite sparse. Bikers are normally friendly, but some are not, and that is a bit worrisome. Shoving my gear under some oak leaves blown there by a recent storm, I run to the nearby edge of the clearing, and duck under a thick pine tree with low boughs. Fortunately, I am wearing a dark green jacket and blue jeans and can blend in. I am equally pleased that no rattlesnake shares my hiding place. I am sure the bikers will just pass through and move on, or at least I hope so. The noise grows louder and louder, and the bikers roll into view. They are wearing black leather jackets with emblems on the back, but it is too far to read the lettering. One carries a beer bottle in one hand—liquid breakfast—and both are laughing.

I silently pray that they follow the old tire tracks and do not careen over the top of my snake nests. No hatchling has yet peaked its head out where it could be run over, but the disturbance may well keep them below ground all day. Snakes are particularly sensitive to vibrations, and they might retreat back into their nest. When I hatched eggs in the laboratory, I found that the young often emerged a few hours after a vibration, such as the heavy carts of the early morning cleaning ladies. Such vibrations may indicate that the nest is no longer safe, it has been discovered by predators, and it is best to beat a hasty retreat.

Abruptly the bikers stop, and one hands his beer to the other.

"That was really fun, we should come back next weekend," the one holding the beer bottle says. "They meet here nearly every week."

"I don't know, I found it a bit scary. They could have hurt that kid."

"Nah, these guys are OK, it is just part of their club thing. An initiation or something. They come here all the time," answers the first, a tall guy with a dark beard. "It's their secret place."

"That seemed more scary than just an initiation, they were hurting him."

"Don't show your fear if we come again, it could be you they were torturing."

"Aren't they afraid someone will find them?"

"Not really. There are only a bunch of old coots out here. They never go anywhere, weird, they just come here to waste away."

"Don't those retirement folks walk in the pines?"

"Nah, they're afraid of snakes and they like the sidewalks. Don't worry so much. Of course, some of those snake people come here sometimes, mostly in July and August."

"You got any more beer?"

"Nah, let's get outta here, it's been a long night, I want to find my ole lady. I still think that one guy was nuts, a real wacko."

"Good thing you didn't bring her here—she would have freaked."

"That's not the half of it—I don't think she would be safe, even with me with her."

With a kick to the bikes, they peel off, down the deer trail toward the main road. The silence is deafening. Thinking over their comments makes me worry—are there more to come? Where have the others gone? There is another way out, just by following the old tire tracks the other way. They must have all come in that way for there were no fresh tracks the way I came in.

I peak out from my pine haven, peering toward the far sand. Even using my binoculars I cannot see the snake nests, they are obscured by the short grass. I wait for my heart to silence, and think about what to do. I could leave, keeping to the woods until I reached the safety of my car, or I could go back and watch for the snakes. It's a long way back to the car, and I decide to stay. I can hear if anyone approaches on the bikes—they make so much noise—and I could easily hide again.

Slowly I creep back to my place beneath the pines near the nests. It is getting hotter, but I keep my jacket on because it is good camouflage, from the snakes as well as bikers. I am sure no one will come, but just in case, I want to be prepared. Now I hear every snap of a pine bough, and imagine others. Trying to break the spell, I eat a lemon Luna bar, humming softly. Feeling I have to be calm and unafraid, I walk over to check one of the nests at the other side of the clearing, but there is no sign of hatchling activity. I am looking for a tiny indentation in the sand that suggests that a snake is moving about below the surface. But there is nothing.

I sneak softly back to the pine tree, and take up the vigil again. The minutes and hours drag on. Nothing happens, and I fight to banish my worry over the bikers. This is "my barrens," I think, what are *they* doing here? I am sure that the first hatchling will emerge in one of these three nests since they were laid a day or two earlier than the others. I count the branches on my tree, diagram the position of the snake nests in the clearing, and finally watch the tiny black ants sliding across the sand. I spend hours watching the small, light tan Fence Lizard whose territory I have invaded. He was a fairly late riser, and then only managed to climb to the top of a log to bask in the sun. He spread out his legs and flattened his body against the log. By facing the greatest amount of his body to the sun, he can warm up quickly. He remains so still that he almost disappears against the dead log, his dappled pattern blending in. Within a few minutes he straightens out his body but remains motionless: he needs more warmth. Then he dashes away and up a tree in search of small insects or other prey.

The sun is nearly overhead. Somehow I have made it to noon. Time to take out my ham sandwich, orange juice, and apple. I have hardly done a thing, but I am famished. I have some more food, but if I eat it now I will never last all day. Reluctantly I decide to save the chocolate bar for later.

Out of the corner of my eye I catch a movement. Taking up binoculars, I peer at the sand. The slight depression seems a bit larger, and before my eyes I see a few sand grains fall in, and then all is still. The minutes pass, but everything is so quiet that I wonder if I imagined the movement. Ten minutes later the sand moves again, and a small black nose appears. It is only a dot, but it rises slowly until two black eyes peer out. It remains absolutely motionless; the sand does not even move. I have to remain still also, or I will frighten it. My arms grow tired, but still I cannot shift. A Blue Jay sails across the clearing, and the snake disappears below the ground, followed by a small avalanche of sand.

Another hour passes with no more movement, and I wonder fleetingly whether I will see any more snakes today. Finally a head pops up, and slowly the snake swivels its head so that it can peer in all directions. It remains absolutely still for 15 minutes. Almost without moving the snake glides farther out, holding its head straight up. Nearly an inch of the snake is above ground, but to a novice it looks like a tiny twig stuck in the sand. The top of its head bends slightly, allowing it to look in my direction. Every movement is very slow and deliberate so as not to attract the attention of any predator flying overhead.

I have been so intent on watching this snake that I did not notice that another head has appeared. It moves up and peers in a direction opposite from the first snake. They remain still for only a minute or two, and then another head appears. The sand cascades down into the hole, now nearly an inch deep. This is a wonderfully exciting moment. Despite my years of study of Pine Snakes in the field and laboratory, I have never witnessed the event before. I imagine very few people have shared this experience, and I can hardly contain myself.

They remain still, peering around for another 10 minutes. I am afraid to move, I might disturb them. My arms grow weary again, but still I hold

14.3. Young hatchlings usually remain in the nest for ten days to two weeks, and emerge when they are ready to shed. Since they cannot eat until after they shed their skin, they are safer in their nests.

up my binoculars. Slowly I inch up my knees to provide some support for my elbows. Fortunately I started the stopwatch with the appearance of the first nose and have been mentally noting the time each new snake appears. It is getting harder to remember all the details, however. Why didn't I bring a tape recorder? Snakes are more sensitive to movement than to sound.

Without warning, one snake slowly moves higher until nearly three inches of it rise above the surface. It lowers itself to the ground and begins to climb from the nest (fig. 14.3). It takes about 10 seconds for the first half of its body to emerge, but only a second or two for the rest. Rapidly it crawls toward the closest lichens, but then moves on; perhaps the rough surfaces were annoying. It slithers completely underneath a patch of leaves, curls up, and disappears from view. It has taken nearly an hour for the first snake to emerge from the burrow. Within two minutes the other two snakes emerge in the same manner. They follow the first one under blueberries, and all disappear quickly. The hole they leave is now larger and looks like a giant ant hole, except that there is no sand piled around the edges.

It is quite adaptive for the hatchlings to be cautious when leaving the nest, for they are relatively safe within, and once they leave they face a number of predators. In a series of laboratory experiments with a stuffed hawk, a model with eyes, a model without eyes, and a person, I found that hatchlings responded most strongly to any stimulus with eyes, and they were most aggressive toward the model with the largest eyes. It took the hatchlings longer to respond to the head without eyes.

Two hours later, and still no new movement. Time to stretch my legs and check the other two nests. It feels good to walk in the sun, listen to the fall migrants, and watch the vulture soaring overhead. I almost wish the walk were longer. There is no activity in the nests, the sand is completely undisturbed, and there is no trace of a small depression that might indicate activity below.

I need a little exercise and decide to check another clearing about half a mile away. In some years the snakes have nested there, but this year we found only one nest in this clearing. But we could have missed the nest if heavy winds filled in the entrance hole quickly. The pines grow denser along my walk, although the warmth of the early afternoon sun still penetrates to the trail. It feels good to walk after sitting still for so long. There must be a healthy deer population this year, as a buck just crossed my path less than 50 yards ahead, apparently unaware of me. I freeze. He stops to eat some leaves, and walks on. It is not yet the hunting season, and the deer are comparatively unconcerned.

Up ahead the trees open into bright sunlight. Only one pine tree grows in the clearing, although there are a couple of small Scrub Oak. The oak leaves are a brilliant green, with no hint of the red tinge they will have in a few weeks once cool weather sets in.

I find another snake nest by searching for old dirt piles, but there is no indication that any snakes have hatched. There is not even a tiny indentation indicating underground activity. Widening my circle, I look for other snake nests that we might have missed. We obviously did, for I find a nest that has been excavated by a fox. There are no scattered eggshells about, indicating that the fox probably ate them all in the late evening or early morning light. The hole is very large, dirt is scattered in all directions, although there is also one large pile.

One solitary trail leads from the opened nest; one baby snake escaped predation and slithered to safety in the cool of the early morning. This predation must have just happened because the sand is a darker shade than the surface sand, and is a bit moist. It hasn't had time to be bleached by the sun. I follow the snake trail until I lose it under some oak leaves. Gently pulling the leaves aside, I find the small hole of a Jumping Mouse. The snake apparently found a safe place, one where it might be able to find food as well.

A recently shed skin in the leaves suggests that the snake hatched eight to ten days ago, the usual time required to shed for the first time. They never eat until they shed. Their skin expanded so much while they were developing in the egg that they are unable to eat until they shed for the first time. Then they respond to the smell or heat from a mouse, striking quickly.

14.4. Predators, such as Raccoons, dig up well over half of the nests to eat the eggs. The tunnel dug by the nesting female is to the right.

It may not be unusual for one or two hatchlings to escape predation, especially if the nest is dug up after the eggs have hatched. When a fox or Raccoon digs up a nest, the sand falls back in as it is digging, and eggs or hatchlings may get buried (fig. 14.4). However, some hatchlings do not stay in the nest once they hatch, but go into side tunnels, away from the nest chamber. I found from my experiments in the laboratory that once Pine Snakes hatch, they dig side burrows away from the nest, and some of these can be a yard or two long. For a long time I wondered why they bothered, but now it is clear. Once the eggs hatch, there are additional odors from the yolk that remain in the shell, which may attract predators. However, if the snakes dig side tunnels away from the main nest chamber, then any predator that finds the nest eats the eggs and hatchlings in the nest, but may not find hatchlings that are a yard or so from the nest.

Hearing the shrill cry of a Red-tailed Hawk, I look up and follow it as it moves across the sky. I have been watching the ground as I moved over the clearing, searching for signs of snake nests or hatchlings, and only now do I see some burned wood. It takes me a few moments to recognize the shape of a cross. The horror slowly grows as I realize this is the place where the bikers were last night.

Beer bottles lie strewn around, fallen in the numerous tire tracks of motorcycles. A few charred logs indicate the center of their activities. On the ground is a sheet, and when I lift it, I see that it is half burned, but it is not burned badly enough to obliterate the two holes for eyes. Remembering the comments of the bikers earlier in the day, I shudder at the midnight ceremony that obviously took place here. A couple of years ago Bob and I found similar evidence at Ed's Place, farther south, but I thought it was an isolated event. Fear tingles down my spine, even though I know that it has been hours since the bikers left.

The barrens are still wild, and in isolated places strange things happen in the dead of night. Even though retirement communities may be only a few miles away, the pines harbor an odd assortment of people who bear grudges against development and the march of time. Few people venture out into the pines except for the occasional deer hunter or snake poacher. Deer hunters travel with guns, and locals know enough to stay out of the woods during the deer season or at night. The snake poachers come out only in the warmth of midday, when they can find snakes resting beneath logs and other debris. Often the snakes are coiled beneath the boards and other objects they have placed there to "sucker" the snakes into a false sense of safety. They check sucker boards regularly, carefully replacing them so there is no clue they have been disturbed.

I am appalled and stand before the cross, still holding the burned sheet in my hands. What prompts such hatred? Much more must have happened here than an initiation ceremony. What midnight ritual do they perform, and for what purpose? Are they play-acting, or is the Klan still alive in the southern Jersey pines? The woods are silent, full sunlight streams into the clearing, and only the soft lullaby of foraging birds breaks the silence. It is eerie to be bathed in such warm sunlight and touched by the evil of the midnight ceremony. Dropping the sheet, I try to walk casually and calmly back toward my post. I have lost my desire to search this clearing further for other nests. I check all the nests in my clearing and settle down to watch the nest where the three hatchlings have emerged. But I am edgy, and it is harder to remain still. The minutes drag on, and all I can picture is the burned cross, silhouetted against the blazing sun.

At 3:30, another hatchling puts up its head, looks around, and remains absolutely still for 23 minutes. It is joined by another, and the two peer around—but the waiting is nearly unbearable. Finally, 44 minutes later, they start slowly, then rapidly, to crawl out of their hole. They crawl out of the other side of the nest from the first batch, but soon they change course and follow the scent trail toward the same blueberries their siblings had sought. Six hatchlings have emerged, leaving another three still in the nest. I should really stay the night to make observations tomorrow, and to make sure that none emerge at night. I have a flashlight, and could check the nest periodically. Some turtles emerge at night to avoid avian predators, and I really want to find out if some snakes do the same.

I start to worry about the long trek back to the car in the darkness; I cannot decide whether I would be safer going when it is light and I can see danger, or going when I can hide in the darkness. The moon will provide enough light to find my car. I need to get my sleeping bag and more food from the cooler. I will be nearly invisible in my brown sleeping bag, hidden by the pine boughs. Even if any bikers came this way they might not see me. They don't expect to find anyone in the pines at night, only their own gang. Any motorcycle sounds would surely wake me.

Images of the charred cross linger, amid thoughts of a ghostlike presence moving across the clearing, covered by a sheet. Stark fear surges through me, and I know I simply cannot remain all night. Better to sleep in the locked car and venture forth in the early morning, before first light. Carefully I put sand in the tiny vortex and smooth it over. This will allow me to tell in the morning whether any hatchlings have emerged and may also prevent any nocturnal predators from finding them. Picking up my gear, I creep back toward the car—hoping I can sleep in the cramped quarters.

Mammals of the Pines

We have come to the Barrens in the dead of winter just to see what it is like, to experience the cold and snow of early February, and to make sure that no one has disturbed our Pine Snake hibernacula. For many years we have followed snakes that spend the winter in a den over six feet below ground. The snow is nearly gone, remaining only in small patches under the low Pitch Pine branches that shade the ground. Blue Jays call loudly from the tree tops and begin to chase one another. Always a bit pesky, they become more so, engaging in long chases and bouts of scolding, sounding like angry neighbors screaming across an invisible fence (fig. 15.1).

The Blue Jays fly noisily to a nearby pine and peck at the bark angrily. Suddenly they disappear, replaced by Gray Squirrels running up and down the larger oaks, chasing one another. Gray Squirrels are not very common in the pines, usually preferring the edge areas that have more tall oaks. Red Squirrels are the more common squirrel of the pines. Although they are mainly gray at this time of year, Gray Squirrels have a reddish brown tinge at the top of the head, back, and tail. Their long, dark gray fur is tipped with silver, and when backlit by the early morning sun, they are surrounded in a silvery glow. They spend the cold winter nights in holes in hollow stumps or in old buildings. When it is not too cold, they stay in leaf nests built among the outer branches of trees. At first these odd affairs look like a few leaves blown there by the wind, but they are actually ball nests carefully constructed by squirrels. The base of these nests is made of small twigs, with leaves piled on top, and the inside is lined with finely shredded bark or lichens. The Gray Squirrels are usually toasty in their winter nests because it is not as cold in the pines as it is farther north, but sometimes when the cold winds whistle through the low pines and oaks, they take refuge in holes in trees or in hollow logs on the ground.

One squirrel has staked out the oak not too far away from me, and a fine oak it is. It is taller than the rest, and the trunk is at least eight inches

15.1. Blue Jays are often the sentinels for other species, calling loudly when danger is near.

thick. Mostly he sits in the branches, peering about, his long tail twitching rhythmically. He cannot seem to remain in one place for long, and he soon scurries up and down the tree, rapidly swishing his tail. Each time his tail twitches, he gives a harsh churring chatter, and his whole body quakes, his tail jerking up and down over his back. He never tires of chattering. Turning, he runs and then stops abruptly, his tail straight out from his body, as if he had been taught perfect posture. He faces downward, spreads his legs for a firmer grip, and pumps his tail up over his shoulder, chattering loudly. He begins to run, and then just as suddenly he stops, sniffs the bark, and begins to nose in the cracks and crevices. Carefully he pulls out a seed, no doubt stored there by an industrious Tufted Titmouse or Carolina Chickadee, but he eats it anyway. Within seconds he resumes his slow walk down the trunk, pumping his tail, and elevating his head in a warning display. When he reaches the bottom, he turns and climbs halfway back up the tree, where he stops, humps his back to form an inverted U, and begins gently to pump his tail up and down in an exaggerated tail bob. Every few seconds he walks higher, and repeats the display. When he reaches a strong horizontal branch, he stops, elevates his tail completely over his back, and pumps it slowly.

On a nearby pine, another squirrel runs down the trunk until he is 10 feet from the ground. Spreading his feet squarely to the side, he elevates his head and pumps his tail rhythmically. For nearly half an hour each runs up and down his respective tree, pumping his tail and churring vigorously one minute and moving slowly and deliberately the next, as if merely searching for food—as if they hadn't a care in the world. This is displacement behavior, that is, an animal performs a behavior that appears unrelated to its previous interactions. Only a stolen glance at the other squirrel gives him away. People do the same thing—when we are embarrassed or angry, we often look away or begin to pay attention to a newspaper or other distraction.

Without warning, the squirrel that seemed so intent on defending his pine descends to the ground and runs swiftly up the oak, chasing the "owner" ahead of him. The top squirrel turns to look down, and they face off (fig. 15.2). Turning again, they race up the tree with lightning speed, and within seconds they are near the top, where the branches are not strong enough to hold their weight. Both tumble down to lower branches, clutch each other as they fall even lower, and quickly dissolve into separate animals running in opposite directions.

15.2. Gray Squirrels chase one another in their defense of territories.

Within minutes both are back, clinging to their respective trees, eyeing each other alertly, their tails twitching slightly. I can recognize the squirrel from the oak tree because his tail has a slight crick in it, as if it was caught in a closing door, or more likely, in the jaws of a predator. He seems more frail, and I secretly root for him. The minutes pass, and both remain immobile, clasping their trees, one with its front feet reaching out in midair, clinging only with its hind legs.

The detente is short lived, and within 15 minutes the "pine" squirrel has run over to the oak tree and is threatening the "oak" squirrel with the bent tail. Bent Tail has now decided to fight, and instead of retreating up the oak, he faces the intruder. For several minutes they face each other again, pumping their tails vigorously and bobbing their heads slightly, then churring. Each grips the branch tighter, and the face-off continues. When the intruder moves in closer, Bent Tail holds his ground and quickly pounces on the other one. The thin branch will not hold their weight, and the whole mass of swirling, scratching squirrels tumbles to the ground once again. But now, instead of going their separate ways, Bent Tail chases the intruder 30 feet away until he goes up another pine. Bent Tail does not follow, however, but runs rapidly back to his own oak, only to find another squirrel clinging to the oak trunk, facing him. Bent Tail is not giving up so easily, and he runs rapidly toward this new intruder, chasing him to the tree top. With one glance back, the intruder leaps downward to a nearby oak sapling. Back and forth they go, the three squirrels chasing one an other up and down six different trees. This is so frenetic that I wonder if they are playing rather than being territorial. The switches are very rapid, and it is not apparent how they choose whether to chase or be chased. When birds defend territories they are more ritualistic, usually fighting only at the edge, and they seldom engage in such long physical encounters. Squirrels, however, are more interested in defending particular trees rather than all the space in between.

After half an hour of this, the squirrels seem to tire and join two other squirrels that are calmly feeding on the ground. They move over the white sand, searching in the lichens, leaves, and low shrubs for berries or acorns hidden last fall. One finds a small dried mushroom from the summer growing season and chews on it. During particularly cold winters when the ground is snow covered for long periods, they even eat the inner bark and green layers of woody plants, but usually they can find acorns they have hidden or that still cling to the branches.

Squirrels were so abundant when the European settlers first arrived that great hordes of them made inroads into corn fields, a sight that we can hardly imagine today. In 1749 they invaded Pennsylvania in such numbers that the state put a bounty on them, and 640,000 squirrel bounties were paid out. Ohio dealt with the problem by requiring each white man to deliver 100 squirrel scalps a year or pay a three-dollar penalty, actually quite a stiff fine in those days. On days when we count 28 squirrels at the bird feeders at our Somerset home, 100 scalps doesn't seem so impossible. When we first moved into our house, we tried trapping squirrels and moving them to a nearby nature reserve, but we ended up with more squirrels than we started with. My guess is that the squirrels that lived around our house had territories and kept the neighbors out. Without "our" squirrels, dozens could move in without fear from territorial ones.

Naturalists' accounts from several decades ago describe large migrations of Gray Squirrels that followed the failure of acorn crops. Such lemminglike migrations still occur today, although in lower numbers and at intervals of many years. These unusual nomadic wanderings are reported in local newspapers. Many years ago hundreds of squirrels were observed crossing the Bear Mountain Bridge over the Hudson River, holding up traffic as they scurried from one side to the other. Only two years ago Mike and I found over 70 dead squirrels along a 50-mile stretch of the New York Thruway, indicating another mass movement. At the same time, my brother Melvin, who traps nuisance wildlife in suburban Schenectady, said he caught record numbers of squirrels in his traps. We have no idea what starts these migrations, or even why they end—maybe too many squirrels in one place with too little food.

There are actually far fewer squirrels in the Pine Barrens than there are in the nearby retirement communities carved out of the Barrens or in central and northern New Jersey. There the squirrels have few predators and a constant supply of bird seed and shrubby oat acorns (fig. 15.3).

I often have my behavioral biology students at Rutgers study squirrels because they are so common, engaging, and active. In residential areas they make their nests under eaves, in attics, or in abandoned buildings. But here in the pines they usually have their young in tree nests. They generally prefer to have their dens in large trees that are 40 to 50 years old, accounting for their low populations in the Pine Barrens. Their brood of four to six young are born in late March or early April. The female is quite protective of her young, and if the nest is disturbed she will carry them, catlike, to another, safer place.

Gray Squirrels maintain a home range of 2 to 8 acres, depending on food supplies, and their ranges overlap. In my suburban Somerset neighborhood, a given squirrel

15.3. *Gray Squirrels forage in suburban developments as well as in the pine woods.*

regularly visits 8 to 10 backyards each day looking for food. The squirrels maintain a social hierarchy that depends on rules based on age and sex. More-dominant squirrels have larger home ranges, and no doubt we have been watching antics designed to determine this dominance. Squirrels serve a very important function in forests because they disperse acorns, burying some where they can later germinate and grow. Biologists call this coevolution: the trees make use of the ability of squirrels to disperse their acorn seeds, and the trees provide the squirrels with acorns.

The fight begins anew among the squirrels I am watching, and they clamber back and forth from tree to tree, until it is difficult to see who is winning. Sometimes they jump from the top of one tree to the top of another in a bold leap that is both strong and graceful. They bound across the ground, their bushy gray tail flowing behind them in a dance that is wonderful to watch. Just as suddenly, they stop, pick up an acorn in their front paws, and, standing on their hind feet, begin to eat while they look around for the competition. They use their tail as a prop. Another not far

15.4. Pitch Pines grow following a fire by sprouting tufts of needles from the nodes of the branches.

away sniffs the ground briefly, digs down through the lichens and sand, and comes up with a nice fat acorn that has been buried for many months. Whether they are digging up their own stores or someone else's is unclear, but I always find it amazing that they can locate an acorn when they really need one.

Leaving the squirrels, we walk to our snake hibernaculum, through an area that burned last year. The pines are sprouting, and the fire did not kill them (fig. 15.4). We are relieved to see that the ground looks undisturbed. Brown and dark-red oak leaves have blown over the small entrance, obscuring it from sight. No mammals have burrowed down, and the snakes are still safe in their underground den, well below the frost line. I like to check the hibernacula a couple of times during the winter so that I can figure out the timing of mammalian predation (if any occurs). Sometimes a large burrow leads downward, suggesting that a fox or skunk has found the snakes resting below.

Smaller Deer Lurk in the Pines

We have lingered longer than we thought we had, watching the antics of the squirrels. The sun is so low that it no longer provides any heat, and the cold begins to seep in. At the edge of a clearing, a White-tailed Deer stands silently, looking in all directions before inching forward. It is nearly dark, and the deer is only visible because of its slight movement. Taking a few tentative steps, it stops to eat some short grass. It is still grayish in late winter, although it will soon turn a reddish brown. I am always surprised at how small the deer in the pines are compared to White-tails near our home. The habitat in the Barrens is marginal for deer, and the winter browse is not quite nutritious enough. Maybe I'm too used to suburban deer that feed on lush backyard gardens in the spring and summer and ornamental shrubs in the fall and winter. The deer on my parents' farm in upstate New York are even larger, but they feed in vast fields of squash, tomatoes, melons, and other vegetables in the summer, alfalfa in the fall, and abandoned crops during the fall and winter.

Behind us, another, smaller doe steps out cautiously, creeping forward into the opening. Within minutes, five females are foraging in what passes as a Barrens meadow. Two are pregnant, having bred in November, but they will not give birth until late May or early June in the pines. During most of the winter they browsed on woody vegetation, acorns, and any herbaceous plants they can find. Even in the summer the pines are not excellent places for deer because there is not a high diversity of herbaceous plants for them to eat; berries are not very big, and they are often reduced to eating acorns. In the fall they eat Greenbrier fruits, as well as grasses and herbs.

White-tails are common from Maine to Florida, and they are equally at home in pines as they are in hardwood forests. Large bucks in the north can weigh 200 pounds, but in the New Jersey Pine Barrens they rarely exceed 100 pounds. Deer were extremely important as a source of protein for paleo-Indians, the Lenape, and the early European settlers. Often, deer meat was the only thing standing between the settlers and starvation. Much of the clothing of the Lenape was made from tanned deer hide, the antlers were fashioned into tools, and the sinews were used for bow strings. It is still the most common game mammal east of the Rockies. Its cunning makes it a worthy hunting opponent, and the antlers of large males are highly prized. In New Jersey alone, annual deer-hunting expenditures exceed $50 million.

In the winter, deer rely heavily on Scrub Oak acorns, but sometimes the crop is poor or the acorns are covered in snow. This leads to poor reproduction; not all females are mated, some abort, and some give birth to fawns that are low in weight. Males that have poor antler development have difficulty fighting other males during the fall rut. A 2½-year-old buck in the Pine Barrens may produce only a single, unbranched or "spike" antler, while the same-aged buck in the forests of northern New Jersey may have antlers with eight to ten points. Some deer in the pines starve in the winter, particularly when deep snow cover makes foraging more difficult. Sometimes there are just too many deer for the habitat, and if there were fewer, those that survived would be healthier and would give birth to twins instead of low-weight single fawns.

Deer browse heavily on small Virginia Pitch Pine, Short-leaf Pine, and Pitch Pine in the winter, but once the seedlings grow over a foot or so tall the deer no longer eat them, and they turn to the sprouts of Scrub Oaks. Mostly, however, the deer retreat into the Atlantic White Cedar swamps that provide cover from the cold winds and drifting snow. In the White Cedar, the deer form herds of 30 or more, trampling the snow to maintain open areas where they can graze. These openings and trails are called "yards." The deer herds sometimes eat so much of the cedars that there no longer are any viable growing points, and the trees die. In many places in the Pine Barrens the high populations of deer overbrowse the young cedar trees, making it difficult for the stands to regenerate after logging or wildfires. Atlantic White Cedar was heavily harvested by the early colonists, but we have no doubt lost additional cedar swamps from the combined actions of the loggers and deer.

After about 200 days of gestation, the females give birth to one or two fawns in early summer. The reddish brown fawns have pale white spots, which they keep until their first molt in the winter. For the first few days the almost helpless fawns lie curled in a ball; the spots allow them to melt into their surroundings because they look like dappled sunlight on the forest floor. The females leave them in the shrubbery or deep within the cedars as they go forth to forage. They return only once a day to suckle them, but otherwise they leave them alone. This affords the young protection because they have no odor that can attract predators, and the mother remains elsewhere to keep her odor from giving away the location of the defenseless fawn. The fawns usually remain absolutely still until they have been discovered, and then they bound quickly and explosively away. Dogs and foxes can pass only a few feet from a fawn hidden in the dense vegetation and fail to smell it.

After the first couple of weeks, the fawns no longer stay hidden in the brush but travel with their mother. They are not weaned until they are about eight months old, and even then, some remain with their mother until she gives birth again the following year. Deer are solitary in the summer, or wander in groups of two or three. Foraging in the summer is relatively easy because there are many fresh green herbs to eat. They eat what is available, but when given a choice, they have an astonishing ability to choose the most nutritious foods.

Young males begin growing their antlers at about 10 months of age, in early April. The antlers, composed of bone containing calcium and phosphorus, are solid and do not have any marrow. During their period of growth the antlers are covered in a layer of blood-vessel-rich skin, called velvet. The antlers are sensitive, and the deer are careful not to touch the tangles of branches as they move through the pines. With the onset of the breeding season in September, the blood supply to the antlers shuts down, the velvet dies, and the buck is quick to scrape it off on tree trunks. During the rutting season the males paw at the ground, making an indentation. They then urinate on their hind leg gland. The urine slowly trickles to the ground, leaving a pungent odor of sexual pheromones and urine on the sand. Females are attracted to these scrapes, and courtship begins.

Although deer can live to be 15 years or older, in the wild most White-tailed Deer live only four to seven years. Bucks usually have a much shorter lifespan because of hunting pressure; most bucks live to be only three to five years old. The hunting pressure is less in the Pine Barrens than in most other parts of New Jersey because the deer are smaller, there are few trophy deer, and it is impossible to penetrate the dwarf pines.

We pause at the edge of a large clearing to watch a group of five does accompanied by two of last year's fawns, which are smaller. They eat quietly, but when they hear the loud, raucous alarm call of a Blue Jay, they all look up, watching and waiting. As if by signal, one turns, raises its white tail, and bounds off, to be followed quickly by the others. Raising the white tail is called "tail-flagging," and it serves many functions. Because it is so conspicuous, it alerts any unwary deer that danger is about. Birds and other mammals also respond, and I have watched birds scatter and Woodchucks run for cover when a deer turned and bounded off with its white tail flag-waving. But more importantly, tail flagging signals predators that they have been detected, and there is really no reason to give chase. I tend to favor the explanation that it is telling the predator that it has been discovered because solitary deer tail-flag when departing as well. A White-tailed Deer can outrun any predators in the pines except men on four-wheel-drive vehicles.

Masked Bandits of the Pines

We creep forward and pause to watch a Raccoon, mostly hidden beneath the vegetation hanging over a small stream, dipping something in the water with its paws. We catch a glimpse of a fish before it disappears, melting into the dense brush with only some waving branches indicating its passage. Raccoon paws are remarkably manipulative, which gave rise to their Algonquin name of "Ah-coon-em," which means "scratches with its hands." The early settlers could not pronounce this, and so shortened it to Raccoon. They are also called "masked bandits" because of their black face mask and their annoying reputation for stealing whatever they can find.

There is little doubt that Raccoons can be very cute, but they make bad pets, particularly the males who are prone to rip up furniture, rugs, and anything else in their way. Female Raccoons were once very popular as pets, and both Calvin Coolidge and Herbert Hoover kept them in the White House. They lived long enough to have second terms—the Raccoons as well as the presidents. Raccoons should not be taken as pets because they may carry rabies. Most of the rabies cases in humans are from Raccoons, and pets can get rabies from them as well. Any strange-acting Raccoon should be avoided, especially one that moves toward you. Run!

Raccoons are widely distributed, not only in pineland communities, but in nearly every habitat from the deepest hardwood forests to urban parks, provided the areas are large enough. They occur over most of the United States, south to South America. Their only requirement seems to be water. They have adapted well to suburbia, going from garbage can to garbage can, and in some places are fed by unthinking people. They are quite adept at coming in "cat doors" and feasting on cat food at night, while the occupants of the house are fast asleep. My friend Patti Murry once came downstairs to find three Raccoons happily eating cat food, while the cat stood by, miffed but avoiding a tangle.

The Raccoon we watch is quite large, so it is probably a male since they are considerably larger than females. In New York and New Jersey, females usually weigh more than 20 pounds, and large males can weigh 50 pounds. Farther south, in Florida, females usually weigh only eight or ten pounds. In general, warm-blooded animals that live closer to the equator are smaller than those living farther north, an adaptation to allow for more heat loss from the greater surface area; smaller animals have more surface area for their bulk or volume. Conversely, larger bodies can conserve heat more efficiently.

Males usually have larger home ranges—defined as the area in which an animal normally lives—than do females. The males require up to four times as much space as females. The home ranges of both male and female Raccoons overlap, and they run into each other now and then with few overt interactions. Females remain close to home, especially when they have young, but the males wander all year, walking farther and faster than females, sometimes moving up to 400 yards an hour.

During the breeding season, the female holes up in a den and waits for the male to find her. He moves in for a few days, they mate, and then he leaves to search for another female in her den. The young are born with their eyes closed and are really quite helpless. They only begin to make short forays from the den when they are eight to twelve weeks old, but they still remain with the female, who defends them against predators. She leaves the den only long enough to find food and then returns to her young. During the day, Raccoons usually sleep in trees, so it is unusual to see one about in the late afternoon. Sometimes, two or three may use the same tree, particularly a mother and her young. These same groups then go out foraging together for three or four hours at night before returning to their resting trees. Although wild Raccoons can live up to 20 years, most live only two or three.

Raccoons are good prey for a variety of predators, such as Bobcat, Coyotes, and Panthers in the south. Humans, rather than predators, pose the greatest problem for Raccoons. Many thousands are killed on highways every year, particularly when the animals are dispersing after the breeding season. They are also hunted, mostly for the sport of treeing them with dogs, but in some places they are eaten by people or are fed to dogs. Depending on the fashion, they are also trapped for their pelts, and some are still used for "coonskin" hats. Despite all these adversities, Raccoon populations are booming everywhere.

We watched the Raccoon for too long, and it is getting dark. In the lingering twilight we pick our way cautiously through the pines to the car, and sit quietly, waiting for nightfall. The cold seeps in quickly, and I am reminded that winter is still around us. The Blue Jays have quieted down, and we listen intently for any night creatures. Very faintly we hear the deep booming "whoo who who whoo whoo" of a Great Horned Owl. I never tire of that sound, for it takes me back to my childhood when I used to lie in bed, listening to owls calling from the oak woods behind our house. I could imagine the owl quietly incubating in a tree not far away, and could visualize the nest then, as I can now, because my father had led me through the dark woods to show me a Great Horned Owl nest on a snowy evening a half century ago. Even today, he still stops while checking on greenhouses to listen to the eerie sound.

We are parked not far from an oak-pine woods where there are some tall Black Oaks that are large enough to support a Great Horned Owl. These owls are not common in the pines, but a few pairs do nest on the edges. The Barred Owl is more abundant, mainly along rivers and streams, but they have not yet begun to call; the Great Horned Owls have the night to themselves. The hooting sounds a long ways off, too far to venture in the mud and on snow patches in the dark. Without moonlight the woods are pitch black.

Owls Rule the Night

Great Horned Owls are quite predictable: they live in the same place, use the same nest in the same tree from year to year, cherish the same mate, and do not bother migrating south. This one may have been here for years. When most other owls, most passerines, and many other birds have gone south for the winter, the Great Horned Owls stay at home. In the dead of winter their thoughts turn to mating, and they begin to court when the ground is still snow covered. They need trees with strong horizontal branches that can support their large, heavy stick nests. But once they have a nest, they just keep adding more twigs and sticks each year to repair it, as well as some cedar branches, a bit of brightly colored string, and feathers.

For centuries they were safe in the oaks at the edge of the pines; the Indians revered owls and did not harm them. The owls were harbingers of spring, foretelling of the renewal just a few weeks away. Even the early settlers ignored them: they were not worth hunting, and they provided no useful products. The owls came out at night to patrol the forest floor for mice and rabbits. Although in other regions they were persecuted because they killed free-ranging chickens, the early pineys kept few fowl, and the owls were tolerated. Habitat loss and logging present problems for the owls because they need tall trees for nesting. Unexpectedly, some Great Horned Owls have adapted to suburban living, nesting in the giant oaks that are left standing and hunting in schoolyards and on abandoned lots by night. Most of the children playing soccer never realize the owls are there. I have known an ornithologist or two who were first turned on to birds by watching a Great Horned Owl hidden in the oaks near their schoolyard.

It is the snowmobilers who have disturbed the tranquil winter nesting trees of Great Horned Owls. They flush from the nest each time a noisy snowmobile shatters the silence, leaving the eggs or young unattended and subject to chilling winds. Logging at the wrong time of year, or other loud disturbances when owls are nesting, can keep them off their eggs for too long as well. Now in February, Great Horned Owls are sitting on eggs already. They are the earliest breeder in the pines, and will no doubt have young in another month. I have watched a female owl incubate, covered by two inches of falling snow, her head hunched down into her back to conserve heat. There may still be snow on the ground when they first start feeding their young, but the male is not deterred from his task of finding rats, mice, rabbits, woodchucks and even skunks to bring back to the female. She rips pieces of meat from the carcasses for the young, and he goes back to searching for more prey.

In early March, when it is a bit warmer, I come back to look for the owl's nest. I am sorry now that Mike and I did not walk back to search for the nest, but it was dark and cold, and the pines were foreboding. The forest is quiet; I cannot find either the owl or a nest, and I wonder if we heard a solitary male searching for a female. Perhaps he did not find one and moved farther north into deeper forests where there are more Great Horned Owls. Instead, I find only a pair of Mallards incubating beside a small wet slough—the male stands guard nearby, a practice only of Mallards in the Northeast. In other, more rural areas, males desert the females shortly after mating (fig. 15.5). I think that the males mate-guard their females because there are so many Mallards in suburban areas. Faced with intense competition from other males, it is prudent to guard their female, much like a jealous boyfriend watches over his sweetheart

15.5. *Female Mallard incubates while her male stands guard nearby.*

in a crowded bar. Both are ready to defend "their" female from any unwanted suitors.

I walk on, enjoying the solitude; it is still too early for many birds to be
back, although the Blue Jays are scolding each other. Deeper in the pines
I come across two Red Squirrels, running up and down the trees. Red
Squirrels are creatures of the pines, and most New Jersey Red Squirrels
are found in the Pine Barrens although they also occur in hardwood
forests of northwestern New Jersey. They are much smaller than the
Gray Squirrel, and far more rusty. Their underparts are pure white, and
they have a white ring around their deep brown eyes. It is the middle of
spring, and they still have the deep black line on their sides, which they
will lose by fall.

Red Squirrels feed on pine seeds, and large piles of opened and dis-
mantled pine cones lie discarded at the base of favored feeding trees or
stumps. Unlike Gray Squirrels, which bury acorns or other seeds anywhere that takes their fancy, Red Squirrels store most of their food in underground caches. I have found caches in abandoned fox dens, in old
Raccoon holes, in Pine Snake burrows, and in wood piles. Most of the
middens I have found contained a stash of seeds the size of a large cabbage or soccer ball, but they can store a bushel or more. They often store

far more than they could possibly need, and they avidly defend these caches against other squirrels, particularly during the winter.

It is interesting that Red Squirrels put their middens in the dens of their predators, but they always use abandoned ones, except for Pine Snake burrows. Over the years we have found many middens of Red Squirrels in Pine Snake hibernacula, some in active snake burrows, others in tunnels the snakes have not used for a year or two. Pine Snakes, however, are not likely to capture a Red Squirrel in the hibernaculum because they do not eat in the winter, and when the snakes leave in the spring, they move very slowly and don't normally eat until they have shed their skin for the first time. Red Squirrels abandon these winter middens long before warm breezes of spring awaken the Pine Snakes enough to leave the dens. The harsh conditions of winter have already passed, and the squirrels are out frolicking in the pines.

Red Squirrels also live in nests in trunks or old stumps, but in a pinch they build a nest of twigs and leaves in the crotch of a tree. They usually produce two litters in one season, one in early spring, and one in early summer. After a gestation period of 40 days, females give birth to up to five young, which stay with them until fall. The life of a Red Squirrel is far more hazardous than that of a Gray Squirrel because they are smaller and have many more predators. They are just the right size for foxes, cats, weasels, Mink, large hawks and owls, and even Bobcat in some places. In the Pine Barrens they are also plagued by tree-climbing snakes, and if they fall into a pond, they are likely to succumb to Snapping Turtles, and even to fish. On a warm sunny day in late March I found a five-foot-long Pine Snake basking on a branch, 30 feet up in a tree, blending in so perfectly it could easily capture an unwary Red Squirrel. Red Squirrels could get into trouble with the Pine Snakes for another reason: they are very curious and often come to investigate anything new in their environment, such as a snake in a tree. The snakes are quick to capture them by striking, coiling, and squeezing the life from them before they can escape.

The squirrels stand nearby, chattering and clucking noisily with an extensive vocabulary that does not seem to repeat itself, giving rise to their nickname of "chatterbox." They sometimes play in groups and often forage together, moving quickly over the pines as if they were jungle gyms. They take quick aim and easily leap great distances in a single jump, landing unerringly in another pine.

Other than Red Squirrels, there are few mammals that dwell predominantly in the New Jersey Pine Barrens. Most mammals that live in the pines also occur in many other habitats in the region. Of the over

50 species of terrestrial mammals that occur in New Jersey, 34 have been recorded in the Pine Barrens, but only 20 are very common. These include Eastern Moles, White-footed Mouse, Red-backed Vole, Pine Vole, Eastern Cottontail, Red Squirrel, Beaver, Gray Fox, Raccoon, Striped Skunk, and White-tailed Deer. The Pine Vole is a specialist in the pines, but we rarely see these creatures, except when we set up traps to catch snakes. It is interesting that so many reptiles and amphibians are unique to the barrens, but there are so few mammals. Perhaps habitat diversity is more important to mammals.

The diversity of mammals in the Pine Barrens is low, as is the diversity of birds. When there are few species in any habitat it is easy to disrupt the balance among the species because the presence of each species is important for other species. When the number of small mammals declines, the populations of snakes and other predators that rely on them for food declines as well. When the number of Raccoons and foxes increases, they exert undue predation pressures on the small mammals, birds, and reptiles that they eat.

It is the disruption of the natural relationships among organisms that has been the most critical impact of man in the pines. The animals can tolerate slight decreases in habitat, even with some fragmentation, but the altering of both the kinds of animals in the pines and the relative populations of these animals is difficult to cope with. Increases in populations of Raccoons brought about by the constant presence of food near habitation can have devastating effects on many ground-nesting animals such as snakes, birds, and lizards. The animals of the pines are adapting to these new challenges, and many are learning to make use of Raccoon dens for their own summer or winter dens.

In the lingering light I watch for hunting Great Horned Owls until it is too dark to see. I feel protected by the darkness and the isolation, for few people wander these woods even during the day. Leaning against the car I listen, hoping to hear an owl. Without the sunlight the barrens are cold and damp, and I imagine small birds huddled together within the dense pine boughs, and rattlesnakes hidden in the cedar roots of the bogs. The moon rising just above the pines is huge and a fiery yellow. The silence is broken by a chorus of Coyotes, composed of eerie yips, howls and mournful wailings. They are never quite in unison, as if there is no leader. The yippy-howls crescendo until they send chills down my back, and then there is silence.

Coyotes are relative newcomers to the Northeast and to the edge of the Barrens, but they have adapted readily to the open pines where they can hunt Cottontail Rabbits and take down the occasional deer weakened by a long winter. They are true generalists, however, and will eat mice, rats, squirrels, carrion, snakes, birds, fruits, and berries, and even watermelons or other vegetables. Radio-tracking data indicate that Coyotes do not eat garbage even when it is readily available. Weighing 30 to 40 pounds, an adult Coyote resembles a German shepherd or a Husky. They can be distinguished because Coyotes hold their tail down when running, while the dogs hold it up, and foxes hold their tails straight out.

In the silence, I wonder what effect these predators will have on the pine barrens ecosystem of the Northeast. Will the rabbits crash beneath the pressure? Over the last ten years, Woodchucks and Cottontails have almost completely disappeared from my parents' and brother Roy's farm, to be replaced by at least two packs of Coyotes that howl on most moonlit nights. They are a success largely because they can live close to people and can fit into the open habitat patches that manage to survive. Coyotes remain within three or four miles of their den, defending their territories by howling, as well as marking with urine and droppings.

As the moon rises well above the trees, a burst of howling sounds way too close, and I am torn between listening to the yipping wails and heading for home. Reluctant to shatter the chorus with the sounds of an engine, I wait and listen for the answering calls of another pack. Finally in the distance, I hear the faint yipping of a different pack. Ten minutes later "my" pack begins yowling anew, but it is farther away from me, moving in the direction of the intruding pack. I imagine their encounter in the depths of the pines, and visions of their standoff linger with me as I thread my way over sandy roads toward home.

16

There Are Snakes below the Ground

Small patches of snow from a late winter storm linger in the shade beneath low-hanging pine boughs and nestle in the crevices beside fallen logs and piles of brush. The branches are so low that in places they form a carpet of green. The ground is covered with wet oak leaves packed like soggy sheets of paper, strewn about in various shades of brown, mauve, and tan. The scraggly oak trees are barren, misshapen, their buds just swollen enough to suggest that spring is not far off. The needles on the pines are a dull green, as if they are tired of the long wait for the warm sun of spring.

The New Jersey Pine Barrens is silent, there is no sign of movement. The birds have not returned from southern climes, and the few Blue Jay calls are scattered to the wind. At the edge of the clearing a small deer stands motionless, watching our strange group. She is partly hidden by the low scrubby pines, and I know she is there only because I saw her tail move once. She has not raised her tail in the characteristic warning, and so I know she will remain where she is. There may be others with her, but they are well hidden. It has been a hard winter with deep snows that lasted for many days at a time, and deer had difficulty finding food. Many of the them survived the harsh winter by raiding ornamental plantings in the senior citizen communities that are encroaching on the barrens. Some houses have foundation plantings of yew bushes, which provide excellent browse when other foods are covered with a blanket of wet snow. Many people treasure the small herds of deer that wander through their yards in the winter as a reminder that some wildlife manages to survive the deep snows and harsh cold of a northern winter. Others do not, and deer are vilified as insatiable marauders of the night.

Turning from the deer, Bob Zappalorti and I peer at the ground, but the mat of leaves is unbroken. We are in the middle of a large clearing, surrounded by endless acres of Pine Barrens interrupted only by soft sand roads that lead deeper into the pines. It is time for our annual late winter ritual—one we perform in late February or early March each year. We are here to dig up our snakes. Since 1986 we have been studying the wintering behavior of Pine Snakes. In the early years we agonized long and hard about our effect on snake lifestyle, but the snakes return each year, and our disturbance is offset by the fact that we rebuild fortified hibernacula (or dens) that skunks and foxes cannot dig up easily. We pick our date depending on how cold the winter has been, when the snow cover disappears, and how warm February is. We wait until the snow has melted, when it is warm enough for us to work, but not so warm that hibernating snakes are awakening. We must dig them up before any have emerged, but after the ground has thawed and it is warm enough to dig. It must also be warm enough so the snakes are not unduly stressed.

Not much is known about wintering behavior of reptiles in the northern regions of North America because it is hard to find just where they hibernate. Many reptiles hibernate solitarily, buried below logs, rocks, old roots, or in the burrows of other animals. Others, like Garter Snakes, sometimes hibernate in old foundations, under wooden steps, or in the cellars of unsuspecting homeowners. Garter Snakes are particularly interesting because at the northern limit of their range in Canada, they hibernate in sinkholes where hundreds and sometimes thousands gather together. They form spectacular masses of writhing snakes when they emerge in the spring. The sex ratio is unbalanced, and hundreds of males may gather around every female, each male trying to be the one to fertilize her. But here, in the New Jersey Pine Barrens, the Garter Snakes live on the edges of the pines and hibernate under old foundations, fallen logs, and in holes in tree trunks that lead underground. Their courting masses are smaller, but I've found up to 20 or 30 males wriggling around one female.

We glance at the nearest pine tree, gauge the distance, and bend to gently pull the oak leaves away, revealing a tiny hole not much bigger than the mouth of a large aspirin bottle. With the leaves removed, the edges of the hole appear smooth and well worn. This is a good sign that indicates that many snakes slithered through this opening last fall. I gently push a yardstick down the hole as far as it will go so that we do not lose track of the entranceway.

We are digging up a snake hibernaculum, defined as a place where reptiles go to hibernate during the cold winter months. They must find a place that is below the frost layer where their body temperature will go low enough so that they do not have to eat and hardly breathe, but will stay high enough so they do not freeze. It must also be safe from predators since they are completely defenseless while hibernating.

Bob and I have brought several people with us to help in the fascinating task.

"Well," I say to the assembled group of students and associates, "let's begin here. First we have to remove the old logs and then we can scrape the oak leaves and needles into a pile so that we can replace them when we are done."

"Are you sure this is where you want to dig? It all looks the same to me," Says Jorge. A tall, dark, handsome student from Puerto Rico, Jorge Saliva is remarkably interested in snakes but is mystified that I like them as well as my beloved seabirds. He thinks I am a bit *loco*. Jorge came out with us despite the cold, for he is not used to the freezing weather. He saw his first snow at our annual Christmas party, and we all enjoyed sharing his pleasure of a new experience.

"Of course I am sure. Why?"

"Well, it doesn't look any different from any other place to me. There are holes all over—we can't dig them all up," Carl answers. Carl Safina, then a biologist with the National Audubon Society, had come out to see Pine Snakes in the wild. He lived with a Gopher Snake for nearly 20 years and he will be thrilled to see a wild Pine Snake. Gopher Snakes are closely related to Pine Snakes, and they live in the western United States. Some herpetologists even think they are the same species. I do not agree, however, because their behavior is very, very different. Carl divides his time between the open ocean and meetings aimed at protecting the creatures of the deep—for fish are wildlife also. Today, many years later, Carl is president of his own Blue Ocean Institute, dedicated to conservation of the oceans.

"Believe me, this is the place. Now that the leaves are out of the way, we can start to dig. We need to clear an area about three feet wide and six feet long, starting here."

"Won't we hurt the snakes?" Jorge asks.

"Not until we get down about two and a half feet. We can use the big shovels and dig without worrying. The snakes are always below that level. Still, be careful. It is possible one of them may have started to move up in the tunnels, preparing to emerge for the spring," I reply.

The clash of shovels echoes across the clearing as we bring tools from the truck. We are alone here, and there is no other sound. The diggers get in each other's way and have to synchronize their shoveling to avoid injuring one another. Their faces are skeptical, but still they dig. What else are students to do?

Bob and I began studying the hibernating behavior of Pine Snakes so that we could understand what kind of hibernation places they needed. With so much residential development in the pines, suitable snake habitat is being destroyed at a rapid rate, and with it, the snakes' hibernation spots. To mitigate these effects, we wanted to build hibernacula that the snakes could use. We learned enough in the early years so that we can construct such hibernacula, and Bob regularly patrols them. Each fall Pine Snakes, Black Racers, and even Corn Snakes bask at the entrances and go far below when the cold weather sets in. It is unusual for several species to overwinter together, but these other species make use of the digging ability of the Pine Snakes (or in this case, of the hibernacula we construct). This management tool has been a success, and the artificial hibernacula are used by many different species. We also want to find out whether the same individuals use the same hibernaculum from year to year, or whether they need several hibernacula in an area. This is a more complicated question, for some move around while others have stayed in the same den for years. Also, we are examining growth of hatchlings, and have followed many for several years.

The suspense builds with each shovel of dirt that is removed. Despite the fact that we have done this for many years, we never know exactly what we will find. There is always the chance that the snakes have abandoned this den or that a predator such as a fox or skunk has entered and either eaten the snakes or prevented them from using it. There is also the possibility that it will hold even more snakes than it did last year. If the previous summer was particularly bad, with low food resources, some snakes may have died, or the young may not have survived even to reach a hibernaculum. Young Pine Snakes hatch in late August and early September. When the weather is too cold to spend much time searching for prey, or the rodent populations are low, the young snakes sometimes enter a hibernaculum without any food and many perish over the winter. When it is a nice warm summer, the eggs hatch earlier, giving the hatchlings more time to hunt for prey before finding a place to hibernate. Well-fed young are more likely to survive the difficult fall and find suitable places to hibernate, often with older snakes.

My experiments in the laboratory demonstrated that young Pine Snakes can locate the odor of adult Pine Snakes, even when only one snake was present for only a few minutes. It is likely that the young snakes find their first hibernaculum by searching for the odor trails of adults. They also can distinguish the odors of predators such as King Snakes and foxes and avoid places where they have been. The young slither about the Pine Barrens, and when they smell a Pine Snake odor trail, they begin to follow it. As they get closer to a den, more and more odor trails converge, and these eventually lead to the entrance. I have seen young hatchlings make a right turn and follow such a trail. I know it was a trail because I placed an adult snake there to move about, making the trail.

These few minutes just before we get down to about the three-foot level are the most nerve-racking for me. I am so sure there will be no snakes, that all have disappeared or been eaten by a fox. We might have missed them. Maybe the warm weather a few weeks ago was enough for some of them to leave the hibernaculum. Maybe they have already emerged and are out foraging. Maybe they emerged so early that the freezing weather last week killed them all, and they may be underneath logs and leaves, frozen to death. There are so many things that could have happened.

"Dig carefully now, you are almost down to where they could be. Put your shovel in very gently, so that you won't hurt one," I warn. Short and muscular, Carl digs tirelessly, shoveling the dirt way over his head, while Steve Garber shovels the dirt away from the hole, hoping to prevent a cave-in. As I watch these young men I am gratified that so many of my old Ph.D. students return year after year.

"I feel something hard," Carl screams. "Maybe I hit one."

"Let me see," I say, and the crowd of students opens up to let me in. "No, that is just the old board that we put on top of the main hibernaculum chamber last year. But wait, we need to get all our equipment together. When I lift this off, there may be a snake underneath—and I want to be prepared to take their body temperature. While Bob and I get things ready, you scrape away all the dirt from the top, but don't lift it up until I say so."

"Bob," I call, "we're ready to lift the board off. You want to come over?" Bob, who has been investigating a hole in the woods to see if it might be an undiscovered hibernaculum, comes running. He is always on the lookout for suspicious holes that may signify that there is another den below. It is quite hard to find these places. Carl is right, there are small holes all over the forest, and most go nowhere. Others are the runs of small rodents that move through the leaves and soil just below the surface. We found most hibernacula by searching for basking snakes in the late fall: our presence disturbed them slightly, and they retreated lethargically down an obscure hole, showing us where a hibernaculum might be.

"This is it," I say, "they'll either be here, or they may still be in their chambers farther down. Open her up, careful now." Delicately Bob raises the board, revealing a mass of swirling snakes, slow moving to be sure,

16.1. We dig up snake hibernacula in late winter to study the fidelity of Pine Snakes and to understand their growth patterns and survival. Between the cement block are several Pine Snake adults and one Black Racer. We are looking straight down into a hibernaculum.

but still moving. It is a tangle of sleek all-black bodies, and vibrant black and white ones (fig. 16.1).

"I can see at least three Pine Snakes and two Black Racers," Bob cries excitedly. "Give me the Schultheis," a long slender thermometer we insert in the cloaca (the snake's equivalent of a rectum) to measure its temperature. We are interested in finding out their normal temperature during hibernation, and how this temperature corresponds to that of the surrounding sand.

Everyone is galvanized into action: Bob sticks the thermometer into the cloaca of the biggest Pine Snake that is the most exposed, Carl measures the distance from the snake to the surface, Jorge puts another thermometer in the sand to get the sand temperature where the snake was, and Susan measures the distance from the snake to the entrance of the burrow. Another graduate student at Rutgers, Susan Elbin, works full time at Wildlife Trust, running its New York Bioscape program. Bending over the tunnel, her long golden hair falls to the sand unnoticed as she measures the length of the tunnel.

"Eight point five degrees," Bob calls out. "It's a female, judging by the thickness of the tail." Males have a bulging tail just below the cloaca, where the hemipenis (organ for sperm transfer) is, while females have a thin tail. When the hemipenis is everted, the sperm travel down an indentation in the top, into the female.

"Ninety-six centimeters from the surface to the snake," says Carl.

While I record the various biological parameters, Bob hands the snake to Mike and begins to take the body temperature of the next snake. Meanwhile, Mike puts the Pine Snake on the ground and records its defensive behaviors. What does the snake do when so rudely awakened from its sleep? Does it remain still? Does it move? How fast does it move? Does it strike? How often and how high can it strike? We are trying to figure out what defensive behavior a Pine Snake has if it is dug up by a predator such as a fox or skunk. This can easily happen, particularly in the early spring when the presence of one snake at the hibernaculum entrance may give the location away to predators that are having trouble finding food. Susan remains with Mike, carefully recording the antipredator behavior of each snake. Emile DeVito, another Rutgers alumnus who works for New Jersey Conservation Foundation, records the time of some of the behaviors. Tall, with dark thick hair and a ready smile, Emile often brings his father or his son or daughter with him. I get a special pleasure in watching his father dig enthusiastically, in Emile's loving gaze on him, in his son's enthusiasm with each new snake. When the behavioral observations are finished, they wave a thick radio-frequency wand over the snake, and with a slight beep, a number appears on a small computer screen— AB0037D67—the unique number of its PIT tag. The PIT tags have been lifesavers for our project, since there is no question of the identity of any snake.

"It's a recapture," Mike calls out, and reads me the number, which I record with all the other information on my data sheets.

Meanwhile, Bob is working with the third Pine Snake, and Emile is holding a Black Racer. It takes a while for us to process these five snakes, and after their behavior is recorded, they are put safely in snake bags, each with a field number. We will take them back to the laboratory to weigh and measure before returning them to their winter dens.

"Clean out all the sand from the hole, and put that rake handle in one of the tunnels that runs off the main chamber, and the stick ruler in the other. We don't want to lose the tunnels; they collapse easily. Since these are good tunnels, we want to follow them because they lead to other snakes that have tucked themselves into the sandy wall. I can feel it, we are going to find 30 snakes here," I say.

"I hope you're right," Bob says. "How many did we get here last year?"

"Only 12, but the year before we had 26," I reply. "So there is hope."

"From now on," I say, "we should use the small hand trowels for all the digging; we don't want to take a chance on hurting any snakes."

"I can see one in this tunnel," Carl calls out. "It is a big one; it must be a Pine."

He works diligently for ten minutes, gradually pulling the sand from around the snake by hand. Although hibernating, these snakes are very strong, and it is impossible to pull them out until they are mostly uncovered. Finally the snake is free, but in fact there are two. They were intertwined in a side chamber off the main tunnel. The tunnel continues farther in, deeper and deeper. Meanwhile, Jorge has been following the other tunnel that went off to the right.

"There are two big Pines coming out of their chambers," Jorge calls, and we scramble to measure them (fig. 16.2).

"I have two hatchlings off to the side." he calls. "Bob, hand me the thermometer."

"No more digging," I say, "until we have processed all of the snakes we have found. I need to get all the measurements and to finish diagramming the tunnel structure. The snakes that are still in their tunnels can wait. As long as they are underground they are fine, and their body temperatures will remain stable."

Carefully I record all the measurements, making sure each column is filled in. I'll never remember the data later, and having columns insures I don't forget anything. I learned early on how important it was to decide initially what information I needed, and to make a column for each. Otherwise, I end up with a hodgepodge of information that varies from year to year.

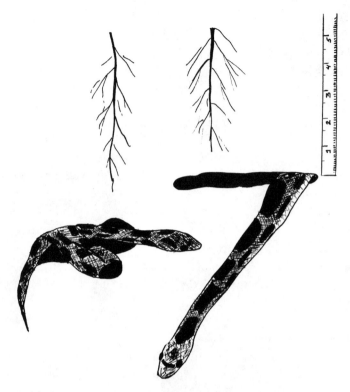

16.2. The Pine Snakes are curled up in side chambers of the hibernacula three to four feet below the surface.

"OK, I'm caught up on the burrow characteristics," I say. "You can begin to dig again, but be very careful. There could be snakes anywhere, including where you are standing."

Carefully Susan scrapes away the dirt from the floor of the hole, and sure enough, there is a big Pine Snake folded in a tight ball exactly where she was standing. There must have been a tunnel that led to the snake, but it collapsed while everyone was digging. The excitement begins anew as Carl, and then Jorge, each find another Pine Snake. The excitement is too much for Steve, and he slips in to start following another tunnel. We work very slowly, making sure that we have information on the exact location of each snake, the temperature of the snake and its chamber, and the number of snakes in each chamber. After an hour the hole is over six feet deep and nearly ten feet long. Great mounds of sand are piled around the edges.

I look around at the students hovering above the hole. We must look an odd sight. There are nine of us, all peering into a hole that looks like a grave site. Over the years nearly all of my graduate students and a fair number of undergraduates have come out for the annual snake dig. Many have gone on to jobs in universities and government, but I follow all of their careers just as I follow the snakes. It is one of the most rewarding experiences a teacher can have—savoring the return of old students now successful in their own careers. Over the years I watch their professional personalities bloom and welcome back their own children to help dig up the snakes each spring.

Two of the students have large, five-foot-long Pine Snakes wound around their necks, another two are holding jet black Racers, and another is holding a shovel. I am sitting on a lawn chair at the very edge, writing furiously on a clipboard. On the outside of the group, four shovels are standing upright, with coats and sweaters hanging from the handles, dangling and swaying in the breezes as if inhabited by spirits of the pines. Every few minutes I glance at the piles of sand, searching for movement. Eventually I am rewarded, and I see a small hatchling pulling itself out of the sand. It is so small that it was shoveled out of the hole with the sand. No doubt it was in a tight ball surrounded by sand. It is unharmed, so we give it a number and put it in a box with the other hatchlings. We have to be quite careful about this—hatchlings must go in a separate shoebox so that the big snakes will not crush them. Racers are separated from the Pine Snakes because they might decide to eat a smaller Pine Snake.

We were so engrossed in digging for snakes that we have completely forgotten lunch, so some of us take the opportunity to grab a sandwich since no snakes are currently exposed. Nellie continues to follow one of the tunnels, using a small hand trowel to delicately push dirt away, moving deeper and deeper into the side of our cavernous hole. We still have two or three tunnels to follow, so several more snakes may still be buried. A tall Greek woman, Nellie Tsipoura is still recovering from Lyme disease, a hazard of fieldwork. Most of us have had it—I had it four times. Except for Lyme, I seldom get sick; I was brought up believing you weren't sick unless you had to go to the hospital.

The last few clouds have disappeared, and the sun is quite warm despite the cool air. We can feel spring coming. Coats are strewn about; jackets are piled on branches, flannel shirts hang from shovels, and gloves and warm scarves decorate the pines. There are incredible variations in temperatures this time of the year in the barrens; in the early morning there was a touch of frost on the silvery lichens, and now it is nearly 60 degrees Fahrenheit and the sun is warm and pleasant. The sun feels comforting on our faces, but we soon turn back to our pit and slowly begin digging again with our hands and trowels. As the day wears on, we pull snake after snake out of the hibernaculum, carefully following and diagramming the elaborate tunnel structure. Before we are done, we have 28 Pine Snakes and eight Black Racers.

Bob and I go into the hole and carefully slice the dirt away from the sides, leaving a smooth surface along the edges. We can see that there are no tunnels leading in any direction. We have reached the hard-packed sand that was not disturbed last year, and it would be easy to see tunnels if there were any. Satisfied that there are no more, we climb out. The tunnels have ended, and there are no more snakes. We begin to shovel dirt back into the hole until we have filled it to within about three feet of the surface. Then we put in four cement blocks to form a square, leaving holes between each block as well as an open space in the center that is about two feet long. We put an old board or piece of metal on top of this, and cover it with sand. We then place cement blocks from the open space to the surface of the ground, aligned so that there is a tunnel from the top to the chamber that can serve as an entrance to the hibernaculum. This has an added advantage: the opening in the cement blocks is too small for a fox or skunk to enter.

We finish shoveling the dirt back in the hole and rake the leaves and old debris back over the ground. Large sun-bleached logs, clumps of lichens, and leaves are strewn around to obliterate our footsteps. We want to camouflage our activities as much as possible. After the first rain it will be impossible to find the place where we were digging. This is important as poachers lurk in the Pine Barrens—poachers who would like to trade or sell the snakes to others from around the country who will pay dearly for a New Jersey Pine Snake. Bob and I are very particular about whom we bring with us on these trips—only people we know very well and can trust are allowed to come. In the early days, some "friends" asked to come who later returned to poach our snakes, taking them across state lines where the thieves could not be prosecuted.

By 4 P.M. it is already chilly, and most of our jackets are back on. When the sun begins to sink low in the sky, it quickly cools off, for the ground is still cold. We pick up the snakes, pack our tools, and head to Bob's house to process them. Bob lives in the Pine Barrens. Pine Snakes roam the woodlands and Spring Peepers call from the pond across the street from his house (fig. 16.3).

We set up an assembly line at the laboratory so that we can process the snakes as quickly as possible. We each have a task, and each snake passes from one person to another. The PIT tag must be read, the snake

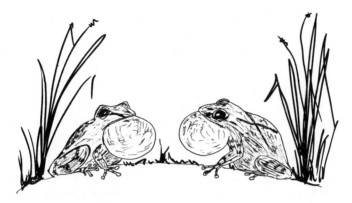

16.3. Male Spring Peepers gather in large numbers in small vernal ponds to call and attract females.

weighed and its length measured, and its head measurements must be taken. PIT tags are like the bar codes in grocery stores, and each snake has a unique number. Since nothing is electronic and there are no batteries, they will read forever. With so many people helping, the task goes quickly, and within two hours all the snakes are measured and weighed and are back in their bags. We put them outside in the garage for the night because it is important to keep them at about the same temperature as their hibernaculum. In the morning Bob will return them to their den and let them go down the cement-block tunnel to the chamber below. Some of the more ambitious ones will dig side chambers, but all of them will continue hibernating for the next few weeks until it is warm enough to emerge. Others will remain in the central chamber until warm breezes stir them to move. Even then, they may come up to bask for a few hours and return to the safety of the hibernaculum chamber in the evenings. By late April they will fan out into the barrens, searching for prey.

We have been studying the hibernating behavior of these snakes since 1985, and every year some of the same snakes return to the same hibernacula, seemingly undisturbed by our work. Back at my Rutgers lab I carefully diagram the elaborate tunnel system. In most dens the entrance tunnel goes nearly straight down for at least three feet, and then it begins to level off. We constructed the initial tunnel to mimic the natural ones we excavated years ago. But following our tunnel, the snakes have constructed their own main tunnel, which usually continues for five to ten feet, with a number of side tunnels and chambers, each chamber occupied by one or more snakes. Fortunately the hatchlings make very small tunnels when they burrow to the side, and the larger snakes do not follow; otherwise the hatchlings would be crushed by the weight of the big snakes. A small hatchling may weigh only about 30 grams—about an ounce—while a large female Pine Snake may weigh as much as 1,400 grams (about three pounds)—certainly enough to crush a hatchling to death over the four to five months of hibernation.

Pine Snakes are relatively safe in their underground burrows. Over the years we have found only six or seven crushed hatchlings, three frozen snakes, two partially eaten hatchlings, and a charred snake. The frozen snakes were near the surface, and we think they came up too early during a warm spell in January and did not go down deep enough when the cold returned at night. We were especially sad to find one of the frozen females whom we had been following for over ten years. She had been hibernating in the same den for a long time.

We found the charred snake at the surface of a hibernaculum. There had been a brush fire only two weeks before we dug them up, and she must have died then. We figure that she came up because hot air from the fire penetrated the burrow, stimulating her to emerge, and she was caught above ground when the fire roared through the underbrush. The other snakes were still below ground and survived the fire. Fire is a problem for all snakes in the Pine Barrens because the dry pine needles burn like tinder. Any snake caught in its path perishes. A snake that is active has a chance of going down a hole, going under a log or wet leaves, or finding a den, but if the fire is hot and fast, it may not escape. Fortunately, Pine Snakes spend a great deal of time under logs, in logs, and under the ground in hibernacula or summer dens where they are safe from the ravages of fire.

Within a week of digging up the snakes we get a late storm, and the barrens are covered with a blanket of snow. The snakes are safe beneath the sand, and they may not come out for several more weeks. They wait for the air to warm up in their tunnels, and then they slowly make their way to the surface. The Black Racers are the first to emerge. They warm up sooner because they are much more slender, and once on the surface their black skin absorbs the heat rapidly. It is fortunate that they leave when they first become active because otherwise they might prey on the defenseless baby Pine Snakes. Racers are voracious snake predators and will even eat their own young or siblings.

By mid-April all the snakes have emerged, although some may spend a few days near the entrance, basking during the day and seeking the safety of the chamber at night. With time, they move farther away. They fan out within a mile or two of the winter den, establishing a home range where they can hunt for baby rabbits, mice, and other small mammals. They sometimes follow rodent runs until they find a nest, and then they kill four or five mice in rapid succession, and eat them one after the other. Others wait in ambush near rodent runs or behind logs where mice scurry by without looking.

In late May males begin to look for females. It is quite rare to find a copulating pair, but once in a while we are lucky. The male and female intertwine for hours, writhing for a few minutes, and then lying quietly for awhile. In the heat of passion, the male gently grasps the female on the head and moves his body up and down hers until his cloaca finds hers. Sperm is transferred over his hemipenis to her cloaca, and they separate only after many hours of copulating. Once mating ends, the male leaves, and the female spends her days eating and lying in the sun, letting the eggs grow. In late June and early July, the females converge on the nesting grounds, searching for a suitable nest site that has full sun penetration to the ground. Reptiles rely on the sun to incubate their eggs, so it is critical to place their nests where there is enough heat.

Female Pine Snakes dig a nest tunnel that is five to eight inches below the ground, and may be three to seven feet long. At the end of the tunnel they construct a chamber where they lay a clutch of about nine or ten eggs, although some lay as few as three and others lay as many as 15. This digging behavior is very unusual for any species of snake, and Pine Snakes are the only American snakes known to dig their own nests. Pine Snakes dig by pushing the sand with the tip of their nose, then curving their head back a few inches to make a shovel with their neck. They pull the sand out of the burrow, depositing it at the edge, and then return to bring out more dirt.

Most snakes rely on finding abandoned burrows of other animals, or they lay their eggs under logs, roots, or tree stumps. However, there are no native mammals or reptiles that dig adequate burrows in the Pine Barrens of New Jersey, at least none that are not predators. Elsewhere, in the Carolinas and Florida, Pine Snakes do not have to dig their own nests because there are many harmless mammals that build burrows they can use. The Pine Snakes simply dig a side chamber for their eggs.

Sitting in my laboratory at Rutgers many years later, I look over the 20 years of our work with Pine Snakes. Females have always laid eggs between 17 June and 14 July, although the egg-laying period in any one year is only about two weeks long. Individual females usually return to the same exact place to lay their eggs each year, truly remarkable in a reptile. It is well known that birds often return to the same place each year, but we were surprised at first that Pine Snakes would also show such a high degree of nest-site fidelity. We often find old hatched eggshells in these nests, indicating that they are indeed safe sites. If predators had found the nests, the eggshells would be scattered above ground. Presumably the females can find these old eggshells in the nest as well, indicating that it is a safe nest site—safe from both predators and poachers.

In some years we have lost 40 percent of our nests to poachers. We find the nests completely dug up, with the eggs all gone and human footprints all around. As a conservation measure we have been moving clutches to the laboratory for incubation, then returning the hatchlings to their own nest to emerge naturally. This reduces both poaching and predation, and results in a much higher number of hatchlings emerging in the wild. Moreover, we feed them before returning them, giving nature an added boost. Since Pine Snakes are threatened in New Jersey, this is an important conservation measure.

Not only must the females find a safe place to nest away from predators such as fox, skunk, and Raccoon, but they must place their nests where they will get enough warmth for the eggs to develop properly. I have been examining this factor for many years in the laboratory. In most reptiles, the sex of the offspring is determined by incubation temperature. At one incubation temperature all the eggs become males, and at another all the eggs become females. This is true for turtles, lizards, and alligators, but not for snakes. This was a tragic discovery, in a way, as it turns out that for many years efforts to artificially hatch sea turtle eggs succeeded in putting only males into the sea because of the incubation temperatures that were used. It would have been far better to produce only females, since one male can fertilize many females, but a female sea turtle can only lay so many eggs.

I reasoned that any factor that was powerful enough to determine sex must have other effects as well. Herpetologists had not examined the effect of incubation temperature on other aspects of the behavior of reptiles because they had to kill them in order to determine their sex. The snakes' internal hemipenis can be everted manually, which we use to sex them. I placed temperature probes in some nests to determine the range of temperatures to which eggs are normally exposed in New Jersey, and then selected three temperatures within this range for examination in the laboratory.

Hatching rate has been remarkably high in the laboratory, but the eggs at low temperatures take nearly a month longer to hatch. I also discovered that almost all aspects of their behavior are affected by incubation temperature. Hatchlings from high and intermediate incubation temperatures do fine, but those that hatch from low temperatures are slow to develop. They are less able to avoid predators, catch and kill their prey, or move rapidly. In short, they would be less able to survive in the wild.

I plotted how long it would take the low-incubation-temperature snakes to hatch, shed their skin for the first time, locate and capture their first meal, and find a hibernaculum. The hatchlings that were incubated at low temperatures take longer to do each of these tasks than do the snakes from the intermediate and high incubation temperatures. To me it seems that snakes that hatch from comparatively cold nests simply do not have time to both eat and find a hibernaculum. Without eating, their chances of making it through the first winter are slim. In the Pine Barrens we have found many snakes that we hatched in the laboratory, and they were incubated at intermediate or high incubation temperatures. We have never found one that was incubated at low temperatures, and we no longer incubate any eggs at the lowest temperature because of their lowered survival.

Our experiments suggest that the reason Pine Snakes do not live farther north than New Jersey is that it is simply too cold for the embryos to develop properly during incubation. I had always wondered why there were none in the barrens of Long Island or Albany—and I believe this is the answer. It also explains why the females spend such a long time searching for just the right nest site. And once they find one, they use it for many years.

With the cold snow blanketing the ground, it is hard to believe that the Pine Barrens soon will be warm and sunny enough for the Pine Snakes to emerge, mate, search for nest sites, and lay eggs. For now, all are safe in their underground hibernacula. It should be a good breeding season because most of the females we weighed were much heavier than they were last winter. Not only did most of them grow in length, but they gained weight, a good indication that they will have enough reserves to lay large eggs, which will produce healthy hatchlings.

In a few weeks the oaks will drop their old brown leaves and burst forth with new green ones, the herbs will spring to life, and the chorus of Spring Peepers will fill the evening. The pine needles will somehow look shiny and bright, and the Mountain Laurel will burst forth in an incredible display of rich pink flowers.

PINE BARRENS
TO THE SOUTH

17

The Pines of Central
South Carolina

I am drawn to the sandhills whenever I come to South Carolina—they remind me of the Albany Pine Bush near my childhood home and the Pine Barrens of New Jersey where I now spend as much time as my teaching and research allow. For most people, the deep deciduous woods are exciting places where one searches for peace, solitude, and exotic animals, but I have never been fond of dark forests. I find them confining, almost suffocating, but the sparse pines always beckon, as if they hold some mystery I have yet to discover. Here in the pines I can see the blue sky, feel the warmth of the noonday sun, and watch the Pine Warblers move through the pine boughs. There is a peace and quiet about the pines; it is a place to think, to feel, to muse about life, and to appreciate all we have been given.

The sandhills of the Carolinas are legendary for naturalists working on their "lists." Herpetologists come for Coachwhip, Northern Pine Snake, and Pine Barrens Treefrog; birders come for the Red-cockaded Woodpecker and Bachman's Sparrow, and botanists look for Turkey Oaks and Wiregrass. The sandhills have not escaped the recent upsurge of interest in butterflies. Visitors come to see the federally endangered Mitchell's Satyr, the very rare King's Hairstreak, and the more common (but very local) Edward's Hairstreak (fig. 17.1). The sandhills of the Carolinas have a butterfly list of over 100 species (there are only about 164 species in North Carolina),[1] and nearly 50 different butterfly species can be found in one day in July when the Sweet Pepperbush burst into bloom.

Just north of the Georgia border in South Carolina is a patch of upper coastal plains tucked between rolling farms, horse pastures, and pine plantations. Along SC highway number 125 there are pine forests on both sides, and a few scattered sandy fields, abandoned long ago. The forests look healthy, with a rich understory of deciduous plants and a

[1] H. LeGrand, "The North Carolina Sandhills," *American Butterflies* 8 (2000):5–15.

17.1. Edward's Hairstreak is a specialty of the pine barrens of Albany, New Jersey, and the Carolinas.

carpet of amber-colored pine needles. The deep layer of pine needles signals that it has been quite a while since a fire swept through, and the next one will be particularly hot because of the plentiful tinder. It is cool at seven in the morning, but the bright sun and clear skies promise a warm day. Since it is early June, the midday temperatures will no doubt reach 70 degrees.

The pine woods are quiet, the needles muting even the wind. As I drive, the land gradually rises into sandhills, with upland plant communities that thrive on the dry soil, dominated by Longleaf Pine and Turkey Oak. The track is undulating and the vehicle moves rhythmically up and down as I cross several knolls. These are actually old sand dunes left when the seas retreated during the interglacial epochs from 10,000 to 100,000 years ago. This part of South Carolina was once seashore, and sand dunes formed from the high tides just as they do today along the Atlantic coast nearly 200 miles away. Then the glaciers formed in the far north, removing water from the oceans, and the sea retreated and abandoned the dunes far from the shore. Three such episodes left behind three wide terraces of sandy soils in South Carolina. The sandhills are remnants of the ancient beach dunes that rimmed the Cretaceous seas, although the sands were moved about by the waves and flooding waters. A few scientists believe the region is the result of the delta of a large river that emptied into the seas. Streams and wind action created the hilly topography. Both groups of scientists believe the sandhills were formed by the blowing sands—only the origin of the sands is in dispute. These upland sands are less fertile than the heavier soils near the stream terraces and flood-plains of the Savannah River.

Longleaf Pine

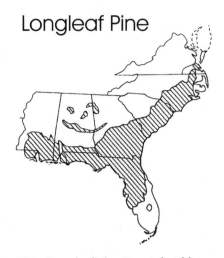

The sandhills are the pine barrens of the region—indeed, they were called pine barrens by the early settlers. They contain the typical nutrient-poor soils that support only scrubby oaks, scattered pines, and a tangled understory of heaths. These same sandhill communities once extended from here down into Florida, but now they are mostly gone. Indeed, the Carolina sandhills contain up to 1,500 plant species, nearly 30 percent of the species that occur in North and South Carolina. Several plants are

17.2. Longleaf Pine Forest that blanketed the Atlantic Coastal Plain from Virginia to Texas (after Means 1996).

found only in the sandhills, such as Pyxie Moss, and like the sandhills and pine scrub of Florida, they are the centers of rare plant diversity within the region. Once much more common on the Savannah River Site, there are only about 1,000 to 2,000 acres of sandhills left, depending on the year and fire regime. Even the sandhills that remain are not pristine, for 50 years ago these habitats were logged sporadically. The sandhills are the highest places in the region, with some as much as 350 feet above sea level.

I abandon the car and wander off the road toward a clearing created by a small fire. The forest is not lush. Before the European settlers arrived, an extensive Longleaf Pine forest blanketed the Atlantic Coastal Plain from Virginia to Texas (fig. 17.2). It was the most extensive single-species forest in North America, and it must have been spectacular, teaming with wildlife and dominated by gigantic trees. Now all that remains are these sandhill communities that are relatively undisturbed because the soils are too poor to support agriculture or a pine plantation.

The signature species of sandhill communities are here: scrubby oaks, Wiregrass, and scattered Reindeer Moss. Most of the Turkey Oaks are only my height, and many of the other species are much shorter. The leaves of the oaks are leathery and hard, well adapted to withstand dry conditions. The Turkey Oaks are still covered with their sharply pointed lobed leaves, although they are dried, brown, and shriveled. In contrast, the Blackjack Oaks lost most of their leaves months ago. Under the dense tangle of oaks, the dead and dried leaves of Bracken Fern are nearly covered with brown pine needles, and small acorns are scattered everywhere.

The pines are relatively young, mostly less than 50 years old—the larger and older trees were removed by lumbering. In contrast, many of the small scrubby oaks are well over 50 years old because the people who lived here years ago had no use for these oaks. It is fortunate that there was no agriculture on these sandhills, since till agriculture destroys the underground root systems of Wiregrass. Once destroyed, Wiregrass seldom moves back in, and whatever remains is soon outcompeted by other grasses. Wiregrass seems to need a fire every two or three years to keep out its competitors. Thus Wiregrass can be used as an indicator of a functioning sandhill community. It is possible to discern both the forestry footprint and the range of agriculture just by looking at the vegetation: Wiregrass and Reindeer Moss will not grow where the soil has been disrupted by agriculture (fig. 17.3), and very old Longleaf Pine are not found where logging has been recent. The Wiregrass is sparse and short, only eight or ten inches tall, but the huckleberries are dense and difficult to walk through. I find a small native Yucca, with a dead flower stalk that is nearly chest high. Short scrubby bushes have a few small clumps of tiny pink flowers, like miniature pom-poms brightening up an otherwise drab habitat of browns and beiges. These small cherries are scattered throughout the woods, lending a splash of color amid the brown oak leaves still clinging to the branches.

Sitting on a small pine log, surrounded by low shrubby huckleberries and scattered Reindeer Moss lichens, I can let my mind wander back over time, imagining what earlier visitors found. From about A.D. 800 to A.D. 1520 the native Indians lived in a cultural system with hereditary chiefs that ruled from temple mound centers, usually located in the rich bottomlands of rivers. Some of these chiefdoms extended for hundreds of square miles and encompassed many villages. Hernando de Soto explored the region for Spain in the mid-1500s, crossing the Savannah River near

17.3. *Reindeer Moss is one of the early invaders in barren habitats.*

what is present-day Augusta, on his way to Mexico. After de Soto left, the Indians in the high country around the Savannah River were left alone for nearly 100 years. Although the English claimed the lands, they remained along the coast. By the mid-1600s the Westo Indians were selling other Indians they captured in raids to the English as slaves. This destabilized the frontier, and the English eventually crushed the remaining Westo Indians.

The poor farmland in the sandhills was not rich enough to support a landowner and his slaves. Even the government inducements in the 1730s and 1740s failed to settle the land, but immigrants from Europe in the 1750s slowly began to populate the sandhill country. The real problem with farming was that good and poor land were intermingled, making it nearly impossible to have a productive farm. Since the soil was so poor, crops soon exhausted the nutrients, and farmers moved from one area to another, abandoning their fields to the pines and scrubby oaks. Since populations were low, there was ample agricultural land that was wet and flat, and the sandhill soils escaped disruption. They used the sandhills for logging and cutting firewood. Removal of wood destroys the pine communities temporarily but leaves the soils intact, and intact soils are essential for natural sandhill communities. The sandhills that burned regularly every two to seven years remained as pine barrens, retaining both their natural soil structure and unique plants and animals.

Typical animals of the sandhill communities are White-tailed Deer, Opossum, Raccoon, Otter, Fox Squirrel, Gray Squirrel, Cottontail Rabbit, and Beaver. White-tails are one of the common species in most pine barrens because they provide sufficient browse for them to survive and reproduce. Today, White-tails are hunted extensively in South Carolina, and in a given year, some 22,747,362 pounds of venison are prepared in kitchens across the state. The equivalent number of cows needed to produce this much meat (34,466 cows) would require the conversion of 41,359 to 68,892 acres of wildlife habitat to cattle ranches. I find this quite amazing, and it gives me pause to think about the implications of hunting in the pinelands along the Atlantic Coast.

Natural plant communities on South Carolina sandhills are rare because in most places the sands are covered with towns, farms, and farmhouses. Some places to see representative sandhills are Weymouth Woods Sandhills Nature Preserve in Moore County (North Carolina) and Carolina Sandhills National Wildlife Refuge and Sandhills State Forest in Chesterfield County (South Carolina). Each of the latter two have 45,000 acres, but only small portions have undisturbed, native sandhill communities. The sandhill communities I walk through today managed to survive because they are tucked within the Savannah River Site, which belongs to the United States Department of Energy and served the nation for nearly half a century as a nuclear production and storage facility.

In the 1940s, this part of South Carolina was populated with a few sleepy agricultural towns, such as Ellenton and Dunbarton, which had dwindling populations and faltering economies. Ellenton was the busiest of the towns, but its population still numbered less than a thousand even though it was on the railroad line. The town was named after Ellen, the daughter of a Mr. Dunbar, who owned the largest plantation around. It was a beautiful town, with stately Magnolias, pines, and Carolina Cherries. The people of the town worked on the railroad, farmed, or cut wood from the large pines on the sandhills. In 1950 hordes of strangers descended upon Ellenton, and for a few months the people wondered whether oil had been discovered, only to learn that the Atomic Energy Commission (the forerunner of the Department of Energy, or DOE) was planning to build an H-bomb factory in their midst. On November 28, 1950, the announcement came over the radio that it would be necessary to relocate about 1,500 families over an 18-month period. Some people put their houses on large tree-length logs and rolled them into Jackson on the edge of the site. When I went into Shane Boring's grandmother's house, it was eerie to see the old beams and cracks left from the move. Shane was a graduate student of mine, and he and I walked slowly through the house and imagined it still nestled in the pines out on the site. The forest has reclaimed the lawns where his grandmother's house once stood, but a few forlorn daffodils and a blooming rosy Redbud still attest to the care that she once gave her home. Some of the curbs still remain along the main street of Ellenton, but huckleberry and other low vegetation obliterates most of it. I marvel at how quickly the forest reclaims the land.

The Atomic Energy Commission acquired over 200,000 acres of land and paid $18,975,000 to move 6,000 people and 6,100 graves from the lands now occupied by the Savannah River Site. Many graves still remain on site because no relatives were left to claim them and to decide where to move them. The graves were once in well-tended cemeteries with flowers and mowed grass, but now they stand amid the forest, overgrown by tangled vegetation under Longleaf Pines and dense oaks (fig. 17.4). The deserted towns, such as Ellenton, can still be located by the old concrete roads, shallow curbs, sidewalks, and old brickwork fallen to the ground. It is eerie to walk through these ghost towns, deserted because the people

17.4. An old cemetery, where daffodils still bloom, is the only reminder of some villages moved by the Department of Energy in the 1950s. Some of the stones have been toppled.

were forced to move, leaving behind daffodils that still flower each spring. Tulips must be far less hardy, for none remain to bloom along the decaying sidewalks. Only a broken branch of a Longleaf Pine remains.

Eugene Odum of the University of Georgia set up a small laboratory to examine the effect of energy activities on ecosystems. Over the years, his group grew little by little until today one of the country's premier ecology research laboratories is located on-site—the Savannah River Ecology Laboratory. Faculty and students from the lab not only study the effects of nuclear production, thermal pollution, and nuclear contamination, but continue to conduct some of the country's longest studies on amphibians and reptiles, and on plant communities. These studies have provided baseline information to evaluate claims of population changes due to global warming, habitat loss, and other human effects. The Department of Energy maintained large buffer zones around the nuclear productions buildings, thereby maintaining natural plant communities as well as the indigenous animals. The site itself occupies 310 square miles. When the DOE acquired the land in 1950, 67 percent was forested and the rest was in pasturelands or farms that grew corn, cotton, and peanuts. Most of the forest stands had been logged, but the swampy areas along the Savannah River belonged to the Alligators and Cottonmouths.

It is odd, really, that these sandhills were preserved by the overzealous security force of the DOE. Odder still that I feel safer here than in other pine barrens because the general public is denied access. Should any stranger wander by, the Wackenhut Security Forces would stop them, with cars or even helicopters. I have no doubt that Wackenhut knows exactly were I am. No one follows my progress in the New Jersey Pine Barrens or knows where I am in the Long Island Barrens.

I stop to study a Longleaf Pine that sprouted following a fire; the long needles resemble tufts of grass. By pushing away the oak leaves and needles I can find the light-yellow bud, buried where it is safe from fires. The "tree" will spend two to three years in this stage, putting its energy into growing an elaborate root system that allows it suddenly to shoot up to 10 feet when it is only four or five years old. In one year it must grow tall enough to be above the ravages of ground fires. After this initial spurt, it will send out side branches and form a "candelabra" growth form. On the lower elevations the soil is wetter, and trees can grow taller. Where the pine forest is a little denser, there are Red-cockaded Woodpecker families, building nests 25 to 35 feet up in the taller, living trees, unlike all other woodpeckers, which build their nests in dead trees. Below the nests the bark is streaked whitish with pitch and droppings.

The woods hide abandoned cemeteries, each surrounded by a wire fence. A small sign identifies one as Pleasant Hill Cemetery #137 and 138. The woods are quiet as I wander among the gravestones, only an occasional Pine Warbler trills softly. An epidemic must have devastated the people—most of the residents of this cemetery died in 1902 and 1903. Some of the headstones are for children who lived only a few months or years, while others are from far older people, but most died at the same time. Many of the headstones are tilted over, pushed aside by growing roots, and only a few stand upright. Longleaf Pines grow from a pile of bricks that must have been a statue or small platform, but there is no one left to tell their story, and no one to mourn. As a child, I had not appreciated my mother Janette's love of the history present in cemeteries, but sitting here I can visualize the past and mourn their passing.

Rising from my log, I walk over the gently undulating hills. I can feel the oaks and pines only by walking among them. Scrub and Turkey Oak dominate the landscape. In a few places there are open sandy spots and I linger, scanning the edges for any movement of Pine Snakes. They are relatively rare in South Carolina, but this would be the perfect place to find them. They should be nesting about now, so the females may be on the move searching for safe nesting places. Unlike the New Jersey Pine Snakes, these may not have to dig their own tunnels—there are plenty of small mammal burrows they can use for nesting. This means, however, that it is not possible to search for their nests by the characteristic dump pile of sand, and finding adults is a chance event.

I stop to rest on the edge of the sandhills, facing a dense pine forest. I find a nice tree to lean against, sit in the warm sand, and settle in. I can see quite a ways up the sandy ridge and I plan on scanning the open sand

17.5. Female Wild Turkey with her brood feeding in the deep forest shadows.

for an hour or two for any movement that could be a Pine Snake. In the shade of the pines it is still surprisingly cool and pleasant, and few flies buzz about. The dry pine needles rustle softly behind me, and I turn to watch a Fox Squirrel climb about a short pine. Larger than a Gray Squirrel, Fox Squirrels vary in color from nearly pure black to a whitish gray, although their faces are always black with white noses and ears. Fox Squirrels are creatures of the ground, where they gather nuts, acorns, seeds, and fungi.

Out of the corner of my eye I see motion in the undergrowth, too small to be a deer. Finally, a female Wild Turkey moves along the edge of the forest searching the leaves for food, her head held down. Soon six young move out of the shadows following her, their shapes barely visible in the dark woods. I would have missed them except for the movement; they were invisible because they blend into the shadows (fig. 17.5). The female is searching for old acorns left from last year's crop, and I watch as she picks up one after another, and then moves off into the darkness of the forest. Turkeys eat a wide variety of foods, including acorns, grain, fruit, and grass and weed seeds. About 10 percent of their diet is insects. They usually prefer the fresh growth of weeds, grasses, and browse, particularly after a fire, and they do best in pine forests that burn every three to five years. Turkeys can be particularly common in pine, oak, and hickory forests because of the abundance of nuts.

How very different the hen's covert motions are from the vigorous display behavior of male turkeys. Only a few months ago I happened upon a flock of 13 toms and 11 hens moving through the pine forest with no regard for anyone but themselves. One male, and then another, displayed to the females, who seemed oblivious to their charms. It was difficult to see the whole group at once since they moved in and out of the pines. It was very clear, however, that the females ate continually while the males merely displayed, over and over again. Older males have a long wiry beard dangling from their throat and are especially attractive to females. The females were intent on eating, searching the ground with each step. Perhaps they were being coy and were acutely aware of the male's displays. Each male lowered his head slightly, fluffed his body feathers, drooped his wings, spread his tail upward, and gobbled loudly while moving forward. In this desolate pine forest miles from any towns or farms, it is possible to harken back to the days before Europeans walked here—Wild Turkeys must have roamed throughout eastern North America in large flocks. They seem so primeval, so much a part of a larger, wilder forest penetrated only by Native Americans slipping silently through deer trails.

The turkeys moved through the pine woods keeping to the more open places where they could display without interruption. Every once in a while a female seemed interested, approaching a male for a few moments before returning to search for grass seeds or berries. Without any apparent interest, a female crouched to the ground, and within two seconds a male came close, circled her deliberately, and then mounted her. Copulation lasted only about 30 seconds, he dismounted, and she returned to feeding, showing no further interest. This period of intense displaying must be hard on males because the females eat while they evaluate the relative merits of each male, but the males must strut around constantly, spreading their tail, gobbling provocatively (fig. 17.6).

During the breeding season turkeys have even smaller home ranges than they do in the winter. Not all females breed each year, and those that do must be better at selecting habitats for they use a smaller area for

17.6. *Male Wild Turkeys displaying to females in the late winter.*

foraging during the spring and summer than females that do not breed. Their nests are on the ground in the dense oak shrubs or against a pine tree, hidden by shrubs, needles, and fallen logs. Most females move to other areas to feed during the winter, where food is more available. Females that are older and larger often manage to have breeding ranges that will provide them with food and other resources they need all year, and they do not have to move to new areas in the winter. This is an advantage for three reasons: they do not have to search for new winter habitats, they can reduce their exposure to predators because they do not move over large distances, and they do not have to find new hiding places.

The Wild Turkey and her brood disappear among the pines and oaks, and the forest is again motionless. The hours pass slowly, and gradually the pines become hotter and hotter. It is difficult to search the sands using binoculars because of the intense heat haze, but I persist, still hoping to see a Pine Snake. It is far too hot now for Pine Snakes to be slithering about—they are more likely curled up in a rotting log or buried a few feet underground where it is much cooler. They will wait for late afternoon to move. Slowly I amble back over the sandhills toward the car, disappointed for now, but knowing full well I will return another day to search for a Pine Snake.

I did not really expect to see one just by sitting here, quietly. But I love to inhale the quiet and solitude of the pines, and to watch the common critters like Fox Squirrels and Pine Warblers. Like Peter Freuchen's Snow Leopard, Pine Snakes are for me the spirit of the pines, and I feel their presence though I rarely see one.

Only a few miles away is the Savannah River, where giant Cypress Trees and Water Tupelo dominate the bottomland swamps. I am anxious to see the primeval Cypress swamps once again, but first I must return to the Savannah River Ecology Laboratory to meet Whit Gibbons, who has promised to show me a Cottonmouth—and I mean to hold him to it. Whit is always enthusiastic, an old-school herpetologist who has made the transition to thinking about broader ecological and evolutionary questions. He greets me with his usual broad smile, his eyes mirroring anticipation for the project ahead. Mike is waiting in the library where he was busy reading as much as possible about the snakes here, and is equally excited about seeing Cottonmouths again, for he has seen them in the Everglades. After loading our field gear in the back of the truck, we are off.

The sky is brooding and dark up ahead, and we are all excited because when it rains, frogs, toads, and snakes cross the road, and the warm rains stimulate the frogs to chorus. In the stillness of the early evening the choruses are nearly deafening, with the penetrating calls of Green Tree Frogs alternating with the loud staccato notes of tiny Cricket Frogs. In the woods a Whip-poor-will is calling and several Chuck Wills Widows, a close relative, are calling as well. It is that wonderful time when day gives way to night, and sounds crescendo as amphibians come to life. We stop to listen to the distant din of frogs coming from a Carolina bay hidden behind the pines. Carolina bays are elliptical wetlands that were once common throughout the coastal plains from Georgia to Virginia, but now the 200 on the Savannah River Site are among the last ones remaining.

"Perhaps," Whit says, "I should not have been so quick to promise a Cottonmouth."

"But promise you did, and I mean to hold you to it," I reply.

"I always find them, but it is these difficult moments when we are first looking," he replies.

The waters of the swamp along the road are dark and still, and Cypress knees emerge from the surface, allowing the trees to obtain oxygen. Otherwise the roots would suffocate and the Cypress trees would slowly die. Each tree has several knees, and their rounded ends stand like so many silent soldiers guarding the swamps. Also here are Water Tupelo, and a few Water Ash, Swamp Black Gum, and Red Maples in between. These swamps are under water for much of the year, forming a band a couple of miles wide along the river. The swamp partially dries up for some of the year, allowing Cypress seedlings to germinate and grow before they are inundated. Without this period of natural drying, the seedlings would be unable to sprout. The trees that live here are adapted to having their feet wet for most of the year, but the short period of dry-down is essential.

Spanish Moss hangs from the trees, giving the swamp a misty, cobweb appearance, with shafts of light penetrating to the water below. Tiny specks of dust dance in the yellow beams. A Whip-poor-will calls close at hand, an eerie voice amid the loud clicking notes of the Cricket Frogs. The darker it gets, the louder the frogs call, some from perches near the water, others while sitting on the low vegetation or even on tree trunks. Leopard and Green Frogs contribute occasionally, and Whit calls our attention to a distant chorus of Barking Tree Frogs. The frogs are always thrilling, but I want to see a Cottonmouth, my first. I have searched the Cypress swamps in the Everglades for years, all to no avail. I have missed several by only a matter of minutes, but miss them I did.

With flashlights in hand so we do not step on an unsuspecting Cottonmouth, we carefully pick our way down the rocks to the muddy swamp. In some places, Cottonmouths are called Water Moccasins, although they do not go into deep water. We are scattered out along the swamp edge and only our moving lights give away our locations, like giant fireflies dancing in a strange ritual. In the eerie darkness I am temporarily transported back to the days before the Civil War, and I can imagine the poor black souls who had only these swamps as passageways to the North and freedom. The courage and determination it must have taken to lower themselves into the dark murky waters with gators and snakes must have been tremendous. The swamps back then stretched on for miles, bordering most of the Savannah River, but now we have only this natural remnant. The irony of it being protected by the need for nuclear "readiness" to face the Cold War is now lost in the beauty of the Cypress and Spanish Moss that still endures.

"Here's one," Whit calls out, "over here, in the culvert." Somehow it does not seem quite right having my first Cottonmouth be a small one swimming along the inside of a giant corrugated metal pipe, searching for prey. Still I find it exciting to watch him slip slowly through the water toward us.

"Here's another one, much nicer, quite big," Whit says. "Come quickly, he's hunting along the bank." We clamber over the rocks and slippery mud to reach Whit just in time to see the four-foot-long, heavy-bodied snake slowly gliding away. He is on the shallow, muddy bank beside a small dark pool, partly hidden beneath fallen branches. He is no doubt hunting, stimulated by the first warm rain in weeks. It is a large male with a wonderful bold color pattern (fig. 17.7).

17.7. Cottonmouth in a hunting posture, watching and waiting for prey to pass by.

Using a snake hook to hold his head secure, Whit reaches down and picks up the venomous snake by the neck, something I would never try.

"The snake is far longer, far brighter, and far fatter than I expected," I exclaim. "He is lovely." The top side of this one is brown with dark olive crossbands. His underbelly is a dull yellow and brown, although the undertail is black. Disturbed now, he gapes open his mouth, exposing the vibrant white lining—his cotton mouth.

"Don't forget your camera," Mike says, and I quickly focus the lens. The snake refuses to stay still to show his brilliant white mouth lining or to coil nicely. It is hard to focus in the dark, but I snap a few pictures anyway. It is not a Pine Snake, but still, it is my first Cottonmouth and that counts for something.

"Have you been watching the sky?" Mike asks, peering overhead.

A bright bolt of lightning flashes over half the sky, plunging to the earth up ahead, and rain begins to come in waves. We stop to listen to the Bird-voiced Frogs singing from the trunks of the trees—this is the only place one can find them on the Savannah River Site. They have a lovely, nearly musical call. But they are frogs, after all, and I am drawn back to look for another Cottonmouth, for another smooth, slithering serpent of the Cypress searching for prey along the muddy banks and dark waters of the Savannah River swamps. Hours later, elated and fatigued, we call it a night and head back to the laboratory.

The next morning we walk through the swamps, watching our every step, looking for Cottonmouths. Even when they are there, they are hard to see because they blend with their surroundings, and when they remain absolutely still they are very hard to pick out. Whit has developed a search image for Cottonmouths, and he finds one long before the rest of us see it. Pointing it out, we all gaze in wonder at its camouflage, while the snake seems completely oblivious to our gazes. Usually this is a good strategy, for most people walk by without even seeing a snake. The color pattern makes it blend in with the leaves and twigs, and the darkness of the swamp makes it even harder to see.

"Take a few minutes to enjoy it," Whit says, "savor the moment."

I appreciate his sensitivity to my pleasure, one I have long awaited. Cottonmouths are the most common venomous snake in southern South Carolina and nearby Georgia. They are particularly interesting because, unlike most snakes, they do not move rapidly away when interrupted. Most other water snakes quickly head for the water and disappear when disturbed, but Cottonmouths remain where they are or retreat slowly. When they do go in the water, they swim just at the surface, unlike other

17.8. Armadillo rooting around in the leaves for small insects.

water snakes that are mostly submerged. Although they are active primarily at night, they are usually stepped on during the day because they are camouflaged as they lie about on the leaves or near Cypress knees.

We move on in search for others, but it is too dry here, and we find no more. They have moved back into the swamp where there are still small pools of water and where it is cooler. Up ahead we hear rustling, and I see movement. I walk hurriedly along the boardwalk, and see an Armadillo slinking slowly through the undergrowth, searching the ground for insects (fig. 17.8). When it sees us, it quickly scurries away, searching for a burrow where it can hide.

"This is great! It's my first sighting of a live Armadillo on the Savannah River Site," exclaims Whit.

"How can that be?" I ask. Still, it is fun to see him so excited and to share this experience with him.

"I saw dead one on the road, but this is my first live one." Armadillos are extending their range northward, as so many other species are, keeping to the pine woods where there are few people. In only a few years Armadillos may be common in the pines of South Carolina, but we savor this first encounter—one of a naturalist's thrills.

18

The Florida Pines

Sitting on top of a sand ridge surrounded by short stubby pines, I am bathed by cool breezes from the Atlantic Ocean. The pines are barely 20 feet tall, and many still bear the blackened bark of fires they survived. Underneath the canopy, a few Saw Palmettos grow in domed clumps, but mostly the sand is covered with a carpet of pale green lichens called Reindeer Moss. Overhead, a Brown-headed Nuthatch works up and down a trunk, picking at the loose bark, tossing bits away as it pecks at a small insect. The scrub pine habitat along coastal Florida is a jewel nestled between the coastal highway and the inland pine flatlands so typical of much of interior Florida.

Looking to the east I see the blue-green Atlantic Ocean, with Brown Pelicans cruising in formation just over the shallow waves. Turning to the west, there is a sea of scrub pines with a few oaks and Rosemary bushes mixed in. It is early January, and Mike and I are searching Okeeheelee Park pines for Gopher Tortoises—a specialty of the south and central Florida pinelands. Okeeheelee Park houses one of the few remaining sandhills mixed with pine flatlands in South Florida, a treasure nestled among golf courses, playing fields, streams, and other recreational facilities on the outskirts of West Palm Beach. When the county parks department took over the land, they began to develop it for local recreation, but fortunately the importance of leaving some in a relatively pristine condition was recognized. This required extensive management: some exotic plants and trees had to be removed, and some native plant species required reestablishment and additional protection once they were growing. The rock shell pits were barren and eroded, and park personnel planted tree species that could help stabilize the soil around the edges. For me, the rocky pits provide a segue to the very bedrock of Florida.

Geologically, Florida is the youngest state in the continental United States, having risen from the sea a mere 30 million years ago. Underneath present-day Florida is the Florida Platform, which extends south from

North America to separate the Atlantic Ocean from the Gulf of Mexico. This platform has existed for tens of millions of years, often lurking just below the shallow seas. The base rocks are early Cambrian granite and volcanic rocks from nearly 2 billion years ago, covered with early Paleozoic sedimentary rocks from over 250 million years ago. In fact, these rocks were part of the original land mass of Gondwana, dating back over 200 million years, when all the land masses of the earth formed two large continents. Some parts of Florida have been above sea level and occupied by plants and animals for 30 million years, while others have been above sea level only for a few thousand years.

Over the eons, water levels have risen and fallen many times, and ancient seas have left behind vast flat areas of former seabeds that are now dry (fig. 18.1). The underlying platform is limestone, overlain everywhere with layers of sand. Sometimes the level of the seas rose about 40 inches a year, but this rate gradually slowed down. When the earth's climate cooled during the last ice ages, vast quantities of water were frozen in the polar ice caps, and sea level fell, exposing more of Florida. From about 10,000 to 3,000 years ago, the level of the sea rose about 10 inches

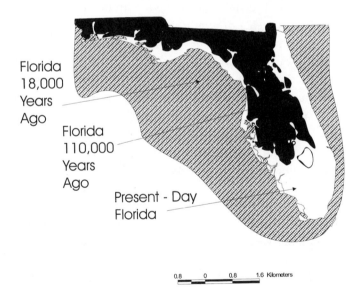

18.1. Schematic of Florida in earlier geological times (after Webb 1990). The black area is the interglacial period about 110,000 years ago when no ice was in glaciers and the sea level was higher. The dotted area is the extent of Florida land surface from 18,000 years ago during the full glacier, and the dark outline is present-day Florida.

every 100 years, a relatively rapid rise that left the coastal zone in constant turmoil. The Florida we see today above the sea occupies the eastern edge of the Florida Platform. Thus the continental shelf drops off relatively rapidly along the Atlantic Coast, while there is extensive shallow water along the west coast. An inland ridge extends 100 miles down through the center of Florida and rises to less than 300 feet above sea level. When the sea level was high before the last ice age, more than 10,000 years ago, these high ridges were islands. Some of these giant sand dunes are still present in two places: the Lake Wales Ridge, and a lower elevation ridge along the Atlantic coast, between the ocean and inland marshes and pine flatlands. The coastal ridge is a relict beach built up during past sea level highs, and it is here where we sit, gazing at the Atlantic Ocean.

All of Florida is part of the Atlantic Coastal Plain, which extends north through Georgia, the Carolinas, and up into New Jersey, Long Island, and Cape Cod. It is this similarity in geology that has shaped the pine communities in these states. There are three major kinds of pinelands in south and central Florida: high pines, pine flatwoods, and scrub pines. In some places the three are intertwined, with only slight differences in elevation giving rise to a dramatic shift in the type of pine forest. Like pinelands everywhere, they occur on relatively infertile soil, well drained or sandy, and they depend on fire for their regeneration and well-being. Fire maintains these pinelands by killing any hardwoods that have invaded, and the heat of even the smallest fires opens the cones, allowing the seeds to sprout. Without fires, the pines in Florida, as in many other places, would be replaced by hardwood forests. It is difficult to watch a fire go wild, ripping through the understory and shooting flames up into the taller pines, but we must. Without the fires, these habitats will be gone.

The main pine forests in Florida are pine flatwoods, and they cover much of central Florida that is still undeveloped. Even with development, the pine flatwoods cover nearly half of the state. Oldtimers called the flatwoods "barrens." But to me, there is something rather stately and graceful about the thousands upon thousands of tall, straight, slender trunks, each surrounded by a suitable space. The ground in pine flatwoods is low lying, poorly drained, and flat. Here the pine trees are lanky and magnificent. Overhead the canopy is relatively open, with blue sky framing the tops of the trees. Even though Florida has more species of trees than any other state, 275 of the 625 found in North America, only three dominate the pinelands of Florida: Longleaf, Slash, and Pond Pine.

Many different kinds of shrubs flourish in the understory, including Wax Myrtle, Saw Palmetto, Rosemary, and Rusty Lyonia. These are the pinewoods that line the highways throughout Florida.

In the pine flatwoods, Pine Woods Treefrog, Pine Snake, Eastern Diamondback Rattlesnake, and Florida Box Turtle lurk in the dry grass or at the edge of the bogs. The wilder areas even have Black Bears and Bobcats, but the more usual mammals are Fox Squirrels and Gray Foxes. The bears eat mostly vegetation, such as roots, acorns, hearts and fruits of Saw Palmetto and Sabal Palms, blueberries, and Tupelo fruit, but they also eat insects such as Walking Sticks, Bessie Bugs, and Carpenter Ants. Bobcats, nocturnal and secretive, weigh only 12 to 25 pounds and look like a cat with a "bobbed" or short tail. With longer legs than a house cat, they can travel great distances. They prefer the wetter pinewoods and often stay close to the streams and river. They are a species of the forest and are found in patches of the pine flatlands that are larger than 250 acres, the average size of a female Bobcat's home range in the Southeast. Conservationists believe that at least 200 Bobcats are necessary to maintain a healthy and stable population.

Bobcats are still quite common in Florida, although they are seldom seen. They often make their dens in the dense palmettos in pine flatwoods, but solitary animals do well near civilization, eating mice, Cotton Rats, Cottontail Rabbits, and squirrels. Unable to take down a healthy deer, they search for the young or injured. Adult Bobcats rarely fall prey to other predators, but Bobcat kittens are eaten by foxes, coyotes, and owls, and are even killed by male Bobcats when not guarded by their mother. The cats are polygamous, each male wandering about in search of females for mating, and they breed from late February to early April. The female carries the young for about 60 days and then gives birth to three babies. The young remain in the den for only four or five weeks, and then begin accompanying their mother on hunts. Bobcats are not particularly long lived: the oldest known one lived only 15 years.

There is little chance of seeing a Bobcat from our sandy ridge lookout, but we can hope. Overhead, Myrtle and Pine Warblers fly from tree to tree. The Myrtle Warblers, often called Yellow-rumped Warblers, come to the Florida pines by the thousands to spend the winter, while the Pine Warblers are the commonest resident breeder in these woods. I listen for Red-cockaded Woodpeckers, but they no longer nest here. These woodpeckers flourish only where the trees are at least 75 or 80 years old, and the Longleaf Pines they prefer can live for 500 years. They are unique among woodpeckers in that they excavate their nest hole in live trees.

Some families of Red-cockaded Woodpeckers use the same nesting pine tree for many generations, and a given nest hole may be used for over 50 years. Red-cockaded Woodpeckers need many old nesting trees because they live in large social groups.

Where the land rises to form rolling hills there are sandhills or high pines. Sandhills also occur in the coastal plains of Georgia, the Carolinas (such as the Savannah River Site described in the previous chapter), Virginia, Alabama, Arkansas, Oklahoma, and Texas. Okeeheelee Park, where we are sitting, is a good example of this habitat (fig. 18.2). The sandhill community looks almost like the pine flatwoods because the same pine trees grow here, and they are as tall. The high refers to the hilly portions of the "barrens," rather than to the height of the trees. The distinctive feature of sandhills is the presence of a lush understory of perennial grasses, primarily Wiregrass. These habitats look a bit like a savannah,

18.2. Map of Sandhill and Sand Scrub habitats in Florida.

with Longleaf Pines scattered amid a grass prairie. Some areas have no oaks, while others have a very dense understory of them. In some places where fire has been eliminated, Turkey Oak has all but disappeared. Longleaf Pine cones can be six to ten inches long. Unlike the other pines in Florida, Longleaf Pine requires fire to open its cones. It shares this serotinous trait with the Pitch Pines of the barrens in the Northeast and Jack Pines of the midwestern United States.

Unlike the scrub pine habitat discussed below, high pines have few animal species that are unique. There are some unusual species that typify the habitat, including Florida Mouse, Sherman's Fox Squirrel, Pocket Gopher, Gopher Tortoise, and Red-cockaded Woodpecker. Gopher Tortoises were hunted for food up until 1987 when they gained protection, but by then they had disappeared from many high pine habitats. It is here that the Gopher Tortoise is making its stand, with the Indigo Snakes, Oak Toads, and Florida Scrub Lizards. Other species, such as Brown-headed Nuthatch and Yellow-breasted Chat also use these habitats primarily but also occur elsewhere.

The pine habitat I love the best is the pine scrub, for it is the most barren of them all, and we will visit this rare habitat in the next chapter. It is also Florida's most distinctive habitat, and about half of its species occur only in this habitat; in other words, they are endemic to the pine scrub. This habitat is dominated by an understory of nearly evergreen oaks and Florida Rosemary. Pine scrub occurs in the highest elevations of central Florida on ridges, where the Sand Pines grow no taller than 20 feet because the loose, sterile soil makes it difficult for large trees of any species to grow.

The color of the soil can be used as an indication of the age of the scrub. When water percolates through, the acids produced by the pine-oak litter remove the iron and organic stains from the sand, bleaching them white. The deeper the layer of white sand, the longer the scrub community has existed. Although the pine scrub soils are well drained and relatively dry, plants living there may not suffer because many have long "sinker" roots that tap moisture at considerable depths. The appearance of stress in scrub communities may be due to lack of nutrients more than to water stress. Most of the plants of the pine scrub also have a network of very shallow roots to capture all the available nutrients.

Most of the pine scrub remaining in Florida is around the Ocala National Forest, on the Lake Wales Ridge, and along the coastal ridge (fig. 18.2). The central Florida ridge is 100 miles long, and up to 13 miles wide. Most has been converted to citrus groves, but some native habitat remains in places like Blue Springs and Highlands Hammock. Pine scrub is recognizable because the understory is always composed of the same seven species: Myrtle and Scrub Oak, Saw Palmetto, Sand Live Oak, Chapman's Oak, Rusty Lyonia, and Florida Rosemary. Sand Pine is the diagnostic element, although it can be replaced by Slash Pine. The ground cover usually contains Gopher Apple and a variety of lichens, including the very fine Florida versions of Reindeer Moss.

Animals that are specialties of the pine scrub are the Florida Mouse, Florida Scrub Lizard, Florida Scrub Jay, Sand Skink, and the Blue-tailed Mole Skink. The latter three are federally listed as threatened. Most of these species require an open or almost nonexistent canopy. They disappear when shrubs get too tall. Widespread animals that also occur in the pine scrub are Black Bear, Bobcat, Gray Fox, Spotted Skunk, and Raccoon. Gopher Tortoises often live here, but prefer to go down the slopes into wetter vegetation to feed.

In the very driest, highest, and sandiest places on the Lake Wales Ridge are the ancient sand dunes, the very oldest habitats in Florida. The sand dunes remain from ancient seas, which built up beaches along its edges many millions of years ago. The soils are pure sand and do not hold any water. Few plants can grow, and those that do are often stunted and their leaves are waxy coated, hairy, or curled to keep in the moisture. Some of the rarest plants in the United States grow here, remnants of a past age, still clinging to a barren habitat. Over 30 species of plants that grow here are found nowhere else in the world. The animals that survive in these ancient dunes often are fossorial, living mainly below the ground to escape the hot searing sun. The Lake Wales National Wildlife Refuge has 13 endangered and threatened species of plants, 13 rare plants, and 4 federally listed animals—the greatest number of listed species in eastern North America.

The first people arrived in Florida about 12,000 years ago, just at the end of the last ice age. Because an ice sheet still covered much of northern North America, waters from the sea were tied up in the ice, sea level was some 200 feet lower than currently, and Florida was much larger than it is today. It provided a very hospitable environment for prehistoric people because it extended down into the warm and productive Caribbean waters. Florida was a mosaic of land and water, but forests fringed a wide savannah in western Florida, providing a wonderful hunting ground for Rabbit, deer, Black Bear and Raccoon, as well as the now-extinct Mammoth, Mastodon, Giant Armadillo, Tapir, and large Ground Sloth. People shared their hunting grounds with Saber-toothed Cats,

Giant Lions, Dire Wolves, and Panthers. By 11,000 years ago a massive extinction of the large land mammals, such as the Mastodons and Mammoths, occurred, and the big carnivorous predators also died out.

About 1,100 years ago, the early Floridians began agriculture, initially with gourds and corn, followed by squash, pumpkins, and beans. Some clans gave up their nomadic ways and cleared more land. They either cut a strip around the base of the pine trees so they would die (called girdling), or they burned them. Burning does not work very well with Longleaf and Slash Pines since they are fire adapted, and this practice resulted in massive regeneration of the seeds liberated when the heat of the fires opened the cones. Gradually, the many different tribes that lived in Florida settled down into villages and developed more and finer forms of agriculture.

Ponce de Leon and his Spanish explorers were the first Europeans to see Florida in 1513. They found the land apparently deserted, and claimed it for Spain as "La Florida," although many tribes were living throughout the area. In 1500 A.D. there may have been as many as 100,000 people living in present-day Florida, but by 1800 nearly all aboriginal Floridians were gone, mainly due to war, disease, and capture for slavery. The Seminoles and Miccosukees are the two American Indian tribes that currently live in south and central Florida. In 1819 the ownership of Florida was transferred from Spain to the United States. The first American governor of Florida, Andrew Jackson, advocated the extermination of the Seminoles, or their placement on "reservations." When extermination failed, the remaining Seminoles were herded into central Florida, far removed from the coasts where they might receive arms.

With the Seminoles forced from their villages, the pinelands of Florida were taken over by Americans from more northern states. Many of the pine forests were cleared by the Spaniards for orange groves. The great freezes in the mid-1800s killed many of the orange trees, and the citrus groves were moved farther south where the danger of frost was less. In the mid-1800s the sand scrub lands along the coast were used for cattle ranching. The ranchers were called "cow hunters" because they had to hunt down the cows that wandered about, and they did not want to be called cow "boys." The ranch hands carried a whip, which they cracked in the air fast enough to sound like a gunshot, giving rise to the term "Florida cracker." Pineapple was planted along the coast, but in the 1920s, nematodes and other worms infested the crops, Cuban pineapple flooded the market, and the Florida pineapple industry collapsed. The fields along the coastal ridge were abandoned and slowly reverted to their natural state. The pine scrub along the central ridge in Polk and Highlands counties was converted to citrus groves and residential development, and much of the rest of the central ridge soon suffered the same fate.

An elaborate system of canals and dikes that radiates from Lake Okeechobee southward through the Everglades was constructed in the late 1800s for flood control. In the early 1900s the state built the Tamiami Trail, creating the longest dike outside of Holland. The twentieth century saw the dewatering of the bottom third of Florida when gigantic water authority districts were set up, with nearly unlimited funds. The land was crisscrossed with canals, with little regard for natural drainage or the importance of water movement through the Everglades. Transforming marshes into agricultural land was viewed as a wonderful thing, a great achievement, and a source of great pride. Today I sit on an Everglades Committee aimed at restoring the water regime to the Everglades; we have come full circle and are now trying to re-create what we once destroyed. The 1950s and 1960s saw tremendous economic and residential growth as snowbirds from the North flocked to winter in this warm wonderland. Developers constructed apartments on the beaches near Miami and built roads to transport the hordes of winter visitors from the north. Much of southern Florida became a retirement community.

Walking slowly through Okeeheelee, away from the highway noise and bustle of retirement communities, we can search quietly for Gophor Tortoises. The low plants are fairly dense, and a variety of prickers and seeds literally fly to my pants as I walk across the field. I scan for any disruption in the vegetation that might indicate the subtle trails of Gopher Tortoises, and finding one, I follow it. The trail is only a foot or so wide, and the vegetation is flattened in the middle, with taller plants bowing over the path, providing a bit of shade. The trail winds circuitously through the sand and vegetation, and then leads abruptly straight into a large hole.

The hole is about 15 inches wide and 8 inches high. Weeds obscure the entrance, and roots and stems hang down over the roof. The many plants and roots that grow down from the roof of the burrow indicate that it has been undisturbed for many months. The dirt pile in front of the burrow is packed and is barely higher than the surrounding soil, tamped down by countless rains. Another burrow nearby seems active because only a few roots hang down, but it too is empty, guarded only by a Scrub Lizard (fig. 18.3).

We move on, searching for other burrows. The trail weaves along, under a Brazilian Pepper, through some bright Vinca, and past some Sand Burs and Beggars Ticks. My pants are covered with small seed ticks that cling, waiting to be carried far from parental plants, an excellent but

18.3. Scrub Lizard guarding the entranceway of a Gopher Tortoise burrow. Only a few roots hang down, indicating that the burrow may be active.

uncomfortable method of seed dispersal. The trail finally widens to nearly a foot and a half, the center is bare of vegetation, and few weeds lie strewn over the path. This path leads directly to another burrow, an active one by the looks of the fresh sand and lack of vegetation around the opening. The sand pile in front of the burrow is much larger and higher, and two trails of footprints suggest the tortoise was here today. The hard rain last night would have obliterated any old prints.

The burrow entrance is about the same size as the others, shaped like a crescent. Gopher Tortoise burrows can be identified because they are not round, as are the burrows of Armadillos and smaller Pocket Gophers. The crescent or oblong shape is required so the tortoise can fit its shell through the hole; its shell is wider than it is high. The width of a burrow is related to the size of the tortoise. The sand pile is nearly five feet long and four feet wide. When burrows are used regularly, the tortoise constantly brings up the yellow sand from below, which has not had sufficient time for the sun to bleach out the iron. Gopher Tortoises, earthworms, and other animals that make burrows are responsible for aerating and mixing the soil, and scientists estimate that burrowing animals turn over nearly half of the soil every decade.

Tortoise footprints lead from the burrow entrance over the sand pile, to the trail beyond. The tracks themselves look like bulldozer treads, about a foot wide, with each footprint a few inches from the last. The prints on the incline are deep, where the turtle had to push extra hard with its back legs to get up and over the lip of the burrow. Flat, hard-packed sand between the two lines of footprints indicates where the lower shell (called the *plastron*) was dragged.

18.4. *Diamond-back Rattlesnakes also use Gopher Tortoise burrows to escape the hot sun, basking at the entrance in the very early morning. This one is using an abandoned burrow, as indicated by the number of roots hanging down in the entrance.*

We peer in, but no one is home, and the burrow is dark. Many of these burrows extend up to 40 feet underground, and may go as deep as 15 feet. The record tunnel is 47 feet, but some may be even longer. Here they are only about 3 to 5 feet deep because the water table is so high. Gopher Tortoises are the tunnel builders for the whole pine community, regularly providing homes for Raccoons, Cotton Rats, lizards, frogs, insects, and many snakes such as Rattlesnakes and Indigo Snakes (fig. 18.4). Over 300 species of invertebrates and 60 species of vertebrates have been reported using Gopher Tortoise burrows throughout its range. They also provide nesting places for a number of lizards and snakes that would otherwise lay their eggs in rotten logs or resort to digging their own nests. Even Burrowing Owls will retreat to these burrows when frightened.

We follow the subtle trails that crisscross the field like footprints on new fallen snow. It reminds me of our childhood game of "Fox and Geese," when we made a series of trails and then dashed around madly trying to avoid the "fox." Now, we are trying just as hard to "find" the tortoise. We wander about for nearly two hours, finding only empty burrows. The sun is getting hotter, and I find the seeds and Sand Burrs more annoying. Finally we stumble upon a burrow with a tortoise (fig. 18.5). I have to get down on my hands and knees to see it, but it is there, filling the entire opening. It is sitting only a foot down the burrow, well out of the direct sun and just far enough to be invisible to most passersby. Its head is extended, and placidly it peers at me, its doleful dark brown eyes unblinking. Its front legs are out, as if it might be thinking of moving, but it holds its ground. Moving away to give Mike a chance to peer in, I notice a lizard

18.5. Gopher Tortoise coming out of its burrow, which may be 30 to 40 feet long.

scurrying away, dashing into another tortoise burrow, but it is too fast for us to identify.

The thrill of seeing my first Gopher Tortoise is exhilarating. They are a Species of Special Concern in Florida, not only because they are a fairly large tortoise that is vulnerable to humans, but because their habitat is dwindling everyday. They need the high, dry pinelands and sandhills for their burrows and nests, and do not live in the low pine flatwoods or the Everglades habitats that are widespread in south Florida. They require high enough sandy places so that their burrows are not below the water table, just the places people want to build homes or grow crops. The Gopher Tortoise has a compressed, oblong *carapace* (top shell) that is gray or black and tan. A large one reaches about 14 inches in length. Its front feet are spadelike, allowing it to dig burrows in the moist soil, while the hind feet are large and flattened to aid in crawling. We, however, are unable to see any of these traits; all we can see is the front of a partly withdrawn head.

We move off a short distance to wait, hoping that it will come out. It is maddening, for now I cannot see him, and if I move closer, I may scare him farther down his tunnel. Soon discouraged, Mike moves on to search for butterflies, but I remain. After about an hour I give up also, and walk softly away. Others have found that Gopher Tortoises leave their burrows only about half of the days a year, and I cannot wait until tomorrow.

Gopher Tortoises are known as a keystone species because their role in the community is so very important. If they were eliminated, many other species would suffer, and some would decline. Not only do they provide burrows for resting and nesting, but these same burrows serve as havens from predators and the cold at night—and safety when a massive fire rips through the pines. The heat can be so intense that many animals would perish if it were not for these underground burrows. Sometimes as many as 250 different species can be found in Gopher Tortoise burrows following a particularly hot fire.

Gopher Tortoises are well worth protecting, but a statewide ban on taking them was not instituted until 1988. Even today they are exposed to many threats. Loss of habitat goes without saying, but they also die from a respiratory disease that is passed from one tortoise to another. The release of a tortoise outside of its own habitat may expose the resident tortoises to the disease and should be undertaken only by the U.S. Fish and Wildlife Service and state agencies that quarantine each tortoise and examine it carefully before release.

I leave my tortoise, and pleased with my find, I abandon my quest for a foraging one, for it is midday, not a good time for a tortoise to be wandering about—or for me, either. It is far too hot, and tortoises must await the cooler temperatures of the late afternoon or the early morning to emerge. I stop to gaze at the calm water of another lake that was created when the park managers dug out the invasive Melaleuca trees, exotics they wanted to remove from the otherwise native habitat. Young native Slash Pines now line the bank. In the shallow water a lush stand of Pickerel Weed provides safe havens for a variety of swimming insects. Pickerel Weed is just beginning to come into flower, and the tall stalks of delicate purplish flowers are visited by a number of bees and other insects. A small mixed flock of Myrtle Warblers, Palm Warblers, and a Yellow-throated Warbler flit in the low branches of the pines. The wintering Myrtles are abundant here, far from the northern coniferous forests in which they nest. Sabal Palms and Saw Palmettos form a dense understory, and here and there is a Gallberry, the native holly. A very small plant that resembles rosemary catches my eye. It is called Penny Royal, and its leaves have a strange odor when crushed. The paleo-Indians and settlers mixed it with a kind of cold cream to make an insect repellent, and it can be grown in the garden to repel a variety of bugs.

The sky suddenly blackens, the clouds move menacingly closer, and too late I realize I should have stayed near the Nature Center. Within a few minutes a gentle rain gives way to a torrential downpour, lightning flashes, and winds rip through the pines. I rip a Palmetto frond from its base to use as an umbrella—it helps even though I worry fleetingly about what kinds of creatures might be living underneath. I hear a crack, too late to move away from the falling branch. Minutes later I find myself on the ground, a large branch lying on my head. I don't know how long I was out, but it was long enough to soak me through to the skin. Slowly I move my arm to try and remove the branch, but it too hurts, and I lie back down, letting the rain soak into my shirt, vaguely aware that I am getting wetter and wetter. After a few minutes, I sit up and remain quiet for a minute, dizzy and disoriented. Finally, my vision clears, and, rising carefully, I start down the trail, looking for Mike. I find him dashing down the trail looking for me, and together we walk to the car, vowing to come back when it is sunny.

Another day we return about noon, and wander the butterfly garden in search of the Atala Butterfly common to the park. Our son David is along, and is anxious to look for the tortoises. A tall man with long curly black hair, David creates Web sites to support his real love—acting off-Broadway. He patiently looks at the Coontie Cycads we point out, but is not impressed with the small cycads the Atala caterpillars have eaten nearly to the ground. Fortunately, there are a lot of the cycads, and many are still lush and growing strong. The orange caterpillars are quite ferocious and chomp on the fronds until little is left. Then they form small chrysalides the size of a blueberry and begin their development. The cold front that passed through a few days ago must have killed all the adults, but the young caterpillars and chrysalides are quite hardy, an excellent adaptation to the sporadic cold winter nights of southern Florida.

Overhead a pair of Turkey Vultures wheel in the sky, their dark wings forming slight V's. They soar higher and higher on the rising thermals and nearly disappear into the billowy clouds. A Fish Crow squawks hoarsely as it flies through the trees to join the large flock congregating on the edge of the forest. At this time of year, Fish Crows in Florida travel in large noisy groups. We retrace our steps from the other day, checking each tortoise burrow in turn. But no one seems to be home—no shadows fill the entranceways. There is no indication of the tortoise that calls this its home range. It is quite unusual to see one of these tortoises, for they stick to the trails in the woods. When they remain absolutely still, they blend in with the sticks and small branches strewn in the underbrush.

Shafts of light penetrate to the needle-strewn path as we amble along, looking and listening for a tortoise moving quietly through the undergrowth. Small shrubs line our path: Wax Myrtle, Cocoplum, Red Bay, Southern Red Maple, and young Cypress. The Red Maple leaves have turned a bright red, Florida's version of late fall color. At the edge of a pond there is a small patch of glades Sawgrass, a tall thin grass with saw-tooth edges that is common in the Everglades. In some places it is nearly eight feet tall, and its razor-sharp edges account for its name. A variety of dragonflies flit from one Pickerel Weed to another, landing occasion-ally. A lone female with a bright red body skims across the surface, dip-ping her abdomen in the water to touch the floating vegetation. She is laying eggs, one at a time. They hatch and drop into the water, where the small predaceous larvae forage for weeks or months before they climb up the stems of Pickerel Weed or Arrowhead to break from their exoskele-ton and emerge as delicate dragonflies.

On a distant log, two medium-sized Red-bellied Turtles are basking in the warm sun. Although the log is nearly 10 feet long, they are together, one with its front legs on the back of the other. They live in the shallow, still waters where they can find carrion and vegetation for food. Unlike the Gopher Tortoises, Red-bellied Turtles have a number of enemies, including Alligators. This pond has no Alligators, and for the moment the adult turtles are safe. The baby turtles are just the right size to be eaten by herons and egrets, and many perish before they are even a few months old.

Female Red-bellied Turtles have to leave the safety of the pond to dig a nest in the packed sand, and they may travel as far as a few hundred feet away from the pond before encountering sand that is to their liking. Females nest from May until October, and they lay about 30 eggs in the nest cup before they cover it with sand. Their eggs normally take only 60 to 70 days to hatch, depending on where they laid them. If there is full sun penetration, then the eggs will hatch sooner because they are kept warmer than those in nests under dense vegetation.

We move on past a dense stand of Saw Palmetto into an area where the larger Slash Pine trunks are blackened; this part of the forest burned nearly 15 years ago. The periodic droughts render the forest vulnerable to fires, ignited by lightning or a careless smoker. The primary trees of the flatwoods have adaptations to deal with fire. The pine bark peels into paper-thin layers as it burns, removing the hottest part of the fire from the trunk. Cabbage Palm leaf fronds direct the fire away from the trunk because they burn up and out; Saw Palmetto burns freely but can bud from any undamaged portion of the trunk or from the underground stems that never burn.

We return to the path, discouraged. It is a lovely day, and the forest is peaceful and deserted. Few people venture within, being more inter-ested in golf, roller-blading, or running on the paths in the open, mowed,

18.6. Gopher Tortoise foraging on grass and other vegetation

well-tended lawns that surround the forest. We sit on a wooden bench and contemplate what South Florida must have been like before we controlled the mosquitoes, drained the Everglades, and managed the water. From around the corner of the path, motion catches my eye. Slowly a Gopher Tortoise shuffles along, stopping to eat some low vegetation, slowly chomping away, oblivious of us. Carefully it pulls the leaves from the weeds and chews, working its jaws up and down. With hardly a glance around, the tortoise moves on toward a Prickly-pear Cactus growing on a barren spot. Ignoring the spines, it takes small bites, lifting its head to the sun while it chews. Prickly-pears and Gopher Apple are two of their favorite foods. We creep slowly forward. When we get within about 30 feet, it stops chewing, raises its head, and deliberately looks around. It returns to feeding when it sees that we are motionless (fig. 18.6).

After sampling the cactus for a while, it moves on, walking to the edge of another path. A small boy scampers up, the first we have seen all day, sees the turtle, and makes a beeline for it. The tortoise quickens its pace, turns at a right angle, and makes for an open path through the underbrush, under the Saw Palmetto. It stops briefly, turns part way around to peer at the youngster, and then resumes its journey, crawling faster than before. We are surprised by how fast it can move, and within two minutes it has slid down into a burrow.

Fortunately there is enough habitat here in the pines for a Gopher Tortoise to wander around, and still find a place to dig a burrow on its own. But in many places there is simply not enough space available, as the pineland patches are too small. The habitats preferred by Gopher Tortoises

have gradually shrunk over the years, leaving them in isolated populations. Most populations are separated by such great distances that there is
no chance of interbreeding or gene exchange, certainly a concern for conservation managers. As these habitat islands shrink, there is an increasing
likelihood that the isolated tortoises will die out as well. When human activity increases, the chances that the tortoises will be taken for pets or are
killed by cars also increases.

Up ahead, an Armadillo ambles slowly along, peering at the ground.
Armadillos range from the southern United States to Argentina in South
America. Fossils show that armadillos lived in Florida for several million
years before becoming extinct at the end of the last ice age some 10,000
years ago. The Armadillos now in Florida made their own way here from
Texas sometime in the mid-1800s, probably aided by intentional intro-
ductions. But this theory is controversial; some biologists fervently believe that Armadillos never made it here on their own, but were brought
by people. With binoculars I can see his long, sticky tongue flash out to
capture a tiny ant, and then he noses on. Armadillos can consume some
200 pounds of insects a year, and they can smell insects as much as six
inches underground. When they locate an insect, they rapidly dig up the
soil with their strong legs and long curved claws, leaving deep holes that
makes them very unpopular with home owners, golf course ground-
keepers, and anyone else trying to maintain a smooth unblemished
lawn. Our daughter Debbie is none too fond of the "dillo" that visits her
lawn each night, leaving a string of holes, but I would love to have one.
Small streams or lagoons do not deter them from finding golf courses, for
they plunge in and simply walk on the bottom under the water, holding
their breath until they reach the other side.

Armadillos were eaten by the earliest aboriginal Floridians, and more
recently, their flexible shells were made into handbags. Today they are
used for medical research because their body temperature is lower than
traditional laboratory animals such as rats and mice, and leprosy bacteria
requires such a temperature. Anti-leprosy drugs are routinely tested on
Armadillos. Moreover, females give birth to genetically identical quadru-
plets, which also makes them important research animals.

In the face of predators or other disturbances, Armadillos either form
an armored ball by rolling up, or they jump up in the air. This jumping
up may be their crude attempt at scaring the enemy. Although the armor prevents dogs, foxes, and other small predators from eating them,
larger predators such as Panthers, Bobcats, and Alligators simply bite
through the shell. On a roadway at night, trapped in the blinding glare

of oncoming headlights, their habit of jumping up into the air often proves fatal. If they had run swiftly or remained quietly on the ground, cars would pass over without injuring them. They are frequently killed on roads, giving rise to the common name "Texas turkey" and "possums on the half-shell." Indeed, cars are a leading cause of death of adult Armadillos. Barring car accidents, disease, and predators, an Armadillo can live for 10 to 15 years in the wild. This one is safe here in the scrub pines, but Route 1 is only a few hundred yards away, well within its home range. Before reaching me, he turns off and heads into the dense undergrowth where he no doubt has a burrow. Armadillos usually come out at dusk to hunt for ants, millipedes, roaches and worms. Sometimes they even eat amphibians and reptiles, including their eggs and those of ground-nesting birds. I wonder idly what effect they are having on the reproduction of the local snakes and lizards. I feel lucky to have seen this Armadillo, and I wait quietly for a few minutes, giving him ample time to find his burrow before rising to continue on.

Lake Wales: The True Barrens of Florida

For many years I dreamed of visiting the Lake Wales area in central Florida, dreamed of seeing the most ancient dune habitat in all of Florida. This sandy ridge is similar to the scrub pine habitats along the Atlantic Coast of Florida, but I wanted to see it because of its unique features. Two to three million years ago, this ridge was all that was left of Florida, and it remained as isolated islands where unique plant and animal communities could develop, surrounded by shallow seas. Powerful oceanic currents swept down along the coasts of Georgia and the Carolinas, bringing tons of siliceous sand, until today the ridge has 30 to 40 feet of sand on top of limestone rocks. When the sea level fell again, the islands were left as the backbone or ridge of central Florida, the highest place in the state. Now the sea is 60 miles away, and the "islands" are surrounded by a sea of citrus groves and homes.

Finally, I stand atop the dunes and survey the mosaic of plant communities that can survive on the sterile, nutrient-poor soils, periodically pounded by heavy summer rains and swept by raging wildfires. Some of the Sand Pine trees are short, sparse, and have the same twisted appearance. These pines do not shed their lower limbs as do the Slash and Longleaf Pines, but keep their lower branches, accounting for their use as Christmas trees. Saw Palmettos form dense stands on the lower elevations, and Florida Rosemary grows on the ridge tops that the locals call "Rosemary Balds." Here the Rosemary is less dense than that along the coast, and is shorter than I. The air is still, no breezes blow in from the faraway ocean, but it is easy to imagine this ridge as a series of islands once surrounded by raging seas.

The Lake Wales ridge extends for nearly 100 miles from Clemont in Lake County, south to Venus in Highlands County. It is never more than 13 miles wide, and sometimes as narrow as 3. The highest point is still just over 300 feet above sea level. It is here in one of the last remaining undisturbed scrub habitats in central Florida that the Archbold Biological

Station was started by Richard Archbold in 1941, the year I was born. Archbold was an aviator who explored New Guinea and eventually acquired the estate of John A. Roebling, an industrialist who lived in Trenton, New Jersey, not far from the New Jersey Pinelands. As the years passed, Archbold became more eccentric, but he retained his love for the scrub, adding more parcels of land to the station with the passing years. When he died, he left permanent funding for the station, a rare and wonderful opportunity for science and for the preservation of some of the last remaining pine scrub that would have fallen to citrus groves were it not for his foresight. Today the station owns 5,000 acres and is a significant natural reserve and research center. Scrub on the Lake Wales ridge once covered 200,000 acres, but now only 29,000 remain, and Archbold Biological Station is a shining jewel located at the southern end of the ridge and an island in a sea of citrus and sprawl.

The Scrub Live Oaks here are even more stunted than on the coastal ridge. Most are shorter than the average basketball player, and there are few pines. Over 300 vascular plants have been collected from pine scrub, and as many as 40 percent occur only in this habitat, defined as endemism. This is a high rate of endemism. Many of these are restricted to the Lake Wales Ridge. At least nine vertebrates are endemic, and scientists can only guess at the number of unique invertebrates that live here. Endemic vertebrates include the Scrub Lizard, Blue-tailed Mole Skink, Sand Skink, Peninsula Crowned Snake, Short-tailed Snake, and Florida Mouse. The three reptiles are sand swimmers, spending most of their lives within the sand. At least six endemic ants have been identified.

Archbold is unique because it is the site of one of the longest and most detailed studies of any bird—the Florida Scrub Jay (fig. 19.1). These jays, long isolated from Scrub Jays breeding in the western United States, are a relict population of a species that once was more widespread. Today, they are considered a separate species, and the closest Scrub Jays outside of Florida are in central Texas. In Florida, Scrub Jays are dependent on short oak scrubland, with scattered pines. When not disturbed by people, Scrub Jays are extremely tame, making them ideal to watch, photograph, and study. They have a fascinating and complex social system that involves helpers at the nest. Besides, they are lovely and engaging birds that readily adjust to human observers.

These characteristics led Glen Woolfenden to begin studying them at Archbold in the late 1960s. Starting out many years ago to explore the evolution of birds by studying bones, Glen gravitated to the jays because he was fascinated by their strange social groupings, so unlike most

19.1. Florida Scrub Jays readily adapt to people, and here one is watching intently in an alert posture.

birds that traveled in mated pairs. At a time when few ornithologists thought of starting long-term studies, Glen set out to mark all the birds in his study area so he could begin to figure out who they all were and why they remained on the same territories throughout the year in small flocks. A tall handsome young man with twinkling eyes, silent strength, and incredible determination, he labored long hours in the hot scrub to band every bird. Several years later he was joined by John Fitzpatrick, known as Fitz, and together they have spent over 30 years following many different family groups on Archbold. When other scientists assumed they had learned all there was, and questioned their persistence, they continued, slowly amassing the personal histories of their beloved jays. I first met Glen in the early 1970s, and over the years we have shared special discussions about social systems, ornithology, and the philosophy of science. His eyes still twinkle and flash as he talks about the jays, and his fervor has not been dulled by the gray in his hair. He has been a strong supporter of my own journey, and I am pleased to see him on his home turf.

Scrub Jays are called communal breeders because they live in family groups, and their offspring often remain in the parental territory to help them with the next brood. Most Jay families have a territory of about 25 acres, or about eight to ten city blocks. Glen and Fitz now know the parents and grandparents, and even the great-grandparents of each Jay. They know more about the genealogy of the Jays than most people know about their own families. With such an investment in the Jays, it is critical that the population be protected and surrounded by a wide buffer zone. Archbold provides this protection. Scrub Jays have rather specific habitat requirements, preferring oak scrub with Archbold Oak, Scrub Live Oak, and Chapman's Oak, along with Saw Palmetto, Sabal or Sand Palmetto, scattered Sand Pines, and Rosemary. They shun the dense Sand Pines where the sky is not visible. In the taller scrub, or where the habitat is dominated by pine, the Scrub Jays are replaced by quite ordinary Blue Jays. Although they are very widespread, Blue Jays have escaped detailed study. Personally, I feel that Blue Jays are one of

19.2. *The sandhills scrub is a habitat similar to the dwarf barrens of New Jersey in that the vegetation is so low I can easily look over it. Only a few scattered pines rise above ten feet.*

our most lovely and fascinating birds and deserve their own long-term study.

The aspect and ambiance of the oak scrub is more like the dwarf Pine Barrens in New Jersey than other pine barrens habitats, although the plant species differ. Standing on top of a ridge, it is possible to look for miles over the scraggly palmettos and short pines (fig. 19.2). We see only the tip of the forest in the pine scrub—more than 75 percent of the oak biomass is buried beneath the soil, ensuring that the oaks can resprout quickly following a wildfire. The Pitch Pines in the dwarf forests of New Jersey employ the same strategy: massive root systems just below the surface are ready to sprout after even the hottest fires that sweep through the pines every 10 to 20 years. Unlike the dwarf pines of New Jersey, Florida pine scrub does best when it is burned only every 30 to 80 years. Otherwise, the dominant scrub plants do not reach reproductive maturity before the next fire. What is remarkably different about the Scrub Jay's habitat is the rapid shifts in aspect. In many other pine barrens regions, the habitat is remarkably uniform for acres and acres. But here, the habitat changes every few yards. The changes are caused by slight differences in elevation of a yard or so.

We bump along with Glen and his wife Jan in an old white truck, clutching at the dashboard to keep from hitting our heads on the roof. Spotting a Scrub Jay perched on the top of a scrubby Archbold Oak, he screeches to a halt, and we all jump out. Glen tosses a peanut to the

ground, and Mike and I watch in amazement as we are instantly surrounded by eight Jays, all hopping at our feet in the pure white sand.
One picks up the peanut, swallows it in one gulp, and flies to a nearby
oak. It raises its bill skyward and makes a rapid mechanical clicking
call, identifying itself as the resident female. The Florida Scrub Jay is 12
inches long, blue and gray with a dusky brown back and long tail, and
without a crest. Delicate blue feathers separate a white throat from gray
underparts. It lacks the white wingspots and white tailfeather tips of the
common Blue Jay, and it is smaller than our northern Blue Jay. It is really quite exquisite—as is our own Blue Jay of the New Jersey Pinelands.

The Scrub Jays make use of the mosaic of habitats by nesting in the
dense scrub bushes and feeding in the more open patches or recently
burned areas where insects are more abundant. The thick scrub provides
protection from predators, but in the open places it is easier for them to
find prey. The open patches of bare sand also provide places for the Jays
to cache acorns for the wintertime when insects are no longer available.
Once Scrub Jays find suitable habitat, they are relatively sedentary, remaining in the same place for years and years. They defend the same territory and the same mate for their entire lives. Finding a new territory is
difficult, partly because the established Jays vigorously defend their territories and remain on them year-round. There are few places for birds
without a home to go—the habitat is full. In the jargon of population
biologists, the habitat has reached carrying capacity: there is no more
room for additional breeding pairs.

The population saturation forces the young to stay at home. Non-
breeding individuals remain on their natal territory and help the breeding pairs raise their young. Such birds are called "helpers." Pairs with
helpers usually raise 50 percent more young than those without. This social system is called *cooperative breeding.* Since there is really nowhere else
to go, they simply wait for the old pair to die, thus they may not breed
until they are three or four years old, and some never breed at all. Much
of their social system derives from this waiting game.

Divorce is very rare, and only when one mate dies does the other take
a new one. The divorces that Glen and Fitz observed over the years usually involved sickness or injury (fig. 19.3). The new mate is not one of
their offspring, but an immigrant who has been a helper on the territory.
This ensures that the population is not inbred. There are many advan-
tages to maintaining the same mate from year to year. Among mated
pairs the courtship period is shorter, lingering courtship throughout the
nesting period seems less necessary, egg laying is earlier, the territory

19.3. Scrub Jay waiting for the trap door to be opened on a trap set by Glen Woolfenden in his long-term study of their population dynamics.

boundaries are less in dispute, and they already have worked out how to raise a brood efficiently. The clutch size is often smaller for newly established pairs, even when the female previously had a mate, and established pairs raise more young than first- or second-time breeders. Increased fledging success means that they will have helpers the following year, and having helpers increases their reproductive success. The pattern becomes circular, and has been found in many species of birds—monogamous birds live longer and raise more young. The parallels with humans are striking—married folks live longer than single ones.

While Jan searches for nests, I wander off into the pines, stopping at each ant mound, peering at the sand rimming the hole. The ants have been busy bringing up the darker sand from below, and it stands out against the bleached surface sand. I am on the lookout for fungus-growing ants that are also leaf-cutting ants. There is a specialized ant, known to scientists as *Trachymyrmex septentrionalis,* that maintains gardens of a unique fungus that cannot survive on its own. The ants tend the fungus, and the fungus provides food for the ants. The ants are intriguing because they exist here in the Florida pine scrub and sandhills, as well as in the Pine Barrens of New Jersey. Their closest relatives occur in Panama and farther south, in dry desert regions.

Suddenly the Jays are very noisy, and I thread my way carefully back to the truck only to discover that two different families are fighting. It soon quiets down, and the nonresident family drifts off into the scrub.

Only the breeding pair of Jays engages in courtship, while the helpers discretely refrain from any sign of impropriety. During the courtship period, the male remains with the female, although actual defense of her seems unnecessary. Copulation occurs in secret, at least from the researchers. Egg-laying begins later in March, and the female lays one egg a day until her clutch is complete. One of the odd things about Scrub Jays is that they lay their eggs in March and incubate in late March and April, when the oaks have lost their leaves. Without leaves to obscure the nests, they are maximally visible to predators. This probably accounts for their habit of building their nests in the densest oaks with the most twigs and spins—defense against hunting Cooper's Hawks. Last week, H.B. Tordoff and Glen watched a Cooper's Hawk take a Mourning Dove that was in the open in the scrub—a rare treat since predation is hard to witness. Tall and slim with snow white hair, H.B. has worked for many years on the reintroduction and conservation of Peregrine Falcons in Minnesota. When he isn't working with the falcons, he is out hunting quail or grouse with dogs. Ornithology is a small world—H.B. was my Ph.D. adviser at the University of Minnesota many years ago, and he also was Glen's Master's degree adviser. This makes Glen and me academic siblings, an amusing thought. H.B. had a critical role in my development for he alone gave me confidence at a time when few women were successful in ornithology, and even fewer were active field researchers.

Nesting of the Jays is timed so that the young hatch just when the oaks have a new flush of catkins and leaves, which corresponds to the time when the most insects are available. The fresh leaves and catkins also help to hide the baby Jays from the eyes of predators, providing an additional measure of protection. Young Jays may be helpers for up to six years, although for most the apprenticeship is much shorter. Some young Jays ultimately leave to disperse or to find mates, and some just die without ever breeding. Females often find a mate within two years, while most males are not so lucky. The male and female helpers each have a different strategy for success. Males seem to wait on their natal territory for the resident male to die, thereby allowing them to take over the territory. Nearly 60 percent of the male Jays finally inherit a territory from their father. If the opportunity never arises, they eventually die as childless uncles. Females, on the other hand, often disperse from their parents' territory into others, where they have a chance of vying for a widower's favors. Nearly all of the females that breed do so outside of their natal territory. This dispersal has a cost in terms of increased energy needs to fly a longer distance and increased risk of predation, and females have a higher mortality rate than males.

In many ways, the Jays are in a dilemma: staying at home is safer and involves a lower death rate, but it also involves waiting longer for the territorial bird to die if you are a male, and almost no chance of breeding if you are a female. On the other hand, leaving involves a much higher death rate, with a slim chance of finding a widowed female if you are a male, and a quite good chance of finding a widowed male if you are a female. When any female dies, the widower is immediately surrounded by many potential suitors and is not unpaired for long.

Jays have to worry mainly about Cooper's Hawks, which are quite adept at flying through the thick oaks in pursuit of young Jays. Sometimes Jays are taken by female Sharp-shinned Hawks or by Merlins, and occasionally by Harriers, Great Horned Owls, and Red-tailed Hawks. Black Racers are the most abundant snake in the pine scrub, followed by Eastern Coachwhips, both excellent tree climbers that eat baby Jays. The few rattlesnakes around are mainly nocturnal and move along the ground. The Jays actually have more predators to worry about in the winter, when migrant hawks from farther north swell the ranks of raptors on site.

While the Jays have to worry about hawks and other predators, they do not have to worry about contaminants. Several years ago, Glen, Mike, and I analyzed the levels of heavy metals in the eggs of Scrub Jays. Because they are endangered, we used only abandoned eggs or those that did not hatch. The levels of contaminants in the eggs were well below those known to cause any adverse effects in birds. We hadn't expected to find high levels, but it is important to rule out contaminants as a possible cause of any population declines.

Scrub Jays prepare for winter mainly by caching acorns in the sand. They put them on the sand, push them under, and then peck with all their might as if they were hammering a nail. Within seconds the acorns disappear, and the Jays pick up another one to cache. During the cold winter they search through the ground for the acorns, throwing sand in every direction. With diligent searching they invariably find an acorn, often one stashed by another family member, but that small bit of information has long since been forgotten, and the Jays eat the acorn anyway. They cache acorns singly, and each Jay may cache between 6,000 and 8,000 acorns a year—an impressive job.

So often today, Scrub Jays are isolated in small suburban forests and are separated from stable populations in nature preserves. This disrupts their social system, and their normal dispersal pattern is altered. Eventually they may die out. Female Scrub Jays in suburban habitats often leave their families at an earlier age and have to travel farther to find suitable habitat. Because they leave home earlier, and fly farther, they suffer high mortality. In contrast, females from preserves leave when they are older and remain closer to home. They never disperse to suburban habitats, leaving the suburban populations even more isolated. Over time, few Scrub Jays survive in these suburbs, even though the habitat appears suitable. Fitzpatrick, Woolfenden, and others have estimated that at least 40 territories are necessary for a population to be viable. Given the average size of territories, between 1,000 and 2,000 acres of suitable habitat are required. Thus, there are not very many conservation areas in Florida that are large enough to support viable populations of Scrub Jays, and less than ten such populations exist.

The jays playing at our feet are captivating, and when they all line up on the tops of the scrub inches from our camera lenses, they are impossible to resist. It is not clear what I can do with four rolls of Scrub Jay portraits, but I cannot resist one last picture of the resident male standing on a nearby pine, surveying the territory he has maintained for 12 years, the same one that was maintained by his father for the previous 13 years. Still, it's time to stop feeding them peanuts. I want to move on to see the most barren habitats here—the sandhills on the red sand ridge. Climbing in the truck, we head for the highest ground around. The Red Hills are so named because this high ridge is composed of red sand, while the scrub pine habitat below is a pure white sand. The ridge runs from here some 100 miles northward, eventually to the Ocala National Forest. The Red Hills have a number of endangered plants that grow nowhere else in the world, remnants of ancient populations that lived on these lands millions of years ago. These plants even managed to survive when the ridge was a series of isolated islands surrounded by the Atlantic Ocean.

As we drive higher on the sandhills, the Sand Pine gives way to Slash Pines, Hickory, and overgrown oaks. There are a few Turkey Oaks, and a few Longleaf Pines. Historically, some of the Longleaf Pines that grew here were four to five feet in diameter, but these quickly fell to the loggers to be used for construction. When the Longleaf Pine forests covered the sandhills, Rufous-sided Towhees, Brown-headed Nuthatches, Mourning Doves, Pine Warblers, Yellowthroats, Wild Turkeys, and Ivory-billed Woodpeckers nested here. The Ivory-bills disappeared along with the giant Longleaf Pines, and the species was thought to be extinct, although there were tantalizing reports and carefully guarded secrets about their possible whereabouts. In the spring of 2005, the first confirmed sightings of a male Ivory-bill were reported from Arkansas. I never gave up hope for them. The Wild Turkeys grew scarcer. Now only the Mourning Doves,

Pine Warblers, and Rufous-sided Towhees are common, moving through the knee-high Wiregrass and tall Slash Pines.

On the highest ridge we find several burrows of Gopher Tortoises, and two are at home. They peer out at me, their dark brown eyes unblinking. They ignore even the flashing camera and wait patiently for the sun to move lower in the sky before coming out to forage on Gopher Apple or Prickly-pear Cactus. For them, the ridge top is still suitable, for it is open and covered with Wiregrass. Farther down the slope, the habitat is too dense for most sandhill species. It will take years to return to the typical sandhill community of a few majestic Longleaf Pines towering over the scraggly Turkey Oaks, with a rich continuous understory of knee-high Wiregrass. But Archbold remains a jewel, harboring a wide diversity of endangered, threatened, and rare plants and animals, and a mosaic of different habitat types from pine flatwoods, through pine scrub, to sandhills. Scientists have the freedom to study the unique flora and fauna without the threat of disturbance or destruction. As they work along with the Florida Fish and Game Commission, the amount of land that is preserved will continue to expand. The habitat islands of the Lakes Wales ridge can continue far into the future. Scrub Jays will prosper in their family groups, Scrub Lizards will search for insects in the lichens and brown oak leaves, and tiny ants will continue to tend their fungus gardens.

It is a breathtaking drive from the high sandy ridges of Lake Wales to the Everglades to the south, through the Longleaf Pine forests. We traverse the same ecological gradient as driving from the dwarf pines of the New Jersey Pine Barrens through the lowland pines to the marshes along the Atlantic Coast. Although the gradient in pines and oaks is most obvious, it is the bird communities that have received the most attention; reptiles and mammals are more active at night, and birds have the decency to be active when we are.

David Hirth, Larry Harris, and Reed Noss studied the bird communities in a mature Longleaf Pine forest in east central Florida, northeast of Brooksville. Birds that breed in Florida, known as permanent residents, constituted the majority of the species they observed, as well as the majority of the individual birds. Even during the winter, migrants did not swamp the native bird community. They found that there were twice as many birds present in the summer compared to the winter, even though the climate in this part of Florida is relatively mild in winter. Pine forests are rich in both the number of insect species and in the number of individual insects present, partly explaining the large number of insect-eating birds. These included warblers, vireos, and tanagers. In the summer the pine trees were dripping with Yellow-throated Warbler, Red-eyed Vireos, Parula, and Pine Warbler, with the calls of White-eyed Vireos and Oven-birds echoing from the understory. Only the White-eyed Vireo, Yellow-throated Warbler, and Pine Warbler remained to glean insects from the pine boughs in the fall and winter, the others departing for winter quarters. Other insect eaters such as Downy and Pileated Woodpeckers moved up and down the trunks throughout the year, searching for insects in their own way.

Overall, Hirth and her colleagues found that permanent residents dominated the bird community in both summer and winter, indicating that the Longleaf Pine community is self-contained. This differs from many other pine communities, even in the southeastern United States. Perhaps food resources do not vary seasonally as much as they do in other pine communities. Certainly they do not vary as much as food resources in forests farther north, where insects decline markedly in the fall and winter. It may also be that the resident birds in Longleaf Pine communities have had generations to adapt to these habitats and are adept at finding and tracking food resources through the seasons. Another possibility is that the resident birds know their territories well enough to outcompete any birds from farther north that might venture into Longleaf Pine forests. Their data is exciting, because it suggests that the old-growth, Longleaf Pine forests are stable, as long as they are not disturbed and fragmented. The birds can remain in these forests year-round, obtaining all of their requirements, without migrating farther south.

It is interesting to contrast the birds of a mature, old-growth Longleaf Pine forest with those of an exotic (nonnative) stand. In Florida there are many choices; several different exotic tree species have invaded pine flatlands, including Brazilian Pepper and Casuarina, also called Australian Pine, although it is not a pine at all. Many people like these trees because they are attractive, and Casuarina is useful as a quick-growing windbreak or a hedge. In a study of a dense Brazilian Pepper stand in South Florida, John Curnutt found only six species breeding: Cardinal, Common Yellowthroat, Red-winged Blackbird, Rufous-sided Towhee, White-eyed Vireo, and Carolina Wren. Native pine flatland habitats normally have about 28 species of breeding birds. Densities of breeding birds in native pine flatlands were nearly ten times as high as they were in the Brazilian Pepper stand. Still, I am amazed that any species are using the Brazilian Pepper, since whenever I pass such stands I seldom see any birds.

Nonnative plants are not the only invaders in Florida. The state estimates that more than 200 nonnative species of wildlife live in Florida,

including troublesome species such as Boa Constrictors and Green Igua-
nas from Central and South America. Monk Parakeets and several other
species of parrots and parakeets from Mexico and tropical South America form dense flocks. Burmese Pythons that reach eight feet in length
are breeding in the Everglades, and they might eventually displace native snakes. Pet owners release or lose many of these species, and others
escape from zoos or pet stores. One dealer lost some 10,000 geckos. As
troublesome as these escapees are, it is the dwindling of native habitat
due to invasive plants that is the major problem.

The first animals that are affected by loss of the pine flatlands are those
that require large, unbroken stretches of habitat. These disappeared first
from much of the landscape as land was cleared for agriculture, phosphate
mines, and residences. The habitat was broken up into smaller and smaller
patches, with fewer connecting corridors. Remnant populations survive
where the pine flatlands are unbroken, but few large patches are left. Perhaps the species that best typifies this problem is the Florida Panther.

The Florida Panther has adapted to the pine flatlands and subtropical
Everglades of Florida, having arrived in the late Pleistocene about 10,000
years ago and then spreading over much of the state. Indeed, it ranged
over much of the Americas, from the Yukon to the tip of South America.
The Panther, which is the same size as the African Leopard, has the greatest natural distribution of any mammal in the Western Hemisphere, except for man. It occurs in vary diverse habitats, from the tropics to elevations of over 13,000 feet in Ecuador. It also goes by the name of Cougar,
Puma, Mountain Lion, or in Latin America simply as Leon. Panthers were
very successful in the pine flatlands of Florida for many centuries and are
recognized today as the Florida Panther because of their separation from
the Cougars that remain in the western states. Studies of Panthers fitted
with radio collars show that Panthers prefer the forest uplands where they
can stalk deer, feral hogs, and Raccoons.

The Panther is tawny brown on top and creamy white below, with a
J-shaped tail (fig. 19.4). A large male can weigh 135 pounds and be nearly
eight feet long from muzzle to the tip of its tail, and it may stand 24 inches
tall at the shoulder. The female is smaller than the male. Male Panthers
have a home range that averages about 135,000 acres (212 square miles),
although females make do with an average of only 74,100 acres (110
square miles). Still, this is a lot of space to search for each other, and it
sometimes takes them a week to get around their home range.

Panthers usually mate in January or February, with a three-month
gestation period. Females may breed when they are two and a half years

19.4. One of the rarer animals in Florida is the Florida Panther, which has been declining despite conservation efforts. Remarkably, they can disappear in the Sawgrass or in the pines.

old, but males usually wait until they are three or older. The females give birth only every other year. Females have only five or six young in their lifetime, but males may be reproductively active until they are 20 years old. The babies are born in a den, which may be no more than a depression in the ground, a crevice under roots or falling logs, or an opening under palmettos. The young can make their own kills by 10 or 11 months of age, but they remain with their mother for a year to 18 months, during which time they learn further hunting skills. Once on their own, the young wander until they can establish a territory.

Cougars, including Florida Panthers, were once common enough to be hunted relentlessly. They were eliminated from the 13 colonies by 1700. Most states had bounties on them, and Florida had a bounty of five dollars up until the end of the 1800s. Some western states still allow sport hunting of Cougars. The total population of Panthers in Florida is between 30 and 50, and most are in the southwestern part of the state. Conservationists believe that a population of 50 to 70 would have a good chance of surviving for at least 200 years, based on population viability models. These are computer models that take into account reproductive rates, migration, life span, and random mortality to predict the probability of extinction for a population of any initial size. Given the small current population estimate, the Panther is in serious trouble. But it is not hopeless, for some other species have rebounded with populations as low as this.

Even though they have been studied so intensively for two decades, Panthers have continued to decline in number. They suffer from a great variety of maladies, including congenital heart defects, low sperm densities, abnormal sperm, thyroid problems, and immune system disfunctions. In addition, some young males are born with their testes not descended, called cryptorchidism. Many of these traits could be caused by inbreeding, and this led scientists to worry that the decline of the Panthers was due to inbreeding. After all, the breeding population was less than 100. Recently, Lou Guillette of the University of Florida and others have discovered a more sinister factor that might be responsible—toxic chemicals. Of medium height, with sandy hair, and eyes that emote intelligence, Lou is very interested in how chemicals disrupt the endocrine system. Although he has worked with Alligators in northern Florida for many years, recently he turned his attention to examining the effect of chemicals on Panthers.

As early as 1962 Rachel Carson reported that cats were far more sensitive to insecticides than other animals, and many died where pesticide use was high. Programs to eradicate the Japanese Beetle succeeded in killing 90 percent of farm cats, but not the beetles. The decline of many birds, particularly pelicans, hawks, and fish-eating birds, led to the ban of DDT and some other highly toxic and persistent chemicals. But other toxic chemicals have been developed and are in widespread use.

The possibility that contaminants might be affecting the Panthers first came to light when a seemingly healthy female in the Everglades without any apparent problems died. As a last effort at determining the cause of death, tissues from the female were given a wide range of chemical tests. Many common contaminants were present, but at relatively low levels. Mercury, however, was very high (110 parts per million in the liver)—as high as the levels that caused the deaths of domestic cats in Minamata, Japan. The cats were the earliest victims of mercury poisoning, providing an early warning of the human harm to follow. Minamata is the bay that gained its notoriety from mercury contamination that was so severe in fish that many people who ate them died, and the fish are still not safe to eat even today, 45 years later. The Panther's death certificate lists mercury as the cause of death. Since then, other Panthers have died with elevated mercury levels.

This prompted a closer look at mercury concentrations at all levels in the Everglades food chain, from small fish to humans who were consuming the fish. These studies are ongoing, but disturbingly high levels of mercury have been found at several levels in the food chain. It is possible that failure of many birds to reproduce at normal levels over the last twenty years may be partly due to mercury in their prey. The possibility that mercury was responsible for some of the problems of reptiles, birds, and mammals led to further analysis of other contaminants, most notably chemicals that are known to cause disruptions in the endocrine glands, such as DDE (a remaining by-product of DDT, now banned) and PCBs. This was an obvious avenue for investigation because so many of the problems (low sperm density, abnormal sperm, lack of testes descending) are endocrine related. Further, work by Lou Guillette and others has shown that some of the sex hormones in male and female Panthers no longer show a difference in levels. Male Panthers are being demasculinized and feminized as a result of exposure to abnormal hormone levels before they are born.

Panthers are predators, and we picture them slinking through the Sawgrass or the Saw Palmettos, stalking deer or Bobcat. They leap to the chase, running down and capturing deer, and drag them to their den. They wander the open Wiregrass prairies beneath the tall Longleaf Pine of the high pine zone. The reality today is somewhat different. Most predators rely heavily on smaller game to tide them over. It may not always have been so, when larger game was more abundant, but it is true now. Most predators eat a wide range of prey, relying on smaller game that is easy to catch and more abundant. This is true of the Panther as well. They eat a lot of Raccoons, which are easier to run down than Bobcat or deer. Raccoons, in turn, eat mainly fish captured from many different habitats. Contaminants move rather rapidly through aquatic food chains because the chemicals can spread quickly in water and are taken up by organisms at every level.

The chemicals concentrate at higher levels in each succeeding step in the food chain. Small fish store the chemicals in their tissues and fat, and more and more accumulates with time. When large fish eat small fish, they get high concentrations, and they also continue to store the chemicals in their own tissues. And so the process goes, with each level on the food chain having higher levels in their tissues than the previous one. This is called biomagnification. The Panther is at the top of the food chain, and can be expected to have the highest levels of any contaminant.

The possibility that chemicals may be at the root of the Panthers' population decline is controversial, and people do not want to believe it. If it is true, what does it say about ourselves? For we are also at the top of the food chain, and we eat fish as well. The picture for the Panther seems clear to me. These are the facts: there are only 30 to 50 animals left in the wild, the remaining habitat is heavily impacted with agricultural chemicals, Raccoons provide a pathway between contaminants in water and the Panther, Panther's have detectable and disturbing levels of some chemicals, and Panthers have a variety of ailments, all of which have been shown to be caused by chemicals in other species. What else are we to think? When will we have enough "proof" that there is a severe and serious problem in South Florida in general, and for the Panthers in particular? The time to act is now; we have studied them enough.

On one calm day in January many years ago, Mike and I spent a morning in a small airplane with National Park Service personnel trying to find our own radio-collared Panther. I was none too happy, since I usually get quite sick in small planes, but I was determined to see one. The view from the plane was magnificent, and the Everglades stretched before us in an unbroken expanse of swaying brown and green grasses, bisected by small meandering Alligator trails leading to wallows, and bordered by hardwoods on the east. From the air, each wooded hammock looked like a small oasis strewn in the middle of a green, yellow, and brown plain.

Our target was the four animals known to be in the Homestead vicinity. We aimed for their last known location and flew back and forth until a beeping was audible in our earphones. We found the first one in a wooded area, then another in tall grass, then a third in a thicket two miles west. Slowly we coursed back and forth, looking for the fourth Panther. Finally our radio picked up the signal from the last animal, and we flew lower, looking intently for any sign. As we flew back and forth, the signal became alternately louder and softer, allowing us to get closer and closer. Excitement mounted as we realized we were about to see our first Panther. Finally the signal was at a peak, the same peak we located each time we flew the transect. Unfortunately the strongest signal came from the only large hammock in the area—the Panther was obviously hanging out under the Cypress. Try as we might, we never did get a look at him. The panther is still my most wanted North American mammal.

These Everglade Panthers are monitored carefully, but even with this care, there have been many deaths. With increasing development and habitat fragmentation, Panthers must cross highways, and this is a significant cause of mortality. Half of the known deaths have been due to car accidents, prompting the highway department to fence highway I-75 and build underground tunnels that allow the Panthers to cross under the highway when they encounter the tall fences that prevent access over the road.

Panthers are elusive, even for a tracker, for they often weave among the grasses without leaving a physical trail. At other times, they follow the old Seminole Indian trails through the glades, past old kills, looking for fresh prey. They try to eat every two or three days. Although they can run as fast as 35 miles an hour, they can only do this for a few hundred yards, so they must catch their prey quickly. They can leap as much as 15 feet when required. Panthers will search for Bobcats that eat their own kills, pouncing on their neck and crushing the spinal cord in one swift bite. They can then eat both the Bobcat and its kill. Though their favorite prey is the White-tailed Deer, they eat whatever they can find, including Armadillo, Raccoon, Wild Turkey, and even wading birds. A male Panther can eat 35 to 50 deer a year, or ten times that many Raccoons. They drag their prey to a sheltered place, perhaps under a Saw Palmetto thicket or other brush, and eat only part of it.

Finding a panther is very, very rare these days. More often, one finds panther droppings or the animal's old kills, long since discarded and eaten by the vultures. Most of us see one only on Florida license plates. Forced as many are into the wilds of the Everglades, Panthers face not only natural predators, but poachers, hunters, and habitat destruction. Females can lose their cubs to cars, snakes, and Alligators, and to more subtle forces such as mercury or other contaminants. This magnificent cat is the state's official animal, so named in the hope that its future can be secured. But wishing does not make it so.

In many ways, the Panther is a success story, for despite great odds, and with very low numbers, the Panthers are hanging on. They are relatively long lived, giving us a little time. Each female only has to replace herself and her mate, and they seem to be doing this. With more and more attention being paid to contaminant levels in the Everglades, to maintenance of appropriate water levels, and to conservation of large habitat patches and safe corridors between them, the Panthers will survive.

Even though I have yet to see one, I eagerly search the Sawgrass meadows every time I am in the Everglades. I sit in mosquito-infested hammocks or along dark wooded trails, waiting for one to pass on its regular nightly rounds. I have been within minutes of seeing one, I have felt its presence, and one day, I will see this magnificent cat walk across the road, through the underbrush, or over a well-trod trail across a hummock. Maybe I will even see one in the pines.

THE FUTURE OF THE
PINE BARRENS

Looking Forward

A brilliant blue sky frames the Pitch Pine, while a faint breeze stirs the needles. A Pine Warbler creeps from the trunk toward the end of an unruly branch, peering intently at small cracks in the mottled bark. It inspects a tuft of needles for a moment, then flies to the next-higher branch. It lunges forward to catch a small insect, swallows, and moves on, intent only on foraging. On a fallen log a Fence Lizard sits motionless, absorbing the early morning sun in the New Jersey Pinelands. A Carpenter Ant scurries away, keeping out of the shaft of sunlight. In other pine barrens from Massachusetts to Florida, other ants scurry around and lizards bask in the warm sun. Only the warblers will make a journey from the northern pine barrens to those in Florida.

My own journey has spanned 50 years, but my course was laid down eons ago, long before the European settlers arrived or the first paleo-Indians roamed the pines. It began with the earliest bedrock that was part of Gondwana over 100 million years ago. Attached to tectonic plates far below the land surface, the Cambrian granite and volcanic rocks eventually tore away from Gondwana, creating the rift we know as the Atlantic Ocean. Once North America drifted west, the coastal lands alternated between exposure and inundation as sea levels rose and fell. Sometimes all of the present-day Coastal Plain was covered with seas, and at other times the land extended over 100 miles east of its present location.

The Coastal Plain was shaped most recently by the four ice sheets that ended with the retreat of the Wisconsin Glacier some 12,000 years ago. Although the glaciers moved only as far south as New Jersey, they influenced the climate and land masses all the way down to the tip of Florida. When the glaciers were the most extensive, they tied up vast quantities of water in their mile-thick phalanges of ice, lowering the sea level so that much more land was exposed. The glaciers also moved the tundra climate farther south, obliterating the desertlike conditions that once covered the southern part of the United States, extending from

20.1. *Woolly Mammoths roamed the pine barrens regions when the glaciers were retreating.*

Florida through Texas and into present-day Mexico. Some of the plants and animals that lived in this vast dry desert still remain on the Lake Wales ridge in central Florida, marooned from their closest counterparts in southern Mexico.

A cold tundra climate blanketed much of eastern North America 15,000 years ago, and lichens and mosses grew at the foot of the glacier, breaking up the rocks and boulders and creating soil for other plants. Farther south, the land was covered with spruces and other cold-adapted trees. Mastodons and Woolly Mammoths wandered through the spruce bogs, pursued by Saber Cats and serenaded by Dire Wolves at night (fig. 20.1). As the glaciers began to retreat northward about 12,000 years ago, paleo-Indians moved into Florida—at least there is archeological evidence of people in the pines from this period. Florida was never covered by glaciers, but the climate was influenced by those farther north. Movement into other regions of the Atlantic Coastal Plain was rapid, and by 10,000 years ago humans occupied the East Coast up to New Jersey and New York. The climate changed rather quickly, and within a mere couple of thousand years, Pitch Pines dominated the barrens of the Northeast, and an unbroken forest of Longleaf Pine stretched from Virginia to Florida, disrupted only by fires.

Throughout the pinelands from New York to Florida, the early paleo-Indians had a similar nomadic lifestyle. They lived in small bands and hunted in the pines in the fall and winter, moving to the coast and estuaries in the spring and summer to fish and collect shellfish. When mosquitoes and other insects became unbearable, they headed back to the pines to gather fruits and nuts and to hunt game. They used the pines to make dugout canoes and poles for their huts, they collected pine resin to attach their arrowheads to shafts and to make other tools, and they gathered berries, herbs, and roots from the pine forest for food, medicine, and dyes. They dried a variety of reeds and rushes to weave baskets and mats and to plait rope. They made nets for catching fish and other shellfish, and for building long funnels to trap deer. In the central and northern regions of the pine barrens, the paleo-Indians used cattails and other reeds to weave cloth and make rope, but from the Carolinas south they used palms and palmettos for weaving. The paleo-Indians in the southern regions had access to more tropical plants, but throughout the region they pounded tubers and buds into mush, and dried other roots for winter use.

Sitting in the warmth of the Jersey pines, surrounded by plants that our predecessors gathered for food, fiber, and tools, I can imagine them stalking noiselessly through the pines in quest of White-tailed Deer, Raccoons, and rabbits. Limited gardening began over three thousand years ago in the Northeast, although evidence for sustained agriculture dates back only 1,000 years. Gradually, the Indians began to live in small villages and to domesticate a few crops: gourds, squash, pumpkins, corn, and beans. Remarkably, agriculture developed at about the same time all along the Atlantic Coastal Plain, in Florida, Georgia, and South Carolina, and New Jersey and New York. Partly, technology traveled rapidly because an extensive network of trade routes connected the different Indian tribes, from the Iroquois Nation in the North to the Creeks in the South.

One theme that runs through the pine barrens all along the Coastal Plain is the scarcity of information about the transition from a nomadic hunting and gathering lifestyle to an agrarian one, but the transition occurred rather rapidly throughout the region. The archeological record for archaic Indians is quite extensive, particularly from Florida, where artifacts were preserved in peat. There are many dugout canoes made of pine; arrowheads and other stone tools; woven ropes, mats and baskets; and seeds, nuts, and other foods revealing dietary practices.

The appearance of agriculture was relatively swift and pervasive. Suddenly people were living in small villages in homes made of wood, with small garden plots nearby. They continued to use the resources of the pinewoods and estuaries, but they relied more and more on crops. The earliest agriculturalists practiced slash and burn, clearing small plots and then abandoning them when they were no longer productive. Since the pinelands had nutrient-poor soils and were dry, people moved often, allowing the old fields to revert to pine barrens.

When European explorers arrived in the early 1500s, they found the Indians living in villages with small gardens, using the resources of the pines and the shore, and engaged in far-reaching trading. The extensive pine barrens along the East Coast looked wild and relatively undisturbed. The European settlers were dismayed by the wilderness they found, and fearful of the pinewoods and the dangerous animals that still prowled the night. That this forest was pristine is only a popular illusion because the Indians burned the pines regularly to open the forest, increase game, and make travel and hunting easier.

The European settlers learned from the Indians, although the degree of friendly cooperation varied from region to region. Mostly, both the indigenous peoples and the settlers wanted to trade goods, creating a détente of sorts. The settlers used the trade routes and passageways of the Indians, and many of their trails are the foundation for today's roads and superhighways. As the European populations increased, they usurped more and more land from the native peoples who did not have the same views of land tenure and private ownership. The Indians were pushed deeper into the pines or into the swamps and marshes where the European settlers were loath to go. In Florida, the local Indians retreated to the Everglades, where some held out until the 1950s when they finally achieved tribal sovereignty. In the northeastern barrens, most of the Indians were forced farther inland, into western New York and Pennsylvania.

The early European settlers did not think of pinelands as hospitable places where they could settle down and farm. They thought they were dark, dismal, and frightening. They called them "barrens" and used them primarily for cutting timber and firewood. In both the New Jersey and the New York pine barrens, the oaks and pines were extensively cut for firewood for bog iron, glass blowing, charcoal production, and heating cabins, leaving the region even more barren. Commerce developed in the pine barrens, particularly in New York and New Jersey, where early industries included bog iron, cranberries, and sand mining for glass. Sand mining and lumbering were also important in the southern Longleaf Pine barrens, while citrus farming predominated in the Florida barrens.

The common threads of human development of the paleo-Indians and the early settlers result, in my view, from common ecological conditions (table 20.1). The soils of the barrens are generally nutrient-poor sands that are well drained in higher places. There is little humus. Although a rich and diverse pine barrens plant community developed on these soils, they were not amenable to traditional agriculture: they were far more suited to the hunting and gathering lifestyle of the Indians. Even today, pine barrens habitats produce abundant game far in excess of what the land could produce if converted to cattle production or crops.

Over the entire region, pine barrens communities are dominated by fire. Without frequent fires the pines and scrub oaks are replaced by hardwoods and dense forests. Before the paleo-Indians arrived, fires were ignited by lightning and burned until they reached natural fire breaks such as rivers or deep ravines, or they were extinguished by heavy rains. Once the paleo-Indians moved into the pines, they started their own fires to open the pinelands and increase populations of game. They took their cue from nature and burned in the summer when lightning fires are most common, making their fires less destructive than burning at the wrong time of year.

True barrens habitats, whether in New York, New Jersey, South Carolina, or Florida, have the same general ambiance. There are a few scattered pine trees, an understory of scrubby oaks, and a rich ground cover of heaths, mosses, and lichens. Reindeer Moss is a signature plant of the pine barrens regions throughout the Atlantic Coastal Plain, for it occurs only where the soil horizon has been undisturbed and the soils are poor, acidic, and sandy. It was left behind by the retreating glaciers and remains today in the barrens as well as on the tundra in northern Canada.

Most pine barrens also have associated bogs—remnants of the glaciers. Many still remain with their traditional plants, such as sundews and Pitcher Plants. The barrens bogs are gradually drying up, and have been doing so since the glaciers retreated. They also face succession, with deciduous shrubs and eventually trees moving in. The streams, bogs, and small lakes increase the diversity of plants and animals of the barrens. Because the sandy soils are so porous, the water percolates through, emerging as springs and streams. The streams, bogs, and lakes provided the early impetus for development, because this is where bog iron, cranberry bogs, and other industries sprang up. They also provided a linkage to

Table 20.1. Summary of Some General Themes That Run through the Pine Barrens Habitats Discussed in This Book

PALEO-INDIANS

1. Occupation immediately followed the retreat of the glaciers.
2. Initially hunters and gatherers.
3. The seasonal movement of paleo-Indians between the pines and the shore.
4. The use of pine products for food, canoes, medicines, resin, and weaving.
5. All used the pines in the winter months.
6. All burned the pines to increase game and open the forest for small garden plots.
7. Agriculture developed from 3,000 to 1,000 years ago, with primary crops being gourds, corn, squash, pumpkins, and beans.
8. There are few artifacts from the transition from early to historical.

EARLY EUROPEAN SETTLERS

1. They learned from Indians how to use products of the pines for food and medicine.
2. All used the pines as trade routes to inland areas.
3. They initially exploited the pines for firewood and lumber, and later for sand.
4. They developed early industries: bog iron, cranberries, sand for glass.
5. Eventually all forced the Indians out, in most places in the 1700s.
6. The pines were often the last retreat of Indians in some places.
7. Ultimately they developed the land for agriculture (citrus in Florida, garden crops in New Jersey) or residential development (in all areas).
8. Wiped out large predators.

ECOLOGICAL CHARACTERISTICS

1. All on Atlantic Coastal Plain.
2. Generally nutrient-poor, sandy soils that are well-drained in higher places.
3. Little humus.
4. Fire-dominated, and fire required to prevent invasion of hardwoods. Fire affects type of forest, size of trees.
5. Several kinds of pines grow along the Atlantic Coastal Plain, but there are only three truly dwarf forests (genetically adapted).
6. Predominant pines have serotinous cones (Pitch Pine in Northeast, Longleaf Pine in Southeast; both require fire to release seeds).
7. All contain ground and shrub layer of scrubby oaks and heaths.
8. Some species unique or last stronghold, or specifically adapted to these extreme.
9. Fewer exotics than most ecosystem types, largely because few dry, scrub, sandy species imported for sale in nurseries.

Table 20.1. (*continued*)

TAXONOMIC SIMILARITIES

1. Most have a unique fungus-growing ant and other insects.
2. Most have high species diversity of plants, insects, and reptiles. Pine Snakes occur from New Jersey Barrens south, others, such as Pine Barrens Tree Frog limited to barrens bogs.
3. Reindeer Moss is signature plant of these dry, sandy, poor soils.
4. Have some unique birds, such as Florida Scrub Jay in Florida, Red-cockaded Woodpecker in southeastern pine barrens.
5. Some species are typical throughout, such as Pine and Prairie Warblers.

POLITICAL SIMILARITIES

1. Control for future land use lies with many authorities: state, local, and federal.
2. All except New Jersey Pine Barrens lack a central authority with complete control over habitat and fire regime.
3. Nature Conservancy and other conservation organization work actively with barrens. Private citizens groups just developing for most pine barrens regions.

coastal areas, and lumber was floated to markets along these waterways. On the edges of the pine barrens there are usually deciduous forests, with large, tall trees that support healthy populations of Great Horned Owls (fig. 20.2), Neotropical migrants, and a wide range of other species that sometimes wander into the pines.

All regions of the Atlantic Coastal Plain have pine barrens trees that are short. The Northeast has three dwarf forests where the Pitch Pines are genetically stunted, and even if planted in other upland areas, the pines remain short and stubby. In the Southeast, particularly in Florida, there are scrub pine habitats where the ambiance is similar; only the species differ. In all of these dwarf forests the trees are less than 20 feet tall, and in many, they are less than 10 feet high. Their stunted growth is a function of poor sandy soils with few nutrients and no ability to retain water, as well as to the evolution of a genotype.

For many species, pine barrens habitats are the last stronghold of remnant populations that remain from the aftermath of glaciation. Three groups are remarkable for flourishing in pine barrens regions: plants, insects, and reptiles. Every one of the pine barrens habitats discussed in this book has unique, threatened, and endangered species belonging to these three groups. In many regions, the barrens habitats have high

*20.2. Great Horned Owls live on the fringes of pine
barrens from Albany and Long Island to Florida,
nesting in tall old trees.*

species diversities of plants, insects, and reptiles, and without these habitats, the local floras and faunas would suffer.

The future of the pine barrens, as with nearly all of our natural ecosystems, lies with people. Since the retreat of the last glacier, the Atlantic Coastal Plain and its pine barrens habitats have been profoundly altered by people. Although the paleo-Indians did not clear the land as extensively as the early European settlers, they managed the pinelands with fire, hunted the game, and harvested many of the plants for food and fiber.

The European settlers first conducted limited industries in the pines, and eventually cleared them for housing and industrial developments in the Northeast and citrus groves and other farming in the Southeast. People planted lawns and gardens, bringing in a variety of exotic and invasive plants, attempting to re-create lush gardens in habitats more conducive to sparse and dry plantings. Only in the last decade do we find a new form of gardening that tries to make peace with this troubled land-scape. Fortunately, few dry scrub plants have been imported from other parts of the world, and so the problem of exotic plants is less severe in pine barrens and the scrub pines than it is in wetter, upland habitats.

All of the pine barrens I visited, studied, and enjoyed are now recognized as critical and important habitats by the relevant state agencies. Only one, the New Jersey Pine Barrens, has been recognized in its entirety as representing a national treasure and was designated a National Reserve. A high degree of protection and management is essential to preserve barrens habitats because it is extremely important to treat them on a landscape scale. Any development within the New Jersey Pine Barrens is considered in light of the system as a whole, leading to protection and preservation of the entire ecosystem. Further, central control increases the likelihood that a fire regime can be instituted that maintains the barrens.

This level of protection does not exist for the other regions, although both state and local agencies have recognized the need for this protection. In some areas, such as the Albany Pine Bush, there are commissions that oversee their management and protect small reserves, but they do not have legal authority to control future land use or fire regimes. Most of the other regions have state or federal parks or reserves that contain pine barrens habitats, but they are not nearly large enough to maintain the integrity of the systems.

Unlike many other ecosystems, pine barrens evolved with a frequent fire regime that creates a mosaic of patches at different successional stages, providing habitat for species that require barren, early successional openings. Although many of the endemic and unique species of plants, insects, reptiles, and other animals have relatively small home ranges, much larger areas are required by other species, such as hawks, Bobcats, foxes, bears, and Florida Panthers.

Many of the pine barrens serve an important role in providing fresh and pure drinking water. The Cohansey Aquifer provides critical water reserves for the citizens of New Jersey, and the aquifer under the Long Island Barrens provides water for rapidly growing populations in Suffolk County. Without these aquifers, pure drinking water would be scarce. For this and many other reasons, protection of the pine barrens is critical.

The Nature Conservancy is overseeing many of the pine barrens habitats, and is taking inventory of the indigenous plants and animals, drawing attention to local endemics or species of special concern. In some places, such as the Albany Pine Bush, the Nature Conservancy is overseeing the fire regime, while in others, such as the Florida Pine Scrub, conservationists are especially concerned with invasive plant species. Most of the regions have citizens groups that are just beginning to work toward the conservation and preservation of pine barrens habitats, but the task is a long way from completion.

The future of the pine barrens that remain intact on the Atlantic Coastal Plain looks bright. Federal, state, and local agencies are beginning to recognize the species diversity, endemism, and charm of their local pinelands. Conservation agencies, private citizens, and even industries are working together to preserve these fragile systems. The pines are remnants of a past age and support isolated populations of plants and animals important to a balanced and sustainable earth.

To me, pine barrens habitats are wonderful. They are peaceful, serene, and contain species that exist nowhere else. They do not appear as lush and expansive as our northeastern deciduous forests, our southern hardwood forests, or the Everglades, nor do they have the cachet of the rain forest. But they have a rich species diversity, particularly of plants, reptiles, and insects, that deserves protection. For too long we have worried about birds and mammals and assumed that what was good for them was good for all other species. This doesn't work for the pines. Conservation has become a balancing act; we must balance the competing needs of many different creatures, including ourselves. Pine Barrens habitats are integral to that balance. I will continue to wander the barrens along the Atlantic Coastal Plain searching for Pine Snakes and the solitude that can be found within the deep barrens.

Picking my way cautiously through the Dwarf Pines of the New Jersey Pine Barrens or the Barrens of Long Island, or walking slowly through the Scrub Pines of Florida, I am reminded of the ribbon of sand from the ancient seas that lies beneath me. The sands are old and have been moved inland and then seaward again by the forces of countless inland seas that rose and fell with the formation of giant ice sheets that covered much of the Northern Hemisphere. My journey is not completed, for there are many intricacies of the interactions among the plants and animals that live in the pine barrens that will always beckon to be studied, to be understood, and to be appreciated. May my journey start you on your own, to discover the wonders that reside in the pinelands that our predecessors appreciated so many thousands of years ago. The Mastodons are long gone, but many wild and wonderful creatures remain.

Appendix
List of Species

Plants

COMMON NAME	SCIENTIFIC NAME
Alder	*Alnus* sp.
American Lotus	*Nelumbo lutea*
Archbold Oak	*Quercus inopina*
Arrowhead	*Sagittaria* sp. (*S. latifolia*)
Aspen (=Quaking Aspen)	*Populus tremuloides*
Atlantic White Cedar	*Chamaecyparis thyoides*
Australian Pine	*Casuarina equisetifolia*
Bayberry	*Myrica pennsylvanica*
Beach Heather	*Hudsonia tomentosa*
Beach Plum	*Prunus maritima*
Bearberry	*Arctostaphylus uva ursi*
Beggars Tick	*Bidens* sp.
Black Huckleberry	*Gaylussacia baccata*
Black Gum	*Nyssa sylvatica*
Black Oak	*Quercus velutina*
Black Locust	*Robinia pseudoacacia*
Blackjack Oak	*Quercus marilandica*
Bladderworts	*Utricularia* sp.
Blueberry	*Vaccinium* sp.
Bluestem Grass	*Andropogon, Schizachyrium*
Bog Asphodel	*Narthecium americanum*
Bracken Fern	*Pteridium aquilinum*
Brazilian Pepper	*Schinus terebinthifolius*
British Soldier Lichen	*Cladonia cristatella, C. inerassata*
Broom Crowberry	*Corema conradii*
Butterfly Weed	*Asclepias tuberosa*
Butternut	*Juglans cinerea*
Cabbage Palm	*Sabal palmetto*
Carolina Cherry	*Prunus caroliniana*

Catbrier	*Smilax* spp.
Cattail (Broad-leafed)	*Typha* sp. (*latifolia*)
Chapman's Oak	*Quercus chapmanii*
Chestnut Oak	*Quercus prinus*
Cinnamon Fern	*Osmunda cinnamomea*
Cocoplum	*Chrysobalanus icaco*
Coltsfoot	*Tussilago farfara*
Common Milkweed	*Asclepias syrianca*
Coontie Cycad	*Zamia* sp.
Cranberry (American)	*Vaccinium macrocarpon*
Curly Grass Fern	*Schizaea pusilla*
Cypress	*Taxodium distichum*
Dandelion	*Taraxacum officinale*
Dangleberry	*Gaylussacia frondosa*
Deadly Nightshade	*Atropa belladona*
Dogbane	*Apocynum cannabinum*
Dwarf Huckleberry	*Gaylussacia dumosa*
Dwarf Pine (=Dwarf Pitch Pine)	*Pinus rigida*
Eelgrass	*Zostera maritima*
Florida Rosemary	*Ceratiola ericoides*
Gallberry	*Ilex glabra*
Garberia	*Garberia heterophylla*
Ginseng	*Panax quinquefolius*
Gray Birch	*Betula populifolia*
Grass-leaved Blazing Star	*Liatris framinifolia*
Greenbrier	*Smilax* spp.
Gopher Apple	*Licania michauxii*
Golden Club	*Orontium aquaticum*
Goldenrod, Rough-leaved	*Solidago patula*
Haircap Moss	*Polytrichum* sp.
Hickory, Shagbark	*Carya ovata*
Highbush Blueberry	*Vaccinium* spp.
Indian Hemp (Dogbane)	*Apocynum cannabinum*
Inkberry	*Ilex glabra*
Jack-in-the-Pulpit	*Arisaema triphyllum*
Jack Pine	*Pinus banksiana*
Jerusalem Artichoke	*Helianthus tuberosus*
Knieskern's Beak	*Rhynchospora kneiskernii*
Leatherleaf	*Chamaedaphne calyculata*
Lobelia	*Lobelia inflata*
Loblolly Pine	*Pinus taeda*
Longleaf Pine	*Pinus australis*
Lowbush Blueberry or Huckleberry	*Vaccinia vacillans*

Magnolia	*Magnolia* spp.
Marsh Marigold	*Caltha palustris*
Morning Glory	*Ipoemea* spp.
Mountain Laurel	*Kalmia latifolia*
Mullein	*Verbascum thapsus*
New England Blazing Star	*Liatris scariosa*
New Jersey Tea	*Ceanothus americanus*
Old-man's Beard	*Usnea barbata*
Orange Milkweed	*Asclepias tuberosa*
Pearly Everlasting	*Gnaphalium polycephalum*
Pennsylvania Sedge	*Carex pennsylvanica*
Penny Royal	*Piloblephis rigida*
Pepper Root	*Cardamine diphylla*
Persimmons	*Diospyros virginiana*
Pickerel Weed	*Pontederia cordata*
Pickering's Morning Glory	*Stylisma pickeringii*
Pine Barrens Gentian	*Gentiana autumnalis*
Pitch Pine	*Pinus rigida*
Pitcher Plant	*Sarracenia purpurea*
Poison Ivy	*Rhus radicans* (=*Toxicodendron radicans*)
Poison Sumac	*Rhus vernix* (=*Toxicodendron vernix*)
Pond Pine	*Pinus serotina*
Ponderosa Pine	*Pinus ponderosa*
Post Oak	*Quercus stellata*
Prickley-pear Cactus	*Opuntia* sp.
Pyxie Moss	*Pyxidanthera barbulata*
Quaking Aspen	*Populus tremuloides*
Red Bay	*Persea borbonia*
Redbud	*Cercus canadensis*
Red Cedar	*Juniperus virginiana*
Red Maple	*Acer rubrum*
Red Oak	*Quercus rubrum*
Reindeer Moss (or lichen)	*Cladonia* sp. (= *Cladina*)
Rose Mallow (=Swamp Rose Mallow)	*Hibiscus moscheutos*
Rosemary	*Ceratiola ericoides*
Round-leaved Sundew	*Drosera rotundifolia*
Rusty Lyonia	*Lyonia ferruginea*
Sabal Palm (=Sand Palmetto)	*Sabal palmetto*
Sabal Palmetto	*Sabal palmetto*
Salt Hay	*Spartina patens*
Sand Bur	*Cenchrus tribuloides*

Sand Live Oak (=Scrub Live Oak)	*Quercus geminata*
Sand Myrtle	*Leiophyllum buxifolium*
Sand Palmetto (=Sabal Palm)	*Sabal palmetto*
Sand Pine	*Pinus clausa*
Saw Palmetto	*Serenoa repens*
Sawgrass	*Cladium jamaicense*
Scarlet Oak	*Quercus coccinea*
Scrub Holly	*Ilex opaca var arenicola*
Scrub Live Oak (=Sand Live Oak)	*Quercus geminata*
Scrub Oak	*Quercus ilicifolia*
Seaside Goldenrod	*Solidago sempervirens*
Sheep Laurel	*Kalmia angustifolia*
Shining Whip Grass	*Scleria nitida*
Short-leaf Pine	*Pinus echinata*
Sickle-leaved Golden Aster	*Chrysopsis falcata*
Silk Bay	*Persea humilis*
Skunk Cabbage	*Symplocarpus foetidus*
Slash Pine	*Pinus elliottii*
Southern Red Maple	*Acer rubrum*
Spanish Moss	*Tillandsia usneoides*
Spatterdock (=Yellow Pond Lily)	*Nuphar variegatum*
Spatulate-leaved Sundew	*Drosera intermedia*
Sphagnum Moss	*Sphagnum* spp.
Spotted Knapweed	*Centaurea maculosa*
Strawberry	*Fragaria virginiana*
Sugar Pine	*Pinus lambertiana*
Sundew	*Drosera* spp.
Swamp Azalea	*Rhododendron viscosum*
Swamp Black Gum (=Tupelo)	*Nyssa sylvatica* variety *biflora*
Swamp-pink	*Helonias bullata*
Sweet Bay (=Swamp Magnolia)	*Magnolia virginiana*
Sweet Fern	*Comptonia peregrina*
Sweet Flag	*Acorus calamus*
Sweet Magnolia	*Magnolia virginiana*
Sweet Pepperbush	*Clethra alnifolia*
Teaberry	*Gaultheria procumbens*
Thread-leaved Sundew	*Drosera filiformis*
Tupelo (Black Gum)	*Nyssa sylvaticus*
Turkey Oak	*Quercus laevis*
Turkeybeard	*Xerophyllum asphodeloides*
Vinca (Periwinkle)	*Vinca minor*
Virginia Creeper	*Parthenocissus quinquefolia*
Water Ash	*Nyssa aquatica*

Water Tupelo	*Fraxinus caroliniana*
Wax Myrtle	*Myrica cerifera*
Western White Pine	*Pinus monticola*
White Cedar (Atlantic)	*Chamaecyparis thyoides*
White Pine	*Pinus strobus*
Widgeon Grass	*Ruppia maritima*
Wild Ginger	*Asarum canadense*
Wild Lupine	*Lupinus perennis*
Wild Morning Glory	*Ipomoea pandurata*
White Oak	*Quercus alba*
Wild Olive	*Osmanthus megacarpa*
Wild Plum	*Prunus* sp.
Wild Rice	*Zizania aquatica*
Wild Strawberry	*Fragaria virginiana*
Wintergreen	*Gaultheria procumbens*
Wiregrass	*Aristida stricta*
Yellow Birch	*Betula alleghaniensis*
Yellow Pond Lily (Spatterdock)	*Nuphar variegatum*

Invertebrates

Atala Butterfly	*Eumaeus atala*
Backswimmer	*Notonecta* sp.
Bessie Bug	*Odontataenius disjunctus*
Blue Crab	*Callinectes sapidus*
Bog Copper	*Lycaena thoe*
Brown Elfin	*Callophrys augustinus*
Buck Moth	*Hemileuca maia*
Cabbage (White) Butterfly	*Pieris rapae*
Carpenter Ant	*Campanotus floridanus*
Delaware Skipper	*Anatrytone logan*
Dotted Skipper	*Hesperia attalus*
Earthworm	*Lumbricus terrestris*
Eastern Tailed Blue	*Everes comyntas*
Edward's Hairstreak	*Satyrium edwardsii*
Fiddler Crab	*Uca* spp.
Grasshopper	*Orthoptera order*
Green-head Fly	*Tabanus americanus*
Hard Clam (=Quahog)	*Mercenaria mercenaria*
Hessel's Hairstreak	*Callophrys hesseli*
Horseshoe Crab	*Limulus polyphemus*
Japanese Beetle	*Popillia japonica*
Juvenal's Duskywings	*Erynnis juvenalis*

Karner Blue Butterfly	*Lycaeides melissa samuelis*
King's Hairstreak	*Satyrium kingi*
Locust Borer	*Megacylline robinae*
Locust Leaf Miner	*Odontota dorsalis*
Mitchell's Satyr	*Neonympha mitchellii*
Monarch	*Danaus plexippus*
Mottled Duskywings	*Erynnis martialis*
Mourning Cloak	*Nymphalis antiopa*
Oyster	*Crassostrea virginica*
Pearl Crescent	*Phyciodes tharos*
Pine Barrens Dagger Moth	*Acronicta albarufa*
Pine Barrens Underwing Moth	*Catocala herodias gerhardi*
Pine Barrens Zale Moth	*Zale* sp 1 nr *lunifera*
Pine Elfin (=Eastern Pine Elfin)	*Callophrys niphon*
Quahog Clam (=Hard Clam)	*Mercenaria mercenaria*
Sleepy Duskywing	*Erynnis brizo*
Tailed Blue, Eastern	*Everes comyntas*
Soft-shelled Clam	*Mya arenaria*
Variable Heterocampa Moth	*Heterocampa varia*
Walking Stick	*Anisomorpha buprestoides*
Water Boatman	*Corixa* sp.
Water Strider	*Gerris* sp.
Whirligig Beetle	*Dineutes* sp.

Fish

Banded Sunfish (=Sphagnum Sunfish)	*Enneacanthus obesus*
Bluefish	*Pomatomus saltatrix*
Bullhead	*Ictalurus nebulosus*
Chub Sucker	*Erimyzon oblongus*
Eel	*Anguilla rostrata*
Northern Yellow Bullhead	*Ictalurus natalis*
Sphagnum Sunfish	*Enneacanthus obesus*
Swordfish	*Xiphias gladius*
White Perch	*Morone americana*

Amphibians

Barking Treefrog	*Hyla gratiosa*
Bird-voiced Frogs	*Hyla avivoca*
Bullfrog	*Rana catesbiana*
Carpenter Frog	*Rana virgatipes*

Chorus Frog	*Pseudacris triseriata* spp.
Cricket Frog	*Acris crepitans*
Fowler's Toad	*Bufo fowlerii*
Green Frog	*Rana clamitans*
Green Treefrog	*Hyla versicolor*
Leopard Frog	*Rana sphenocephala*
Marbled Salamander	*Ambystoma opacum*
Oak Toad	*Bufo quercicus*
Pine Barrens Treefrog	*Hyla andersoni*
Pine Woods Treefrog	*Hyla femoralis*
Southern Leopard Frog	*Rana sphenocephala* (=*Rana utricularia*)
Spadefoot Toad	*Scaphiopus holbrookii*
Spotted Salamander	*Ambystoma maculatum*
Spring Peeper	*Hyla crucifer*
Tiger Salamander	*Ambystoma tigrinum*
Wood Frog	*Rana sylvatica*

Reptiles

Alligator	*Alligator mississippiensis*
Black Pine Snake	*Pituophis melanoleucus lodingi*
Black Racer	*Coluber constrictor*
Black Rat Snake	*Elaphe obsoleta obsoleta*
Blue-tailed Mole Skink	*Eumeces egregius*
Boa Constrictor	*Boa constrictor*
Box Turtle	*Terrapene carolina*
Burmese Pythons	*Python molurus bivittatus*
Coachwhip	*Masticophis flagellum*
Corn Snake	*Elaphe guttata*
Cottonmouth	*Agkistrodon piscivorus*
Diamondback Terrapin	*Malaclemys terrapin*
Duck-billed Dinosaur	*Hadrosaurus* spp.
Eastern Coachwhip	*Masticophis flagellum flagellum*
Eastern Diamondback Rattlesnake	*Crotalis adamanteus*
Eastern Worm (also simply worm)	*Carphophis amoenus amoenus*
Fence Lizard	*Sceloporus undulatus*
Florida Box Turtle	*Terrapene carolina bauri*
Florida Scrub Lizard	*Sceloporus woodi*
Garter Snake	*Thamnophis sirtalis*
Gopher Tortoise	*Gopherus polyphemus*
Gopher Snake	*Pituophis melanoleucus*
Green Iguana	*Iguana iguana*

Hognose Snake	*Heterodon platyrhinos*
Indigo Snake	*Drymarchon corais*
King Snake	*Lampropeltis getulus*
Midland Painted Turtle	*Chrysemys picta marginata*
Milk Snake	*Lampropeltis triangulum*
Mud Turtle	*Kinosternon subrubrum*
Peninsula Crowned Snake	*Tantilla relicta relicta*
Pine Snake	*Pituophis melanoleucus*
Puff Adder	*Bitis arietans*
Rattlesnake	*Crotalis adamanteus*
Red-bellied Snake	*Storeria occipitomaculata*
Red-bellied Turtle	*Pseudemys rubriventris*
Sand Skink	*Neoseps reynoldsi*
Scrub Lizard (=Florida Scrub Lizard)	*Sceloporus woodi*
Short-tailed Snake	*Stilosoma extenuatum*
Snapping Turtle	*Chelydra serpentina*
Timber Rattlesnake	*Crotalus horridus*
Water Moccasin (Cottonmouth)	*Agkistrodon piscivorus*
Western Gopher Tortoise	*Gopherus agassizii*
Worm Snake	*Carphophis amoenus amoenus*

Birds

Bachman's Sparrow	*Aimophila aestivalis*
Bald Eagle	*Haliaeetus leucocephalus*
Baltimore Oriole	*Icterus galbula*
Barred Owl	*Strix varia*
Belted Kingfisher	*Ceryle alcyon*
Black Skimmers	*Rynchops niger*
Black and White Warbler	*Mniotilta varia*
Black-capped Chickadee	*Parus atricapillus* (=*Pooecetes*)
Blue Jay	*Cyanocitta cristata*
Bobwhite Quail	*Colinus virginianus*
Brown Pelican	*Pelecanus occidentalis*
Brown Thrasher	*Toxostoma rufum*
Brown-headed Cowbird	*Molothrus ater*
Brown-headed Nuthatch	*Sitta pusilla*
Burrowing Owl	*Athene cunicularia* (=*Speotyta*)
Canada Goose	*Branta canadensis*
Cardinal	*Cardinalis cardinalis*
Carolina Chickadee	*Parus carolinensis* (=*Pooecetes*)
Carolina Wren	*Thryothorus ludovicianus*
Catbird	*Dumetella carolinensis*

Cattle Egret	*Bubulcus ibis*
Chickadee, see Black-capped Chickadee	
Chipping Sparrow	*Spizella passerina*
Chuck Will's Widow	*Caprimulgus carolinensis*
Clapper Rail	*Rallus longirostris*
Common Nighthawk	*Chordeiles minor*
Common Tern	*Sterna hirundo*
Common Yellowthroat	*Geothlypis trichas*
Cooper's Hawk	*Accipiter cooperi*
Crow (American)	*Corvus brachyrhynchos*
Downy Woodpecker	*Picoides pubescens* (=*Dendrocopus*)
Eastern Bluebird	*Sialia sialis*
Eastern Wood Peewee	*Contopus virens*
English Sparrow	*Passer domesticus*
Field Sparrow	*Spizella pusilla*
Fish Crow	*Corvus ossifragus*
Florida Scrub Jay	*Aphelococoma coerulescens coerulescens*
Forster's Tern	*Sterna forsteri*
Franklin's Gull	*Larus pipixcan*
Great Blue Heron	*Ardea herodias*
Great Horned Owl	*Bubo virginiensis*
Green Heron	*Butorides virescens*
Hairy Woodpecker	*Dendrocopu villosus*
Harrier (=Marsh Hawk)	*Circus cyaneus*
Heath Hen	*Tympanuchus cupido cupido*
Herring Gull	*Larus argentatus*
House Sparrow	*Passer domesticus*
Ivory-billed Woodpecker	*Campephilus principalis*
Kestrel	*Falco sparverius*
Kirtland's Warbler	*Dendroica kirtlandii*
Laughing Gull	*Larus atricilla*
Long-billed Marsh Wren	*Cistothorus platensis*
Mallard	*Anas platyrhynchos*
Marsh Hawk (Northern Harrier)	*Circus cyaneus*
Merlin	*Falco columbarus*
Mockingbird	*Mimus gilvus*
Monk Parakeet	*Myiopsitta monachus*
Mourning Dove	*Zenaida macroura*
Myrtle Warbler	*Dendroica coronata*
Northern Harrier (Marsh Hawk)	*Circus cyaneus*
Ovenbird	*Seiurus aurocapillus*
Oystercatcher	*Haemotopus palliatus*

Palm Warbler	*Dendroica palmarum*
Parula Warbler	*Parula americana*
Passenger Pigeon	*Ectopistes migratorius*
Peregrine Falcon	*Falco peregrinus*
Pileated Woodpecker	*Dryocopus pileatus*
Pine Warbler	*Dendroica pinus*
Piping Plover	*Charodrius melodus*
Prairie Chicken (=Greater Prairie Chicken)	*Tympanuchus cupido*
Prairie Warbler	*Dendroica discolor*
Purple Martin	*Progne subis*
Red-cockaded Woodpecker	*Dendrocopos borealis*
Red-eyed Vireo	*Vireo olivaceus*
Red-shouldered Hawk	*Buteo lineatus*
Red-tailed Hawk	*Buteo jamaicensis*
Red-winged Blackbird	*Ageliaus phoeniceus*
Redstart	*Selophaga ruticilla*
Ring-necked Pheasant	*Phasianus colchicus*
Robin	*Turdus migratorius*
Roseate Tern	*Sterna dougallii*
Ruffed Grouse	*Bonasa umbellus*
Rufous-sided Towhee	*Pipilo erythropthalmus*
Sanderling	*Calidris albus* (*Crecetnia*)
Scarlet Tanager	*Piranga olivacea*
Screech Owl	*Otis asio*
Scrub Jay	*Aphelocoma coerulescens*
Sharp-shinned Hawk	*Accipiter striatus*
Slate-colored Junco	*Junco hyemalis*
Snowy Egret	*Egretta thula*
Song Sparrow	*Melospiza melodia*
Spotted Owl	*Strix occidentralis*
Starling	*Sturnus vulgaris*
Tree Swallow	*Iridiprocne bicolor*
Tufted Titmouse	*Baeolophus bicolor*
Tundra Swan	*Olor columbianus*
Turkey Vulture	*Cathartes aura*
Yellow Warbler	*Dendroica petechia*
Yellow-breasted Chat	*Icteria virens*
Yellow-rumped Warbler (Myrtle)	*Dendroica coronatus*
Yellowthroat (=Common Yellowthroat)	*Geothlypis trichas*
Yellow-throated Vireo	*Vireo flavifrons*
Yellow-throated Warbler	*Dendroica dominica*

Western Meadowlark	*Sturnella neglecta*
White-breasted Nuthatch	*Sitta carolinensis*
White-eyed Vireo	*Vireo griseus*
Whip-poor-will	*Caprimulgus vociferus*
Wild Turkey	*Meleagris gallopava*
Woodcock	*Scolopax minor*

Mammals

African Leopard	*Panthera pardus*
Armadillo	*Dasypus novemcinctus*
Beaver	*Castor canadensis*
Big Brown Bat	*Eptesicus fuscus*
Black Bear	*Ursus americanus*
Bobcat	*Lynx rufa*
Caribou	*Rangifer tarandus*
Cotton Rat (=hispid cotton rat)	*Sigmodon hispidus*
Cottontail Rabbit (Eastern)	*Sylvilagus floridanus*
Cougar	*Felis concolor*
Coyote	*Canis latrans*
Dire Wolf	*Canis dirus*
Eastern Chipmunk	*Tamias striatus*
Eastern Mole	*Scalopus aquaticus*
Elephant	*Loxodonta africana*
Florida Mouse	*Podomys floridanus*
Florida Panther	*Felix concolor*
Flying Squirrel	*Glaucomys volans*
Fox Squirrel	*Sciurus niger*
Giant Armadillo	*Holmsina setptentrionalis*
Giant Beaver	*Castoroides ohioensis*
Giant Lion	*Felis atrox*
Gray Fox	*Urocyon cinereoargenteus*
Gray Squirrel (=Eastern)	*Sciurus carolinensis*
Ground Sloth (=Giant or Jefferson's)	*Megalonyx jeffersoni*
Jumping Mouse	*Zapus hudsonius*
Leopard	*Panthera pardus*
Long-tailed Weasel	*Mustela frenata*
Masked Shrew	*Sorex cinerus*
Mastodon	*Mammut* sp.
Meadow Vole	*Microtus pennsylvanicus*
Mink	*Mustela vison*
Muskrat	*Ondatra zibethica*
Opossum	*Didelphis virginiana*

Otter	*Lutra canadensis*
Panther	*Felis concolor*
Pocket Gopher	*Geomys pinetis*
Porcupine	*Erethizon dorsatum*
Pine Vole	*Pitymys pinetorum*
Rabbit	*Sylvilagus* spp.
Raccoon	*Procyon lotor*
Red Bat	*Lasiurus borealis*
Red Fox	*Vulpes vulpes*
Red Squirrel	*Tamasciurus hudsonicus*
Red-backed Mouse (or vole)	*Clethrronomys gapperi*
Rhinoceros	*Diceros bicornis*
Saber-toothed Cat (=Saber Cat)	*Smilodon floridanus*
Sherman's Fox Squirrel	*Sciurus niger*
Short-tailed Shrew	*Blarina brevicauda*
Skunk (=Striped)	*Mephitus mephitus*
Snow Leopard	*Panthera uncia*
Southern Flying Squirrel	*Glaucomys volans*
Spotted Skunk	*Spilogale putorius*
Star-nosed Mole	*Condylura cristata*
Striped Skunk	*Mephitus mephitus*
Tapir	*Tapirus* spp.
White-footed Mouse	*Peromyscus leucopus*
White-tailed Deer	*Odocoileus virginianus*
Wolf (=Gray Wolf)	*Canis lupus*
Woodchuck	*Marmota monax*
Woodland Caribou	*Rangifer tarandus caribou*
Woolly Mammoth	*Mammuthus* spp.

Suggested Readings

General and Chapters 1 and 2

Barnes, J. K. 2003. *Natural History of the Albany Pine Bush*. Albany, N.Y.: New York State Museum Bulletin 502.

Beans, B., and L. Niles. 2003. *Endangered and Threatened Wildlife of New Jersey*. New Brunswick, N.J.: Rutgers University Press.

Boyd, H. P. 1991. *A Field Guide to the Pine Barrens of New Jersey*. Medford, N.J.: Plexus Publishing.

———. 1997. *A Pine Barrens Odyssey: A Naturalist's Year in the Pine Barrens of New Jersey*. Medford, N.J.: Plexus Publishing.

Burger, J. 1996. *A Naturalist along the Jersey Shore*. New Brunswick, N.J.: Rutgers University Press.

———. 1999. *Animals in Towns and Cities*. Dubuque, Iowa: Kendall/Hunt.

Forman, R.T.T., ed. 1996. *Pine Barrens: Ecosystem and Landscape*. New Brunswick, N.J.: Rutgers University Press.

Martin, A. C., H. S. Zim, and A. L. Nelson. 1961. *American Wildlife and Plants: A Guide to Wildlife Food Habits*. New York: Dover Publications.

McPhee, J. 1967. *The Pine Barrens*. New York: Noonday Press.

Myers, R. L., and J. J. Ewel, eds. 1991. *Ecosystems of Florida*. Orlando: University of Central Florida Press.

Palmer, E. L., and H. S. Fowler. 1975. *Fieldbook of Natural History*. New York: McGraw-Hill.

Russell, E.W.B. 1983. Indian-set fires in the forests of the Northeastern United States. *Ecology* 64:78–88.

Chapter 3

Albany Pine Bush Preserve Commission. 1996. *The Albany Pine Bush Preserve: Protection and Project Review Implementation Guidelines and Final Environmental Impact Statement*. Albany, N.Y.: Albany Pine Bush Preserve Commission.

———. 1998. *The Albany Pine Bush*. Albany, N.Y.: Albany Pine Bush Preserve Commission.

American Pine Barrens Society. 1980. Index to Pine Barrens literature and related (Pinelands, pine-oak and oak-pine forests, sandplains, and heathlands) ecosystems. *Skenectada* 2:19–24.

Barnes, J. K. 2003. *Natural History of the Albany Pine Bush.* Albany, N.Y.: New York State Museum Bulletin 502.

Breen, P. 1973. The Albany Pine Barrens. *The Conservationist* 28:3–5.

Cook, J. H. 1930. *The Glacial Geology of the Capital District.* Albany, N.Y.: New York State Museum Bulletin 185:181–213.

Dineen, R., ed. 1975. *Geology and Land Uses in the Pine Bush, Albany County, New York.* Albany, N.Y.: New York State Museum and Science Service Circular 47, 1–27.

Pine Bush Historic Preservation Project. 1976. *Pine Bush: Albany's Last Frontier.* Albany, N.Y.: Pine Bush Historic Preservation.

Seischab, F. K., and J. M. Bernard. 1991. Pitch pine (*Pinus rigida* Mill.) communities in central and western New York. *Bulletin of the Torrey Botanical Club* 116:412–423.

Chapter 4

Anonymous. 1997. Burden Ironworks. In *Dictionary of New York Historic Places,* 3:1370. St. Clair Shores, Mich.: Somerset Publishers.

Beale, G., and M. R. Boswell. 1999 *The Earth Shall Blossom: Shaker Herbs and Gardening.* Woodstock, vt.: Countryman Press.

Day, G. M. 1953. The indians as an ecological factor in the northeastern forest. *Ecology* 34:329–346.

Dineen, R., ed. 1975. *Geology and Land Uses in the Pine Bush, Albany County, New York.* Albany, N.Y.: New York State Museum and Science Service Circular 47:1–27.

Duke, J. A. 1985. *CRC Handbook of Medicinal Herbs.* Boca Raton, Fla.: CRC Press.

Gibbons, E. 1966. *Stalking the Healthful Herbs.* New York: David McKay.

Nevin, C. M. 1925. *Albany Molding Sands of the Hudson Valley.* Albany, N.Y.: New York State Museum Bulletin 263:1–81.

Rittner, D., ed. 1976. *Pine Bush: Albany's Last Frontier.* Albany, N.Y.: Pine Bush Historical Preservation Project.

Chapter 5

Andow, D. A., R. J. Baker, and C. P. Lane, eds. 1994. *Karner Blue Butterfly: Symbol of a Vanishing Landscape.* St. Paul: University of Minnesota Agricultural Experiment Station Technical Publ. 84.

Andrle, R. F., and J. R. Carroll. 1988. *The Atlas of Breeding Birds in New York State.* Ithaca, N.Y.: Cornell University Press.

Bull, J. 1974. *Birds of New York State.* New York: American Museum of Natural History.

Dirig, R. 1973. The endangered Karner Blue. *The Conservationist* 28:6.

Gochfeld, M., and J. Burger. 1997. *Butterflies of New Jersey.* New Brunswick, N.J.: Rutgers University Press.

Kerlinger, P., and C. Doremus. 1981. The breeding birds of three pine barrens in New York State. *Kingbird* 31:126–135.

Nabokov, D., and M. J. Bruccoli, eds. 1989. *Vladimir Nabokov: Selected Letters, 1940–1977.* San Diego, Calif.: Harcourt Brace Jovanovich.

North American Butterfly Association (NABA). 2003. *2003 Report: NABA Butterfly Counts.* Morristown, N.J.: NABA.

Rittner, D. 1979. Karner blue butterfly nominated as threatened species. *Skenectada* 1:46–65.

————, ed. 1976. *Pine Bush: Albany's Last Frontier.* Albany, N.J.: Pine Bush Historical Preservation Project.

Stewart, M. M. 1988. Dearth of the Blues. *Natural History* 97:64–70.

Stewart, M. M., and J. Rossi. 1981. The Albany Pine Bush: A northern outpost for southern species of amphibians and reptiles in New York. *American Midland Naturalist* 106:282–292.

Chapter 6

Black, J. A., and J. W. Pavacic. 1997. The Long Island Pine Barrens: An anthropogenic artifact or natural ecosystem. In *Proceedings of Fire Effects on Rare and Endangered Species and Habitat Conference,* 221–226. Cour de Alene, Idaho: IAWF.

Kurczewski, F. E., and H. F. Boyle. 2000. Historical changes in the Pine Barrens of central Suffolk County, New York. *Northeast Naturalist* 7:95–112.

Chapter 7

Anderle, R. F., and J. R. Carroll. 1988. *The Atlas of Breeding Birds in New York State.* Ithaca, N.Y.: Cornell University Press.

Bishop, S. C. 1941. *The Salamanders of New York.* New York State Museum Bulletin 324:1–365.

Bull, J. 1974. *Birds of New York State.* New York: American Museum of Natural History.

Burnley, J. 1966. Salamanders of Long Island. *Bulletin of the New York Herpetological Society* 2:15.

Central Pine Barrens Joint Planning and Policy Commission. 1995. *Central Pine Barrens Comprehensive Land Use Plan.* Great River, N.Y.: Central Pine Barrens Joint Planning and Policy Commission.

Dove, A. 1995. *The Cranberry Bog Preserve.* West Sayville, N.Y.: Suffolk County Department of Parks, Recreation and Conservation.

Kurczewski, F. E., and H. F. Boyle. 2000. Historical changes in the Pine Barrens of central Suffolk County, New York. *Northeast Naturalist* 7:95–112.

Olsvig, L. S., J. F. Cryan, and R. H. Whittaker. 1979. Vegetational gradients of the pine plains and barrens of Long Island, New York. In *Pine Barrens: Ecosystem and Landscape,* ed. R.T.T. Forman, 265–282. New Brunswick, N.J.: Rutgers University Press.

Chapter 8

Boyd, H. P. 1991. *A Field Guide to the Pine Barrens of New Jersey.* Medford, N.J.: Plexus Publishing.

———. 1997. *A Pine Barrens Odyssey: A Naturalist's Year in the Pine Barrens of New Jersey.* Medford, N.J.: Plexus Publishing.

Collins, B. R., and K. H. Anderson. 1994. *Plant Communities of New Jersey.* New Brunswick, N.J.: Rutgers University Press.

Dighton, J., A. S. M. Bonilla, R. A. Jiminez-Nunez, and N. Martinez. 2000. Determinants of leaf litter patchiness in mixed species New Jersey pine barrens forest and its possible influence on soil and soil biota. *Biology of Fertile Soils* 31:288–293.

Dighton, J., A. R. Tuininga, D. M. Gray, R. E. Huskins, and T. Belton. 2004. Impacts of atmospheric deposition on New Jersey pine barrens forest soils and communities of ectomycorrhizae. *Forest Ecology and Management* 201:131–144.

Forman, R.T.T., ed. 1996. *Pine Barrens: Ecosystem and Landscape.* New Brunswick, N.J.: Rutgers University Press.

Gallagher, W. B. 1997. *When Dinosaurs Roamed New Jersey.* New Brunswick, N.J.: Rutgers University Press.

Gibson, D. J., R. A. Zampella, and A. G. Windisch. 1999. New Jersey pine plains: The "true barrens" of the New Jersey Pine Barrens. In *Savannas, Barrens and Rock Outcrop Plant Communities of North America,* ed. R. C. Anderson, J. S. Fralish, and J. M. Baskin, 23–51. Cambridge, U.K.: Cambridge University Press.

McPhee, J. 1967. *The Pine Barrens.* New York: Noonday Press.

Mohlenbrock, R. H. 2003. Bogs and burning woods. *Natural History* 112:58–59.

Moore, D. F. 1997. Preservation in the Pinelands: Great things are happening. *New Jersey Conservation* (Summer 1997):2–3.

Pettigrew, L. 1998. *New Jersey Wildlife Viewing Guide.* Helena, Mont.: Falcon.

Pierson, G., and G. Zimmermann. 1993. Restoring Jersey's Atlantic White-Cedar. *New Jersey Outdoors* 20:17–19.

Roberts, Richard. 1981. Don't call it "the Barrens." *Audubon* (July 1981):1–4.

Widmer, K. 1964. *The Geology and Geography of New Jersey.* Princeton, N.J.: D. Van Nostrand.

Chapter 9

Burger, J., and M. Gochfeld. 2000. *25 Nature Spectacles in New Jersey.* New Brunswick, N.J.: Rutgers University Press.

Burger, J., R. Norgaard, E. Ostrom, D. Policansky, and B. D. Goldstein. 2001. *Protecting the Commons: A Framework for Resource Management in the Americas.* Washington, D.C.: Island Press.

Cohen, D. S. 1983. *The Folklore and Folklife of New Jersey.* New Brunswick, N.J.: Rutgers University Press.

Eck, P. 1990. *The American Cranberry.* New Brunswick, N.J.: Rutgers University Press.

Harington, M. R. 1966. *The Indians of New Jersey: Dickon among the Lenapes.* New Brunswick, N.J.: Rutgers University Press.

Miller, P. S. 1994. *Double Trouble State Park.* Trenton, N.J.: Division of Parks and Forestry.

Moonsammy, R. Z., D. S. Cohen, and L. E. Williams, eds. 1987. *Pinelands Folklife.* New Brunswick, N.J.: Rutgers University Press.

Pierce, A. D. 1984. *Iron in the Pines.* New Brunswick, N.J.: Rutgers University Press.

Russell, E.W.B. 1981. Vegetation of Northern New Jersey before European settlement. *American Midland Naturalist* 105:1–12.

Schmidt, R. M. 1991. *Cranberry Cookery.* Barnegat Light, N.J.: Pine Barrens Press.

Still, C. C. 1998. *Botany and Healing: Medicinal Plants of New Jersey and the Region.* New Brunswick, N.J.: Rutgers University Press.

Teal, J., and M. Teal. 1969. *Life and Death of the Salt Marsh.* New York: Ballantine Books.

Whitesbog Preservation Trust. 1997. *Fire Ecology of the New Jersey Pine Barrens.* Browns Mills, N.J.: Whitesbog Preservation Trust.

Chapter 10

Dunne, M. 1989. New Jersey toads. *New Jersey Outdoors* 16:40.

Juelg, G. R. 2002. *New Jersey Pinelands: Threatened and Endangered Species.* Pemberton, N.J.: Pinelands Preservation Alliance.

Kenney, L. P., and M. R. Burne. 2002. *Salamanders, Frogs, and Turtles of New Jersey's Vernal Pools.* Trenton, N.J.: Department of Environmental Protection.

New Jersey Pinelands Commission. 1998. *The Pine Barrens Treefrog.* Bellmawr, N.J.: Pinelands Commission.

Schwartz, V., and D. M. Golden. 2002. *Field Guide to Reptiles and Amphibians of New Jersey.* Trenton, N.J.: New Jersey Division of Fish and Wildlife.

Zappalorti, R. T. 1982. Spring voices in the night. *Wildlife in New Jersey* 9:11–13.

Chapter 11

Juelg, G. R. 2002. *New Jersey Pinelands: Threatened and Endangered Species.* Pemberton, N.J.: Pinelands Preservation Alliance.

Garber, S. D. 1987. *The Urban Naturalist.* Mineola, N.Y.: Dover Publications.

Schwartz, V., and D. M. Golden. 2002. *Field Guide to Reptiles and Amphibians of New Jersey.* Trenton, N.J.: New Jersey Division of Fish and Wildlife.

Chapter 12

Beck, H. C. 1983. *Jersey Genesis: The Story of the Mullica River.* New Brunswick, N.J.: Rutgers University Press.

Burger, J. 1976. Behavior of hatching Diamondback Terrapins (*Malaclemys terrapin*) in the field. *Copeia* 1976:743–748.

———. 1976. Temperature relationships in nests of Diamondback Terrapin, *Malaclemys terrapin. Herpetologica* 32:412–418.

———. 1977. Determinants of hatching success in Diamondback Terrapin, *Malaclemys terrapin. American Midland Naturalist* 94:446–464.

———. 1979. Salt marshes—havens for waterbirds. *New Jersey Outdoors* 6:6–7.

———. 1984. Diamondback terrapins: Behavior and reproductive success. *New Jersey Outdoors* 11:5–6.

———. 1985. Habitat selection in temperate marshes. In *Nest Site Selection in Birds,* ed. M. Cody, 253–281. New York: Academic Press.

———. 1991. Coastal landscapes, coastal colonies, and seabirds. *Aquatic Reviews* 4:23–43.

———. 1996. *A Naturalist along the Jersey Shore.* New Brunswick, N.J.: Rutgers University Press.

———. 1996. Laughing Gull. In *Birds of North America,* ed. A. Poole and F. Gill. No. 225:1–28.

———. 2002. Effects of motorboats and personal watercraft on nesting terns: Conflict resolution and the need for vigilance. *Journal of Coastal Research* 37:7–17.

———. 2002. Food chain differences affect heavy metals in bird eggs in Barnegat Bay, New Jersey. *Environmental Research* 90:33–39.

Burger J., and W. Montevecchi. 1975. Nest site selection in the terrapin *Malaclemys terrapin. Copeia* 1975:113–119.

Burger J., and M. Gochfeld. 1990. *The Black Skimmer: Social Dynamics of a Colonial Species.* New York: Columbia University Press.

————. 1991. *The Common Tern: Its Breeding Biology and Behavior.* New York: Columbia University Press.

————. 2004. Metal levels in eggs of common terns (*Sterna hirundo*) in New Jersey: Temporal trends from 1971 to 2002. *Environmental Research* 94:336–343.

Burger, J., M. Gochfeld, and L. Niles. 1995. Ecotourism and birds in coastal New Jersey: Contrasting responses of birds, tourists, and managers. *Environmental Conservation* 22:56–64.

Burger, J., C. D. Jenkins, Jr., F. Lesser, and M. Gochfeld. 2001. Status and trends of colonially-nesting birds in Barnegat Bay. *Journal of Coastal Research* 32:197–211.

DiIonno, M. 1997. *New Jersey's Coastal Heritage.* New Brunswick, N.J.: Rutgers University Press.

Garber, S. D. 1988. Diamondback Terrapin exploitation. *Plastron Papers* 17:18–22.

Gosner, K. L. 1979. *A Field Guide to the Atlantic Seashore.* Boston: Houghton Mifflin.

Kennish, M. J., and R. A. Lutz, eds. 1987. *Ecology of Barnegat Bay.* New York: Springer-Verlag.

Montevecchi, W., and J. Burger. 1975. Aspects of the reproductive biology of the Northern Diamondback Terrapin, *Malaclemys terrapin. American Midland Naturalist* 94:166–178.

Nordstrom, K. R., P. A. Gares, N. P. Psuty, O. H. Pilkey, Jr., W. J. Neal, and O. H. Pilkey, Sr. 1986. *Living with the New Jersey Shore.* Durham, N.C.: Duke University Press.

Roberts, R. 1995. *Discover the Hidden New Jersey.* New Brunswick, N.J.: Rutgers University Press.

Roberts, R., and R. Youmans. 1993. *Down the Jersey Shore.* New Brunswick, N.J.: Rutgers University Press.

Chapter 13

Clark, K. E. 1991. Jersey: A way station for migratory birds. *New Jersey Outdoors* 18:28–31.

Dunne, P. J., ed. 1989. *New Jersey at the Crossroads of Migration.* Franklin Lakes, N.J.: New Jersey Audubon.

Ehrlich, P. R., D. S. Dobkin, and D. Wheye. 1988. *The Birder's Handbook: A Field Guide to the Natural History of North American Birds.* New York: Simon and Schuster.

Kerlinger, P. 1989. *Flight Strategies of Migrating Hawks.* Chicago: University of Chicago Press.

Kerlinger, P., and C. Doremus. 1981. Habitat disturbance and the decline of dominant avian species in pine barrens of the northeastern United States. *American Birds* 35:16–20.

Leahy, C. W. 2004. *The Birdwatcher's Companion to North American Birdlife.* Princeton, N.J.: Princeton University Press.

Leck, C. 1975. *The Birds of New Jersey: Their Habits and Habitats.* New Brunswick, N.J.: Rutgers University Press.

———. 1984. *The Status and Distribution of New Jersey's Birds.* New Brunswick, N.J.: Rutgers University Press.

Niles, L. J., J. Burger, and K. E. Clark. 1996. The influence of weather, geography, and habitat on migrating raptors on Cape May Peninsula. *Condor* 98:382–394.

Robbins, C. S., D. K. Dawson, and B. A. Dowell. 1989. Habitat area requirements of breeding forest birds in the Middle Atlantic states. *Wildlife Monographs* 103:1–34.

Chapter 14

Burger, J. 1989. Following of conspecifics and avoidance of predator chemical cues by Pine Snakes (*Pituophis melanoleucus*). *Journal of Chemical Ecology* 15:799–806.

———. 1989. Incubation temperature has long-term effects on behavior of young Pine Snakes (*Pituophis melanoleucus*). *Behavioral Ecology and Sociobiology* 24:201–208.

———. 1991. Effects of incubation temperature on behavior of hatchling Pine Snakes: Implications for reptilian distribution. *Behavioral Ecology and Sociobiology* 28:297–303.

———. 1998. Effects of incubation temperature on behavior of hatchling Pine Snakes: Implications for survival. *Behavioral Ecology and Sociobiology* 43:11–18.

Burger, J., and R. T. Zappolorti. 1986. Nest site selection by Pine Snakes, *Pituophis melanoleucus,* in the New Jersey Pine Barrens. *Copeia* 1:116–121.

———. 1986. On the importance of disturbed sites to habitat selection in Pine Snakes in the Pine Barrens of New Jersey. *Environmental Conservation* 12:358–361.

———. 1988. Effects of incubation temperature on Pine Snake development: Differential vulnerability of males and females. *American Naturalist* 132:492–505.

———. 1991. Nesting behavior of Pine Snakes (*Pituophis m. melanoleucus*) in the New Jersey Pine Barrens. *Journal of Herpetology* 25:152–160.

Burger, J., R.T. Zappalorti, and M. Gochfeld. 1987. Developmental effects of incubation temperature on hatchling Pine Snakes *Pituophus melanoleucus.* *Comparative Biochemistry and Physiology* 87A:727–732.

Chapter 15

Bogan, D. A., and R. Kays. 2002. Home range and diet of eastern coyotes from a suburban forest preserve. *Northeast Natural History Conference in New York State Museum Circular* 64:77.

Juelg, G. R. 2002. *New Jersey Pinelands: Threatened and Endangered Species.* Pemberton, N.J.: Pinelands Preservation Alliance.

Kays, R., and D. Bogan. 2003. Coyote. In *Natural History of the Albany Pine Bush,* ed. B. K. Barnes, 161–162. Albany, N.Y.: New York State Museum Bulletin 502.

McCullough, D. R., D. H. Hirth, and S. J. Newhouse. 1989. Resource partitioning between sexes in White-tailed Deer. *Journal of Wildlife Management* 53:277–283.

Chapter 16

Burger, J., and R. T. Zappalorti. 1992. Philopatry and nesting phenology of Pine Snakes *Pituophis melanoleucus* in the New Jersey Pine Barrens. *Behavioral Ecology and Sociobiology* 30:331–336.

Burger, J., R. T. Zappalorti, J. Dowdell, J. Hill, T. Georgiadis, and M. Gochfeld. 1992. Subterranean predation on Pine snakes (*Pituophus melanoleucus*). *Journal of Herpetology* 26:259–263.

Burger, J., R.T. Zappalorti, and M. Gochfeld. 2000. The defensive behaviors of Pine Snakes (*Pituophis Melanoleucus*) and Black Racers (*Coluber Constrictor*) to disturbance during hibernation. *Herpetologyical Natural History* 7:59–66.

Burger, J., R.T. Zappalorti, M. Gochfeld, W. Boarman, M. Caffrey, V. Doig, S. Garber, M. Mikovsky, C. Safina, and J. Saliva. 1988. Hibernacula and summer dens of Pine Snakes (*Pituophus melanoleucus*) in the New Jersey Pine Barrens. *Journal of Herpetology* 22:425–433.

Mara, W. P. 1994. *Pine Snakes: A Complete Guide.* Neptune City, N.J.: T.F.H. Publications.

Chapter 17

Kane, S., and R. Keeton. 1994. *In Those Days: African-American Life near the Savannah River.* Atlanta, Ga.: National Park Service.

LeGrand, H. 2000. The North Carolina sandhills. *American Butterflies* 8:5–15.

Martof, B. S., W. M. Palmer, J. R. Bailey, and J. R. Harrison III. 1980. *Amphibians and Reptiles of the Carolinas and Virginia.* Chapel Hill: University of North Carolina Press.

Means, D. B. 1996. Longleaf pine forest, going, going, ... In *Eastern Old-Growth Forests,* ed. M. B. Davis, 210–229. Washington, D.C.: Island Press.

Rohde, F. C., R. G. Arndt, D. G. Lindquist, and J. F. Parnell. 1994. *Freshwater Fishes of the Carolinas, Virginia, Maryland, and Delaware.* Chapel Hill: University of North Carolina Press.

South Carolina Department of Natural Resources. 1992. Wild Turkey. *Wildlife Management* Guide 1–4.

Vaitkus, M. R., and K. W. McLeod. 1995. Phyotosynthesis and water-use efficiency of two sandhill oaks following additions of water and nutrients. *Bulletin of the Torrey Botanical Club* 122:30–39.

Chapter 18

Ashton, R. E,. Jr., and P. S. Ashton. 1985. *Handbook of Reptiles and Amphibians of Florida: Lizards, Turtles and Crocodiles.* Miami, Fla.: Windward Publishing Company.

Carr, M. H. ed. 1994. *A Naturalist in Florida: A Celebration of Eden.* New Haven, Conn.: Yale University Press.

Greenberg, C. H., D. G. Neary, L. D. Harris, and S. P. Linda. 1995. Vegetation recovery following high-intensity wildfire and silvicultural treatments in Sand Pine Scrub. *American Midland Naturalist* 133:149–163.

Guyer, C., and S. M. Hermann. 1997. Patterns of size and longevity of Gopher Tortoise (*Gopherus polyphemus*) burrows: Implications for the Longleaf Pine ecosystem. *Chelonian Conservation and Biology* 2:507–513.

Hewell, S. D. 1995. *Exploring Wild Central Florida.* Sarasota, Fla.: Pineapple Press.

Means, D. B. 1996. Longleaf pine forest, going, going, ... In *Eastern Old-Growth Forests,* ed. M. B. Davis, 210–229. Washington, D.C.: Island Press.

Myers, R. L., and J. J. Ewel, eds. 1991. *Ecosystems of Florida.* Orlando, Fla.: University of Central Florida Press.

Neill, W. T. 1956. *Florida's Seminole Indians.* St. Petersburg, Fla.: Great Outdoors Publishing.

Smith, K. R., J. A. Hurley, and R. A. Seigel. 1997. Reproductive biology and demography of Gopher Tortoises (*Gopherus polyphemus*) from the western portion of their range. *Chelonian Conservation and Biology* 2:596–600.

Webb, S. D. 1990. Historical biogeography. In *Ecosystems of Florida,* ed. R. L. Myers and J. J. Ewel. Orlands: University of Central Florida Press.

Chapter 19

Anderson, R. C., J. S. Fralish, and J. M. Baskin. 1999. *Savannas, Barrens, and Rock Outcrop Plant Communities of North America.* Cambridge, U.K.: Cambridge University Press.

Cerulean, S., and A. Morrow. 1998. *Florida Wildlife Viewing Guide.* Helena, Mont.: Falcon.

Deyrup, M. 1989. Arthropods endemic to Florida scrub. *Florida Scientist* 52:254–270.

Deyrup, M., and T. Eisner. 1993. Last stand in the sand. *Natural History* 102:42–47.

Florida Game and Fresh Water Fish Commission. 1990. Living treasures of the Florida scrub. *Wild Florida* 1:1–6.

Greenberg, C. H., S. H. Crownover, and D. R. Gordon. 1997. Roadside soils: A corridor for invasion of xeric scrub by nonindigenous plants. *Natural Areas Journal* 17:99–109.

Hirth, D. H., L. D. Harris, and R. F. Noss. 1991. Avian community dynamics in a peninsular Florida Longleaf Pine forest. *Florida Field Naturalist* 19:33–48.

Menges, E. S. 1999. Ecology and conservation of Florida scrub. In *Savannas, Barrens and Rock Outcrop Plant Communities of North America*, ed. R. C. Anderson, J. S. Fralish, and J. M. Baskin, 7–22. Cambridge, U.K.: Cambridge University Press.

Stap, D. 1994. Along a ridge in Florida, an ecological house built on sand. *Smithsonian* 25:36–45.

Woolfenden, G. E., and J. W. Fitzpatrick. 1984. *The Florida Scrub Jay: Demography of a Cooperatively-Breeding Bird.* Monographs in Population Biology 20. Princeton, N.J.: Princeton University Press.

Chapter 20 (same as for Chapters 1 and 2)

Subject Index

Species Index

About the Author

Joanna Burger is a Distinguished Professor of Biological Sciences at Rutgers University. Her 17 books include *A Naturalist along the Jersey Shore, Oil Spills,* and *25 Nature Spectacles in New Jersey* (all Rutgers University Press) and *The Parrot Who Owns Me* (Random House). She lives in Somerset New Jersey with her husband, Michael Gochfeld, and parrot, Tiko.